COMAP, Inc.

UMAP

MODULES

TOOLS FOR TEACHING 1985

Consortium for Mathematics
and Its Applications, Inc.
60 Lowell Street
Arlington, MA 02174

This material was prepared with the partial support of National Science Foundation Grants No. SED80-07731 and SPE-8304192. Recommendations expressed are those of the authors and do not necessarily reflect the views of the NSF or the copyright holder.

ISBN 0-912843-08-X
Printed in USA

Table of Contents

Introduction

The instructional modules in this volume were developed by the Undergraduate Mathematics and Its Applications (UMAP) project. UMAP has been funded by grants from the National Science Foundation to Education Development Center, Inc. (1976-February 1983) and to the Consortium for Mathematics and Its Applications, (COMAP) Inc. (February 1983-February 1985). Project UMAP develops and disseminates instructional modules and expository monographs in the mathematical sciences and their applications for undergraduate students and instructors.

UMAP modules are self-contained (except for stated prerequisites), lesson-length, instructional units from which undergraduate students learn professional applications of mathematics and statistics to such fields as biomathematics, economics, American politics, numerical methods, computer science, earth science, social sciences, and psychology. The modules are written and reviewed by classroom instructors in colleges and high schools throughout the United States and abroad. In addition, a number of people from industry are involved in the development of instructional modules.

In addition to the annual collection of UMAP modules, COMAP also distributes individual UMAP instructional modules, *The UMAP Journal,* and the UMAP expository monograph series. Thousands of instructors and students have shared their reactions to the use of these instructional materials in the classroom. Comments and suggestions for changes are incorporated as part of the development and improvement of the materials.

The substance and momentum of the UMAP Project comes from the thousands of individuals involved in the development and use of UMAP's instructional materials. In order to capture this momentum and succeed beyond the period of federal funding, we established COMAP as a non-profit organization. COMAP is committed to the improvement of mathematics education, to the continuation of the development and dissemination of instructional materials, and to fostering and enlarging the network of people involved in the development and use of materials. COMAP deals with science and mathematics education in secondary schools, teacher training, continuing education, and industrial and government training programs.

Incorporated in 1980, COMAP is governed by a Board of Trustees:

Instructional programs are guided by the Consortium Council, whose members are variously elected by the broad COMAP membership, or appointed by cooperating organizations (Mathematical Association of America, Society for Industrial and Applied Mathematics, National Council of Teachers of Mathematics, the American Mathematical Association of Two-Year Colleges, and the Institute of Management Sciences). The 1986 Consortium Council is chaired by Joseph Malkevitch (York College, CUNY), and its members are:

Joseph Malkevitch, Chair	York College, CUNY
Robert Borelli	Harvey Mudd College
Alphonse Buccino	University of Georgia
Paul J. Campbell	Beloit College
Frank R. Giordano	U.S. Military Academy
Joanne Growney	Bloomsberg University
Eugene A. Herman	Grinnell College
Irwin Hoffman	Geo. Washington H.S. Denver, CO
Zaven Karian	Dennison University
Peter Lindstrom	North Lake College
William Lucas	Claremont Graduate School
Warren Page	NYC Technical College CUNY
Louise Raphael	Howard University
Fred S. Roberts	Rutgers University
Stephen Rodi	Austin Community College
Robert T. Shanks	Edison Public Schools Edison, NJ.

This collection of modules represents the spirit and ability of scores of volunteer authors, reviewers, and field-testers (both instructors and students). The modules also present various fields of application as well as different levels of mathematics. COMAP is very interested in receiving information on the use of modules in various settings. We invite you to contact us.

UMAP

Modules in Undergraduate Mathematics and Its Applications

Module 522

Unconstrained Optimization

Joan R. Hundhausen and
Robert A. Walsh

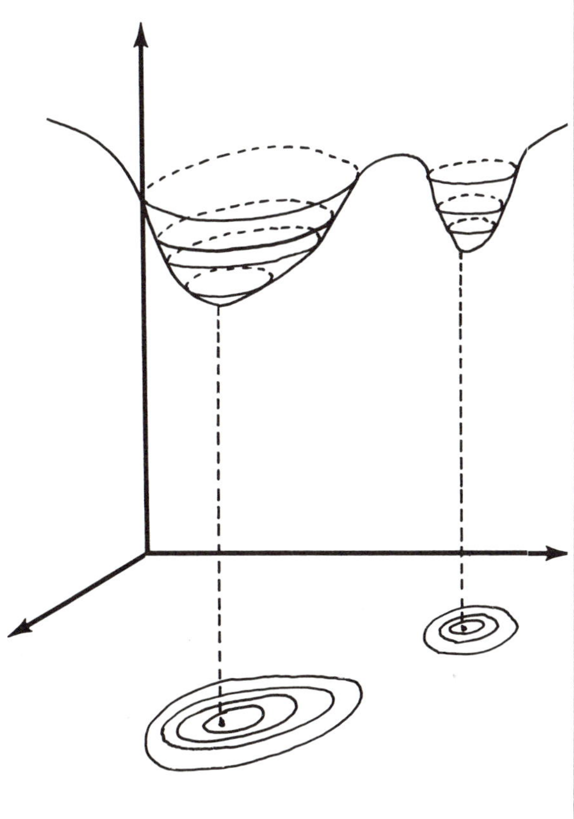

Published in cooperation with the Society for Industrial and Applied Mathematics, the Mathematical Association of America, the National Council of Teachers of Mathematics, the American Mathematical Association of Two-Year Colleges, and The Institute of Management Sciences.

COMAP

INTERMODULAR DESCRIPTION SHEET:	UMAP Unit 522
TITLE:	UNCONSTRAINED OPTIMIZATION
AUTHORS:	Joan R. Hundhausen Dept. of Mathematics Colorado School of Mines Golden, CO 80401 Robert A. Walsh 1203 1/2 Washington Ave. #4 Golden, CO 80401
MATH FIELD:	Second-semester calculus
APPLICATIONS FIELD:	Gradient searches, optimization
TARGET AUDIENCE:	Students in courses that introduce or apply the notion of gradient.
ABSTRACT:	This unit introduces Gradient Search Procedures, with examples and applications. Students are introduced to the use of computational algorithms, basic optimization theory, and how to find successive approximations to extreme points.
PREREQUISITES:	Acquaintance with elementary partial differentiation, chain rules, Taylor series, gradients, and vector dot products.
RELATED UNITS:	The Gradient and Some of Its Applications (Unit 431)

Unconstrained Optimization

Joan R. Hundhausen
Department of Mathematics
Colorado School of Mines
Golden, Colorado 80401

Robert A. Walsh
1203 1/2 Washington Ave. #4
Golden Colorado 80401

Table of Contents

MODULES AND MONOGRAPHS IN UNDERGRADUATE MATHEMATICS AND ITS APPLICATIONS PROJECT (UMAP)

The goal of UMAP was to develop, through a community of users and developers, a system of instructional modules in undergraduate mathematics and its applications to be used to supplement existing courses and from which complete courses may eventually be built.

The Project was guided by a National Advisory Board of mathematicians, scientists, and educators. UMAP was funded by a grant from the National Science Foundation and is now supported by the Consortium for Mathematics and Its Applications, Inc. (COMAP), a nonprofit corporation engaged in research and development in mathematics education.

The Project would like to thank Judith Elkins of Sweet Briar College, Peter F. Ash of Kennedy-King College, and Carroll O. Wilde of the Naval Postgraduate School for their reviews, and all others who assisted in the production of this unit.

This unit was field-tested and/or student reviewed in preliminary form by Michael B. Ward of Bucknell University and Richard A. Alo' of Lamar University and has been revised on the basis of data received from these sites.

This material was prepared with the partial support of National Science Foundation Grants No. SED8007731 and No. SPE8304192. Recommendations expressed are those of the author and do not necessarily reflect the views of the NSF or the copyright holder.

1. Introduction

Consider the equation of a surface $z = f(x,y)$ in 3-dimensional space. In general, when we wish to find a local extreme point (x^*,y^*), (maximum, minimum, or saddle point) of a differentiable surface, $z = f(x,y)$, we set $\vec{\nabla} f(x,y) = \vec{0}$ and try to obtain all possible solutions for the unknowns x and y. If a candidate for an extreme point is extracted from the system

$$\vec{\nabla} f(x,y) = \vec{0} \longrightarrow \begin{cases} f_x(x,y) = 0 \\ f_y(x,y) = 0 \end{cases} \qquad \text{System } (A)$$

(and only too often the equations are non-linear and the calculations are rather involved) then we subject the candidate (x^*,y^*) to a further test involving second partial derivatives in order to determine whether the local extreme point represents a maximum, minimum, or saddle point of $z = f(x,y)$.

In this module we explore a technique for approximating solutions of System (A) when it is difficult to solve by the usual arithmetic approaches. In particular, we shall describe and illustrate the bare outlines of such a procedure, called *Gradient Search.* The Gradient Search procedure usually only *approximates* an extreme point, but is very useful, because often for practical reasons we wish to achieve only a reasonable approximation to the point (x^*,y^*).

"... often for practical reasons we wish to achieve only a reasonable approximation ..."

You should recall that the *Gradient vector points locally in the direction of the greatest rate of increase of the surface,* while the *negative of the Gradient vector points in the direction of greatest rate of decrease of the surface.* Realizing this, you have already some intuitive notion about what direction should be followed (at least locally) in seeking the extreme point (x^*,y^*). The material that follows will provide both validity and precision to your intuition!

Keeping these above intentions as a guide, and considering the constraints on the length of this presentation, we have chosen to exemplify the technique of Gradient Search by treating several types of carefully selected surfaces $z = f(x,y)$. These surfaces are not necessarily related to any specific area of application for the method of Gradient Search, but were selected because they exhibit certain properties of the method with great clarity.

In Section 10 we describe a collection of specific topics for application of an elementary optimization technique such as the Gradient Search. Each of those topics in itself could be the subject of extensive exploration and discussion of various advantages and

"...in some cases, one would quickly be led to consider more sophisticated techniques..."

disadvantages (or possible modifications) of the Gradient Search Procedure. Indeed, in some cases, one would quickly be led to consider more sophisticated techniques of optimization. Pursuit of any of these areas of application could be the subject of an additional project for the class, or for independent study.

You may wish to peruse Section 10 to get some idea of the specific applications *before* you proceed with the main body of this module; such a preliminary reading may provide motivation for this study as well as incentive for further exploration.

2. Gradient Search Procedure

We first choose to present a condensed "recipe" (algorithm) for the procedure, assuming that we are searching for a point of minimization (x^*,y^*), with detailed explanations and examples to follow in subsequent sections. (Modifications of the procedure when we seek a maximum point (x^*,y^*) will be mentioned shortly.) The function to be minimized, $z = f(x,y)$, which represents a surface S in 3-dimensional space, is called the *Objective Function;* $f(x,y)$ has a local minimum at (x^*,y^*) if there is some open region R containing (x^*,y^*) such that $f(x^*,y^*) \leq f(x,y)$ for all other (x,y) in R. Local minima correspond to the low points on the surface S; see Fig. 1.

"The function to be minimized ... is called the Objective Function..."

To find an approximate local minimization point (x^*,y^*) for $f(x,y)$:

1. Select a point (x_0,y_0) arbitrarily, or at a minimum approximately known or suspected, from, say, physical reasons.

2. Compute $\vec{\nabla} f(x_0,y_0)$ and $f(x_0,y_0)$.

3. Form the function of a *single* variable t, as follows:

$$\psi(t) = f\{x_0 + f_x(x_0,y_0)t,\ y_0 + f_y(x_0,y_0)t\};\ t < 0.$$

   This function $\psi(t)$ is called the *Davidon function*. (Davidon was a corporate research worker; for further information, you might check the text by Wilde and Beightler, listed in Section 8 of this module.) Find its minimum.

4. Call t^* the value for which the Davidon function is minimized.

5. Using that value of t^*, form the new coordinates

$$x_1 = x_0 + f_x(x_0,y_0)t^* \qquad y_1 = y_0 + f_y(x_0,y_0)t^*.$$

6. To see whether appropriate progress toward the minimum has been achieved, check whether $f(x_1,y_1)$ is significantly less than $f(x_0,y_0)$. If so, go to 1 and repeat all steps with (x_1,y_1) replacing (x_0,y_0). If not, stop.

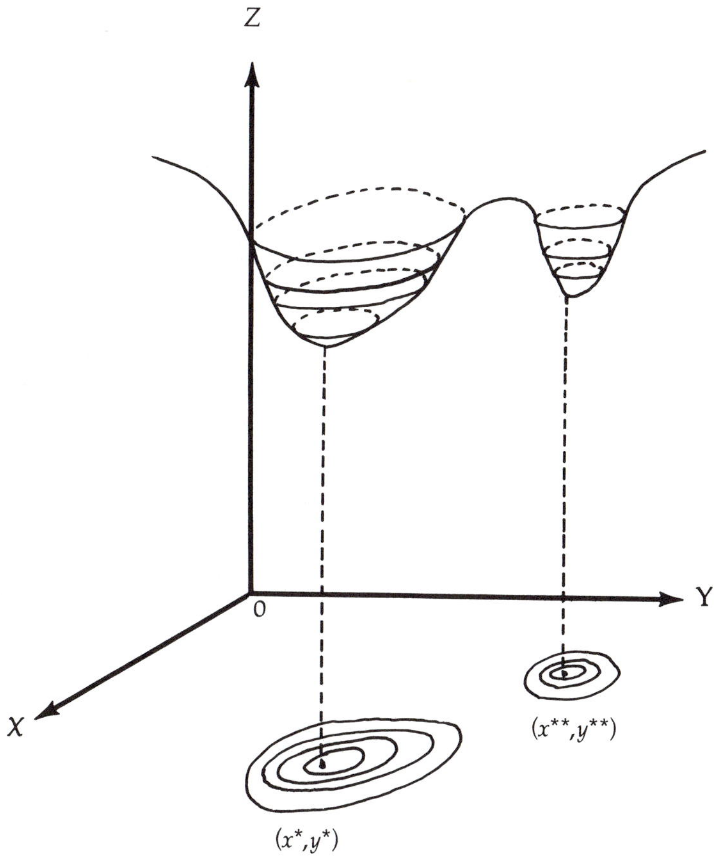

Figure 1. The objective function $z = f(x,y)$ represents a 3-D surface S, with low points (local minima) at (x^*,y^*) and (x^{**},y^{**}).

Brief Comments on the Above...

In Step 3, the actual minimum is usually difficult to find; in practice, we numerically step a small negative distance t a few times, and if the objective function is decreased each time, use the final t (as t^*), save t^* and proceed.

In Step 6, you must decide the tolerance, a priori. A decision as to whether the process should be repeated will usually involve consideration of the effort (and expense) necessary to carry out all of the steps of the procedure as compared to the possible improvement of the objective function. Also, the physical interpretation of the problem may indicate that even a *small* decrease in the objective function (say .10) would be considered a significant improvement and further refinement undesirable. Along this line, the actual cost of obtaining an improvement in the objective function might be prohibitive. Suppose, for example, that in a practical application of this procedure, the objective function z depended upon not only two but perhaps fifteen variables and that it represented a "cost function" measured in units of tens of thousands of dollars per month; in this case, the actual cost of obtaining an improvement (decrease) in the objective function, even though that cost be quite large, might *not* be prohibitive! The decision on whether to proceed with another iteration of the algorithm or not is often a difficult one for the practitioner; he weighs many factors, such as cost of computer time, man-hours, possible advantages to be gained, known capability of a competing firm, production deadlines,... you can name some others which might influence his or her decision.

"The decision on whether to proceed with another iteration of the algorithm or not is often a difficult one..."

In general, the Gradient Search never converges to the *exact* (x^*,y^*) after n steps and moreover converges very slowly to (x^*,y^*) after the first few cycles (steps 1-6). Certain methods are available for "accelerating" convergence; one of these will be illustrated in detail in Section 5.

In searching for a maximum point, replace *each* usage of the word "minimum" in the above outline to "maximum"; also the inequalities in Steps 3 and 6 should be reversed. Even these relatively simple modifications may be avoided by realizing that a maximum point for the function $f(x,y)$ is a minimum point for the function $-f(x,y)$. (Prove this!)

3. A Closer Look at Gradient Search

In this section we establish two important theoretical aspects of the Gradient Search Procedure that will be useful as you follow through the examples and comments presented in later sections. The first indicates the way the objective function changes with t, while the second shows the geometric relationship between successive directions of the gradient.

3.1 The Objective Function Must Decrease

If the parameter t is appropriately chosen small and negative, say $\hat{t}$, the objective function *must decrease* as we move in the direction of the Gradient.

Proof:
Since $z = f(x,y)$ is assumed to be a differentiable function, we can expand $f(x,y)$ in a *Taylor series* about the point (x_0,y_0):

$$f(x_1,y_1) = f(x_0,y_0) + f_x(x_0,y_0)\,(x_1-x_0)$$

$$+ f_y(x_0,y_0)\,(y_1-y_0)$$

$$+ \text{ terms containing } (x_1-x_0)^2,\ (y_1-y_0)^2$$

$$\text{or } (x_1-x_0)\,(y_1-y_0).$$

By definition, from step 5, $x_1-x_0 = f_x(x_0,y_0)\,\hat{t}$ and $y_1-y_0 = f_y(x_0,y_0)\,\hat{t}$, and replacement of these expressions in the above formula yields

$$f(x_1,y_1) - f(x_0,y_0)$$

$$= [f_x(x_0,y_0)]^2\hat{t} + [f_y(x_0,y_0)]^2\hat{t}$$

$+$ terms containing $(\hat{t})^2$ and higher derivatives of $f(x,y)$ evaluated at (x_0,y_0).

.

.

.

$$= |\vec{\nabla} f(x_0,y_0)|^2\hat{t} + \text{ terms containing } (\hat{t})^2.$$

Now if $|\hat{t}|$ is small and the higher derivatives of f are small, then the terms containing $\hat{t}$ will dominate those containing $(\hat{t})^2$, and thus $f(x_1,y_1) - f(x_0,y_0) < 0$ for small negative $\hat{t}$. (Note that for positive t, we have $f(x_1,y_1) - f(x_0,y_0) > 0$.)

Note:
The concept of the *directional derivative* at a particular point, denoted by df/ds, is also useful here to justify the decrease in the objective function. Recall that

$$\frac{df}{ds} = \vec{\nabla} f \cdot \vec{u}$$

where $\vec{u}$ is a unit vector in the s-direction. We can see that df/ds will be negative (i.e., the function f will decrease) if the direction s is chosen opposite to that of the gradient at a particular point. (The choice of a negative parameter t in the gradient search procedure has the effect of reversing the direction of the gradient).

However, we prefer the *Taylor series* approach presented above because it better illustrates the involvement of the parameter t, which is central to the Gradient Search Procedure.

We emphasize that the Gradient Direction is *normal* to a level curve of the surface. Recall also that a move in the direction *opposite* to that of the Gradient vector at a point is a move in the direction of the *steepest descent* on the surface at that point.

3.2 The Directions of Successive Gradients

If t^* yields the *exact* minimum of the Davidon function $\psi(t)$ in step 3, then

$$\vec{\nabla} f(x_0, y_0) \cdot \vec{\nabla} f(x_1, y_1) = 0;$$

i.e., successive gradients are perpendicular to each other. (See Fig. 2.)

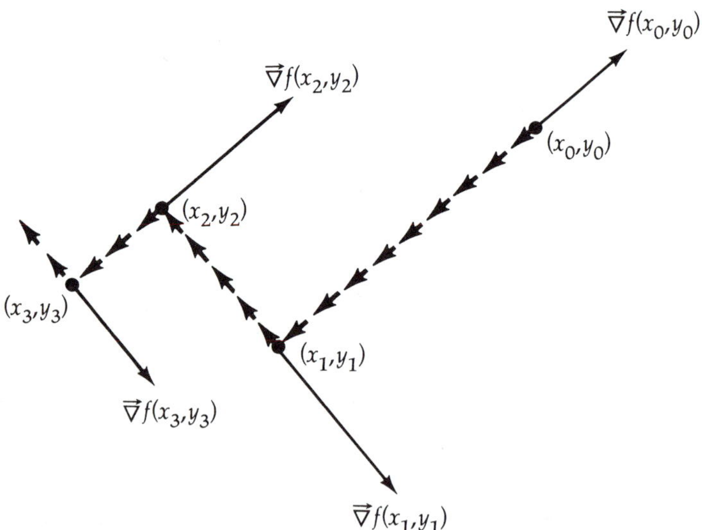

Figure 2. Solid arrows mark successive gradient directions starting from the point (x_0,y_0); broken arrows indicate the path followed by the Gradient Search Procedure.

Proof:

The Davidon function in step 3 can be written as $\psi(t) = f[u(t),v(t)]$, where $u(t) \equiv x_0 + f_x(x_0,y_0)t$ and $v(t) \equiv y_0 + f_y(x_0,y_0)t$. We note also (from Step 5) that $u(t^*) = x_1$ and $v(t^*) = y_1$; so the condition that t^* be a critical point for $\psi(t)$ becomes

$$\left.\frac{d\psi}{dt}\right|_{t=t^*} = \left.\frac{d}{dt} f[u(t),v(t)]\right|_{t=t^*} = 0.$$

By the chain rule, the latter condition can be written

$$(B) \qquad \left.\frac{\partial}{\partial u} f(u,v)\,\frac{du}{dt} + \frac{\partial}{\partial v} f(u,v)\,\frac{dv}{dt}\right|_{t=t^*} = 0.$$

But $\frac{du}{dt} = f_x(x_0,y_0)$ and $\frac{dv}{dt} = f_y(x_0,y_0)$; also

$$\left.\frac{\partial}{\partial u} f(u,v)\right|_{t=t^*} = \left.\frac{\partial f}{\partial x}(x,y)\right|_{\substack{x=u(t^*)\,=\,x_1 \\ y=v(t^*)\,=\,y_1}} = f_x(x_1,y_1),$$

and $$\left.\frac{\partial}{\partial v} f(u,v)\right|_{t=t^*} = \left.\frac{\partial f}{\partial y}(x,y)\right|_{\substack{x=u(t^*)\,=\,x_1 \\ y=v(t^*)\,=\,y_1}} = f_y(x_1,y_1)$$

so that (B) becomes

$$f_x(x_1,y_1)f_x(x_0,y_0) + f_y(x_1,y_1)f_y(x_0,y_0) = 0 \text{ or}$$
$$\vec{\nabla} f(x_0,y_0) \cdot \vec{\nabla} f(x_1,y_1) = 0.$$

4. Examples of the Gradient Search Procedure

4.1 A Function Whose Level Curves Are Ellipses

As a first example, we now apply the *Gradient Search* to the minimization of $z = (1/2)(x^2+2y^2)$. The objective function is non-negative for all x and y, and it is easy to see that the point of minimization is $(x^*,y^*) = (0,0)$. We shall, however, use this somewhat simple example because it illustrates the computational aspects while providing some valuable geometric insight into the procedure. (See Fig. 3.)

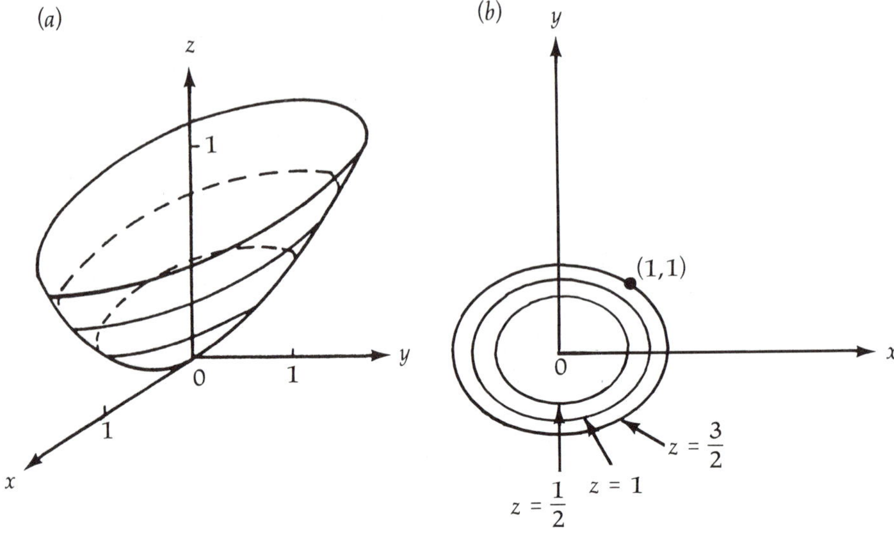

Figure 3a. The surface S: $z = \frac{1}{2}(x^2+2y^2)$.

Figure 3b. Some level curves for the function $z = \frac{1}{2}(x^2+2y^2)$.

We begin with the (somewhat crude) approximation $(x_0,y_0) = (1,1)$. While you might surmise that one iteration of the Gradient Search would enable us to reach (x^*,y^*), we shall see that this is not the case.

Example 1.
Using $z = (1/2)(x^2+2y^2)$, let us follow the recipe which was presented in Section 2.

1. $(x_0,y_0) = (1,1)$.

2. $\vec{\nabla}f(x_0,y_0) = x\hat{i} + 2y\,\hat{j}\Big|_{(1,1)} = 1\hat{i} + 2\hat{j}$;

$f(x_0,y_0) = \frac{3}{2}$.

3. $\psi(t) = \frac{1}{2}\left[(1+t)^2 + 2(1+2t)^2\right]$. The condition $\dot{\psi}(t) = 0$ yields the equation $(1+t) + 4(1+2t) = 0$ or $5 + 9t = 0$, and $t^* = -\frac{5}{9}$.

4. $t^* = -5/9$, in this case the *exact* minimizing point for $\psi(t)$.

5. New coordinates are $(x_1,y_1) = \left(1+1\left(-\frac{5}{9}\right), 1+2\left(-\frac{5}{9}\right)\right)$

$$= \left(\frac{4}{9}, -\frac{1}{9}\right).$$

6. $f(x_1,y_1) = (1/2)\,(x_1{}^2+2y_1{}^2) = 1/9 < 3/2 = f(x_0,y_0).$

Having achieved a decrease in the objective function, we repeat the process, with $(x_1,y_1) = (4/9, -1/9)$ replacing (x_0,y_0).

At this point, we suggest that to gain confidence, you might perform Steps 2-6 of the algorithm yourself as an exercise. Use the starting point $(4/9, -1/9)$, and you can check your results with ours at each step. (In fact, we suggest you use this approach throughout the module; instead of interrupting the flow of the text with many short and relatively simple exercises, we leave it to your discretion to practice and duplicate some of the computations.)

2′. $\vec{\nabla} f(x_1,y_1) = \frac{4}{9}\hat{i} - \frac{2}{9}\hat{j}, \quad f(x_1,y_1) = \frac{1}{9}.$

3′. $\psi(t) = \frac{1}{2}\left[\left(\frac{4}{9} + \frac{4}{9}t\right)^2 + 2\left(-\frac{1}{9} - \frac{2}{9}t\right)^2\right]$

$$= \frac{1}{2(81)}\left[16(1+t)^2 + 2(1+2t)^2\right].$$

The condition $\dot{\psi}(t) = 0$ becomes $\frac{1}{2(81)}\left[32(1+t)+8(1+2t)\right] = 0$

or $48t + 40 = 0$,

$$t^* = -\frac{5}{6},$$

where again this value of t represents an *exact* point of minimization for $\psi(t)$.

4′. $t^* = -\frac{5}{6}.$

5′. New coordinates are

$$(x_2,y_2) = \left[\frac{4}{9} + \frac{4}{9}\left(\frac{-5}{6}\right), -\frac{1}{9} - \frac{2}{9}\left(\frac{-5}{6}\right)\right] = \left(\frac{2}{27}, \frac{2}{27}\right).$$

6′. $f(x_2,y_2) = \frac{1}{2}\left(x_2^2+2y_2^2\right) = \frac{2}{243} < \frac{1}{9} = f(x_1,y_1).$

We interrupt the algorithm to note that (x_2, y_2) is a multiple of (x_0, y_0). To compare the locations of the approximating points (x_0, y_0), (x_1, y_1) and (x_2, y_2), refer to Fig. 4. Upon the next iteration, you will find that $(x_3, y_3) = (2/27)(4/9, -1/9)$ is a multiple of (x_1, y_1). In fact, it can be shown that (x_{m+2}, y_{m+2}) is a multiple of (x_m, y_m), $m \geq 0$. (See Exercise 2.)

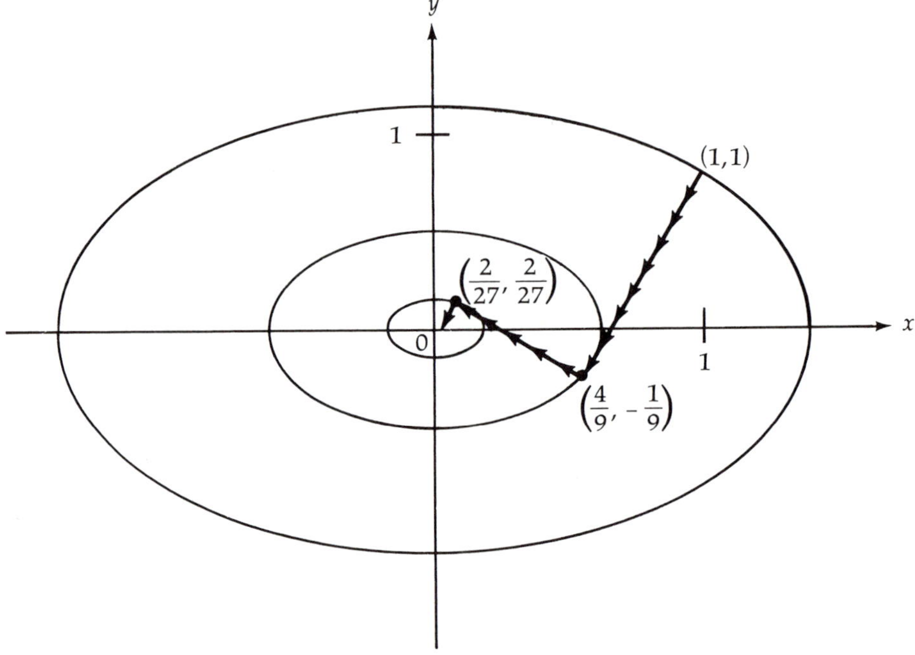

Figure 4. Successive approximating points for Example 1.

Proceeding with one more iteration of the algorithm, we find

2″. $\vec{\nabla} f(x_2, y_2) = \frac{2}{27}\hat{i} + \frac{4}{27}\hat{j}, \quad f(x_2, y_2) = \frac{2}{243}.$

3″. $\psi(t) = \frac{1}{2}\left[\left(\frac{2}{27} + \frac{2}{27}t\right)^2 + 2\left(\frac{2}{27} + \frac{4}{27}t\right)^2\right]$

$$= \frac{2}{(27)^2}\ \left[(1+t)^2 + 2(1+2t)^2\right].$$

The condition $\dot{\psi}(t) = 0$ becomes $1 + t + 4(1+2t) = 0$

$$5 + 9t = 0$$

$$t = -\frac{5}{9}.$$

4″. $t^* = -\frac{5}{9}$.

5″. New coordinates are

$$(x_3,y_3) = \left[\left(\frac{2}{27} - \frac{2}{27}\left(\frac{5}{9}\right)\right), \left(\frac{2}{27} - \frac{4}{27}\left(\frac{5}{9}\right)\right)\right]$$

$$= \frac{2}{27}\left[\left(1 - \frac{5}{9}\right), \left(1 - \frac{10}{9}\right)\right] = \frac{2}{27}\left(\frac{4}{9}, -\frac{1}{9}\right),$$

which is a multiple of (x_1,y_1). Also, you may show that $f(x_3,y_3) < f(x_2,y_2)$.

4.2 The Gradient Corridor

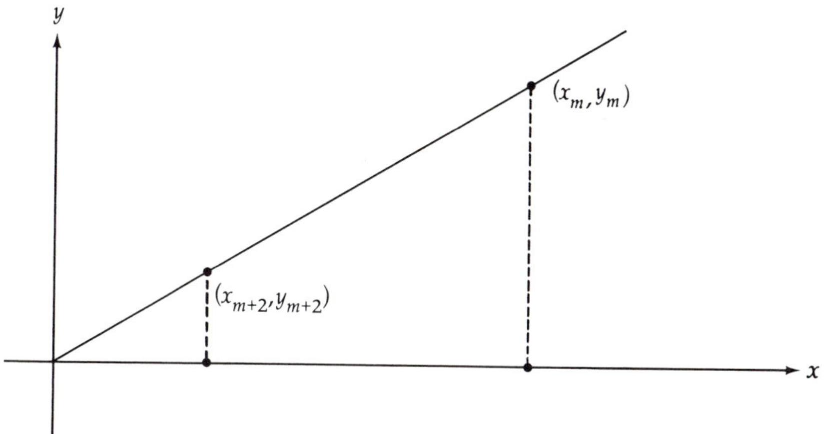

Figure 5. Similar triangles formed by the approximating points.

We shall now take advantage of the pattern that has evolved, and anticipate the result of Exercise 2 to make a geometric construction of the path followed by the points (x_0,y_0), (x_1,y_1), . . . , (x_m,y_m) as they approach the true minimum value for $f(x,y)$, viz., (0,0). You will note that the result of Exercise 2 shows that $x_{m+2}/x_m = y_{m+2}/y_m = p > 0$, which is equivalent to the similarity of the two triangles in Fig. 5. Thus we see that the odd-subscripted points are collinear; apparently the single line which they define, which is directed along the hypotenuse of each triangle, leads directly to the true minimum. (The same could be said of the even-subscripted points.) Let us find the equation of the straight line joining odd-subscripted points, and then do the same for the even-subscripted points.

The straight line through the points (x_1,y_1) and (x_3,y_3) has equation

$$\frac{y-y_1}{y_3-y_1} = \frac{x-x_1}{x_3-x_1} \text{ or } y = -\frac{1}{4}x.$$

Similarly, the line through (x_0,y_0) and (x_2,y_2) is $y = x$. Fig. 6 depicts these lines graphed in the xy plane. The shaded space between these lines is called the "Gradient Corridor" and you can trace the zig-zag pattern by the successive approximating points (x_m,y_m) as we approach the minimum value (0,0). Note also the perpendicularity of the paths connecting the successive points!

"...the convergence... is assured only if we are sufficiently close to an extreme point..."

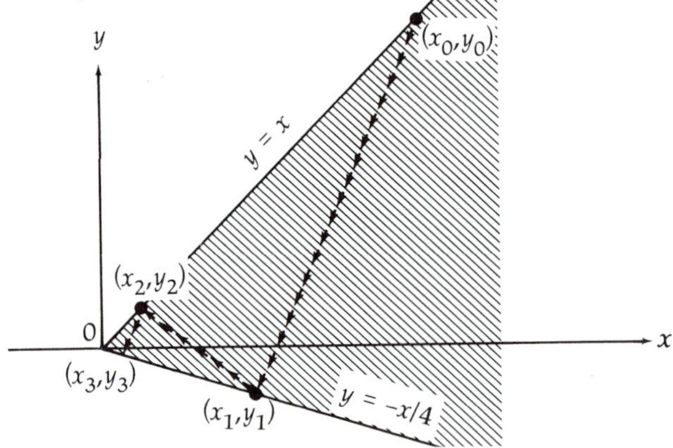

Figure 6. The lines y = x and y = −(1/4)x which bound the "gradient corridor" for Example 1.

Exercise

1. Calculate the slope of the path connecting (x_1,y_1) to (x_2,y_2) and the slope of the path connecting (x_2,y_2) to (x_3,y_3) and show that the paths are perpendicular. Why is this true?

Example 1 is particularly instructive because of the geometric insight it contributes; you can indeed predict the path followed by the approximating points as they "home in" towards the true minimum. This straight-line corridor pattern is characteristic of any objective function of the form $f(x,y) = x^2 + \mu y^2$, whose level curves are ellipses. $(\mu > 0.)$

For level curves having the *general* equation $f(x,y) = C$, the Gradient Corridor will be meaningful only for points very close to a local maximum or minimum point (x_0,y_0). Again we emphasize that the convergence of the Gradient Method along the "nearly" straight bounding lines of the Gradient Corridor is assured only if we are sufficiently close to an extreme point.

Exercise

2. Show that, for functions of the type $z = f(x,y) = x^2 + \mu y^2$ (take $\mu > 1$), the Gradient Corridor lies between 2 straight lines; i.e., show that the approximating point (x_{m+2}, y_{m+2}) is a multiple of the approximating point (x_m, y_m), for $m \geq 0$ in the sense that $x_{m+2} = px_m$, $y_{m+2} = py_m$, where $p > 0$. (Hint: Start with the point (x_m, y_m); use the procedure as illustrated in this example successively to find (x_{m+1}, y_{m+1}) and (x_{m+2}, y_{m+2}); further guidance will be found in the ANSWERS section.)

A few more examples and exercises will increase your understanding of the use of the Gradient Search Procedure and illustrate both its power and its limitations under specific circumstances.

4.3 An Example Possessing Circular Level Curves

The previous example illustrated the optimization of a function whose level curves were ellipses. (See Fig. 3b.) When the level curves are circular, the Gradient Search Procedure is even more effective. In fact, a single application of the procedure, starting from *any* initial point, leads to the exact location of the optimum:

Example 2.
Find the maximum value of the objective function $z = f(x,y) = -x^2 - y^2 - 4x + 2y$. By completing the square, you can verify that $z = 5 - (x+2)^2 - (y-1)^2$, so its maximum value is 5 which occurs at the point $(-2,1)$. Because of the nature of this function (its level curves are circles), you will find that only one application of the gradient search procedure leads directly to the optimum point.

Exercise

3. Following the procedure outlined in Section 2 start with $(x_0, y_0) = (4,-4)$ and show that
   a) $\vec{\nabla} f(4,-4) = -12\hat{i} + 10\hat{j}$; (use the direction vector $-6\hat{i} + 5\hat{j}$);
   b) The Davidon function $\psi(t) = -(4-6t)^2 - (-4+5t)^2 - 4(4-6t) + 2(-4+5t) = -61t^2 + 122t - 56$;
   c) $t^* = 1$;
   d) $(x_1, y_1) = (-2,1) = (x^*, y^*)$, the maximum point for z.

Here the "gradient corridor" in Exercise 3 degenerates to a single straight line; (see Fig. 7). It is only fair to mention that this rarely happens in practice!

"Gradient Search Procedure can be both necessary and effective..."

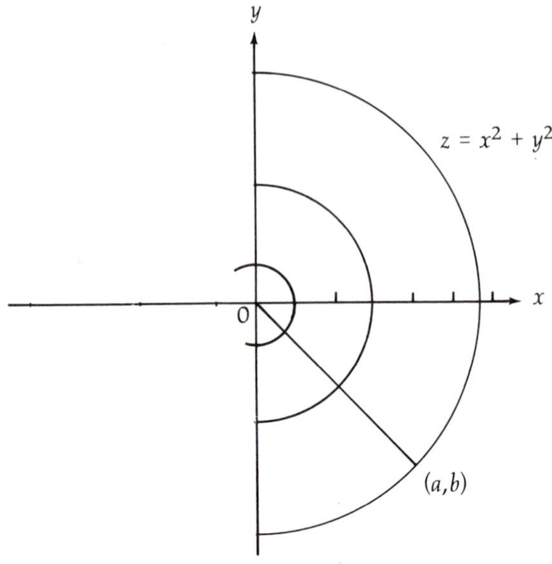

Figure 7. "The gradient corridor" reduces to a straight line when level curves are circular.

Question:
What would happen were we to attempt to continue the Gradient Search Procedure using the "approximating point" (-2,1)?

In summary, we note that an objective function with circular or elliptical level curves can be optimized quite simply by using the analytical tools of the calculus; no approximation method such as the Gradient Search Procedure needs to be considered. What we are trying to do is to illustrate the application of the method with simple examples and to provide you with some geometric insight. In the cases of more complicated objective functions, for which the Gradient Search Procedure can be both necessary and effective, the level curves are neither circular nor elliptical (see Section 6), and it is unlikely that any simple transformation can make them so. But having observed and understood the action of the Procedure for these simple cases, you will be better able to appreciate how it operates in the more complicated cases. This remark also applies to the method we illustrate in the next Section.

5. Speeding Things Up!

Having noted the progress of the iterations down the gradient corridor in Example 1 as well as the dramatic leap to the optimum in Example 2, you might well ask if it wouldn't be more efficient to compute a few approximation points (x_i, y_i), use them to determine the boundary lines of the gradient corridor, and then slide down the corridor to reach the optimum. In the next example we show that your conjecture is well-founded! The process to be illustrated is called "acceleration to the optimum point."

Example 3.
Consider the objective function $z = f(x,y) = (1/2)\,(x^2 + 2xy + 2y^2) - 3x - 2y + 6$, and begin the search at the point (2,1). Following the usual procedure, we have

$$\vec{\nabla} f(x,y) = (x+y-3)\hat{i} + (x+2y-2)\hat{j};$$

$$\vec{\nabla} f(2,1) = 2\hat{j}$$

$$(x_1,y_1) = (2-0t,\ 1+2t),$$

$$\psi(t) = (1/2)\left[2^2+2(2)(1+2t)+2(1+2t)^2\right] - 6 - 2(1+2t) + 6$$

$$= 4t^2 + 4t + 3$$

$$\psi'(t) = 8t + 4;\ t^* = -1/2$$

$$(x_1,y_1) = (2,0).$$

$$\vec{\nabla} f(2,0) = (2-3)\hat{i} + (2-2)\hat{j}$$

$$= -1\hat{i}$$

$$(x_2,y_2) = (2-t,\ 0)$$

$$\psi(t) = (1/2)\left[(2-t)^2\right] - 3(2-t) + 6]$$

$$= (1/2)t^2 + t + 2$$

$$\psi'(t) = t + 1;\ t^* = -1$$

$$(x_2,y_2) = (3,0).$$

Let us now find the direction of one of the bounding lines of the gradient corridor, and we shall optimize along *that* direction rather than compute another gradient direction. The vector directed between points (x_0,y_0) and (x_2,y_2) is $(3-2)\hat{i} + (0-1)\hat{j} = \hat{i} - \hat{j}$, but since the objective function can be expected to decrease with *negative t* (Section 3.1) we form the vector $t(-\hat{i} + \hat{j})$ to indicate the new direction for optimization:

$$(x_3,y_3) = (3-t,\ 0+t);$$

$$\psi(t) = \frac{1}{2}\left[(3-t)^2 + 2(3-t)t + 2t^2\right] - 3(3-t) - 2t + 6 = \frac{t^2}{2} + t + \frac{3}{2}.$$

$\psi'(t) = t + 1;\ t^* = -1.$

$(x_3, y_3) = (4, -1).$

Exercise

4. Using the methods of calculus, verify that (4,–1) is indeed the minimum point for the objective function of Example 3.

6. A More Complicated Objective Function and Some Practical Advice

Our final example will illustrate some difficulties which might accompany application of the Gradient Search Procedure to more complicated objective functions. As we work through it, we will make several digressions; these will serve to deepen your understanding of the method and to expand your horizons with respect to the concept of optimization in general.

6.1 The Importance of a Good Start

Example 4.

Let $z = f(x,y) = x^2 + y^3 - 3xy$. It is known that this function has a saddle point at (0,0) as well as one local minimum at (9/4, 3/2) where $f(x,y) = -1.6875$. Suppose we are seeking this local minimum. (See Fig. 8.) First we shall illustrate what can happen if the first approximation to the local minimum point is not chosen sufficiently close to that minimum point itself.

"... deepen your understanding ... expand your horizons with respect to the concept of optimization..."

Now $\vec{\nabla} f(x,y) = (2x-3y)\hat{i} + (3y^2-3x)\hat{j}$. Suppose $(x_0, y_0) = (0,-1)$; then $\vec{\nabla} f(0,-1) = 3\hat{i} + 3\hat{j}$, which has the direction of $\hat{i} + \hat{j}$. Then

$$(x_1, y_1) = (t, -1+t).$$
$$\psi(t) = t^2 + (t-1)^3 - 3t(t-1).$$
$$\psi'(t) = 2t + 3(t-1)^2 - 3(2t-1).$$
$$= 3t^2 - 10t + 6;$$
$$\psi''(t) = 6t - 10.$$
$$\psi'(t) = 0 \text{ yields } t_1 = \frac{10 - \sqrt{100-72}}{6} > 0,$$
$$t_2 = \frac{10 + \sqrt{100-72}}{6} > 0.$$

The second derivative test indicates that the first of these is a maximum for $\psi(t)$, the second is a minimum for $\psi(t)$, but since neither of these values for t is *negative* we can only conclude that

$\psi(t)$ has no local minima for $t < 0$! We cannot hope to "home in" on the point (9/4, 3/2) from this starting location.

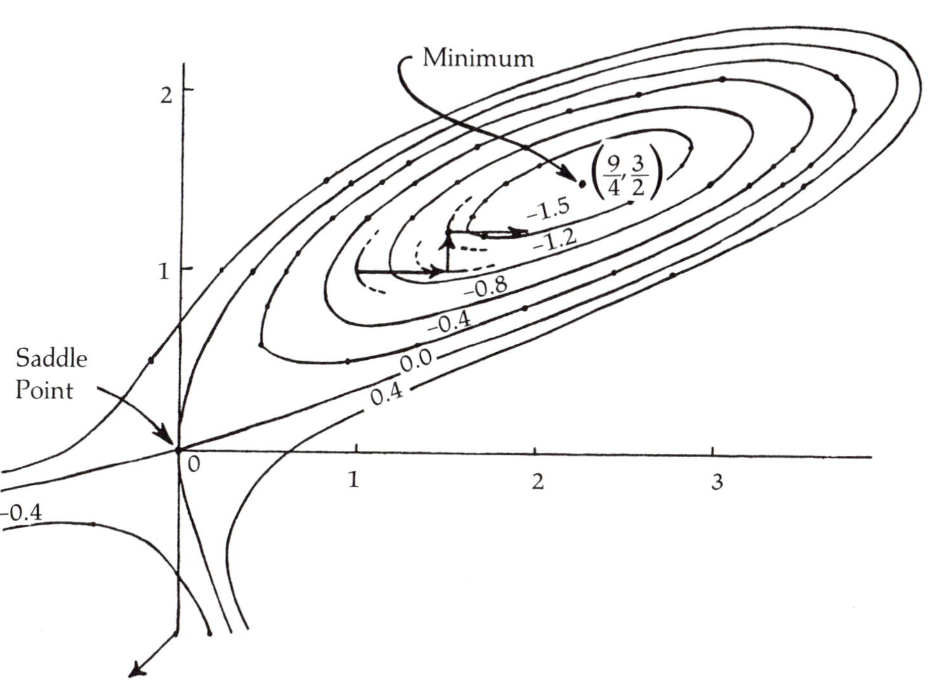

Figure 8. A quantitative rendition of the level curves of the function $z = x^2 + y^3 - 3xy$, considered in Example 4, with functional values labeled on the curves. From the *poor* starting point (−1,0), the gradient heads down the saddle, never to approach the local minimum point; from the better starting point (1,1), the successive gradient paths do approach the local minimum. Note especially the near-elliptical shape of the level curves in the vicinity of the minimum, and that the successive gradients are perpendicular to level curves.

What would happen if we were to *persist* in following the negative gradient direction in seeking a minimum for $f(x,y)$? Suppose a small step (say $t=-1$) were to be taken in that direction, from the starting point (0,−1) to the point $(x_1,y_1) = (-1, -2)$. Then we would see that while $f(x_0,y_0) = -1$, $f(x_1,y_1) = -13$. The choice $t = -2$ would yield a still larger negative value $f(x,y)$, and we begin to realize that the Gradient Search Procedure is not at all effective here, in locating the minimum point (9/4, 3/2). What is happening is that the successive approximating points are following a precipitous path down the saddle! (See Fig. 8.)

We now discuss this "pitfall" briefly. In the previous examples, you have seen how the Gradient Search Procedure is both effective and efficient when applied to functions whose level curves are elliptical. Here we point out that, in the *vicinity* of an extremum, a well-behaved function (continuous first and second derivatives) will possess level curves which "resemble" ellipses; i.e., the local behavior of even a very complicated but well-behaved function can be expected to resemble that of the simpler functions treated in this module. Thus if we have prior knowledge of the approximate location of a local maximum or minimum, the Gradient Search Procedure will improve our educated guess if we start "close enough" to the point. However, if we are not "close enough" to the local max or min, we cannot always expect the Gradient Search to lead us nearer to this particular local optimum point.

"...the gradient search procedure will improve our educated guess..."

We now try a better choice for the first approximation.

Let $(x_0,y_0) = (1,1)$; then $\vec{\nabla} f(1,1) = -\hat{i}$, and $f(1,1) = -1$.

Then $(x_1,y_1) = (1-t, 1)$.

$$\psi(t) = (1-t)^2 + 1 - 3(1-t);$$

$$\psi'(t) = 2t + 1,\ t^* = -\frac{1}{2}.$$

Then $(x_1,y_1) = \left(\frac{3}{2}, 1\right)$; and $f\left(\frac{3}{2}, 1\right) = \frac{-5}{4} < -1$,

so that some progress toward the minimum has been achieved. Another iteration of the gradient search procedure will be instructive.

$$\vec{\nabla} f(x_1,y_1) = -\frac{3}{2}\hat{j}, \text{ which has the direction of } -\hat{j}.$$

Then $(x_2,y_2) = \left(\frac{3}{2}, 1 - t\right)$.

$$\psi(t) = \frac{9}{4} + (1-t)^3 - \frac{9}{2}(1-t)$$

$$\psi'(t) = -3(1-t)^2 + \frac{9}{2}$$

$$\psi'(t) = 0 \text{ yields 2 roots: } t_1 = 1 + \sqrt{\frac{3}{2}},\ t_2 = 1 - \sqrt{\frac{3}{2}}$$

only one of which is negative.

Since $\psi''(t) = 6(1-t)$ and $\psi''(1-(\sqrt{3/2})) = 6(\sqrt{3/2}) > 0$, $\psi(t)$ does have a local minimum value, and we conclude that $t^* = 1 - \sqrt{3/2}$.

Then

$$(x_2,y_2) = \left(\frac{3}{2}, \sqrt{\frac{3}{2}}\right), \text{ and } f\left(\frac{3}{2}, \sqrt{\frac{3}{2}}\right) = \frac{9}{4} - 3\sqrt{\frac{3}{2}} = -1.424.$$

The next iteration yields

$$\vec{\nabla} f(x_2,y_2) = 3\left(1 - \sqrt{\frac{3}{2}}\right)\hat{i}, \text{ or the direction of } -\hat{i}.$$

Then $(x_3,y_3) = \left(\frac{3}{2} - t, \sqrt{\frac{3}{2}}\right)$.

$$\psi(t) = \left(\frac{3}{2} - t\right)^2 + \left(\sqrt{\frac{3}{2}}\right)^3 - 3\left(\frac{3}{2} - t\right)\sqrt{\frac{3}{2}}.$$

$$\psi'(t) = -2\left(\frac{3}{2} - t\right) + 3\sqrt{\frac{3}{2}}; \text{ setting } \psi'(t) = 0,$$

we find the root

$$t^* = \frac{3}{2} - \frac{3}{2}\sqrt{\frac{3}{2}}.$$

Since $\psi''(t^*) = 2$, we do have a local minimum for $\psi(t)$.

Then $(x_3,y_3) = \left(\frac{3}{2}\sqrt{\frac{3}{2}}, \sqrt{\frac{3}{2}}\right) = \left(\frac{3}{4}\sqrt{6}, \frac{\sqrt{6}}{2}\right) = (1.82, 1.2)$,

and $f(x_3,y_3) = -1.53$.

Note that progress toward the true minimum is quite regular. (Recall that the true minimum value of $f(x,y)$ is -1.6875, achieved at $(x,y) = (9/4, 3/2)$.) Such is not always the case. This is an opportune moment for further discussion of slow convergence — a deficiency which can sometimes be remedied.

6.2 Slow Convergence; Discussion

The Gradient Search Procedure, while yielding substantial initial progress toward the desired minimum, often appears to converge very slowly. Alas, this fact is true in general for gradient search patterns. Perhaps some acceleration procedure could be used to advantage. In the Model Exam, we ask you to perform the type of acceleration illustrated in Example 3. However, we note here that other acceleration schemes might be more efficient. Also these could be used in *combination* with the Gradient Search Procedure to achieve a more efficient optimization algorithm. We mention the Newton-Raphson procedure as one example, and refer you to the text "Foundations of Optimization" by D. Wilde and C. Beightler.

In actual practice, the applied mathematician is often faced with decisions which are rooted in the realities of economics. If an objective function represents the cost (or the profit) related to some industrial operation, sometimes even a relatively small improvement can be measured in terms of thousands of dollars. Perhaps even a *single* application of the Gradient Search Procedure (or some other sophisticated optimization procedure) will yield satisfactory (if not optimal) results.

"...the applied mathematician is often faced with decisions which are rooted in the realities of economics..."

Sometimes, preliminary scaling of a problem may be necessary to achieve a desirable configuration of near-ellipses for level curves. The advantage of the scaling procedure can be easily illustrated by attention to a simple example such as $z = x^2/10^6 + y^2/4$; whose level curves are extremely narrow ellipses. The change of variable $x = 10^3x'$ eliminates the severe distortion; now $z = (x')^2 + y^2/4$ (see Figure 9). Without going into detail, we remark that an extreme discrepancy between magnitude of numerical coefficients in a problem can lead to computational difficulties, such as loss of accuracy due to round-off errors. We also note that in many practical cases it is far from obvious just how to scale appropriately in the vicinity of an extreme point.

In summary, we suggest giving some close attention to two preliminary aspects of a practical problem before applying the gradient search or any other optimization procedure.

a) *Try* to scale the variables;

b) If at all possible, choose an initial approximating point which is *close* to the optimum.

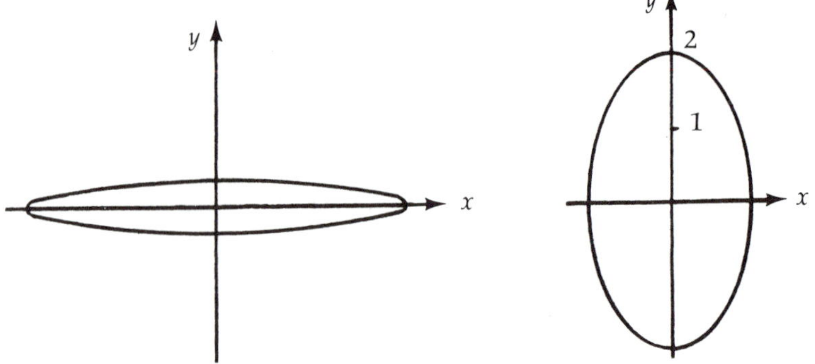

Figure 9. The effects of scaling the variables.

6.3 Other Considerations

Whether or not further iterations or further refinements of an optimization procedure should be pursued depends on many factors. In general, a prime consideration would be the amount of computer usage required to generate the successive approximating points. Naturally we have tried to keep the hand computations in this module to a minimum. However, it is not difficult to imagine formidable computations arising in the formulation of the Davidon function $\psi(t)$, its derivative $\psi'(t)$, and/or the determination of those negative roots t^* which are crucial in the process. Generally the equation $\psi'(t) = 0$ is not linear nor even quadratic (unlike our examples) and a numerical procedure for its solution must be initiated. This could be both costly and time-consuming in terms of computer usage; in fact, a routine to compute the gradient itself could be expensive.

"Both intuition and experience serve as guides..."

In practice the solution may not even be attempted, but instead, a small negative value for t might be selected and tried, based upon the assurance that the objective function must show some improvement when the optimum is pursued in the direction of the negative gradient, (Section 3.1). (Successive gradients cannot, then, be expected to be perpendicular; see Section 3.2). Both intuition and experience serve as guides in these matters; familiarity with the physical characteristics of a problem and an awareness of the approximate location of the optimum can be extremely valuable.

7. Concluding Remarks

The Gradient Search Procedure as outlined here does extend to n-dimensional problems. Our intention is that the geometric insight you have gained from an examination of the two-dimensional case will guide your understanding and appreciation of the possibilities of optimization in more general circumstances. The acceleration procedures, however, become relatively more complicated in higher dimensions. For descriptions of both PARTAN and conjugate gradient procedures, we again refer you to the wealth of existing literature on the subject of optimization. (See Section 8, References). Constrained optimization, in which other conditions are placed upon the independent variables, is also a large area we have left untouched.

Finally, we would like to point out that our treatment in this module is strictly in the spirit of an introduction to the topic, and

"Some would call the whole discipline of optimization an art form..."

hope that you will be motivated to explore further. We have mentioned briefly some of the difficulties, and some deciding factors in using the procedures outlined. The important topics of numerical precision and round-off have not been discussed.

Some would call the whole discipline of optimization an art form; others would quickly add that it is fraught with perils and pitfalls. Even though its methods are sometimes time-consuming and expensive, we often have no choice. Each "optimizer" must do the best possible, and will evolve a "bag of tricks" of his own, as he becomes more deeply involved in the subject.

8. References

The following text is well worth reading and you should derive from it some excellent incentive for further exploration of the subject of optimization.

Wilde, D. and Beightler, C. 1967. *Foundations of Optimization* Prentice-Hall, Inc. Cf. especially pages 271-344.

Also our earlier UMAP module "The Gradient and Some of Its Applications" (Unit 431) would provide helpful background information on vector notation, the Gradient itself, level curves, and the chain rule.

Other recommended reference texts:

Adby, P.R. and Dempster, M.A.H. 1974. *Introduction to Optimization Methods*. Halsted Press.

Cooper, L. and Steinberg, D. 1970. *Introduction to Methods of Optimization*. W.B. Saunders Company.

Hadley, G., and Whitten, T.M. 1963. *Analysis of Inventory Systems.* Prentice- Hall, Inc. 42-47.

Jacoby, S.L.S., Kowalik, J.S., and Pizzo, J.T. 1972. *Iterative Methods for Non-Linear Optimization Problems.* Prentice-Hall, Inc.

9. Optional Additional Exercises

Exercises:

5. For Examples 1, 2, and 3, choose an alternate initial approximating point (x_0,y_0) and perform a few iterations of the Gradient Search Procedure. Discuss the "progress" toward the

optimum point. You may also wish to implement the acceleration procedure.

6. In Section 3.1, we presented a rather general proof concerning the (local) decrease of the objective function for negative t. Prove *directly* that for objective functions whose level curves are elliptical in the vicinity of a minimum point, application of the Gradient Search Procedure does effect a decrease. As in Exercise 2, take $z = f(x,y) = x^2 + \mu y^2$; $\mu > 0$, $\mu \neq 1$. Use successive points (x_m, y_m) and (x_{m+2}, y_{m+2}) which lie along one edge of the Gradient Corridor and show that $f(x_{m+2}, y_{m+2}) < f(x_m, y_m)$. The hints given for Exercise 2 should be helpful.

7. Write a computer program to perform the computations for one of the examples or exercises which we have illustrated in previous sections. Could your program be easily modified to solve similar problems? (Optional)

10. Specific Applications

In this section, we outline a few applications which should be accessible to students of elementary calculus. It is not difficult to list examples which would quickly lead us into the more complex aspects of the field of Operations Research; since that is indeed more than we intend with this module, we present some examples for which you can find correct answers by a direct application of methods of calculus, and suggest that alternatively, you then apply to them the details of the Gradient Search Procedure which you have learned.

1. Consider the problem of solving two non-linear equations for a root (x^*,y^*):

$$g(x,y) = 0.$$
$$h(x,y) = 0.$$

Following a "function norm" method, we could form the objective function

$$f(x,y) = [g(x,y)]^2 + [h(x,y)]^2,$$

and proceed to minimize $f(x,y)$ using the Gradient Search. (The reader should give intuitive reasons why this technique might or might not be reasonable for approximating (x^*,y^*).)

You can see that, depending on the nature of the functions $g(x,y)$ and $h(x,y)$, the formation of the gradient of $f(x,y)$ and the Davidon function could be rather formidable.

Example:
Solve the (linear, this time) equations

$$x + y = 2$$
$$2x - y = 1$$

using the "function norm" method; i.e., find (x^*,y^*).

Solution:
Set $f(x,y) = (x+y-2)^2 + (2x-y-1)^2$ and start the Gradient Search at the point $(x_0,y_0) = (0,0)$.

Example:
Solve the equations

$$x^2 + y^2 = 4$$
$$xy = 1$$

using the "function norm" method; what are the four choices for (x^*,y^*)?

Solution:
Set $f(x,y) = (x^2 + y^2 - 4)^2 + (xy-1)^2$ and start the Gradient Search at the point $(x_0,y_0) = (2,0)$.

2. Find the shortest distance from the point $(\bar{x},\bar{y},\bar{z})$ to the surface $z = h(x,y)$.

Example:
Let the surface $h(x,y) = xy$ and the point $(\bar{x},\bar{y},\bar{z}) = (1,0,1)$.

Solution:
To find the shortest distance from the point to the surface we form the objective function

$$f(x,y) = (x-\bar{x})^2 + (y-\bar{y})^2 + (\bar{z}-h(x,y))^2$$
$$= (x-1)^2 + (y-0)^2 + (1-xy)^2$$

(which is the square of the usual formula for the distance between two points, with z replaced by $h(x,y)$) and begin the Gradient Search at the point $(x_0,y_0) = (0,0)$.

3. The "Least Squares" Procedure. Suppose we desire to fit a set of data points to a suitable straight line. Find constants m and b in the linear equation $y = mx + b$ such that the y-distance from the graph of $y = mx + b$ to the pre-assigned data points is minimized locally in a precise way.

Example:
Suppose the data points are given by (0,1) (2,3), (3,6); then determine "best" values of m and b by minimizing the objective function

$$f(m,b) = (b-1)^2 + (2m+b-3)^2 + (3m+b-6)^2.$$

Hint:
Look up the Least Squares Procedure and find the *exact* answer by methods of calculus; then compute $\vec{\nabla} f(m,b)$ using the starting point $(m_0,b_0) = (1,2)$. Is the Gradient Search Procedure a good way to find these constants m and b? Discuss this!

4. In the text by Hadley and Whitten (see References) you will find an interesting example of an objective function called a "penalty," or "cost" function. To illustrate, let

$$z = \frac{a}{x} + \frac{b}{x}(x-y)^2 + \frac{1}{x}(cy+dy^2),$$

where z is the average annual cost, x is the quantity of stock ordered at any one time, y is the number of back-orders that accumulate before an order for more stock is placed; and a,b,d,c are parameters (constants) of the system. The problem of minimizing cost is to determine $x > 0$ and $y \geq 0$ that minimize z. We suggest that you refer to the above-mentioned text for further discussion of problems of this type, and have a computer handy for the calculations!

Finally, in the text by Cooper and Steinberg (see References) you will find a chapter entitled "Search Techniques." It will be very instructive for you to get an overview of the various search techniques and their merits and disadvantages. There the Gradient Search Procedure is called the "Method of Steepest Descent." An exercise (number 9) at the end of the Chapter suggests fitting some realistic chemical data to an exponential curve by using several different search techniques, among them the Gradient Search Procedure.

11. Model Exam

a) Find a local maximum for the function $z = f(x,y) = 3xy - x^2 - y^3$; begin at the point (3,2), and calculate 2 additional approximating points. (Do not use a calculator here.)

b) Use the direction of the gradient corridor (as formed by the line joining $(3,2) = (x_0,y_0)$ and your second calculated approximating point (x_2,y_2) to accelerate the progress toward the optimum point.

[Note of encouragement: You will find that if you perform the calculations carefully and do not introduce round-off error by using a calculator, the procedure will "home-in" to the exact point you are seeking!]

12. Hints and Answers to Exercises

Exercises:

1. The slopes of paths joining these pairs of points (in the order mentioned) are −1/2 and 2; respectively. The reason for the perpendicularity of the paths lies in part 1 of Section 3.

2. Note that

$\nabla f(x_m,y_m) = 2x_m\hat{i} + 2\mu y_m\hat{j}$, and we can use the direction

$x_m\hat{i} + \mu y_m\hat{j}$; then

$$x_{m+1} = x_m + x_m t = x_m(1+t),$$

$$y_{m+1} = y_m + \mu y_m t = y_m(1+\mu t).$$

The value of t which minimizes the Davidon function is

$$t^* = -\left[\frac{x_m^2 + \mu^2 y_m^2}{x_m^2 + \mu^3 y_m^2}\right]$$ so that the new coordinates become

$$x_{m+1} = x_m \left[\frac{\mu^3 y_m^2 - \mu^2 y_m{}^2}{x_m^2 + \mu^3\, y_m^2}\right] = y_m \mu^2 \alpha_m$$

$$y_{m+1} = y_m \left[\frac{x_m^2 - \mu x_m^2}{x_m{}^2 + \mu^3 y_m{}^2}\right] = -x_m \alpha_m$$

where

$$\alpha_m = \frac{x_m y_m(\mu-1)}{x_m^2 + \mu^3 y_m^2}.$$

Repeating these steps for the next iteration, one finds

$$x_{m+2} = \mu^2 y_{m+1}\alpha_{m+1} = (-\mu^2\alpha_m\alpha_{m+1})x_m$$

$$y_{m+2} = -x_{m+1}\alpha_{m+1} = (-\mu^2\alpha_m\alpha_{m+1})y_m.$$

So that $p = -\mu^2\alpha_m\alpha_{m+1}$ and $p > 0$ since $\alpha_m\alpha_{m+1} < 0$, (verify this)!

The 2 straight lines, (based upon the argument preceding Figure 5), can be found by simply joining the points (x_0,y_0) and (x_1,y_1) to the origin.

3. (Outlined in the text)

4. $f_x(x,y) = x + y - 3$; $f_y(x,y) = x + 2y - 2$. Simultaneous solution of the system $f_x(x,y) = 0 = f_y(x,y)$ yields $(x,y) = (4,-1)$. By the second derivative test for functions of two variables, $(4,-1)$ is a local minimum.

6. As in the answer for Exercise 2, we have

$$x_{m+1} = \mu^2 y_m\alpha_m, \qquad y_{m+1} = -x_m\alpha_m$$

and

$$x_{m+2} = -\mu^2\alpha_m\alpha_{m+1}x_m, \qquad y_{m+2} = -\mu^2\alpha_m\alpha_{m+1}y_m,$$

where

$$\alpha_i = \frac{x_i y_i(\mu-1)}{x_i^2 + \mu^3 y_i^2}, \qquad i = m,\ m+1.$$

Then

$$\frac{f(x_{m+2},\ y_{m+2})}{f(x_m,y_m)} = (\mu^2\alpha_m\alpha_{m+1})^2$$

and we wish to show that $|\mu^2\alpha_m\alpha_{m+1}| < 1$.

By replacement of α_m and α_{m+1} and cancellation of some common terms, we have

$$|\mu^2\alpha_m\alpha_{m+1}| = \frac{\mu(\mu-1)^2\, x_m^2 y_m^2}{(x_m^2 + \mu^3 y_m^2)\,(x_m^2 + \mu y_m^2)}$$

which can be rewritten

$$= \frac{\mu(\mu-1)^2}{\left[1 + \mu^3\left(\frac{y_m}{x_m}\right)^2\right]\left[\mu + \left(\frac{x_m}{y_m}\right)^2\right]}$$

Now if $0 < \mu < 1$, a further re-arrangement of the latter clearly indicates that its value is < 1:

$$|\mu^2\alpha_m\alpha_{m+1}| = \frac{(\mu-1)^2}{\left[1 + \mu^3\left(\frac{y_m}{x_m}\right)^2\right]\left[1 + \frac{1}{\mu}\left(\frac{x_m}{y_m}\right)^2\right]} < 1.$$

And if $\mu > 1$,

$$= \frac{\left(1-\frac{1}{\mu}\right)^2}{1 + \left\{\frac{1}{\mu^3}\left(\frac{x_m}{y_m}\right)^2 + \frac{1}{\mu^2} + \mu\left(\frac{y_m}{x_m}\right)^2\right\}} < 1.$$

and the proof is complete.

13. Answers to Model Exam

a) $\vec{\nabla} f(x,y) = (3y - 2x)\hat{i} + (3x - 3y^2)\hat{j}$

$\vec{\nabla} f(3,2) = -3\hat{j}$ (use direction $-1\hat{j}$)

$x_1 = 3,\ y_1 = 2 - t.$

$\psi(t) = 9(2-t) - 9 - (2-t)^3$

which has a maximum at $t^* = 2 - \sqrt{3} > 0.$

$(x_1,y_1) = (3, \sqrt{3})$

$\vec{\nabla} f(3,\sqrt{3}) = (3\sqrt{3} - 6)\hat{i} + 0\,\hat{j}$ (use direction $-\hat{i}$)

The next value of t^* is $(3/2)(2 - \sqrt{3})$, and

$(x_2,y_2) = ((3/2)\sqrt{3}, \sqrt{3}).$

Note also that $f(3,2) = 1$, $f(3,\sqrt{3}) = 6\sqrt{3} - 9 = 1.392$, and

$f((3/2)\sqrt{3},\sqrt{3}) = 27/4 - 3\sqrt{3} = 1.554$, where a calculator has been used to compute the decimal equivalents only for purposes of comparison.

b) Acceleration direction, along line joining (3,2) and $((3/2)\sqrt{3}, \sqrt{3})$, represented by vector

$((3/2)\sqrt{3} - 3)\hat{i} + (\sqrt{3} - 2)\hat{j}.$

Then $x(t) = 3 + ((3/2)\sqrt{3} - 3)t$

$y(t) = 2 + (\sqrt{3} - 2)t$

Before inserting these expressions in the Davidon function $\psi(t)$, we suggest some modification in their forms, to reduce the computational difficulty *while retaining accuracy.*

Note that $x(t) = 3 + \frac{3}{2}(\sqrt{3} - 2)t$

$y(t) = 2 + (\sqrt{3} - 2)t,$

Letting $\lambda = (2 - \sqrt{3})t$, (a positive multiple of t)

$x(\lambda) = 3 - \frac{3}{2}\lambda$

$y(\lambda) = 2 - \lambda$

and again a simplification is possible by letting $\mu = 2 - \lambda$, so that finally

$x(\mu) = \frac{3}{2}\mu$

$y(\mu) = \mu.$

Then, finally, $\psi(\mu) = \frac{9}{2}\mu^2 - \frac{9}{4}\mu^2 - \mu^3$

$$= \frac{9}{4}\mu^2 - \mu^3$$

which has a maximum at $\mu^* = \frac{3}{2}$.

Then $(x,y) = \left(\frac{9}{4}, \frac{3}{2}\right)$, which is the optimum point.

(Note that $\mu^* = \frac{3}{2} \rightarrow \lambda^* = \frac{1}{2} \rightarrow t^* = \frac{1}{2(2-\sqrt{3})}$,

a positive value as would be expected in searching for a maximum. You can now understand that the optimum point would probably not be reached exactly if a calculator had been used, due to round-off errors.)

Acknowledgement

We would like to acknowledge the helpful suggestions regarding applications which were offered by Professors Carroll O. Wilde, Frank D. Faulkner, and Guillermo Owen, all of the Naval Postgraduate School.

UMAP

Modules in Undergraduate Mathematics and Its Applications

Module 534

Descriptive Models for Perception of Optical Illusions: I

David A. Smith

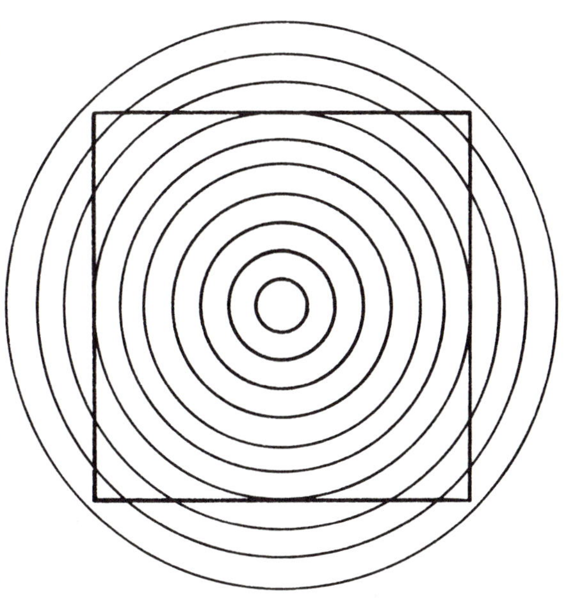

Published in cooperation with the Society for Industrial and Applied Mathematics, the Mathematical Association of America, the National Council of Teachers of Mathematics, the American Mathematical Association of Two-Year Colleges, and The Institute of Management Sciences.

COMAP

INTERMODULAR DESCRIPTION SHEET:	UMAP Unit 534
TITLE:	DESCRIPTIVE MODELS FOR PERCEPTIONS OF OPTICAL ILLUSIONS: I
AUTHOR:	David A. Smith Department of Mathematics Duke University Durham, NC 27706
REVIEW STAGE/DATE:	III 9/30/81
CLASSIFICATION:	APPL VECTOR DIFF CALC & ELEM DIFF EQUA/ VIS PERCEPTION
TARGET AUDIENCE:	This module is an appropriate supplement for the third semester of calculus or the first semester of differential equations.
ABSTRACT:	The historical background of the study of stable illusions of angle is sketched to show how a 19th century concept leads to formalization of a first order differential equation model for the apparent curves in such illusions. Some difficulties with the model are identified, and these lead to a refined formulation based on parametrization by arc length and polar coordinate transformations to solve the refined equations.
PREREQUISITES:	Vector differential calculus in the plane, parametric representations, polar coordinates, variable separable differential equations, techniques of integration, all at the level normally covered in the first three semesters of calculus.
RELATED UNITS:	Descriptive Models for Perception of Optical Illusions: II (Unit 535)

DESCRIPTIVE MODELS FOR PERCEPTION OF OPTICAL ILLUSIONS: I

David A. Smith
Department of Mathematics
Duke University
Durham, NC 27706

Table of Contents

MODULES AND MONOGRAPHS IN UNDERGRADUATE MATHEMATICS AND ITS APPLICATIONS PROJECT (UMAP)

The goal of UMAP is to develop, through a community of users and developers, a system of instructional modules in undergraduate mathematics and its applications that may be used to supplement existing courses and from which complete courses may eventually be built.

The Project is guided by a National Advisory Board of mathematicians, scientists, and educators. UMAP is funded by a grant from the National Science Foundation to the Consortium for Mathematics and Its Applications, Inc. (COMAP), a nonprofit corporation engaged in research and development in mathematics education.

UMAP ADVISORY BOARD

The Project and author would like to thank Eric Nummela of New England College and C.C. Rousseau of Memphis State University for their reviews and all others who assisted in the production of this unit.

1. Background of the Problem

The picture on the cover (also Figure 1) is an optical illusion, one that is sometimes described as a "stable illusion of angle." It is "stable" in the sense that it is perceived in only one way, in contrast to the familiar Necker cubes, perception of which "jumps" spontaneously between two equally plausible interpretations. It is an illusion because almost everyone sees the lines in the figure as slightly bowed, when they are in fact straight. (You may check that by placing a straightedge along each line or by placing the cover flat at eye level and sighting along each line.) It is an "illusion of angle" because the misperception is evidently caused in some way by the distortion pattern of concentric circles, which has many angular crossings with the distorted lines. (A stable illusion having nothing to do with angles can be constructed by drawing line segments of exactly the same length, one vertical and one horizontal, next to each other. They will appear to have different lengths.)

"... in order to perceive a distortion, one must 'know' the 'true' shape of the distorted curve(s)."

This module will explore some descriptive models of perception of stable illusions of angle consisting of a distortion pattern and distorted lines. In principle, the distorted figure could be made up of more general curves; but in order to perceive a distortion, one must "know" the "true" shape of the distorted curve(s). Thus, it would be possible to detect circles that are slightly out-of-round; but it is unlikely that we could perceive distortions in hyperbolas or sine waves, for example. In any case, the models under consideration will be demonstrated adequately by illusions with bowed lines. Our models are "descriptive" in the sense that they attempt to describe both quantitatively and qualitatively what we perceive, but they do not attempt to explain the misperception phenomenon in terms of the neurophysiology of the human optical system.

"Describing misperception accurately is an important step in understanding how the human optical system functions, since we all share this particular trait."

Describing misperception accurately is an important step in understanding how the human optical system functions, since we all seem to share this particular trait. ("All" in this context means adults in civilized societies; there is some experimental evidence that young children and members of primitive societies do not have this "flaw" in their visual systems.) The problem has a long history of study, involving many apparently different theories, and it is still not adequately resolved. Indeed, there is a substantial amount of controversy among the proponents of competing models and theories, including those to be presented here. It will not be possible to survey the study of perception, even that part dealing with just stable illusions of angle. We will content ourselves with a few brief remarks to provide a historical context for the models to be presented.

Perception of optical illusions was the object of intensive study by psychologists in the nineteenth century, especially in Germany. By the 1890s, there were perhaps a dozen competing theories to explain stable illusions of angle, one of which is in fact the basis for the models to be studied here. We quote it in rough translation from a paper of Franz Brentano (Ref. 1):

> "... the phenomenon is a consequence of the well-known fact of overestimation of the smaller and underestimation of the larger angles."

For future reference, we call this *Brentano's Hypothesis*. Here "smaller" and "larger" have to be interpreted as referring to acute and obtuse angles, respectively. Thus, Brentano's Hypothesis asserts that we perceive angles to be more nearly rectangular than they really are. That is consistent with the experimental observation that this is an acquired trait among those who live in largely rectangular surroundings, one that is not seen in those lacking a certain maturity or in those who spend their lives in jungles.

Leaving aside the question of how "well-known" the hypothesis is (there is some contradictory evidence in the experimental literature), let us see how it could explain what we perceive in Figure 1. When you look at the figure, your eyes transmit to your brain certain information about the object viewed, including the angles at which the lines and circles cross; and it is this data that is slightly in error. You also see that each of the lines is continuous, not broken. You may *know* that the lines are straight; but the visual system has to reject that information, because it is inconsistent with the correct observation of continuity and the slightly incorrect angular data. It is plausible to suppose that the brain processes the available data to produce the simplest possible consistent visual image, which in this case would require slightly bowed lines. Before reading further, verify that if the figure really had the bowed lines you perceive, all of the angles would be slightly closer to right angles than if the lines were straight.

"... the brain processes the available data to produce the simplest possible consistent visual image..."

In the 1930's the attempt to place the social sciences, including psychology, on the same sort of logical foundation as the physical sciences was begun in earnest. In some cases physical models were literally copied. Thus, W.D. Orbison (who first published Figure 1) gave the following interpretation (Ref. 5): The distortion pattern is (or is like, the distinction is not made clear) a physical force field distorting the lines in the directions of "positions of cohesive equilibrium," exactly as a magnetic field arranges iron filings into lines of magnetic equilibrium. Orbison's equilibrium positions had a geometric meaning as well, one that we would call "orthogonal trajectories." Thus the equilibrium positions for the pattern of concentric circles are the lines passing through the common center of the circles. Distortion of a crossing line toward one of these lines (through the same crossing point) is the same thing as making the crossing angle more nearly a right angle, i.e. this is just another formulation of Brentano's Hypothesis.

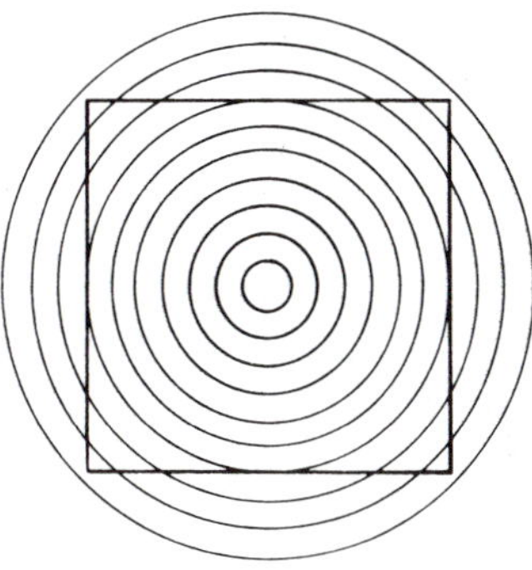

Figure 1. A stable illusion of angle: the Orbison illusion.

In a series of papers starting in the late 1960s, W.C. Hoffman has attempted to put visual (and other) perception on a modern mathematical foundation involving differential geometry and Lie transformation groups, subjects that are beyond the level of this module. However, the application of Hoffman's perceptual theories to stable illusions of angle can be described in terms of vectors in the plane, in much the same way one describes forces in a physics course. Thus Hoffman's model is a logical successor to Orbison's, and we will see that it too is consistent with Brentano's Hypothesis, even though Hoffman specifically contradicts the hypothesis in one of his applications of the model (Ref. 3). Some difficulties in the application of Hoffman's model will be observed, and resolution of those difficulties will lead to our own model (Ref. 6), based directly on Brentano's Hypothesis.

2. The Hoffman Model

2.1 Vector Interpretation of the Brentano Hypothesis

Figure 2 illustrates the way Brentano's Hypothesis will be formulated by vectors in the plane. The slope of a curve (or line) in the plane at any given point is determined by either a tangent vector (same slope) or a normal vector (negative reciprocal slope) at that point. In the Figure, $\vec{N}$ represents a normal vector to the distorted line at one of the crossing points in the illusion, and $\vec{T}$ represents a tangent vector to the distortion curve at the same point Both $\vec{N}$ and $\vec{T}$ and can be chosen in either of two directions, and we choose a pair of directions so that the two vectors make an acute angle. (There are two ways to make this choice, but the acute angle is the same in both cases. Our description of the illusion turns out not to depend on which choice is made.) Now we suppose that $\vec{N}$ is distorted by adding to it a small component in the direction of $\vec{T}$ to produce an "apparent normal":

$$\vec{N}_a = \vec{N} + \epsilon\vec{T} \tag{1}$$

(Think of ϵ as a small positive number; later we will discuss how small it should be.)

The assumption of Brentano's Hypothesis is that we perceive at least a small section of the distorted line as being perpendicular to $\vec{N}_a$ instead of $\vec{N}$ (the dashed segment in Figure 2, which of course exaggerates the distortion effect.) This is *all* that is required mathematically by Brentano's Hypothesis; the distinctions between the models to be discussed come down to different decisions about the lengths of the vectors $\vec{N}$ and $\vec{T}$ and whether ϵ is constant or dependent on position in the illusion.

2.2 Parametrization of Curves

The most convenient way to represent the curves in a distortion pattern (such as the pattern of concentric circles) is by a parametrization using derivatives. This makes it possible to discuss slopes and directions for a whole family of curves without singling out any particular one. We will illustrate this with the concentric circle pattern. If the origin of the coordinate system is assumed to be at the center of the circles, then each such circle can be represented parametrically by:

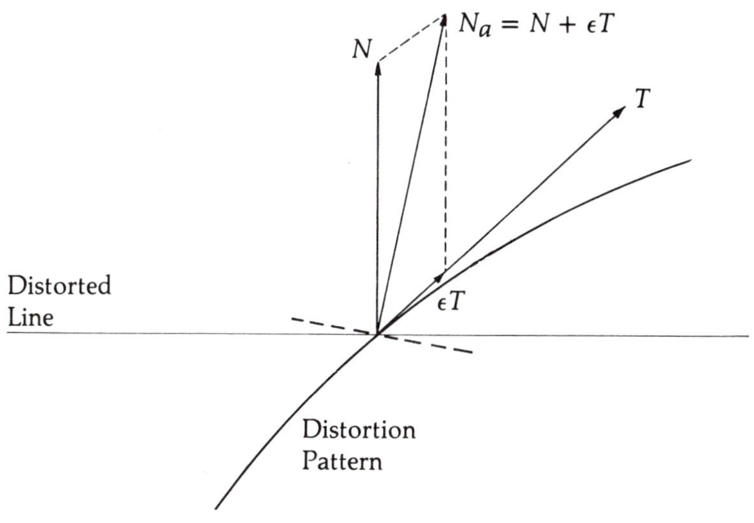

Figure 2. Apparent normal resulting from the Brentano Hypothesis.

$$x = a \cos t,\ y = a \sin t,\ 0 \leq t < 2\pi, \tag{2}$$

where a is the radius. Then

$$dx/dt = -a \sin t = -y, \tag{3}$$

and

$$dy/dt = a \cos t = x, \tag{4}$$

so every circle in the family satisfies the conditions

$$x' = -y, \quad y' = x, \tag{5}$$

where the prime denotes differentiation with respect to the parameter t.

Exercise 1:

Show that no other curve satisfies equations (5), i.e., the set of solutions (x,y) consists of circles centered at the origin. [S-1]

Using the previous example as a guide, we now explain what constitutes a "suitable representation" of a family of curves. The description (2) of the family of concentric circles actually involves *two* parameters, one of which (a) identifies individual curves in the family, and the other of which (t) identifies points on an individual curve. Equations (2) may be thought of as infinitely many sets (one for each a) of parametric equations (with t as parameter), one set for each curve in the family. By contrast, equations (5) are a single set of two (differential) equations that describes the entire family. Note that the curve-identifying parameter a does not appear in (5).

We define a "suitable representation" of a family of curves to be a pair of simultaneous, first-order, differential equations,

$$x' = f(x,y), \quad y' = g(x,y), \tag{6}$$

with the property that a given curve

$$x = F(t), \quad y = G(t), \tag{7}$$

belongs to the family if and only if its coordinate functions (7) satisfy the system (6) identically, that is,

$$F'(t) = f(F(t),G(t)), \quad G'(t) = g(F(t),G(t)). \tag{8}$$

The coordinate functions (7) may involve one or more curve-identifying parameters (like a), but these must not appear in the differential system (6), nor may t appear in any way other than as the independent variable of differentiation. Our example above shows that the family of concentric circles, $x^2 + y^2 = a^2$, which may be parametrized by (2), has the suitable representation (5). Other examples will be introduced below (and in Part II) as needed.

For any curve described by a parametric representation,

$$x = F(t), \; y = G(t), \tag{9}$$

a tangent vector at a given point can be constructed by:

$$\vec{T} = x'\vec{i} + y'\vec{j}, \tag{10}$$

where the derivatives are evaluated at the given point. For the concentric circle pattern, substitution of (5) in (10) gives:

$$\vec{T} = -y\vec{i} + x\vec{j}. \tag{11}$$

Note that this formula requires only the coordinates of the point of tangency, *not* the corresponding value of t.

Exercise 2: Show that the tangent vectors to circles given by (11) always point in the counterclockwise direction. [S-2]

It makes little difference which of the four lines in Figure 1 we study as the distorted line, due to the symmetry of the figure. For convenience, we restrict our attention to the upper horizontal line, for which we may take

$$\vec{N} = \vec{j}\ . \tag{12}$$

However, this does not automatically satisfy the restriction that $\vec{N}$ and $\vec{T}$ should form an acute angle. Rather than worry about this every time a new family of curves is considered, we can reinterpret equation (1) to allow ϵ to be either positive or negative, as long as $\vec{N}$ and $\epsilon\vec{T}$ form an acute angle.

Exercise 3: Verify that the angle between $\vec{T}$ and $\vec{N}$, as given by equations (11) and (12), is acute in the first quadrant, obtuse in the second quadrant. Thus, for the upper horizontal line, we require ϵ to be positive to the right of the y-axis, negative to the left of the y-axis.

Now our application of Brentano's Hypothesis to the Orbison illusion produces an apparent normal at any crossing point (x,y) given by:

$$\begin{aligned}\vec{N} &= \vec{j} + \epsilon\,(-y\vec{i} + x\vec{j}) \qquad (13)\\ &= -\epsilon y\vec{i} + (1 + \epsilon x)\,\vec{j}\ .\end{aligned}$$

Since a vector $a\vec{i} + b\vec{j}$ has slope b/a, the slope of a line perpendicular to the vector is $-a/b$. It follows from (10) that the slope of the apparent line at a crossing point (x,y) is $\epsilon y/(1 + \epsilon x)$.

2.3 The Differential Equation Model

The number of crossing points in a given illusion is clearly finite, so the situation we are studying is inherently discrete. Indeed, if there are too many curves in the distortion pattern, they will completely obliterate the crossing lines, and there will be no illusion. On the other hand, if there are too few curves (only one or two, say), there is no illusion either; the bending effect depends on the fact that the distorting curves are relatively close together. Therefore, it is reasonable to *model* the discrete situation by a continuous one, that is, to assume the Brentano effect on the slopes applies at *every* point along the distorted line. For the case of the Orbison illusion discussed above, this leads to the conclusion that the apparent curve must satisfy

"... if there are too many curves in the distortion pattern, they will completely obliterate the crossing lines, and there will be no illusion... if there are too few curves... there is no illusion either..."

$$dy/dx = \epsilon y/(1 + \epsilon x), \tag{14}$$

where the sign of ϵ is the same as that of x. We assume in the following discussion that ϵ is constant on each of the intervals $x < 0$ and $x > 0$.

Equation (14) is a simple differential equation, one that may be solved by a technique commonly studied in the first calculus course: separation of variables. Thus, we first multiply through by dx and divide through by y to get:

$$dy/y = \epsilon dx/(1 + \epsilon x). \tag{15}$$

Now we may integrate both sides of (15) to get:

$$ln\ |y| = ln\ |1 + \epsilon x| + C. \tag{16}$$

For the top horizontal line (real or apparent), y will always be positive, and our sign restriction makes $1 + \epsilon x$ also positive, so the absolute value bars may be dropped. We may now solve for y in equation (16) by taking exponentials on both sides:

$$y = k(1 + \epsilon x), \tag{17}$$

where $k = \exp C$ is a positive constant. (Note that k is also the value of y when $x = 0$ on the apparent curve.) The apparent curves, according to this model, are straight lines with slopes $k\epsilon$, that is, a small negative slope to the left of the y-axis and a small positive slope to the right. Look again at Figure 1. Is that what you see in the upper part of the figure?

2.4 Another Example: The Hering Illusion

Figure 3 shows another classical optical illusion, the Hering illusion. The distortion pattern in this case consists of lines through the origin, that is, of the orthogonal trajectories of the circles in the Orbison illusion. Thus a suitable representation for this family of curves (lines) can be derived from equations (5) by taking negative reciprocal slopes:

$$x' = x, \ y' = y. \tag{18}$$

Then the apparent normal can be computed as:

$$\begin{aligned} \vec{N}_a &= \vec{N} + \epsilon\vec{T} \\ &= \vec{j} + \epsilon\,(x\vec{i} + \vec{j}\,) \\ &= \epsilon x\vec{i} + (1 + \epsilon y)\vec{j}\ . \end{aligned}$$

Exercise 4: Show that ϵ is positive at all points on the upper horizontal, that is, $\vec{N}$ and $\vec{T}$ form an acute angle (except when $x = 0$).

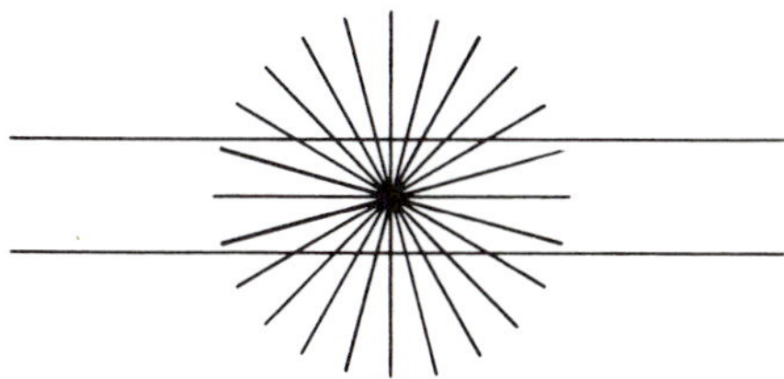

Figure 3. The classical Hering illusion.

The apparent normal vector leads to an apparent slope

$$dy/dx = -\epsilon x/(1 + \epsilon y). \tag{19}$$

Exercise 5: Solve equation (19) by separation of variables, and show that the solutions are arcs of circles with very large radii and centers on the negative y-axis. Does this agree with what you see in Figure 3? [S-3]

2.5 Some Difficulties with the Hoffman Model

"... the computation and conclusion for the Hering illusion exactly parallel a corresponding example in Hoffman's 1971 paper, and the conclusion for the Orbison illusion seems to be what Hoffman would have computed if he had included that example."

It is perhaps a little unfair to Professor Hoffman to attach his name to the model just illustrated with the Orbison and Hering illusions, since his work is based on higher mathematics that we have not discussed. However, the computation and conclusion for the Hering illusion exactly parallel a corresponding example in Hoffman's 1971 paper, and the conclusion for the Orbison illusion seems to be what Hoffman would have computed if he had included that example.

On the other hand, as noted above, Hoffman specifically denies the validity of the Brentano Hypothesis as a general principle. Up to this point, we have used the hypothesis only to resolve the sign of ϵ, having said nothing at all about its magnitude or about the magnitudes of $\vec{N}$ and $\vec{T}$. (Thus we are working with a qualitative model only at this point; the quantitative aspect will come later.) Hoffman chooses to resolve the sign of ϵ by appeal to "subjective impressions" of direction or motion. In the case of the Hering illusion, this requires that one senses the upper line as being directed from left to right, while the lower line is directed from right to left. Take a good look at Figure 3. Do you get that subjective impression of direction? Since Hoffman did not include the Orbison illusion in his paper, we cannot know what subjective impression would lead to a change of sign for ϵ in the middle of each of the lines. But, as we have seen, the Brentano Hypothesis settles the question of which way the distortion should go, and in an unambiguous manner.

More serious objections can be raised to the Hoffman model. First, the distortion effect on the real normal $\vec{N}$ is proportional to $\vec{T}$, so the magnitude of the effect is proportional to the length of $\vec{T}$. In each of the examples considered, the length of $\vec{T}$ at a point (x,y) is the distance from the origin to that point (verify). Is it reasonable that the strength of the distortion effect should depend on how far the crossing point is from an arbitrarily selected origin? The answer to that question is not obvious, since the origin in each case was also the center of the figure, which might have some bearing on the matter. However, we will see in exercises later that the "natural" origin for the coordinate system need not be in the center of the figure, indeed not be in the picture at all! The choice of parametrizations of the circles and lines, while natural, was also rather arbitrary. Do the conclusions depend on this choice? Unfortunately, they do; different parametrizations actually lead to qualitatively different results. (Hoffman would consider the parametrizations used so far to be "canonical," that is to say, inevitable; but we will see in the next chapter how a different choice can lead to superior results and resolve the difficulties being considered here in a logically satisfactory manner.)

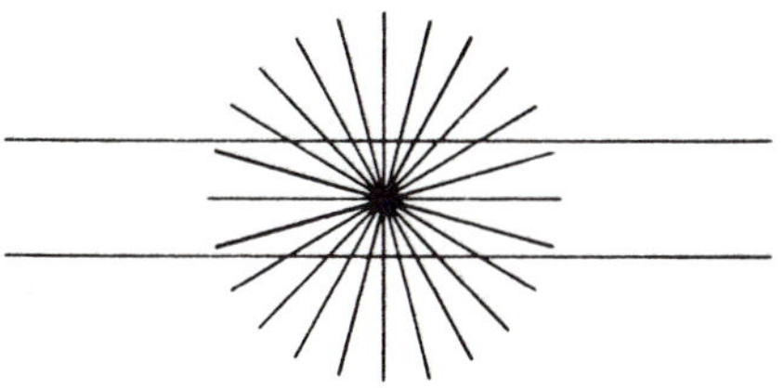

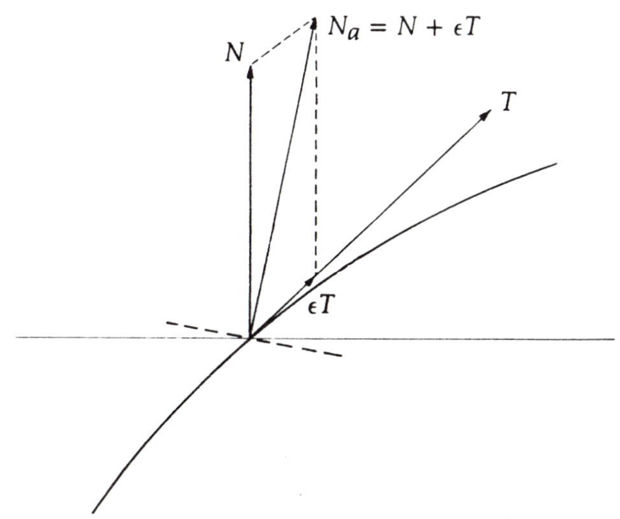

11

3. The Normalized Model

3.1 Removing Dependency on Position in the Plane

The problem with the Hoffman model identified in the previous section is that the choice of tangent vector to the distortion pattern depends on the choice of parametrization of the pattern. Since the tangent vectors actually used had lengths equal to the distance from the origin, the magnitude of the distortion effect on $\vec{N}$ was proportional to distance from the origin. This dependence on position can be eliminated by the simple expedient of "normalizing" $\vec{T}$, that is, requiring that $\vec{T}$ should be a unit vector. As you know from your calculus course, a unit tangent vector can be obtained from any tangent vector by dividing by its length. Of course, this changes the parametrization of the curves as well. For example, consider the family of concentric circles represented by equation (11) again. If $\vec{T}$ is replaced by $\vec{T}/|\vec{T}|$, the new representation in terms of unit tangent vectors is

$$\vec{T}' = \frac{-y}{\sqrt{x^2+y^2}}\,\vec{i} + \frac{x}{\sqrt{x^2+y^2}}\,\vec{j}\,. \tag{20}$$

This is equivalent to the suitable (but not simple) representation

$$x' = -y/\sqrt{x^2+y^2}, \quad y' = x/\sqrt{x^2+y^2}. \tag{21}$$

Of course, for any given circle of radius a, equations (21) are equivalent to the simple (but no longer suitable) representation

$$x' = -y/a, \quad y' = x/a. \tag{22}$$

A parametrization of concentric circles that leads to any of the representations (20) – (22) is

$$x = a\cos(s/a), \quad y = a\sin(s/a), \quad 0 < s < 2\pi a. \tag{23}$$

(Verify.)

In general, it would not be an easy matter to write down an explicit parametrization for a given family of curves that would lead to unit tangent vectors at every point. Fortunately, it is not necessary to do this, since we can always normalize the tangent vectors arising from any suitable representation as we did above, by dividing each vector by its length. However, it is useful to consider in the abstract how this normalized representation results from a certain parametrization, because that reinforces the idea that we are now working with inherent geometric properties of the curves that do not depend on any particular choice of coordinate system. Clearly a correct model of perception of optical illusions must not depend on how one chooses parametrizations of the curves.

"...it is useful to consider in the abstract how this normalized representation results from a certain parametrization ..."

Let $\vec{R} = x\vec{i} + y\vec{j}$ be the position vector for points (x,y) on a curve, and let s denote arc length along the curve, measured from some fixed starting point. We can also think of s as time if the curve is being traversed by a moving point whose speed is one unit of distance per unit of time. Now the curve may be parametrized with s as parameter, in the sense that the coordinates x and y are functions of s, which is either the distance travelled from the starting point or the elapsed time. Recall from your calculus course that $d\vec{R}/dt$ is always a tangent vector to the curve for any choice of parameter t (in fact, it is the vector we denoted by $\vec{T}$ in Section 2.2), and for the particular choice of s as parameter, $d\vec{R}/ds$ is a *unit* tangent vector. To summarize, a parametrization that leads to unit tangent vectors at every point can be obtained in two conceptually different ways: (a) parametrize by arc length; or (b) choose an arbitrary parametrization and normalize. Except for possible differences of direction of travel or location of starting point (which we can take care of on an ad hoc basis), these must lead to the *same* parametrization, since the vector representation is the same.

"...the value of considering the same parametrization ...can be stated very simply: Method (a) characterizes the curve in terms of an intrinsic geometry property (arc length) that does not depend on choice of origin or coordinate system. Method (b) gives a simple way of computing the representation."

Finally, the value of considering the same parametrization in these two ways can be stated very simply: Method (a) characterizes the curve in terms of an intrinsic geometric property (arc length) that does not depend on choice of origin or coordinate system. Method (b) gives a simple way of computing the representation. For purposes of constructing a normalized Brentano model, we need only select a parametrization for method (b) that leads to a suitable representation for the family of curves; normalization will clearly preserve this suitability.

We have concentrated so far on the representation of the distortion pattern by unit tangent vectors. Of course, the distorted line should also be parametrized by arc length, but it was already represented by a unit vector at each point ($\vec{N} = \vec{j}$), so it is not necessary to make any change in that part of the model. We consider now the effect of the reparametrization on the two examples discussed in the previous chapter.

3.2 The Orbison Illusion

We have just seen that the distortion pattern of concentric circles has a suitable representation (20) by unit tangent vectors. We may now compute the apparent normal as before:

$$\vec{N}_a = \vec{N} + \epsilon\vec{T} \tag{24}$$

$$= \vec{j} + \epsilon(-y\vec{i} + x\vec{j})/\sqrt{x^2+y^2}$$

$$= (-\epsilon y/\sqrt{x^2+y^2})\vec{i} + (1+\epsilon x/\sqrt{x^2+y^2})\vec{j}\ .$$

Now when we use (24) to determine the apparent slope at each point, we find (after a little simplification) that:

$$dy/dx = \epsilon\, y/(\sqrt{x^2+y^2} + \epsilon\, x). \tag{25}$$

Equation (25) presents us with a new problem. Unlike the differential equation (14) given by the Hoffman model, the variables are not separable now. The appropriate method for solving this equation involves a transformation to polar coordinates, which we will take up after deriving the corresponding equation for the Hering illusion.

3.3 The Hering Illusion

As with the Orbison illusion, we form a unit tangent vector $\vec{T}$ from equations (18) by dividing through by the length of $d\vec{R}/dt$:

$$\vec{T} = (x\vec{i} + y\vec{j})\ /\sqrt{x^2+y^2}. \tag{26}$$

Then the apparent normal is:

$$\vec{N}_a = (\epsilon x/\sqrt{x^2+y^2})\vec{i} + (1+\epsilon y/\sqrt{x^2+y^2})\vec{j}\ . \tag{27}$$

From (27) we find the differential equation for the apparent curve:

$$dy/dx = -\epsilon x/(\sqrt{x^2+y^2} + \epsilon y), \tag{28}$$

which is just as complicated as equation (25), and roughly of the same form.

3.4 Polar Coordinate Transformations

We pause now in our development of the models to consider a technique for solving equations (25) and (28). All of the necessary information about polar coordinate transformations is in your calculus book, but this specific application may not be.

From the expression for x and y in terms of r and θ,

$$x = r \cos \theta, \; y = r \sin \theta, \tag{29}$$

we may compute (total) differentials of x and y:

$$dx = \cos \theta \, dr - r \sin \theta \, d\theta, \tag{30}$$

$$dy = \sin \theta \, dr + r \cos \theta \, d\theta. \tag{31}$$

The chain rule assures us that it is legitimate to divide these expressions to find dy/dx:

$$\frac{dy}{dx} = \frac{\sin \theta \, dr + r \cos \theta \, d\theta}{\cos \theta \, dr - r \sin \theta \, d\theta} . \tag{32}$$

Now we divide numerator and denominator on the right in (32) by $d\theta$ and write r' for $dr/d\theta$ to get:

$$\frac{dy}{dx} = \frac{r' \sin \theta + r \cos \theta}{r' \cos \theta - r \sin \theta} . \tag{33}$$

This doesn't look very promising as a simplification, but bear with us!

Exercises 6-9:

6. Substitute for dy/dx, x, and y in equation (25) from equations (29) and (33). Simplify by clearing fractions, cancelling, and using an appropriate trigonometric identity. You should end up with:

$$r' \sin\theta + r\cos\theta + r\epsilon = 0. \tag{34}$$

Now solve for r' to get:

$$dr/d\theta = -r(\epsilon + \cos\theta)/\sin\theta. \tag{35}$$

Note that equation (35) is variable separable. Separate the variables and integrate both sides to obtain:

$$r = K/(\sin\theta\,(\csc\theta - \cot\theta)^{\epsilon}). \tag{36}$$

Then multiply through by $\sin\theta$, and multiply and divide by $(\csc\theta + \cot\theta)^{\epsilon}$ to get the solution in the form:

$$y = K\,(\csc\theta + \cot\theta)^{\epsilon}. \tag{37}$$

This gives the y-coordinates on the apparent curve explicitly as a function of the central angle θ. Note that K is the apparent value of y when $\theta = \pi/2$, that is, when $x = 0$. [S-4]

7. Eliminate θ in equation (37) to find an explicit equation in x and y for the apparent curve. (This equation cannot be solved for y as a function of x, and it is not much help in determining the shape of the apparent curve.) [S-5]

8. Make the polar coordinate transformation in the differential equation (28) for the Hering illusion, and solve as in Exercise 6 for y as a function of θ. [S-6]

9. Eliminate θ from the answer in Exercise 8 to get an equation in x and y for the apparent Hering curve. [S-7]

Further Exercises

10. Figure 4 shows an illusion with a distortion pattern consisting of hyperbolas with equations of the form $xy = a$. Find: (**a**) a suitable representation of the distortion pattern; (**b**) the differential equation whose solutions give the apparent curves; (**c**) the appropriate signs for ϵ. [S-8]

11. Rotate Figure 4 through 45 degrees, so the hyperbolas now belong to the family $x^2 - y^2 = a$ (where a may be either positive or negative). Repeat Exercise 10. [S-9]

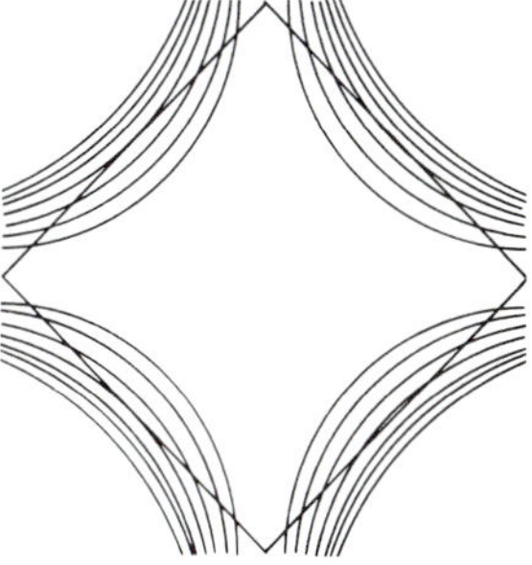

Figure 4. Hyperbola illusion.

12. Figure 5 shows an illusion with distortion pattern consisting of sine waves of the same period, but varying amplitude, $y = A \sin x$. Repeat Exercise 10 for this case. [S-10]

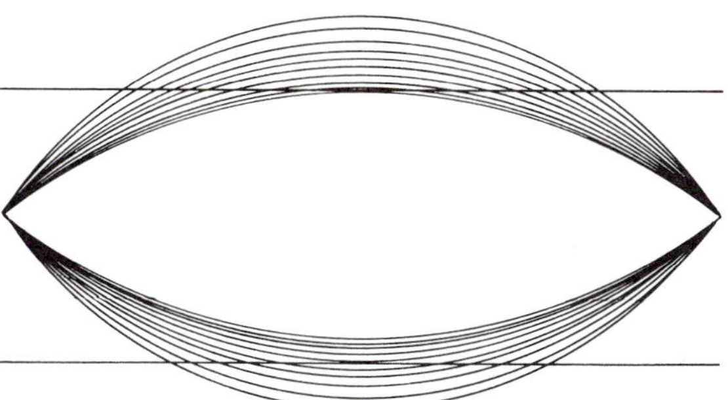

Figure 5. Sine illusion.

13. Figure 6 shows another sine wave illusion. Here the sine waves are parallel (equal period and amplitude, but displaced vertically and cut off at the x-axis). Write down an equation for this family of curves, and repeat Exercise 10. [S-11]

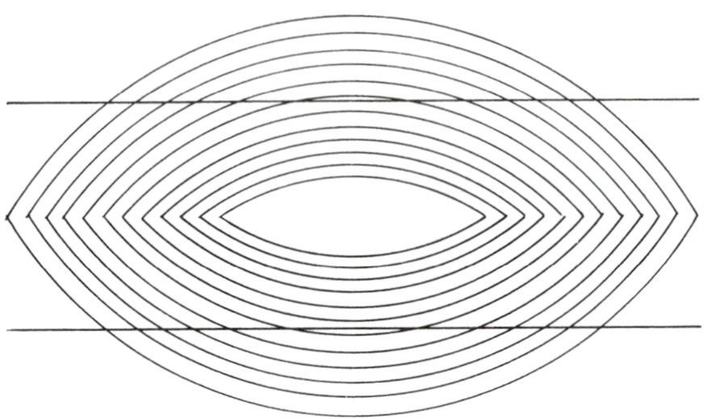

Figure 6. Second sine illusion.

14. The classical Ponzo illusion is an illusion of length (rather than angle) that consists of two equal and parallel line segments placed between two lines that appear to meet at some point in the distance. Figure 7 shows a variant of this illusion in which the horizontal segments have been connected by verticals to form a square, and the pair of converging lines has been expanded to include more members of the same family. Note that the horizontals appear to be of different lengths, and the verticals appear not to be parallel. A possible interpretation of this illusion is that it is created by the Brentano effect of the diagonal lines intersecting the sides of the square. (Is it possible that we provide the sides and extra diagonals unconsciously when they are not actually there?)

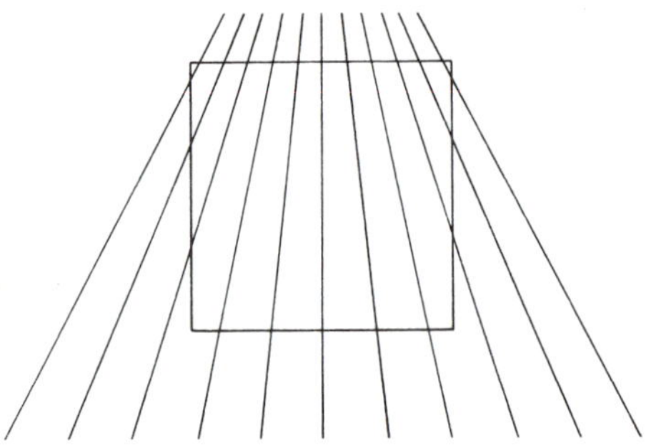

Figure 7. Ponzo illusion.

(a) Rotate the figure 90 degrees, and show that the distorted and distorting curves (lines) are exactly the same as in the Hering illusion, so the apparent curves are given by equation (28). Observe that the natural origin for the coordinate system in this case is the point at which the distortion lines intersect, a point that is not even in the picture, let alone the center of gaze.

(b) Trace the outer two diagonals and the horizontals in Figure 7 to create a classical Ponzo illusion. Is the effect the same?

(c) The Ponzo illusion has sometimes been interpreted as unconscious depth perception, as if the diagonals represented the rails of a railroad track or the sides of a long bridge, so the upper line appears to be farther away, and is therefore interpreted by the brain as longer. If that is correct, the illusion should disappear if the figure is turned upside down. Rotate Figure 7 (or your classical Ponzo figure) through 180 degrees to see if the illusion disappears, weakens, stays the same, or strengthens.

15. Suppose the distorted curve in an illusion is a horizontal line and the distortion pattern is given by a suitable representation (6).

(a) Show that the Hoffman model leads to apparent curves which are solutions of the differential equation:

$$dy/dx = -\epsilon f(x,y)/[1+\epsilon g(x,y)]. \tag{38}$$

(b) Show that the normalized model, with the same representation, and with the strength parameter represented by δ, leads to the differential equation:

$$\frac{dy}{dx} = \frac{-\delta f(x,y)}{\sqrt{f(x,y)^2 + g(x,y)^2} + \delta g(x,y)}. \tag{39}$$

(c) Show that replacement of ϵ in equation (38) by:

$$\delta\Big/\sqrt{f(x,y)^2 + g(x,y)^2} \tag{40}$$

leads to equation (39). Thus, if ϵ is not required to be constant, the Hoffman model includes the normalized model (and vice versa). [S-12]

16. A first order differential equation is called *homogeneous* if it can be written in the form

$$dy/dx = F(y/x). \quad (41)$$

(a) Show that the substitution $u = y/x$ transforms equation (41) into the variable separable equation

$$dx/x = du/[F(u) - u]. \quad (42)$$

(b) Show that equations (25) and (28) are both homogeneous, and find the function F for each.

(c) For equation (25), substitute the appropriate F in equation (42), simplify, and solve. Set $u = y/x$ in the result, and simplify.

(d) Carry out the same procedure for equation (28) as far as you can.

(e) Is this procedure better or worse than the polar coordinate substitution for solving these equations? [S-13]

5. Preview of Unit 535

The preceding section shows that is is possible (but just barely) to normalize the Hoffman model for apparent curves in stable optical illusions and solve the resulting differential equations. The solutions are sufficiently complicated that we can no longer easily identify the shapes as was the case with the line segments and circular arcs arising from the (unnormalized) Hoffman model. How can we tell if the normalized model gives good descriptions or not? The apparent curves can be plotted by a computer plotter, but it turns out to be easier to do this directly from the differential equations than from their solutions, so we will consider how to do that in Unit 535. We will find that the apparent curves are less useful than so-called "correction curves" that can be obtained by reversing the sign of ϵ and plotted on the distortion pattern to see if they appear to be straight.

The descriptive models considered here have a very appealing feature for experimental social scientists: They are "one-parameter" models, that is, there is a single quantity ϵ whose value completely determines the solution quantitatively. (Without knowing ϵ, the solution is only determined qualitatively, that is, the shape is determined, but not the magnitude of the distortion.) We define $|\epsilon|$ to be the *strength* of an illusion, since this quantity is the length of the vector by which the real normal $\vec{N}$ is distorted into the apparent normal $\vec{N}_a$. Unfortunately, no neurophysiological significance has yet been determined for "strength." Most likely, it is a composite of various physiological factors. In Unit 535 we will describe a simple experiment to determine reasonable values for the strength parameter. (Keep in mind that we only need to determine the magnitude of ϵ; its sign is determined by the Brentano Hypothesis.)

Finally, we will apply the ideas of correction curve and strength determination to all the illusions considered above, and some others as well.

6. Answers to Exercises

1. See [S-1].

2. Check the signs of the horizontal $(-y)$ and vertical (x) components of $\vec{T}$ at points (x,y) in each of the four quadrants.

3. $\vec{T} \bullet \vec{N} = x = |\vec{T}| \cos\theta$, where θ is the angle between $\vec{T}$ and $\vec{N}$. Thus $0 < \theta < \pi/2$ for $x > 0$ and $\pi/2 < \theta < \pi$ for $x < 0$. (Or use Exercise 2: T points up in the first quadrant, down in the second.)

4. $\vec{T} \bullet \vec{N} = y = |\vec{T}| \cos\theta > 0$ on the upper horizontal, so $\theta < \pi/2$.

5. Solutions are of the form $x^2 + (y - k)^2 = a^2$, where $k = -1/\epsilon$, $a = \sqrt{1 + 2C\epsilon}/\epsilon$. ($C$ is a constant of integration.)

6. See [S-4].

7. $y^{1+\epsilon} = K(x + \sqrt{x^2 + y^2})^{\epsilon}$.

8. $y = K \sin\theta/(\epsilon + \sin\theta)$.

9. $y + \epsilon\sqrt{x^2 + y^2} = K$.

10. (a) $x' = x$, $y' = -y$.

    (b) $\dfrac{dy}{dx} = \dfrac{\sqrt{2}\,\epsilon x + \sqrt{x^2 + y^2}}{\sqrt{2}\epsilon y - \sqrt{x^2 + y^2}}$.

    (c) $\operatorname{sgn}\epsilon = \operatorname{sgn}(x - y)$.

11. (a) $x' = y$, $y' = x$.

    (b) $\dfrac{dy}{dx} = \dfrac{-\epsilon y}{\sqrt{x^2 + y^2} + \epsilon x}$

    (c) $\operatorname{sgn}\epsilon = \operatorname{sgn} x$.

12. (a) $x' = \sin x$, $y' = y\cos x$.

    (b) $\dfrac{dy}{dx} = \dfrac{-\epsilon \sin x}{\sqrt{\sin^2 x + y^2 \cos^2 x} + \epsilon y \cos x}$ ·

    (c) $\operatorname{sgn}\epsilon = \operatorname{sgn}(\pi/2 - x)$.

13. (**a**) $x' = 1,\ y' = \cos x.$

(**b**) $\dfrac{dy}{dx} = \dfrac{\epsilon}{\sqrt{1 + \cos^2 x} + \epsilon \cos x}\cdot$

(c) Same as 12(c).

15. See [S-12].

16. (**a**) See [S-13].

(**b**) First case: $F(u) = \epsilon u / (\sqrt{1 + u^2} + \epsilon).$

Second case: $F(u) = -\epsilon / \sqrt{1 + u^2} + \epsilon u).$

(c) $x^{1-\epsilon} = K\, e^{y/x}\, (y + \sqrt{x^2 + y^2})^{\epsilon}.$

7. References

1. Brentano, F., "Über ein optisches Paradoxon." *Zeitschrift für Psychologie*, 3 (1892), 349-358; 5 (1893), 61-82.

2. Hoffman, W. C., "The Lie algebra of visual perception." *Journal of Mathematical Psychology* 3 (1966), 65-98, 4 (1967), 348-349.

3. Hoffman, W.C., "Visual illusions of angle as an application of Lie transformation groups." *SIAM Review* 13 (1971), 169-184.

4. Hurley, J.F., *Intermediate Calculus*. Philadelphia: Saunders, 1980.

5. Orbison, W. D., "Shape as a function of the vector field." *American Journal of Psychology* 52 (1939), 31-45.

6. Smith, D. A., "A descriptive model for perception of optical illusions." *Journal of Mathematical Psychology* 17 (1978), 64-85.

7. Thomas, G. E., Jr., and Finney, R. L., *Calculus and Analytic Geometry, Fifth Edition.* Reading, Mass.: Addison-Wesley, 1979.

Appendix A: Special Assistance Supplement

[S-1] Solution to Exercise 1.

If $dx/dt = -y$ and $dy/dt = x$, then

$$\frac{dy}{dx} = \frac{dy/dt}{dx/dt} = -\frac{x}{y} .$$

Separate the variables, integrate, and simplify:

$$y\,dy = -x\,dx ,$$

$$y^2/2 = -x^2/2 + C,$$

$$x^2 + y^2 = 2C .$$

Therefore, every curve that satisfies (5) is a circle centered at the origin.

[S-2] Details of the Solution to Exercise 2.

Examine the signs of the components of $\vec{T}$ in each quadrant. The horizontal component determines whether $\vec{T}$ points right or left, the vertical component whether up or down.

Quadrant		Horizontal		Vertical	
I	$(x>0, y>0)$	left	$(-)$	up	$(+)$
II	$(x<0, y>0)$	left	$(-)$	down	$(-)$
III	$(x<0, y<0)$	right	$(+)$	down	$(-)$
IV	$(x>0, y<0)$	right	$(+)$	up	$(+)$

In each case, $\vec{T}$ points in the counterclockwise direction along a circle centered at the origin.

[S-3] Solution to Exercise 5.

$$\int(1 + \epsilon y)\, dy = -\epsilon \int x\, dx$$

$$y + \epsilon y^2/2 = -\epsilon x^2/2 + C$$

$$x^2 + y^2 + 2y/\epsilon = 2C/\epsilon$$

$$x^2 + (y + 1/\epsilon)^2 = (1 + 2C\epsilon)/\epsilon^2$$

$$x^2 + (y - k)^2 = a^2,$$

where $k = -1/\epsilon$ (large and negative), and $a = \sqrt{1 + 2C\epsilon}/\epsilon$ (large and positive). The center of the circle is at $(0,k)$.

[S-4] Solution to Exercise 6.

The indicated substitutions give:

$$\frac{r' \sin\theta + r\cos\theta}{r'\cos\theta - r\sin\theta} = \frac{\epsilon r\sin\theta}{r + \epsilon r\cos\theta} = \frac{\sin\theta}{1 + \epsilon\cos\theta}$$

Clear fractions:

$$(r'\sin\theta + r\cos\theta)\,(1 + \epsilon\cos\theta)$$
$$= (\epsilon\sin\theta)(r'\cos\theta - r\sin\theta).$$

Multiply out, cancel like terms, and use $\sin^2\theta + \cos^2\theta = 1$:

$$r'\sin\theta + r\cos\theta + r\epsilon = 0. \tag{34}$$

Solve for r':

$$\frac{dr}{d\theta} = \frac{-r(\epsilon + \cos\theta)}{\sin\theta}. \tag{35}$$

Separate the variables and integrate:

$$\int dr/r = -\int(\epsilon\csc\theta + \cot\theta)\, d\theta,$$

$$\ln r = -\epsilon \ln|\csc\theta - \cot\theta| - \ln|\sin\theta| + C.$$

Take exponentials to get:

$$r = K/((\sin\theta)(\csc\theta - \cot\theta)^{\epsilon}). \quad (K = e^C) \tag{36}$$

Note that, for $0 < \theta < \pi$, $\sin\theta > 0$ and $\csc\theta > \cot\theta$, so the absolute value bars may be dropped. Now multiply and divide by $(\csc\theta + \cot\theta)^{\epsilon}$, and use the fact that $\csc^2\theta - \cot^2\theta = 1$. Also, multiply through by $\sin\theta$ and use (29) to get:

$$y = K(\csc\theta + \cot\theta)^{\epsilon}. \quad (37)$$

[S-5] Solution to Exercise 7.

From (29), $\csc\theta = 1/\sin\theta = r/y = \sqrt{x^2 + y^2}/y$, and $\cot\theta = \cos\theta/\sin\theta = x/y$. Thus

$$y = K\left(\frac{\sqrt{x^2 + y^2}}{y} + \frac{x}{y}\right)^{\epsilon},$$

or

$$y^{1+\epsilon} = K(x + \sqrt{x^2 + y^2})^{\epsilon}.$$

[S-6] Solution to Exercise 8.

Substitute (29) and (33) in (28):

$$\frac{r'\sin\theta + r\cos\theta}{r'\cos\theta - r\sin\theta} = \frac{-\epsilon r\cos\theta}{r + \epsilon r\sin\theta} = \frac{-\epsilon\cos\theta}{1 + \epsilon\sin\theta}.$$

Multiply out:

$$r'\sin\theta + r\cos\theta + r'\epsilon\sin^2\theta = -r'\epsilon\cos^2\theta.$$

Simplify:

$$r'\sin\theta + r\cos\theta + r'\epsilon = 0.$$

Solve for r':

$$dr/d\theta = -r\cos\theta/(\epsilon + \sin\theta).$$

Separate variables and integrate:

$$ln\, r = -ln(\epsilon + \sin\theta) + C.$$

Take exponentials:

$$r = K/(\epsilon + \sin\theta).$$

Multiply through by $\sin\theta$ to solve for y:

$$y = K\sin\theta/(\epsilon + \sin\theta).$$

Note that $K = y(0)\,(1 + \epsilon)$, where $y(0)$ is the apparent y-coordinate when x is 0.

[S-7] Solution To Exercise 9.

Write $\sin\theta = y/r = y/\sqrt{x^2 + y^2}$, and substitute in the answer to Exercise 8:

$$y = \frac{Ky/\sqrt{x^2 + y^2}}{\epsilon + y/\sqrt{x^2 + y^2}} = \frac{Ky}{y + \epsilon\sqrt{x^2 + y^2}}.$$

Cancel a factor of y and clear fractions:

$$y + \epsilon\sqrt{x^2 + y^2} = K.$$

[S-8] Solution to Exercise 10.

(a) Differentiate (with respect to a parameter t) the defining equation $xy = a$, and get a relation among x, y, x', and y':

$$xy' + yx' = 0.$$

An easy way to solve this equation identically (this step may be done in many different ways) is to choose:

$$x' = x,\ y' = -y.$$

Now solve this system to verify that the solutions are precisely the desired hyperbolas $xy = a$:

$$dy/dx = y'/x' = -y/x$$

$$\int dy/y = -\int dx/x$$

$$ln\ |y| = -ln\ |x| + ln\ |a|,$$

where $C = ln\ |a|$ represents the constant of integration. Then

$$|y| = |a|/|x|,$$

$$|xy| = |a|.$$

Since both signs are allowed for x, y, and/or a, this is equivalent to $xy = a$.

(b) A unit tangent vector to the distortion pattern is given by:

$$\vec{T} = (x\vec{i} - y\vec{j})/\sqrt{x^2 + y^2}.$$

If we restrict attention to the distorted line in the first quadrant, a unit normal vector is given by:

$$\vec{N} = (\vec{i} + \vec{j})/\sqrt{2}.$$

Setting aside for part (c) the question of sign of ϵ, the form of the apparent normal is:

$$\vec{N}_a = \left(\frac{1}{\sqrt{2}} + \frac{\epsilon x}{\sqrt{x^2 + y^2}}\right)\vec{i} + \left(\frac{1}{\sqrt{2}} - \frac{\epsilon y}{\sqrt{x^2 + y^2}}\right)\vec{j}.$$

Thus the differential equation for the apparent curve is given by:

$$\frac{dy}{dx} = -\frac{1/\sqrt{2} + \epsilon x/\sqrt{x^2 + y^2}}{1/\sqrt{2} - \epsilon y/\sqrt{x^2 + y^2}} = \frac{\sqrt{2}\,\epsilon x + \sqrt{x^2 + y^2}}{\sqrt{2}\,\epsilon y - \sqrt{x^2 + y^2}}.$$

(c) $\vec{T} \bullet \vec{N} = (x - y)/\sqrt{2}\sqrt{x^2 + y^2}$, and this is the cosine of the angle between $\vec{T}$ and $\vec{N}$. Thus the angle is acute, and thus ϵ is positive, if $x > y$; it is obtuse, and thus ϵ is negative if $x < y$.

[S-9] Solution to Exercise 11

(a) Differentiate $x^2 - y^2 = a$ with respect to t, to eliminate a:

$$2xx' - 2yy' = 0.$$

This equation is satisfied by

$$x' = y,\ y' = x.$$

The solutions of this system coincide with the solutions of

$$dy/dx = x/y.$$

Rather than go through the details of the solution, we may observe that this is the differential equation for the orthogonal trajectories of the solutions in Exercise 10, that is, the family of hyperbolas $x^2 - y^2 = a$. Thus the system is a suitable representation.

(b) From $\vec{T} = (y\vec{i} + x\vec{j})/\sqrt{x^2 + y^2}$ and $\vec{N} = \vec{j}$ (for the upper horizontal line), we have:

$$\vec{N}_a = (\epsilon y/\sqrt{x^2 + y^2})\vec{i} + (1 + \epsilon x/\sqrt{x^2 + y^2})\vec{j},$$

so the apparent curves are given by:

$$\frac{dy}{dx} = \frac{-\epsilon y/\sqrt{x^2 + y^2}}{1 + \epsilon x/\sqrt{x^2 + y^2}} = \frac{-\epsilon y}{\sqrt{x^2 + y^2} + \epsilon x}.$$

(c) $\vec{T} \bullet \vec{N} = x/\sqrt{x^2 + y^2}$, so the angle between $\vec{T}$ and $\vec{N}$ is acute when x is positive, obtuse when x is negative. Thus the sign of ϵ is the sign of x.

[S-10] Solution to Exercise 12.

(a) Write the defining equation as $y \csc x = a$ and differentiate:

$$-(y \csc x \cot x)x' + (\csc x)y' = 0.$$

Then multiply through by $\sin^2 x$ to get:

$$-(y \cos x)x' + (\sin x)y' = 0.$$

This is satisfied identically by:

$$x' = \sin x,\ y' = y \cos x.$$

As in the previous problems, one may verify that the solutions of this system are precisely the curves of the distortion pattern.

(b) From part (a) we have:

$$\vec{T} = \frac{(\sin x)\vec{i} + (y \cos x)\vec{j}}{\sqrt{\sin^2 x + y^2 \cos^2 x}}.$$

Taking $\vec{N} = \vec{j}$ for the upper distorted line, we compute the apparent normal in the usual way and solve for the differential equation for the apparent curves:

$$\frac{dy}{dx} = \frac{-\epsilon \sin x}{\sqrt{\sin^2 x + y^2 \cos^2 x} + \epsilon y \cos x}$$

(c) The sign of $\vec{T} \bullet \vec{N}$ is that of $y \cos x$, since the radical in the denominator is always positive. On the upper distorted line, y is always positive, so the sign of ϵ is determined by that of $\cos x$, which is positive for $0 < x < \pi/2$, and negative for $\pi/2 < x < \pi$.

[S-11] Solution to Exercise 13.

(a) The family of curves is given by $y = \sin x + C$. This equation may be differentiated with respect to t to get:

$$y' = x' \cos x.$$

This is satisfied identically by:

$$x' = 1, \; y' = \cos x.$$

(b) From part (a) we have $\vec{T} = (\vec{i} + \vec{j} \cos x)/\sqrt{1 + \cos^2 x}$. With $\vec{N} = \vec{j}$, this leads to an apparent normal in the usual way, from which we get the differential equation:

$$dy/dx = \epsilon/(\sqrt{1 + \cos^2 x} + \epsilon \cos x).$$

(c) Similar to Exercise 12(c).

[S-12] Solution to Exercise 15.

(a) We are given

$$x' = f(x,y),\ y' = g(x,y). \tag{6}$$

For simplicity of notation, the right-hand members of (6) will be abbreviated to f and g, respectively. The Hoffman model gives

$$\vec{T} = f\vec{i} + g\vec{j},\ \vec{N} = \vec{j},$$

hence the apparent normal

$$\vec{N}_a = \epsilon f\vec{i} + (1 + \epsilon g)\vec{j},$$

and the differential equation

$$dy/dx = -\epsilon f/(1 + \epsilon g).$$

(b) For the normalized model, we replace $\vec{T}$ above by the corresponding unit vector:

$$\vec{T} = (f\vec{i} + g\vec{j})/\sqrt{f^2 + g^2}.$$

Thus,

$$\vec{N}_a = (\delta f/\sqrt{f^2 + g^2})\vec{i} + (1 + \delta g/\sqrt{f^2 + g^2})\vec{j},$$

and

$$dy/dx = -\delta f/(\sqrt{f^2 + g^2} + \delta g).$$

Part (c) is straightforward.

[S-13] Solution to Exercise 16.

(a) Write $y = xu$. Then $dy/dx = x\,du/dx + u$ by the product rule, and this is $F(u)$ by (41). Hence $x\,du/dx = F(u) - u$. Separation of the variables now leads to (42).

(b) Equation (25) may be written

$$\frac{dy}{dx} = \frac{\epsilon y/x}{\sqrt{1 + (y/x)^2} + \epsilon},$$

from which we get

$$F(u) = \epsilon u/(\sqrt{1 + u^2} + \epsilon).$$

Equation (28) may be written

$$\frac{dy}{dx} = \frac{-\epsilon}{\sqrt{1 + (y/x)^2} + \epsilon y/x},$$

from which we get

$$F(u) = -\epsilon/(\sqrt{1 + u^2} + \epsilon u).$$

(c)

$$F(u) - u = u\sqrt{1 + u^2}/(\sqrt{1 + u^2} + \epsilon)$$

$$\int \frac{dx}{x} = \int \frac{du}{F(u) - u} = \int \frac{\sqrt{1 + u^2} + \epsilon}{\sqrt{1 + u^2}}\, du$$

$$= \int \left(1 + \frac{\epsilon}{\sqrt{1 + u^2}}\right) du$$

$$\begin{aligned}
ln\ |x| &= u + \epsilon\, ln\ |u + \sqrt{1 + u^2}\,| + C \\
&= y/x + \epsilon\, ln\ |y/x + \sqrt{1 + (y/x)^2}\,| + C \\
&= y/x + \epsilon\, ln\ |\,(y + \sqrt{x^2 + y^2})/x| + C \\
x &= K\, e^{y/x}\, [(y + \sqrt{x^2 + y^2})/x]^{\epsilon} \\
x^{1-\epsilon} &= K\, e^{y/x}\, (y + \sqrt{x^2 + y^2})^{\epsilon}
\end{aligned}$$

(d) If the same steps are followed for equation (28), a solution may be found, but the time and effort required is much greater. No cancellation takes place in the expression for $F(u) - u$, and the resulting integral is too complicated to be found in a table of integrals. A tangent substitution will turn it into a rational function of tangents and secants, which is equivalent to a rational function of sines and cosines, which in turn may be integrated by using a tan (z/2) substitution. All of this is much more complicated than the polar coordinate substitution.

Order Information

All modules are for sale and can be ordered from COMAP, Inc. at the address below.

COMAP, Inc.
60 Lowell Street
Arlington, MA 02174

Where to Send a Manuscript

Most UMAP units teach applications, and, insofar as they do, the applications are timely and genuine. A number of units in pure mathematics are needed and welcome, however, and UMAP reviewers are happy to consider any manuscript that might meet a current educational need. UMAP is interested in precalculus mathematics and in the needs of beginning undergraduates, as well as in the needs of students who are more advanced. The UMAP office will provide editorial and redactory services to all contributing authors. If you are thinking of writing for UMAP, or already have a manuscript, please contact the COMAP office. Copies of the UMAP Author's Manual are free. We urge you to become involved in the development of UMAP materials.

UMAP

Modules in Undergraduate Mathematics and Its Applications

Module 562

Finding the Shortest Distance on the Earth's Surface from Here to Timbuktu

Paul R. Patten

Published in cooperation with the Society for Industrial and Applied Mathematics, the Mathematical Association of America, the National Council of Teachers of Mathematics, the American Mathematical Association of Two-Year Colleges, and The Institute of Management Sciences.

COMAP

INTERMODULAR DESCRIPTION SHEET:	UMAP Unit 562
TITLE:	Finding the Shortest Distance on the Earth's Surface from Here to Timbuktu
AUTHOR:	Paul R. Patten Department of Mathematics North Georgia College Dahlonega, GA 30533
CLASSIFICATION:	Applications of Trigonometry to Geography
PREREQUISITE SKILLS:	1. Right triangle trigonometry. 2. Half-angle formulas. 3. The ability to find geographic coordinates of places in an Atlas.
OUTPUT SKILLS:	1. To use the spherical law of cosines to find great circle distances between points whose geographic coordinates are given.

Finding the Shortest Distance on the Earth's Surface from Here to Timbuktu

Paul R. Patten
Department of Mathematics
North Georgia College
Dahlonega, GA 30533

Table of Contents

Modules and Monographs in Undergraduate Mathematics and its Applications Project (UMAP)

The goal of UMAP was to develop, through a community of users and developers, a system of instructional modules in undergraduate mathematics and its applications to be used to supplement existing courses and from which complete courses may eventually be built.

The Project was guided by a National Advisory Board of mathematicians, scientists, and educators. UMAP was funded by a grant from the National Science Foundation and is now supported by the Consortium for Mathematics and Its Applications, Inc. (COMAP), a nonprofit corporation engaged in research and development in mathematics education.

The Project would like to thank Peter A. Lindstrom of North Lake College, Irving, Texas, George W. Chase of St. Paul's School, Concord, New Hampshire; Barbara Juister of Elgin Community College, Elgin, Illinois; R. E. Romien of Riverside Secondary School, Windsor, Ontario; and Louis M. Edwards of Valencia Community College, Orlando, Florida, for their reviews, and all others who assisted in the production of this unit.

This material was prepared with the partial support of National Science Foundation Grant No. SED76-19615 A02 and No. SED80-07731. Recommendations expressed are those of the author and do not necessarily reflect the views of the NSF or the copyright holder.

1. Introduction

Locations on the earth's surface are given in terms of *latitude* and *longitude*. The *latitude* of a point on the earth's surface is the measure of the angle POE formed by the point, P, the earth's center, O, and a point, E, on the equator either directly north or south of the point. All latitudes are no more than 90°.

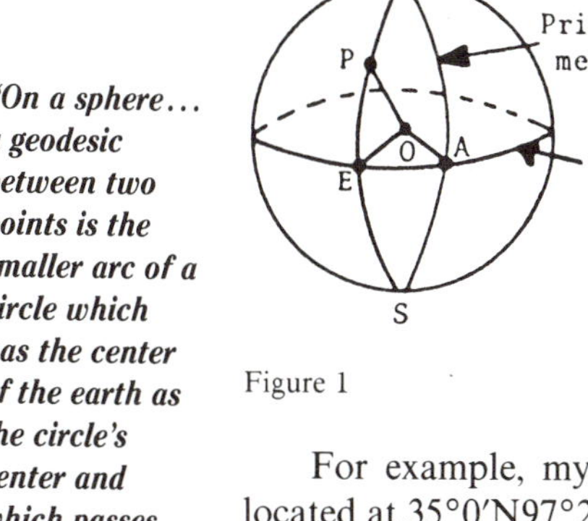

Figure 1

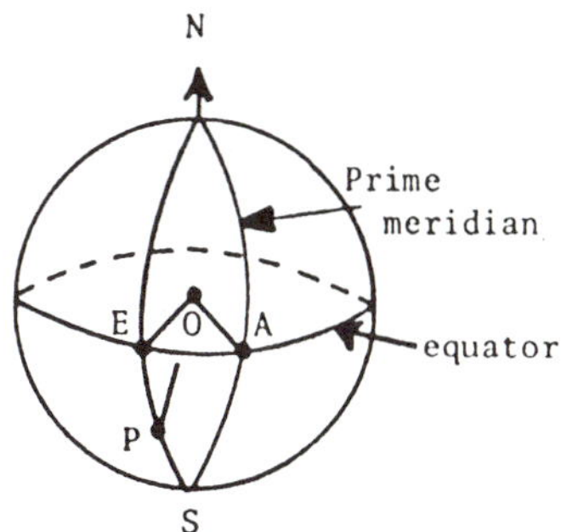

Figure 2

"On a sphere... a geodesic between two points is the smaller arc of a circle which has the center of the earth as the circle's center and which passes through the two points."

For example, my home town, a small town in Oklahoma, is located at 35°0′N97°22′W. We give the latitude first, in degrees and minutes, while we give the longitude secondly, in degrees and minutes. We are going to use these geographic coordinates to answer the following type of question. How far is it from my home town, located at 35°0′N97°22′W, to Timbuktu, which is located at 16°49′N3°0′W, if I follow the shortest path along the earth's surface?

2. The Shortest Distance on the Earth's Surface

When we measure distances along a curved surface, the path of shortest distance is called a geodesic. On a sphere, which is the approximate shape of the earth, a geodesic between two points is the smaller arc of a circle which has the center of the earth as the circle's center and which passes through the two points. Circles on the earth's surface which have the earth's center as a center are called *great circles*. A great circle route is a route that follows the smaller arc (minor arc) of a great circle.

The *longitude* is the measure of the angle AOE, where A is the point where the prime meridian (a north-south "line" which passes through Greenwich, England) intersects the equator. If P is east of the prime meridian, the longitude is east (E) longitude. If P is west of the prime meridian, the longitude is called west (W) longitude. All longitudes are no more than 180°.

The latitude and longitude are like the x and y coordinates on a rectangular coordinate graph. The prime meridian is the "x-axis" and the equator is the "y-axis." Since we are on the sphere, however, the range of values for the coordinates is bounded.

When we measure the lengths of arcs of great circles, it will be convenient to measure the lengths (or distances) as multiples of the earth's radius. We use e.r. to indicate the distance in terms of earth radii. The following conversion factors will be useful:

"...the radian measure of an angle is the length of arc along a unit circle subtended by a congruent central angle."

$$3957 \text{ miles} = 1 \text{ e.r.}$$
$$6367 \text{ kilometers} = 1 \text{ e.r.}$$

Arcs of circles can be used to measure angles. In fact, the *radian measure* of an angle is the length of arc along a unit circle subtended by a congruent central angle. While longitude and latitude are given in degrees, minutes, and seconds, we will find that radian measure is more useful for measuring the length of an arc. For the moment we will measure distances in terms of earth radii; thus, 3957 miles = 1 e.r. (earth radius), and 6367 kilometers = 1 e.r. Doing this will allow us to view the earth as a unit sphere and great circles as unit circles on the surface of that sphere.

Thus in terms of earth radii, the shortest distance between two points along the surface of the earth is the radian measure of the central angle formed by the two points (see Figure 3). Some convenient formulas for converting between radian measure and degree measure are:

$$\text{radian measure of an angle} = \frac{\text{degree measure}}{180} \cdot \pi$$

$$\text{degree measure of an angle} = \frac{\text{degree measure}}{\pi} \cdot 180.$$

Before using the first formula you must change minutes into degrees by dividing the minutes of arc by 60. As an example of using these formulas, we will convert 97°22′ to radians. First we divide 22 by 60, and find that $97°22' = 97.366\overline{6}°$. Second, we divide $97.366\overline{6}$ by 180 and multiply by π, and find that $97.366\overline{6}° = 1.69936\ldots$ radians. Of course, this is the type of work that your electronic calculator is good at doing.

If we use the North Pole and the two given points, a spherical triangle is formed by the lines of longitude (meridians) through the two points and the geodesic connecting them (see Figure 4). Notice

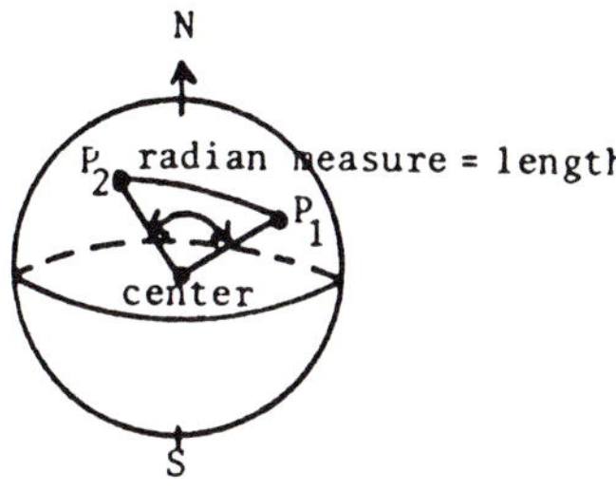

Figure 3

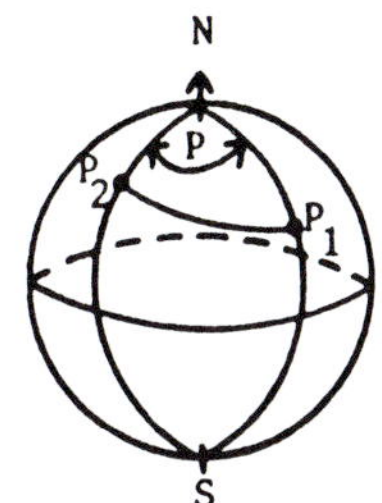

Figure 4

that since the meridians are arcs of great circles, we can find the shortest distance to the North Pole by subtracting from $\pi/2$ the latitude expressed in radians. For the starting location in our problem, 35°, the radian measure is approximately 0.610865 radians; thus the shortest distance to the North Pole is approximately $\pi/2 - 0.610865 = 0.959931$ e.r. Similarly, the distance from the North Pole to Timbuktu is approximately 1.27729 e.r. We can also find the polar angle, P, by finding the difference in longitude: In this case $P = 97°22' - 3° \simeq 1.647009$ radians.

Exercises

1. Atlanta, Georgia is located at 32°11′N latitude and 82°34′W longitude. Find the shortest distance on the surface of the earth from Atlanta to the North Pole. Express your answer in e.r., miles, and kilometers.

2. In an Atlas such as *Goode's World Atlas*, look up the latitude and longitude of your home town and find the shortest surface distance from your home town to the North Pole.

3. Work both problems 1 and 2, but find the distance to the South Pole.

4. What is the maximum geodesic distance between two points on the earth's surface? Express your answer in earth radii.

3. Three-Dimensional Coordinate Systems

Because we live in a three-dimensional space, points on the earth can also be located in terms of three coordinates. There are many ways to do this, but we will examine two of these ways in this section.

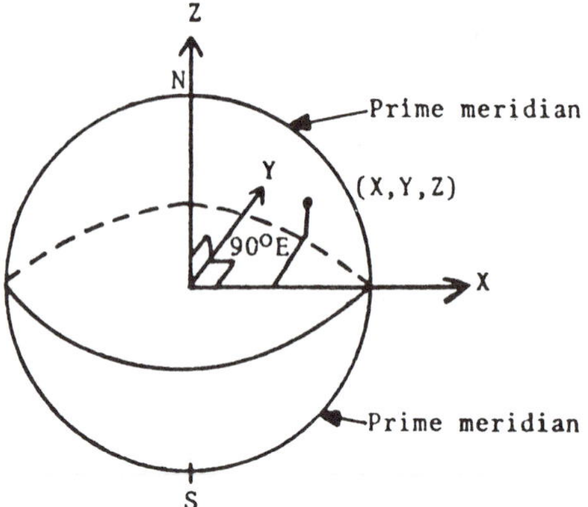

Figure 5

We identify an origin (or beginning point) for our system, and we also identify three directed lines which are mutually perpendicular (form three right angles at the origin). One system is shown in Figure 5. In this system the x-axis passes through the prime meridian and the y-axis passes through 0°N90°E. The third axis, z-axis, passes through the North Pole. This system is called a *right-handed system* because if you curl your right hand from the x-axis to the y-axis, your thumb will point in the direction of the z-axis (north).

Another system, (Figure 6), the kind we will use in the next section, can be formed by letting the y-axis pass through 90°W

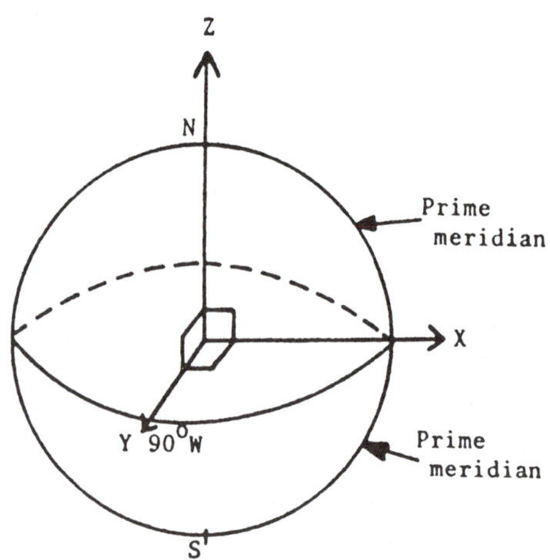

Figure 6

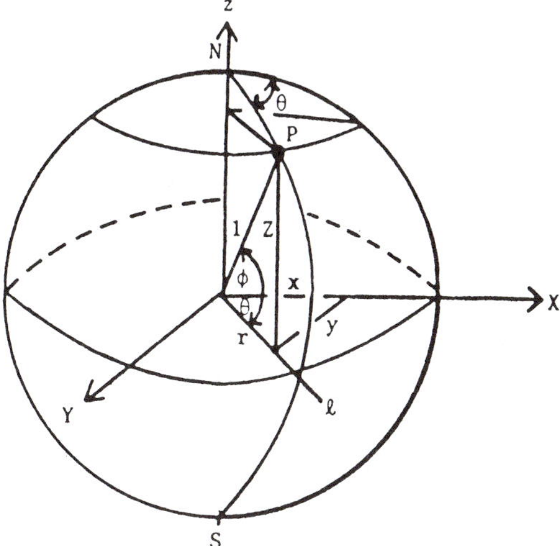

Figure 7

rather than 90°E. In this system if you curl your left hand from the positive x-axis, to the positive y-axis, your left thumb will point in the direction of the z-axis (north). This is a left-handed system.

In the next section we will need to change from geographic latitude and longitude to the three coordinates of the point in a *left-handed coordinate system*. We will now show how to do this. We let ϕ be the latitude of the point on the earth's surface. We also let θ represent the longitude (or change in longitude if the x-axis passes through some other meridian). (See Figure 7.)

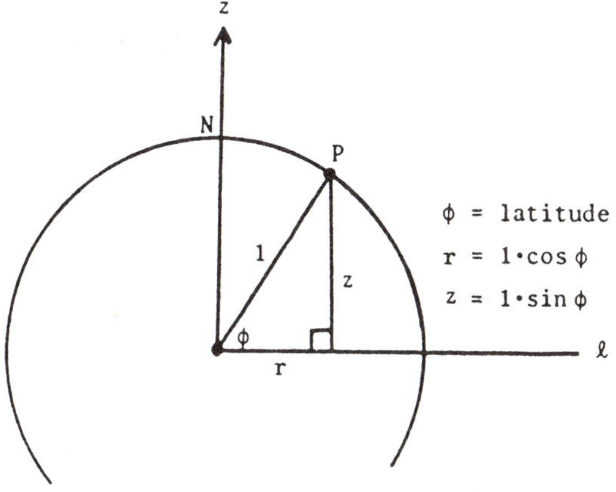

Figure 8

Using Figure 8 and some right triangle trigonometry, we can calculate r and z. In fact, $r = 1 \cdot \cos\phi$ and $z = 1 \cdot \sin\phi = \sin\phi$. (We are measuring distance in earth radii.)

Using Figure 9 and right triangle trigonometry, we find that

$$x = r\cos\theta = \cos\phi\cos\theta, \tag{A}$$

$$y = r\sin\theta = \cos\phi\sin\theta, \text{ and of course} \tag{B}$$

$$z = \sin\phi. \tag{C}$$

The number r is the radius of the circle of latitude (parallel) which passes through P.

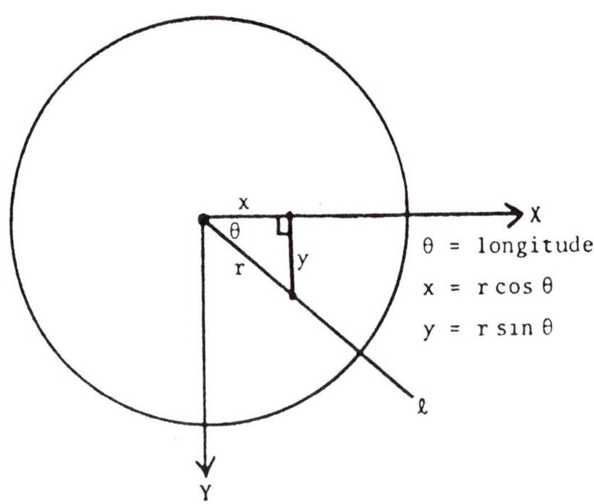

Figure 9

4. The Law of Cosines

In plane trigonometry, if we know two sides and the included angle of a triangle, we can use the law of cosines to find the third side. This is a completely analogous situation, but the triangle involved does not have "straight line" sides. Our task, therefore will be to derive a law of cosines for spherical triangles.

In this section, the center of the earth will form the center of a left-handed rectangular coordinate system for three dimensional space. The latitude of a point P_1 will be represented by ϕ_1, and the longitude of P_1 will be represented by θ_1. Starting at P_1, longitude will increase as we move westward and decrease as we move eastward. (East longitudes will be assigned negative values, as will

South latitudes.) It is because of this occidental viewpoint that a left-handed rather than a right-handed coordinate system has been chosen.

Let P_2 be another point (not either Pole) on the earth's surface. Let (ϕ_2, θ_2) represent the geographic coordinates of P_2. We let the x-axis pass through the meridian which passes through P_1. The y-axis will pass through the meridian which is 90° west of P_1. Also, let θ be the smaller of the two angles between the meridians containing P_1 and P_2. In fact, θ will be the smaller of $|\theta_2 - \theta_1|$ and $360° - |\theta_2 - \theta_1|$. If angles are in radians, θ = minimum of $|\theta_2 - \theta_1|$, $2\pi - |\theta_2 - \theta_1|$.

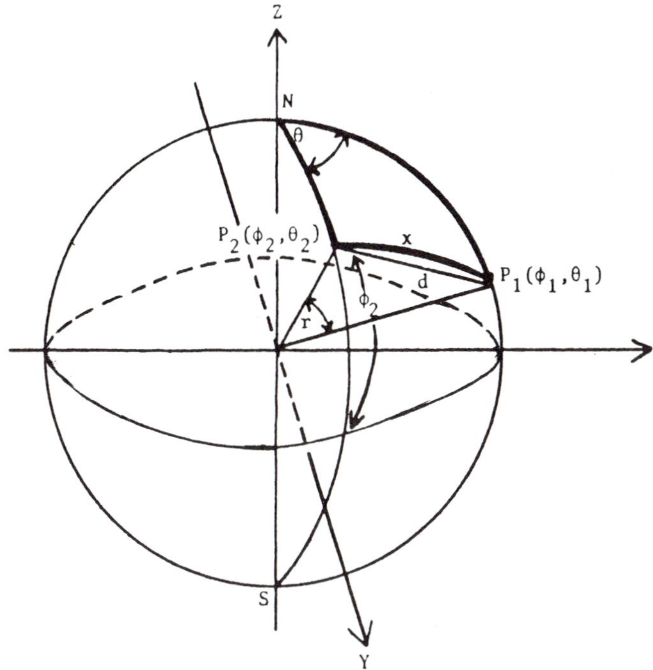

Figure 10

The coordinates of P_1 in the rectangular coordinate system are $x = \cos\phi_1$, $y = 0$, $z = \sin\phi_1$, while the coordinates of P_2 are $x = r \cdot \cos\theta$, $y = r \cdot \sin\theta$, $z = \sin\phi_2$ where r is the radius of the circle which forms the parallel of latitude, ϕ_2. Since $r = \cos\phi_2$, the coordinates of P_2 can be written as $x = \cos\phi_2 \cdot \cos\theta$, $y = \cos\phi_2 \cdot \sin\theta$, $z = \sin\phi_2$.

We can use the distance formula to find the straight line distance, d, from P_1 to P_2. That is:

$$d^2 = (\cos\phi_2 \cdot \cos\theta - \cos\phi_1)^2 + (\cos\phi_2 \cdot \sin\theta - 0)^2 + (\sin\phi_2 - \sin\phi_1)^2$$

$$d^2 = \cos^2\phi_2 \cdot \cos^2\theta - 2\cos\phi_1 \cdot \cos\phi_2 \cdot \cos\theta + \cos^2\phi_1$$
$$+\cos^2\phi_2 \sin^2\theta + \sin^2\phi_2 - 2\sin\phi_1 \cdot \sin\phi_2 + \sin^2\phi_1$$

$$d^2 = \cos^2\phi_2 \cdot \cos^2\theta + \cos^2\phi_2 \cdot \sin^2\theta + \cos^2\phi_1$$
$$+\sin^2\phi_1 + \sin^2\phi_2 - 2\cos\phi_1 \cdot \cos\phi_2 \cdot \cos\theta$$
$$-2\sin\phi_1 - \sin\phi_2$$

$$d^2 = \cos^2\phi_2 + 1 + \sin^2\phi_2 - 2\cos\phi_1 \cdot \cos\phi_2 \cdot \cos\theta$$
$$-2\sin\phi_1 \cdot \sin\phi_2$$

$$d^2 = 2 - 2\cos\phi_1 \cdot \cos\phi_2 \cdot \cos\theta - 2\sin\phi_1 \sin\phi_2. \qquad \text{(D)}$$

(Recall the identity $\cos^2\alpha + \sin^2\alpha = 1$.) However, since we cannot dig a straight line tunnel from here to Timbuktu, the value of d is not what we are looking for. Instead, we need to find the radian measure of the angle x which is formed by P_1, the earth's center, and P_2. Using Figure 11, we find that $d^2 = 4\sin^2(.5x)$.

It is now time for the half-angle formulas:

$$\sin^2(.5x) = (1 - \cos x)/2 \quad \text{and} \quad \cos^2(.5x) = (1 + \cos x)/2.$$

From the half-angle formula for sine and Equation (D) from above, we can conclude that:

$$2(1 - \cos x) = 2 - 2\cos\phi_1 \cdot \cos\phi_2 \cdot \cos\theta \cdot 2\sin\phi_1 \sin\phi_2. \qquad \text{(E)}$$

Solving (E) for $\cos x$ we have:

$$\cos x = \sin\phi_1 \cdot \sin\phi_2 + \cos\phi_1 \cdot \cos\phi_2 \cdot \cos\theta. \qquad \text{(F)}$$

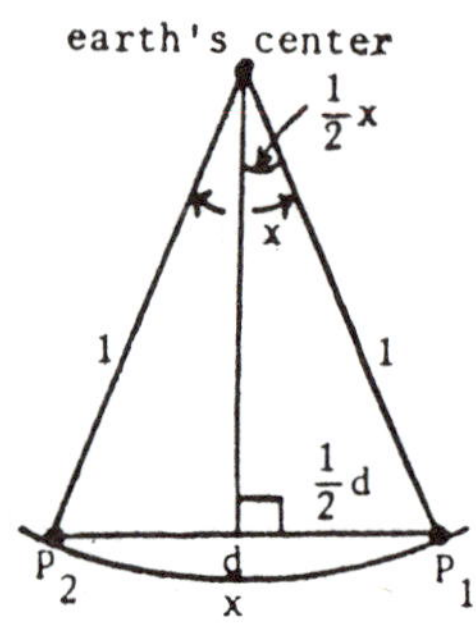

Figure 11

Since the maximum distance between two points of the earth's surface is never more than π e.r., x can never be greater than π. We solve for x using inverse cosine (or Arccosine), and we obtain:

$$x = \text{Arccos}\,(\sin\phi_1 \cdot \sin\phi_2 + \cos\phi_1 \cdot \cos\phi_2 \cdot \cos\theta), \qquad \text{(G)}$$

where θ = minimum of $|\theta_2 - \theta_1|$ and $2\pi - |\theta_2 - \theta_1|$.

Notice that in the final formula (G), ϕ_1, ϕ_2, θ_1, and θ_2 could all be measured in degrees, the trigonometric functions using degree measurement could be applied, but upon taking the inverse cosine it would be necessary to use radian measure for x. In the exercises that follow, a program for the TI-57 calculator is presented which does exactly this. At the end of the exercises is a program in BASIC which must convert all angle measurement into radian measure.

Exercises

5. Using either a calculator or trigonometric table, find the solution to the problem given in the introduction.

6. (Optional) The following is a program for the TI-57 calculator which implements the formula (G) given in this section:

PRESS	CODE
LRN	
2nd Lbl 0	00 86 0
2nd Deg	01 50
R/S	02 81
2nd Dms	03 26
STO 1	04 32 1
R/S	05 81
2nd Dms	06 26
STO 2	07 32 2
R/S	08 81
2nd Dms	09 26
STO 3	10 32 3
R/S	11 81
2ns Dms	12 26
—	13 65
RCL 2	14 33 2
=	15 85
2nd $\|x\|$	16 40
2nd $x \geq t$	17 76
GTO 2	18 51 2
2nd Lbl 3	19 86 3
2nd Cos	20 29

x	21	55	
RCL 1	22	33	1
2nd Cos	23	29	
x	24	55	
RCL 3	25	33	3
2nd Cos	26	29	
+	27	75	
RCL 1	28	33	1
2nd Sin	29	28	
x	30	55	
RCL 3	31	33	3
2nd Sin	32	28	
=	33	85	
2nd Rad	34	60	
INV 2nd Cos	35	−29	
x	36	55	
RCL 4	37	33	4
=	38	85	
INV SBR	39	−61	
2nd Lbl 2	40	86	2
+/−	41	84	
+	42	75	
2	43	02	
x	44	55	
RCL 7	45	33	7
=	46	85	
GTO 3	47	51	3

To operate the program, do one of the following: store 1 in 4, store 3957 in 4, or store 6367 in 4. Store 180 in 7. Example: Suppose P_1 is at 45°N60°W, P_2 is at 30°N120°W, and the distance is to be measured in kilometers. Step 1: 6367 STO 4. Step 2: 180 STO 7. Step 3: SBR 0. Step 4: 45 R/S. Step 5: 60 R/S. Step 6: 30 R/S. Step 7: 120 R/S. The calculator now calculates and displays 5414.0137 (kilometers). We round this answer to 5414 kilometers.

a) Find the distance from 0°N0°W to 0°N1°W in kilometers. Find the same distance in miles.

b) Find the distance from 10°N10°W to 11°N10°W in kilometers and miles.

c) If you travel 1° in longitude, how far do you travel? (In both miles and kilometers.)

7. If a non-stop airline travels from Atlanta, GA. (33°11′N82°34′W) to San Antonio, TX (29°25′N98°30′W) along a great circle route, what is the surface distance traveled (in miles)? If the airplane flies at 3.6 miles above the earth's surface, how far does the airplane fly?

8. Find the geodesic distance from your home to Savannah, GA. (32°5′N81°6′W).

5. Answers to Exercises

1. 32°11′ = 32.183333 . . . ° = .5617051 earth radii (radians). The distance from Atlanta to the North Pole is $\pi/2$ − .5617051 e.r. = 1.0090912 e.r. = 3.992.97 mi = 6424.88 km.

4. No two points can be separated by a minor arc of a great circle of length greater than π radians. In terms of earth radii this is

$$\pi \text{ e.r.} = 12431 + \text{miles} = 20002.5 + \text{km}.$$

5.

```
 READY.
RUN

PROGRAM GEDIST

LOCATION?
? PURCELL
LATITUDE?
? 35
LONGITUDE?
? 97.22
DESTINATION?
? TIMBUKTU
LATITUDE?
? 16.49
LONGITUDE
? 3
THE DISTANCE FROM PURCELL TO TIMBUKTU IS 5794.46 MILES OR
 9323.56 KILOMETERS.
LOCATION?
? ATLANTA
LATITUDE?
? 33.11
LONGITUDE?
? 82.34
DESTINATION?
? SAN ANTONIO
LATITUDE?
? 29.25
LONGITUDE?
```

```
? 98.3
THE DISTANCE FROM ATLANTA TO SAN ANTONIO IS 974.43 MILES OR
 1567.9 KILOMETERS.
LOCATION?
? ATLANTA
LATITUDE?
? 33.11
LONGITUDE?
? 82.34
DESTINATION?
? SAVANNAH
LATITUDE?
? 32.05
LONGITUDE?
? 81.06
THE DISTANCE FROM ATLANTA TO SAVANNAH IS 114.224 MILES OR
 183.791 KILOMETERS.
LOCATION?
? STOP
LATITUDE?
? 0
TOO MUCH DATA, RETYPE INPUT AT 172
? 0
LONGITUDE?
? 0

SRU    0.149 UNTS.

 RUN COMPLETE

PROGRAM GEDIST

100REM THIS PROGRAM CALCULATES GREAT CIRCLE DISTANCES
110C = 3.1415926/180
140DEF FNF(X) = ((X - INT(X))*100/60 + INT(X))*C
145REMFNF CHANGES DEGREES AND MINUTES TO RADIANS
150DEF FNG(X) = ATN(SQR(1 - X*X)/X)
160REM FNG COMPUTES ARCCOSINE
169PRINT"LOCATION?"
170INPUTN1$
171PRINT"LATITUDE?".
172INPUTD1
173PRINT"LONGITUDE?"
174INPUTR1
175IFN1$ ="STOP"THEN260
180PRINT"DESTINATION?"
181INPUTN2$
182PRINT"LATITUDE?"
183INPUTD2
184PRINT"LONGITUDE?"
185INPUTR2
190D1 = FNF(D1)
200R1 = FNF(R1)
210D2 = FNF(D2)
```

```
220R2 = FNF(R2)
224R = R2 - R1
226IFR > 3.1415926THENR = 2*3.1415926 - R
230L = FNG(SIN(D1)*SIN(D2) + COS(D1)*COS(D2)*COS(R))
240PRINT" THE DISTANCE FROM ";
250PRINTN1$;" TO ";N2$;" IS ";L*3957;" MILES OR ";L*6367;"
 KILOMETERS. "
255GOTO169
260END
```

6. **a**) 111.12 km, 69.06 miles
   b) 111.12 km, 69.06 miles
   c) 111.12 km, 69.06 miles

7. 974.43 miles is the surface distance from Atlanta to San Antonio; 975.32 + 7.2 = 982.52 miles if the airplane flies 3.6 miles above the earth's surface.

BIG MATH ATTACK PACKS!

Preparing your students for the world of High School teaching is hard enough — why not let our **Big Math Attack Packs** help out? These packs, geared to the High School-level student, give prospective teachers an opportunity to see how applications can best teach mathematics at the secondary level.

ORDER NOW!

Pack A ** Regular $18.00 Value * Now Only $14.40

1. Module 539 I Will if You Will... Individual Thresholds and Group Behavior
2. Module 560 Some Card Tricks: Algebra in Disguise
3. Module 562 Finding the Shortest Distance on the Earth's Surface From Here to Timbuktu
4. Module 577 Harmonic Motion and the Circular Function
5. Module 641 Cassette Tapes: Predicting Recording Time
6. Module 657 Controlling the Effects of Interruption
7. Module 658 Windchill
8. Module 659 The Mathematics of Focusing a Camera
9. Module 660 Applications of High School Mathematics in Geometrical Probability

Pack B ** Regular $26.00 Value * Now Only $20.80

1. Module 367-369 Concepts of Mathematics for Business: Background Mathematics
2. Module 370-372 Concepts of Mathematics for Business: The Mathematics of Finance
3. Module 373-374 Concepts of Mathematics for Business: Equations and Inequalities in the Plane: An Introduction to Breakeven Analysis and Linear Programming
4. Module 375 Interior Design: Preparing an Estimate
5. Module 479 Line Reflections in the Cartesian Plane
6. Module 546 Measurement Scales
7. Module 567 Zeller's Congruence and Modular Systems
8. Module 584 Concentration of Solutions
9. Module 607 Determining the Size for a Mussel Culture Farm in a Tidal Estuary Based on Local Biological Factors
10. Module 639 The Consumer Price Index: What Does it Mean?

Pack A: Intermediate/Upper Intermediate High School Level $14.40

Pack B: Beginning/Intermediate High School Level $20.80

Shipping & Handling = $ 2.50

Send check or purchase order to COMAP Inc., 60 Lowell Street, Arlington, MA 02174

UMAP

Modules in Undergraduate Mathematics and Its Applications

Module 571

The Use of Continued Fractions in Botany

Roger V. Jean

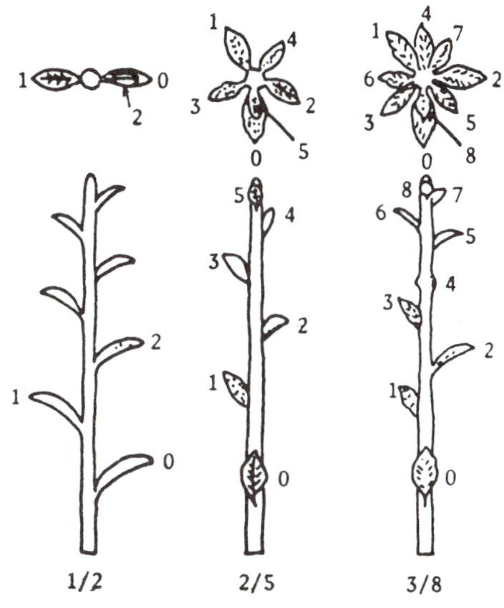

Published in cooperation with the Society for Industrial and Applied Mathematics, the Mathematical Association of America, the National Council of Teachers of Mathematics, the American Mathematical Association of Two-Year Colleges, and The Institute of Management Sciences.

COMAP

INTERMODULAR DESCRIPTION SHEET: UMAP Unit 571

TITLE: THE USE OF CONTINUED FRACTIONS IN BOTANY

AUTHOR: Roger V. Jean
Department of Pure Sciences
University of Québec
Rimouski, Québec, G5L 3A1

CLASSIFICATION: APPLICATIONS OF FINITE MATH & GEOMETRY/PLANT BIOLOGY

ABSTRACT: The use of continued fractions in botany has allowed workers to make important steps in the direction of the solution of the so-called problem of phyllotaxis. This problem is characterized by the emergence of the series 1, 1, 2, 3, 5, 8, 13, 21, . . . in the secondary spirals seen on plants. The question is: "Why does this series arise in 95% of the observations on plants?" It has become a major preoccupation for a lot of research workers in biomathematics. Even if there is not yet a complete answer to that question, there are results, some of which will be put here into light by an accessible, original, straightforward, and pedagogical presentation. Students will become acquainted with some of the most interesting aspects of continued fractions, realize and appreciate the role of some mathematical concepts in botany, develop observational capacities in the surrounding nature, acquire the fundamental notions that will eventually allow them to investigate an important field of research in biomathematics.

PREREQUISITE SKILLS: A familiarity with the notions of continued fraction and lattice; elementary analytic geometry, calculus, and number theory.

The Use of Continued Fractions in Botany

Roger V. Jean
Department of Pure Sciences
University of Québec
Rimouski, Québec, G5L 3A1

Table of Contents

Modules and Monographs in Undergraduate Mathematics and Its Applications Project (UMAP)

The goal of UMAP was to develop, through a community of users and developers, a system of instructional modules in undergraduate mathematics and its applications to be used to supplement existing courses and from which complete courses may eventually be built.

The Project was guided by a National Advisory Board of mathematicians, scientists, and educators. UMAP was funded by a grant from the National Science Foundation and is now supported by the Consortium for Mathematics and Its Applications, Inc. (COMAP), a nonprofit corporation engaged in research and development in mathematics education.

The Project would like to thank Eric C. Nummela of New England College, William C. Ramaley of Fort Lewis College, Alan Osborne of Ohio State University, and one anonymous reviewer for their reviews, and all others who assisted in the production of this unit.

This material was prepared with the partial support of National Science Foundation Grant No. SED80-07731. Recommendations expressed are those of the author and do not necessarily reflect the views of the NSF or the copyright holder.

1. Introduction

We define a few of the mathematical notions, derived from the observation of plants, that constitute the language used in this part of biomathematics known as phyllotaxis or botanometry. In Sections 2.1 and 2.2 we will show how the series 1, 1, 2, 3, 5, 8,... arises from observations on plants. Then our aim will be to produce what is called here Bravais's approximation formula, which in turn will be used to deduce basic results in the field. For that purpose we will introduce the continued fractions in Section 2.3.

Bravais's approximation formula, used for calculating the divergence of a plant, can be found by scrutinizing an article by L. and A. Bravais, in an old French scientific journal (*Ann. Sci. Nat. Bot.*, 7, 42–110, 1837). This text, which has presided to the initiation of botanometry, had been almost forgotten when Tait resuscitated it in a very short article (*Proc. Roy. Soc. Edinburg*, 7, 391–393, 1872). Very recently Jean (*Phytomathématique*, les Presses de l'Universite de Québec, Montréal, 1978) took this formula out of the abstruse and official context of periodicals meant for a narrow circle of specialists, and made an accessible presentation of it. The rigorous presentation of Section 3, pedagogically oriented, makes rapidly available an important result concerning the conspicuous pairs of parastichies (Jean's Theorem). This result is closely related to Adler's theorem (*J. Theor. Biol.* 45, 1–79, 1974) with his extensive theory of visible opposed parastichy triangles. Jean's theorem establishes the geometric relation between two major notions: the divergence and the phyllotaxis of a plant (defined in Sections 2.1 and 2.2). The theorem follows here as an immediate and elegant by-product of the setting put forward to obtain Bravais's formula (Section 3.2).

Section 4 presents a first explanation of the phenomenon of phyllotaxis; that is, of the emergence of the divergences $(t+\phi^{-1})^{-1}$ together with the series $\langle S_{t,k}\rangle$, a particular case of which is the almost omni-present Fibonacci sequence

$$\langle F(k)\rangle = \langle 1, 1, 2, 3, 5, 8, 13, 21, \dots\rangle$$

and divergence $1/\phi^2$ (these symbols are explained further on). The key to this presentation is Klein's theorem (Section 2.4) on continued fractions which allows us to reach rapidly the very essence of Coxeter's contribution to botanometry (Chapter XI of *Introduction to Geometry*, Wiley, N.Y. 1961 and 1969; *J. Algebra*, 20, 167–175, 1972). In Section 4.2, I have deduced indeed the role of intermediate convergents in botany, as an easy corollary of previous exercises. In Section 4.3, I generalize what is called here Coxeter's formula, to normal types of phyllotaxis, with minimal reference to the Fibonacci number theory.

This module is the first rigorous self-contained introductory presentation to an amazing subject, for efficient use in undergraduate university classes, in one of the most fascinating areas of applied mathematics. I think that users of the module will enjoy this excursion that will eventually lead them to the sophisticated theories of phyllotaxis and plant growth. Before that, if they would like to pursue their introductory inquiry in the domain, I suggest that they read my *Phytomathématique* (reviewed in *Math Biosci.*, 46, 301–302, 1979). A complete account can be found in R. V. Jean's *Mathematical Approach to Pattern and Form in Plant Growth* (John Wiley and Sons, New York, 1984).

Phyllotaxis is the bugbear of botany, and our ability to solve the problem it raises appears to be an important test-case in biomathematics.

As to the pedagogical approach to the module, it may be preferable though not necessary, to go through the exercises at the end of each section (solved in Section 6), before going to the next section. The exercises quite often contain results that are important for an adequate understanding of the subsequent sections. First of all let us make some observations and get acquainted with the main concepts in the field.

2. Fundamental Concepts

2.1 Phyllotaxis of a System

If one looks at a pineapple, a sunflower, a pine cone or a daisy, for example, he will notice two families of spirals winding in opposite directions. The botanist calls these spirals, the *parastichies* (pȧ · răś · tĭ · kĭz). An idea that may come to the observer is to count them. This has been done, for pineapples, by a worker in Hawaii, over a period of two years. He certifies that, without exception, the numbers obtained were 5, 8, 13, 21 or 34, according to the size of the fruit. Such observations were also done systematically on the trunk of the palm trees, where the palms leave traces determining parastichies. Without exception the numbers obtained were 2, 3, 5, 8, 13, and 21. In the case of the cones the numbers were 2, 3, 5, 8 or 13. Figure 1 is a transverse section of a cone, showing what is called the *primordia* (here the future scales) arranged according to 8 clockwise parastichies and 5 counterclockwise. Table 1 shows the number of right and left parastichies in the sunflower, according to its size. These observations lead to the important concept presented in the following definition.

The *phyllotaxis* of a plant, like a cone or a daisy, is a pair of integers, denoted m/n, $m > n$, where m and n are the numbers of conspicuous opposed parastichies determined by the primordia (scales, florets, leaves,

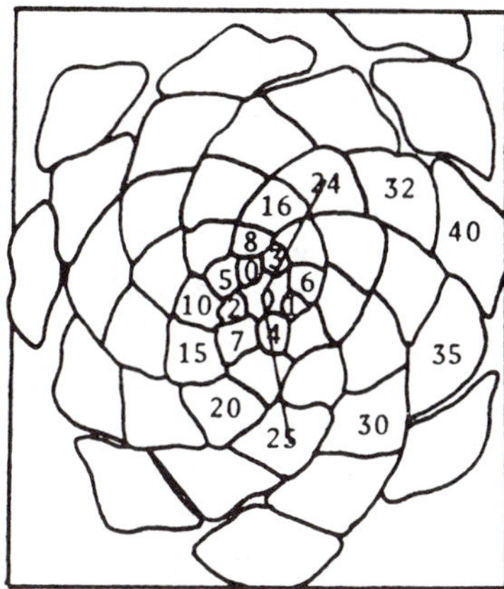

Figure 1. *Pinus pinea*, showing the phyllotaxis 8/5 (notice the 8 counterclockwise spirals and the 5 clockwise), the divergence $1/\phi^2$ (see Section 2.2) and the numbering of the primordia according to the order of their births (in the center of the figure). (After Church, A. H., *On the Relation of Phyllotaxis to Mechanical Laws*, Williams and Norgate, London, 1904.)

etc.) of the plant. In a plant there are many pairs of opposed parastichies; the phyllotaxis is determined by the conspicuous pair, also called the contact parastichy pair. It sometimes happens that two pairs of conspicuous parastichies can be observed. See Exercise 1.

Table 1

The Phyllotaxis of Sunflowers (from Jean, *Phytomathématique*, 1978)

Size of the head of the sunflower	Number of Parastichies positive direction	negative direction
very small	13	21
small	21	34
normal (14 to 15 cm in diameter)	34	55
large	55	89
very large	89	144

2.2 Divergence and Phyllotactic Fraction

Another parameter that comes out of the observation of plants, and which is important for their description, is the divergence. It is an angle that is most of the time equal to 137°30′27″. The *divergence* of a plant is the angle at the center, in a transverse section of the bud of the plant, made by the centers of two consecutively born primordia (such as the angle in Figure 1 between primordia 24 and 25). Most of the time this angle is expressed as a fraction of a turn, that is, as a number between 0 and 1, more precisely between 0 and 1/2.

The divergence observed in a bud, at the origin of the growth, is necessarily an irrational number, since the primordia are arranged on spirals. If the bud becomes a leafy stem, then we can obtain an approximation of the value of the divergence by marking two leaves looking approximately superposed. They thus determine what is called an *orthostichy*, that is a line approximately parallel to the axis of the cylindrical stem, like leaves 0 and 8 in Figure 2. In a movement up

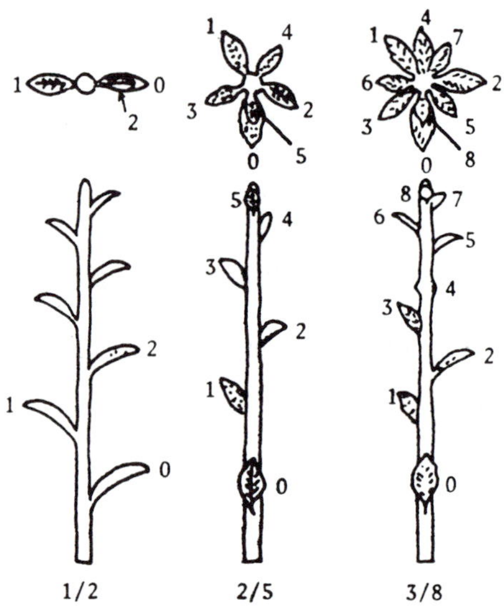

Figure 2. Illustration of the notion of phyllotactic fraction. (From Northrop, E. P., *Riddles in Mathematics*, Kreiger, N.Y. 1975; reprinted by permission of van Nostrand Reinhold Co., 1944.)

around the stem following the *genetic spiral*, determined by the shortest path through two consecutively born primordia, we go from leaf 0 to leaf 8 by doing three turns around the stem to meet 8 leaves. The value 3/8 is an approximation of the divergence. This brings us to the following definition. A *phyllotactic fraction* of a leafy stem (or of a plant in a cylindrical lattice: Sections 3.2 and 4.1), obtained by determining two leaves on an orthostichy, is the ratio of the number of turns around the stem to the number of leaves met, by following the genetic spiral from one leaf to the other. Experiments show that the most common phyllotactic fractions are the members of the sequence 1/2, 1/3, 2/5, 3/8, ... See Exercise 4.

2.3 Convergents of a Continued Fraction

Every positive real number ω can be written, using Euclid's algorithm, in the form

$$\omega = a_0 + \cfrac{1}{a_1 + \cfrac{1}{a_2 + \cfrac{1}{a_3 + \dots}}} \tag{1}$$

where $a_0, a_1, a_2, \dots$ are positive integers. To obtain this development we separate out the largest positive integer a_0 contained in ω and write

$$\omega = a_0 + r_0 \quad \text{where } 0 \le r_0 < 1. \tag{2}$$

Then, if $r_0 \neq 0$, we treat $1/r_0$ as we did ω:

$$1/r_0 = a_1 + r_1 \quad \text{where } 0 \le r_1 < 1, \tag{3}$$

and continue in the same way:

$$\begin{aligned} 1/r_1 &= a_2 + r_2 \quad \text{where } 0 \le r_2 < 1, \\ 1/r_2 &= a_3 + r_3 \quad \text{where } 0 \le r_3 < 1, \dots \end{aligned} \tag{4}$$

According to whether ω is rational or not, the process terminates or goes on indefinitely. An infinite continued fraction is often written $\omega = [a_0; a_1, a_2, \dots]$, and a terminating continued fraction is written $\omega = [a_0; a_1, a_2, \dots, a_m]$. We shall call the continued fractions $[a_0; a_1, a_2, \dots, a_k]$, whose values will be denoted by the rational numbers p_k/q_k, $k = 0, 1, 2, \dots$, the *convergents or principal convergents* of ω. In the case where ω is rational we have $0 \le k \le m$. Obviously

$$p_0 = a_0, \quad q_0 = 1, \quad p_1 = a_0 a_1 + 1, \quad q_1 = a_1. \tag{5}$$

We quote the next useful law, without proof, for $k \ge 2$.

Law of formation of the convergents

$$\begin{aligned} p_k &= a_k p_{k-1} + p_{k-2}, \\ q_k &= a_k q_{k-1} + q_{k-2}. \end{aligned} \tag{6}$$

It can also be proved that the convergents of even order p_{2n}/q_{2n}, $n = 0, 1, 2, \dots$, form an increasing sequence converging towards ω, and that the convergents of odd order form a decreasing sequence also converging toward ω. The *intermediate convergents* of ω are the ratios $p_{k,c}/q_{k,c}$

where $0 < c < a_k$ and c is an integer (when it exists). They are given by

$$p_{k,c} = cp_{k-1} + p_{k-2} \quad \text{and} \quad q_{k,c} = cq_{k-1} + q_{k-2}, k > 1. \tag{7}$$

For a supplement on continued fractions see Section 5.

2.4 Klein's Diagram

In 1896, Klein gave a remarkable geometrical interpretation of the way the convergents of the continued fraction of an irrational number converge towards that number. Let us imagine with him, pegs or needles inserted at all points of the (x, y) plane having integral and

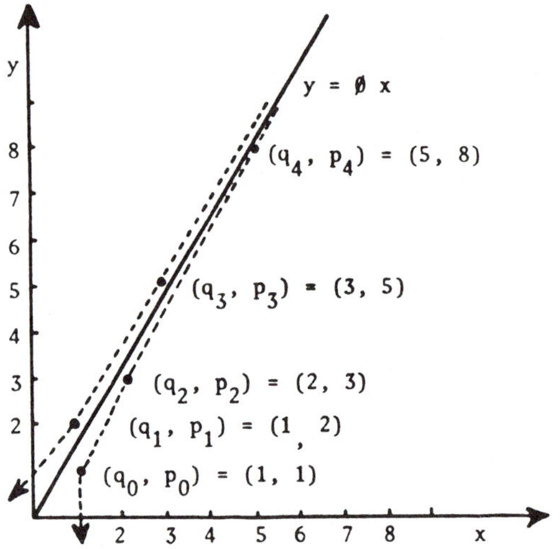

Figure 3. Klein's diagram of the continued fraction of $\phi = (\sqrt{5} + 1)/2$ in the square lattice, showing the first few vertices of the two infinite polygons.

non-negative coordinates. We obtain a *square lattice* of well-aligned pegs, like the trees in an orchard. Looking from the origin, one sees points of the lattice in all rational directions and only in such directions. The field of view is everywhere "densely" but not completely and continuously filled with "stars." One might be inclined to compare this view with that of the "milky way" (Klein, F.). One can use the number-theoretic properties of p_i and q_i to prove the following theorem (given without proof).

Klein's theorem: Given the square lattice and the irrational number $\omega > 0$, wrap a tightly drawn string about the sets of pegs to the right and to the left of $y = \omega x$. Then the vertices of the two infinite string-polygons that bound the two sets will be the points (q_i, p_i) whose coordinates are the denominators and the numerators of the convergents of the continued fraction of ω, the right infinite polygon having the even convergents and the other the odd convergents.

Exercises

1. Laboratory experience for the entire class: bring into the classroom many specimens of cones and pineapples and determine their phyllotaxis.

2. Prove that the fraction of a turn $1/\phi^2$, where $\phi = (\sqrt{5} + 1)/2$, corresponds to the divergence angle mentioned in the text.

3. Establish that the divergence $1/\phi^2$ is related to the phyllotaxis $F(k + 1)/F(k)$ by the formula

$$1/\phi^2 = \lim_{k\to\infty} \left(1 - \frac{1}{F(k+1)/F(k)}\right)$$

where $F(1) = F(2) = 1$, and $F(k + 1) = F(k) + F(k - 1)$ (the answer to Exercise 1, given in Section 6, can help).

4. Ask your students to determine the phyllotactic fractions of the leafy trees they can possibly meet on their way home.

5. Show that the series of common phyllotactic fractions (see the answer to Exercise 4) converges toward $1/\phi^2$.

6. Show that

$$\phi = 1 + \cfrac{1}{1 + \cfrac{1}{1 + \cfrac{1}{1 + \ddots}}} \quad \text{and} \quad \sqrt{2} = 1 + \cfrac{1}{2 + \cfrac{1}{2 + \cfrac{1}{2 + \cfrac{1}{2 + \ddots}}}}.$$

7. Show that for all $k \geq 0$

$$q_k p_{k-1} - p_k q_{k-1} = (-1)^k.$$

8. Show that the successive convergents of ϕ and of $1/\phi^2$ are respectively the series of fractions given in the answers to Exercises 1 and 4. Show that the convergents of $(t + \phi^{-1})^{-1}$ are $F(k)/S_{t,k}$ where $S_{t,k} = F(k)t + F(k - 1)$, t is a positive integer, and $F(0) = 0$, $F(-1) = 1$.

9. Write the first few intermediate convergents of $\sqrt{5}$ and $1/(e - 1)$. Verify that $67/29 = [2; 3, 4, 2]$.

10. Show that every real number ω that has no intermediate convergent has the form $\omega = [a_0; a_1, 1, 1, 1, 1, \ldots]$.

11. Construct Klein's diagram for the continued fraction of $1/(e-1)$. Find two points on the infinite polygonal lines, that are not vertices.

12. Let $\omega = [a_0; a_1, a_2, \ldots]$, p_n/q_n and $p_{n,c}/q_{n,c}$ its convergents. Show that the points $(q_{n,c}, p_{n,c})$ of the square lattice, are on the segment of the infinite polygonal line, determined by the points (q_{n-2}, p_{n-2}) and (q_n, p_n).

3. Bravais's Approximation Formula for the Divergence

3.1 Illustration of the Formula

This formula gives a good approximation of the value of the divergence d between two consecutively born primordia, in a system whose phyllotaxis is known. The formula is

$$d \simeq \frac{c\mu + s\nu}{cm + sn}. \tag{8}$$

The right side of (8) is a phyllotactic fraction determined by six integral parameters defined in the following way:

—m/n is the phyllotaxis of the system: m and n are determined experimentally;
—μ/ν is the convergent of the continued fraction of m/n, satisfying one of the relations $m\nu - n\mu = \pm 1$ that will make $d < 1/2$: $\mu < m$ and $\nu < n$ can also be determined by examination of the corresponding cylindrical lattice (defined in Section 3.2);
—c and s are the numbers satisfying the relation $cm + sn = k$, where k is the number of primordia between the two primordia determining a chosen orthostichy: these parameters can also be determined experimentally or by examination of the cylindrical lattice, as the next example will show.

Before giving the example, we need one simple tool, which is called here Bravais's theorem, after the two French botanists who formulated it in 1837. It allows us to number the scales of pineapples, cones, cycads, etc. according to the order of their consecutive births.

Bravais's Theorem: The numbers on the consecutive scales of any given parastichy, differ by the number of parastichies in the family of the given one.

Here is how this theorem applies. Let us take a cone, like the one in Figure 4, and determine its phyllotaxis m/n, $m > n$. Here $m/n = 8/5$, that is a family of 8 counterclockwise parastichies and a family of 5 clockwise parastichies. Take any scale near the base of the cone and

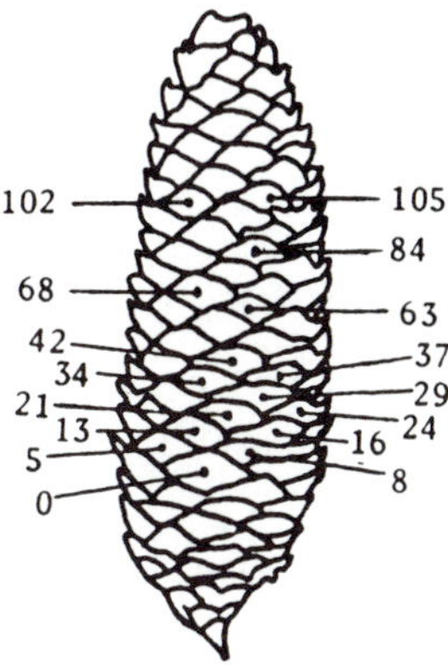

Figure 4. The numbering of the scales of a cone according to Bravais's theorem.

put the number 0 on it. Inscribe the numbers 5 and 8 on the neighboring scales belonging to the opposed parastichies meeting at scale 0. Figure 4 shows in the obvious way how the other scales must be numbered according to Bravais's theorem (a difference of 8 or of 5 between the consecutive scales of a parastichy). It also shows two orthostichies. In the case here, an *orthostichy* is a straight line, determined by nearly superposed scales, which is approximately parallel to the axis of the cone (considered as a cylinder). The scales 0, 21, 42, 63, . . . form one orthostichy; the scales 0, 34, 68, 102, . . . , another.

Given a cone and the numbering of its scales, let us now determine the values of the six parameters defined earlier. First we choose an orthostichy; for definiteness we will take 0, 21, 42, 63, ... It follows that

$$cm + sn = 21,$$

which, in this case, is

$$8c + 5s = 21.$$

This is a diophantine equation whose only solution is $c = 2$ and $s = 1$. Notice that the examination of the cone gives these values, since scale 21 is on the second (2) clockwise parastichy parallel to the one passing by scales 0 and 5, and on the first (1) counterclockwise parastichy parallel to the one passing by scales 0 and 8. The convergents of the continued fraction of 8/5 are 1/1, 2/1, 3/2, and 8/5. The convergent 3/2 gives $\mu = 3$, $\nu = 2$, $m\nu - n\mu = 1$ and $(c\mu + s\nu)/(cm + sn) < 1/2$.

So the needed values are $\mu = 3$, $\nu = 2$ and the approximation of d given by formula (8) is 8/21.

Considering the numbers on the scales of the pineapple in the answer to Exercise 1 (Figure 9 of Section 6), we see that $m/n = 13/8$ or 8/5. Supposing that scale 56 is superposed to scale 22 we have $cm + sn = 34$. When $m/n = 13/8$, $c = 2$ and $s = 1$; when $m/n = 8/5$, we have $c = 3$, $s = 2$. In the first case $u = 5$, $v = 3$ and the approximation of d is 13/34. The second case gives $u = 3$, $v = 2$ and $d \simeq 13/34$.

3.2 Explanation of the Procedure and Jean's Theorem

Figure 5 represents the cone in Figure 4 considered as a cylinder sectioned along the generator passing by scale 0, and unrolled in the plane. Scale 0 thus appears in a and in A. The spirals linking the scales 0 and 5 and the scales 0 and 8 become straight lines meeting at scale

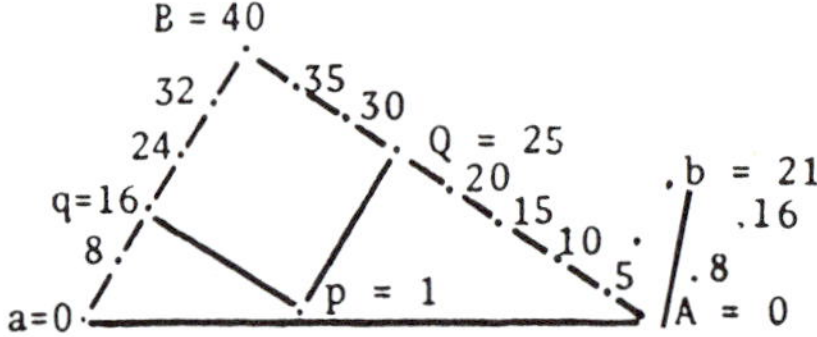

Figure 5. The visible opposed parastichy triangle for the pair 8/5. (From Jean, 1978.)

40. They determine the triangle aBA called (by Adler, 1974) the *visible opposed parastichy triangle* belonging to the pair 8/5. There are 5 lines parallel to $\overline{AB}$ and meeting all the scales; there are 8 lines parallel to $\overline{aB}$ and doing the same. For simplicity and without loss of generality we suppose that $\overline{aA} = 1$. Thus the scales (of the cone or the pineapple) are represented by their centers in an infinite vertical strip of well-aligned points. This is the so-called *normalized cylindrical lattice* where the divergence of the plant is the difference between the abscissae of two consecutive scales and the ordinate of point k is kr, with $r > 0$, the coordinates of scale 1 being (d, r) (we will see in Section 4.1 the relation of this lattice to the square lattice of Section 2.4).

To approximate d, we make the following argument, which for definiteness will be based on the example. The number of complete revolutions around the axis of the cone, to go from scale 0 to scale 21 (determining the chosen orthostichy: the approximately vertical line $\overline{Ab}$ in Figure 5) is given by $\{(cm + sn)d\}$, where c and s are such that $cm + sn = 21$ and $\{\cdot\}$ means the integer nearest to $(cm + sn)d$. It follows that the phyllotactic fraction $\{(cm + sn)d\}/(cm + sn)$ approximates d. Also the approximation will be better if

$$|(cm + sn)d - \{(cm + sn)d\}|$$

is smaller, that is, if the orthostichy approximates a vertical line more accurately in the cylindrical lattice. By the properties of the (approximately) similar triangles aqp and aBA we have

$$d \simeq \overline{aq}/nl \simeq \overline{qp}/ml^* \tag{9}$$

(respectively equal to 2/5 and 3/8 in the example), where l and l^* are the lengths of the regular *steps* on the respective parastichies (the distances between scales 0 and 8 and between scales 0 and 5 respectively). Putting $\overline{aq} = \nu l$ and $\overline{qp} = \mu l^*$ we have:

$$\{(cm + sn)d\} \simeq \{c\mu + s\nu\} = c\mu + s\nu. \tag{10}$$

It follows that $d \simeq (c\mu + s\nu)/(cm + sn)$. The same approximation is obtained by comparing the triangles pQA and aBA. (Note, however, that the meanings of μ and ν have changed). We need to show that μ/ν is a convergent of the continued fraction of m/n. Since $m\nu - n\mu = \pm 1$ (see Exercise 16) we have the result (compare with Exercise 7).

Determination of μ, ν, c and s from the cylindrical lattice. They can be determined by the inspection of the visible opposed parastichy triangle. The parameter $\nu < n$ is the number of steps in the direction of the m parastichies, to go from a to q or from p to Q (depending on whether one compares triangle aBA to triangle aqp or to pQA to obtain $d < 1/2$; that is, depending on the sense of the genetic spiral). The parameter $\mu < m$ is the number of steps in the direction of the n parastichies, to go from p to q or from A to Q (corresponding to the previous choice of triangles). The parameters c and s are the numbers of steps in the direction of the m parastichies and n parastichies, respectively, to go from a or A (either one) to the point determining the orthostichy.

From the setting above we can deduce the following theorem relating the divergence to the phyllotaxis of a system. In this theorem the expression $F(k)t + F(k-1)$ is denoted by $S_{t,k}$. For the proof, see Exercises 17 and 18.

Jean's Theorem: If $m/n = S_{t,k}/S_{t,k-1}$, where $t \geq 2$ is an integer, then d is equal to $F(k)/S_{t,k}$ or $F(k-1)/S_{t,k-1}$ or lies between these two values. When k tends towards infinity, d takes on the limiting value $d = (t + \phi^{-1})^{-1}$.

Exercises

13. Give another approximation of d for the cone of Figure 4.

14. Try out the material in this section on different specimens of cones or pineapples: number the scales, draw the visible opposed parastichy triangle, determine by different methods the parameters μ, ν, c and s, determine orthostichies, apply the formula, and compare the results.

15. At the blackboard, in front of your fellow students, make your presentation of the approximation formula.

16. Referring to the symbolism used in this section, prove that $m\nu - n\mu = \pm 1$.

17. Referring to Figure 5, show that

$$\mu/m \leq d \leq \nu/n \quad \text{or} \quad \nu/n \leq d \leq \mu/m.$$

18. Prove Jean's theorem.

19. Verify that the values of d obtained in Exercise 14 satisfy Jean's theorem.

4. A First Explanation in Phyllotaxis

4.1 Bravais's Cylindrical Lattice in Botany vs. Klein's Square Lattice for Continued Fractions

Consider the following transformation of the xy-plane of Section 2.4 into the XY-plane of the cylindrical lattice of Section 3.2:

$$X = \omega x - y, \quad Y = rx \quad \text{where } r > 0. \tag{11}$$

The line $y = \omega x$ of the xy-plane becomes the line $X = 0$, that is, the Y-axis of the XY-plane. The vertices (q_i, p_i) of the infinite polygons of the continued fraction of ω in Klein's square lattice, become the vertices $q_i = (\omega q_i - p_i, rq_i)$ of two infinite half-polygons, asymptotic to the Y-axis and containing between them only one image of that lattice, that is the point $(0, 0)$. All the points of the lattice on these polygonal lines will be called the *neighbors of the Y-axis*. In the region $0 \leq X < 1$, $Y \geq 0$, the coordinates of the points corresponding to those of the square lattice are

$$(\omega x - y - [\omega x - y], rx) = (\omega x - [\omega x], rx), \tag{12}$$

where [ ] means the integral part, and where x and y are non-negative integers. Those two or three points that correspond to those of the square lattice and that are nearest to (0, 0) in the XY-plane are called the *neighbors of the origin.* The lattice of points with integral coordinates becomes an infinite vertical strip in the region $0 \leq X < 1$, repeated in the other regions $n \leq X < n + 1$, where n is an integer, which are identified to the former region. The points (0, 0) and (1, 0) of the XY-plane represent the same scale, point 1 is $(\omega - [\omega], r)$, and we have the cylindrical lattice met in Section 3.2.

In the light of Klein's theorem of Section 2.4 and the theorem below we are now able to understand better why, as a pineapple or a cone grows, the phyllotaxis goes from m/n to $(m + n)/m$, where m and n are consecutive numbers of the series of integers given in Exercise 1, and why a better approximation of the divergence $1/\phi^2$ is obtained by taking orthostichies made with higher numbers of the series $\langle F(k) \rangle$. The proof of the theorem is left to the Exercises.

Theorem. If $\omega = \phi$, then the point $(F(k), F(k + 1))$ of Klein's diagram for ω, in the square lattice, becomes the neighbor $F(k) = ((-1)^{k+1}\phi^{-k}, F(k)r)$ of the Y-axis in the cylindrical lattice. As r decreases, the neighbors of the origin are consecutive terms of the sequence $\langle F(k) \rangle$ and the orthostichy determined by the origin and $F(k)$ tends towards the Y-axis as k tends towards infinity.

Figure 6 shows the cylindrical lattice corresponding to Klein's diagram for $y = \phi x$. It represents a cone or a pineapple. The coordinates of scale 1 are $(1/\phi, r)$, or $(-1/\phi^2, r)$ (the genetic spiral is clockwise). The figure shows the rhythmic alternation of the neighbors $F(k)$ about the Y-axis. As r decreases, $F(k + 1)$ and $F(k + 2)$ will replace $F(k)$ and $F(k + 1)$ as neighbors of the origin, and the phyllotaxis of the system will always be made of consecutive terms of the sequence $\langle F(k) \rangle$, as it is emphasized in the preceding theorem. Notice also that in this figure, $F(k + 1)$ is closer than $F(k)$ to the Y-axis.

4.2 Coxeter's Formula and the Hexagonal Scales of the Pineapple

To begin the derivation of the formula we need to make the following observation in the cylindrical lattice of Figure 6 of Section 4.1. The points $F(k - 1)$, $F(k)$, and $F(k + 1)$ are neighbors of the origin if r is such that the angle made by the points $F(k - 1)$, 0, and $F(k)$ is obtuse and the angle made by the point $F(k)$, 0, and $F(k + 1)$ is acute. This is realized in Figure 6 and in Figure 12 (Section 6); Figure 9 (Section 5) shows these two angles on a pineapple, A obtuse and a acute). Such a value of r is between two values r_k and r_{k+1} where

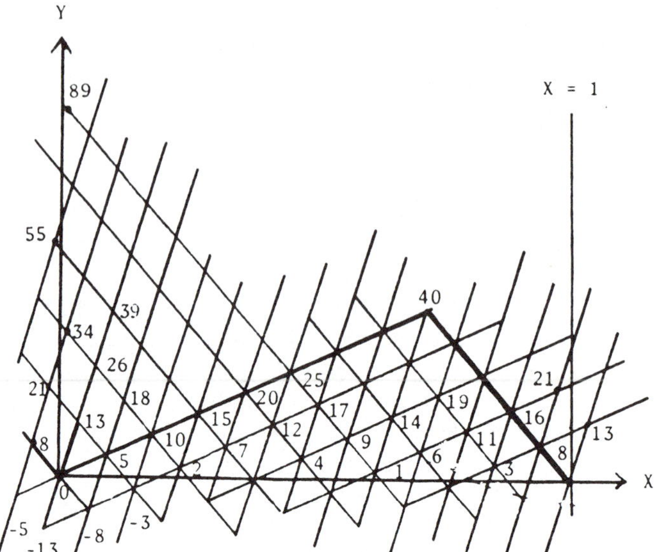

Figure 6. Cylindrical lattice of a cone, having the divergence $1/\phi^2$ and a clockwise genetic spiral. The points 5, 8, 13 are neighbors of the origin (0, 0) or (1, 0): the phyllotaxis is rising from 8/5 to 13/8 with the growth of the fruit (r decreases). We have drawn the visible opposed parastichy triangle belonging to the pair 8/5, as in Section 3.2 (where the genetic spiral is counterclockwise). (From Jean, *Phytomathématique*, Les Presses de l'Université du Québec, 1978).

these two angles are right. One can show that

$$r_k = (F(k-1)F(k))^{-(1/2)}\phi^{-k+(1/2)} \tag{13}$$

and

$$r_{k+1} = (F(k)F(k+1))^{-(1/2)}\phi^{-k-(1/2)}. \tag{14}$$

This I have called *Coexeter's formula* (see Exercise 24). It follows that the three given points will be neighbors of the origin if an appropriate value of r is chosen, such as

$$r = 1/F(k)\phi^k.$$

Let us look now at the concrete significance of this value of r. We have said that the points of the cylindrical lattice can be considered as the centers of the scales of a pineapple. They determine a tessellation of congruent parallelograms or rectangles called the *fundamental regions*. Each of these points, like point p in Figure 7, belongs to six triangles, as is easily seen by looking carefully at the figure. If we join the meeting points of the six medians of the sides of the triangles meeting at p, we

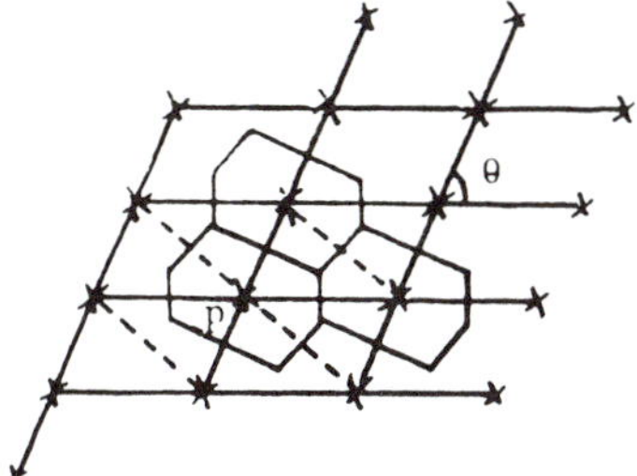

Figure 7. Dirichlet's regions corresponding to points of the cylindrical lattice. Here they are hexagonal, like the scales of the pineapple usually are. (From Jean, *Phytomathématique*, 1978.)

obtain what is called the *Dirichlet region* of point p. It is a polygon whose interior is nearer to point p than to any other point of the lattice. These regions will be rectangles or hexagons depending on whether the angle θ is right or not; then point p has 4 or 6 neighbors respectively in the cylindrical lattice, and the fundamental region is a rectangle or a parallelogram. It follows that our choice of r, between r_k and r_{k+1} where the scales are rectangles, is such that these scales are hexagons, as they usually are at the grocery or in Hawaii. In particular we will have three families of 8, 13 and 21 conspicuous parastichies for $r = 1/F(7)\phi^7$. Then the coordinates of scale n of the pineapple, unrolled in the plane, are $(\phi n - [\phi n], n/F(7)\phi^7)$; those of scale 13 are $(1/\phi^7, 1/\phi^7)$.

4.3 Normal Types of Phyllotaxis

Figure 8 shows a cylindrical lattice with the neighbors of the origin (4, 7, and 11) and the neighbors of the Y-axis. The phyllotaxis of the system is 7/4 and will eventually become, with the growth of the

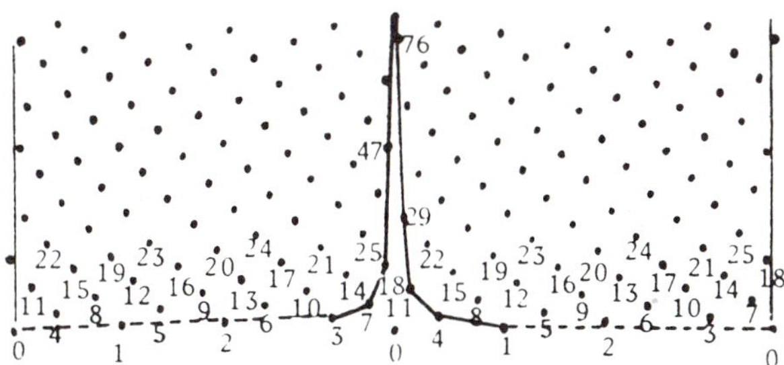

Figure 8. A normal type of phyllotaxis (7/4). Polygonal lines showing Schoute's accessory series 1, 3, 4, 7, 11, 18, ... defined by the relation $S(k+1) = S(k) + S(k-1)$ with $S(1) = 1$, $S(2) = 3$. (From Coxeter, 1972.)

plant, 11/7. Obviously this type of phyllotaxis, occurring in nature, is different from the one discussed in the preceding section (arising in 95% of the cases and characterized by the sequence $\langle F(k)\rangle$ and $1/\phi^2$). The normal types of phyllotaxis are also generally given by the sequences 1, 3, 4, 7, 11, 18, . . . , or 1, 4, 5, 9, 14, 23, ... An anomalous type of phyllotaxis, very rare, is known to exist, defined by the sequence 2, 5, 7, 12, 19, 31, ... In almost all cases, the sequences obtained are given by $S_{t,k} = F(k)t + F(k-1)$ with $k = 0, 1, 2, 3, \ldots$, and $d = (t + \phi^{-1})^{-1}$.

Suppose that $\omega = (t + \phi^{-1})^{-1}$ on the square lattice (of Section 2.4). Then, in the cylindrical lattice, the neighbors of the Y-axis will be the points $S_{t,k}$ (see Exercise 8). The abscissa of $S_{t,k}$ is $S_{t,k}(t + \phi^{-1})^{-1}$ minus the integer nearest to this expression, that is, $(-1)^k/\phi^{k-1}(\phi t + 1)$ (see Exercise 26). It follows that $S_{t,k}$ and $S_{t,k-1}$ make a right angle with the origin for

$$r_{k+1} = (S_{t,k}S_{t,k-1})^{-(1/2)}\phi^{-k+(3/2)}/(\phi t + 1), \qquad (15)$$

a formula which generalizes Coxeter's formula (put $t = 1$). We do the same with the neighbors $S_{t,k-1}$ and $S_{t,k-2}$ to obtain r_k. Finally we choose, as we did in Section 4.2,

$$r = 1/S_{t,k-1}\phi^{k-2}(\phi t + 1),$$

a good value for which $S_{t,k}S_{t,k-1}$ and $S_{t,k-2}$ are neighbors of the origin. In Figure 8 we have $t = 3$, $k = 4$ and we can calculate that $r \simeq 1/100$, the value used by Coxeter to build the lattice.

Why does the divergence $d = (t + \phi^{-1})^{-1}$ arise almost exclusively? Here is a partial explanation, based on observations made by the French botanists Bravais and de Candolle in the nineteenth century. These observations amount to saying that the divergences $d < 1/2$ encountered in nature are irrational numbers and that the neighbors of the Y-axis in the cylindrical lattice must alternate on either side of this axis (as do 8, 13, 21, 34, 55, 89, . . . in Figure 6). With these observations in mind, d cannot have intermediate convergents, because if d had intermediate convergents ($a_n > 1$ for $n \geq 2$), by Exercise 23, when going upward on the Y-axis, if we "see" q_{n-1} on the left, we will "see" consecutively on the left

$$q_{n,1}, q_{n,2}, \ldots, q_{n,a_n-1}$$

(on the segment determined by q_{n-1} and q_{n+1} in Exercise 12) before "seeing" q_n on the right. After, we will "see"

$$q_{n+1,1}, q_{n+1,2}, \ldots, q_{n+1,a_{n+1}-1}$$

on the right before "seeing" q_{n+1} on the left. This contradicts the second observation. By Exercise 10 we have $d = [0; t, 1, 1, 1, \ldots]$.

Exercises

20. Prove the theorem of Section 4.1.

21. With $\omega = \phi$, as in the theorem of Exercise 20, calculate the interval of values in which r must be chosen, so that the normalized cylindrical lattice shows 5 and 3 as neighbors of the origin. Draw the lattice. For which value of r, does point 8 replace point 3; that is, for which value of r the phyllotaxis passes from 5/3 to 8/5? Calculate the value of r for which $F(k+1)$ replaces $F(k-1)$ as a neighbor of the origin.

22. Show that if the Y-axis contains only one point of the cylindrical lattice, that is, $(0, 0)$, then the divergence is irrational.

23. Show that the neighbors of the Y-axis in the cylindrical lattice are ordered as follows:

$$q_{n-1} < q_{n,1} < q_{n,2} < \ldots < q_{n,a_n-1} < q_n < q_{n+1,1} < \ldots < q_{n+1}$$

(where these numbers are the denominators of the convergents and of the intermediate convergents of the continued fraction of ω in the square lattice).

24. Prove Coxeter's formula.

25. In the lattice of Figure 8, show that $d = 1/\phi\sqrt{5} = 1/(3 + \phi^{-1})$.

26. Referring to Section 4.3, show that the abscissa of $S_{t,k}$ is $(-1)^k/\phi^{k-1}(\phi t + 1)$. Compare with Exercise 20 for $t = 1$.

27. Referring to Exercise 26, show that the distance of $S_{t,k}$ to the Y-axis, is, up to a constant factor, the distance of $(S_{t,k}, F(k))$ to $y = (t + \phi^{-1})^{-1}x$.

5. Special Assistance Supplement

What is the continued fraction of 27/8? Using Euclid's algorithm, that is the ordinary process of division, we find that

$$\frac{27}{8} = 3 + \frac{3}{8} = 3 + \frac{1}{(8/3)}.$$

Repeating the process with 8/3 we find that

$$\frac{8}{3} = 2 + \frac{2}{3} = 2 + \frac{1}{(3/2)},$$

$$\frac{27}{8} = 3 + \frac{1}{(8/3)} = 3 + \cfrac{1}{2 + \cfrac{1}{(3/2)}}.$$

Finally we have

$$\frac{3}{2} = 1 + \frac{1}{2},$$

$$\frac{27}{8} = 3 + \cfrac{1}{2 + \cfrac{1}{1 + 1/2}}.$$

Using the notation introduced in Section 2.3 we can write

$$\frac{27}{8} = [3; 2, 1, 2].$$

In that specific example the process of division ends given the fact that the number $\omega = 27/8$ is rational. So we have $a_0 = 3, a_1 = 2, a_2 = 1$ and $a_3 = 2$. Using Expressions 5 and 6 in the text, we have the principal convergents:

$$\frac{p_0}{q_0} = \frac{a_0}{1} = \frac{3}{1}, \quad \frac{p_1}{q_1} = \frac{a_0 a_1 + 1}{a_1} = \frac{7}{2},$$

$$\frac{p_2}{q_2} = \frac{a_2 p_1 + p_0}{a_2 q_1 + q_0} = \frac{7 + 3}{2 + 1} = \frac{10}{3},$$

and finally

$$\frac{p_3}{q_3} = \frac{a_3 p_2 + p_1}{a_3 q_2 + q_1} = \frac{2 \times 10 + 7}{2 \times 3 + 2} = \frac{27}{8}.$$

What are the intermediate convergents (see Expression 7)? Here k can only take the values 2 and 3 (since $k > 1$). For $k = 2$, c in $p_{2,c}$ and in $q_{2,c}$ can take the integral values between 0 and $a_2 = 1$: there is thus no intermediate convergent when $k = 2$. For $k = 3$, c in $p_{3,c}$ and $q_{3,c}$ can only take the value $c = 1$ ($0 < c < a_3 = 2$, c integer). It follows that

$$p_{3,1} = p_2 + p_1 = 10 + 7 = 17,$$

$$q_{3,1} = q_2 + q_1 = 3 + 2 = 5.$$

The only intermediate convergent of $\omega = 27/8$ is $p_{3,1}/q_{3,1} = 17/5$.

Let us consider now a more complex example. What is the continued fraction of π? Using the computer we can easily make the following calculations:

$$\pi = 3 + 0.141592654,$$

$$\pi = 3 + \cfrac{1}{\left(\cfrac{1}{0.141592654}\right)},$$

$$\pi = 3 + \cfrac{1}{7 + 0.062513285},$$

$$\pi = 3 + \cfrac{1}{7 + \cfrac{1}{\left(\cfrac{1}{0.062513285}\right)}},$$

$$\pi = 3 \cfrac{1}{7 + \cfrac{1}{15 + 0.99659976}}.$$

The process does not end since that π is irrational. It is thus found that $\pi = [3; 7, 15, 1, 293, \ldots]$, and $a_0 = 3$, $a_1 = 7$, $a_2 = 15$, $a_3 = 1$, $a_4 = 293$, etc. Using Expressions 5 and 6 the values of p_k and q_k follow. The point (q_k, p_k) can be set in Klein's square lattice (see Section 2.4) and two infinite polygonal lines can be drawn around the line $y = \pi x$, having (q_k, p_k), $k = 0, 1, 2, 3, \ldots$ as vertices. These polygonal lines contain the points $(q_{k,c}, p_{k,c})$ determined by the denominators and numerators of the intermediate convergents. Expression 7 allows us to calculate them. For example, with $k = 3$, c can take all the integral values between 0 and $a_3 = 1$: no intermediate convergent. For $k = 4$ there are 292 intermediate convergents. Check that the even convergents form an increasing sequence and that they are all smaller than π; the odd convergents form a decreasing sequence, each convergent being larger than π.

6. Answers to Exercises

1. The phyllotaxis of the specimens will always be determined by two consecutive members of the sequence $\langle F(k) \rangle$:

$$1, 1, 2, 3, 5, 8, 13, 21, \ldots,$$

defined by the recurrence relation

$$F(k+1) = F(k) + F(k-1),\ F(1) = F(2) = 1.$$

In a word, the phyllotaxis of the plants under observation will be found to be equal to one of the following:

$$2/1, 3/2, 5/3, 8/5, 13/8, \ldots, F(k+1)/F(k), \ldots$$

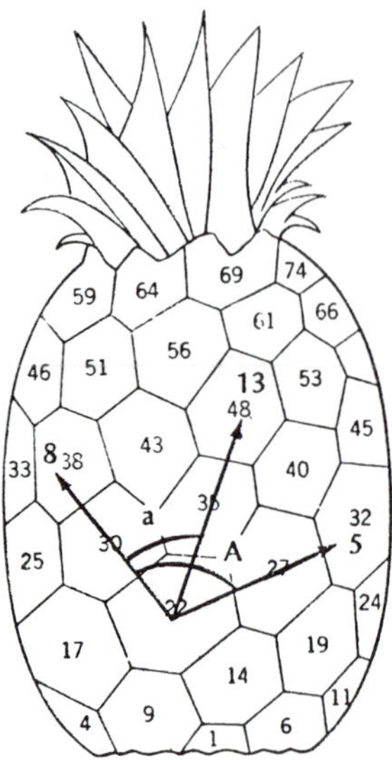

Figure 9. Given the hexagonal shape of the scales of the pineapple shown here, phyllotaxis 13/8 and phyllotaxis 8/5 are conspicuous. The meaning of angles *a* and *A* is explained in Section 4.2. The divergence angle between the scales can be approximated by the fraction 13/34 (see Section 3.1).

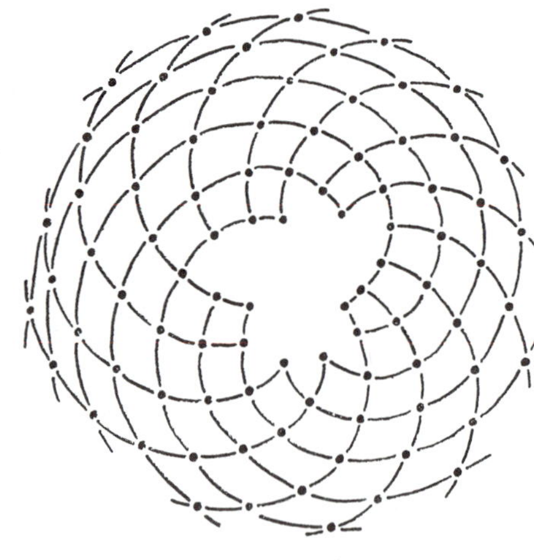

Figure 10. Spiral patterns on a cactus, schematized on the right, showing phyllotaxis 13/8. Can you depict a family of 21 spirals on the cactus? (From H. W. Franke's article published in *Kakteen*, 1969).

3. Prove first that $\lim_{k\to\infty} F(k+1)/F(k) = \phi$. From the relation $F(k+1) = F(k) + F(k-1)$ we get $F(k+1)/F(k) = 1 + 1/(F(k)/F(k-1))$, and, at the limit, putting $\lim_{k\to\infty} F(k)/F(k-1) = x$, we get $x = 1 + 1/x$, an equation whose positive solution is ϕ.

4. To proceed more easily, attach a white thread to the base of a leaf, close to the stem, and twist it around by the shortest path to the following leaf, upward to the leaf recognized as making an orthostichy with the first leaf. Table 2 presents the phyllotactic fractions of commonly known species. The most usual phyllotactic fractions belong to the sequence $1/2$, $1/3$, $2/5$, $3/8$, $5/13$, $8/21, \ldots, F(k)/F(k+2), \ldots$

Table 2

Common Species and Their Phyllotactic Fractions (from Jean, 1978)

Phyllotactic fraction	Species
1/2	Elm, linden-tree,
1/3	Alder-tree, beech, hazel, birch tree
2/5	Plum-tree, oak, cherry-tree, apple-tree, apricot-tree,
3/8	Poplar, pear-tree (see Figure 11),
5/13	Willow, almond-tree.

5. $\lim_{k\to\infty} F(k)/F(k+2) = \lim_{k\to\infty} 1/(F(k+2)/F(k)) = 1/\phi^2$, as it is to be expected, since the phyllotactic fractions approximate the divergence.

6. For the positive root ω of a quadratic equation of the form

$$x^2 = ax + 1 \text{ or } x = a + 1/x,$$

we obtain the expression

$$\omega = a + \cfrac{1}{a + \cfrac{1}{a + \cfrac{1}{a + \ddots}}}.$$

Setting $a = 1$ gives ϕ and $a = 2$ gives $\sqrt{2}$. These remarkable formulae connect ϕ and $\sqrt{2}$ with the integers in a much more striking way than the decimal expansions of these numbers do, since they display no regularity in the succession of their digits.

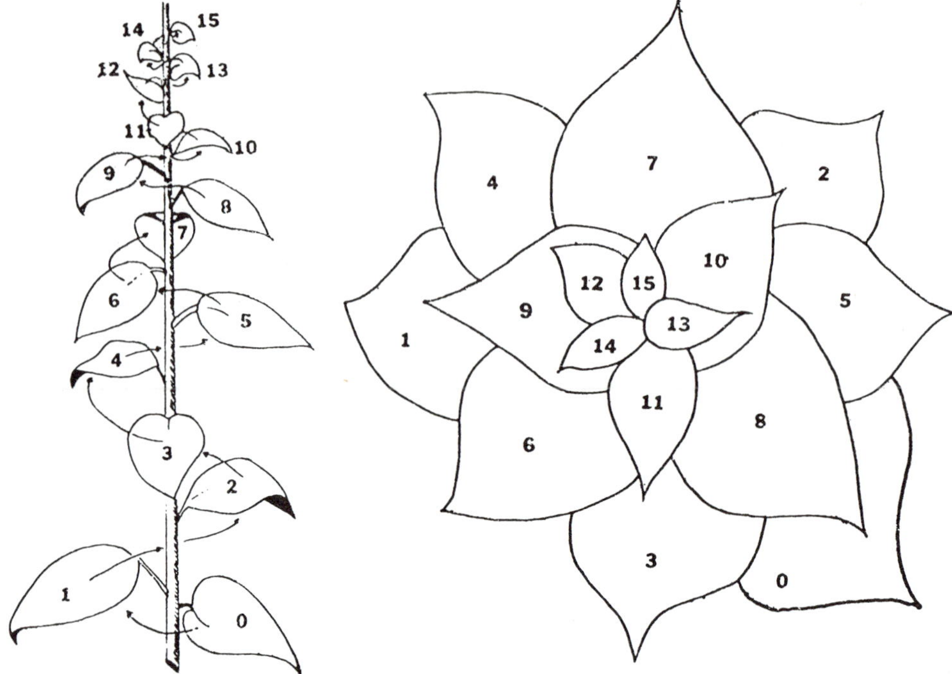

Figure 11. The top view on the right of the stem on the left clearly shows many pairs of superposed leaves such as 3 and 11, 0 and 8, 5 and 13. From the first leaf of such a pair, 3 turns around the stem are needed to reach the second, meeting 8 leaves on our way up the stem. The fraction of one turn between two consecutive leaves is thus 3/8, a phyllotactic fraction representing 135° (that is 360° times 3/8). (From R. V. Jean's *Mathematical Approach to Pattern and Form in Plant Growth,* John Wiley and Sons, New York, 1984).

7. Considering the law of formation of the convergents, multiply the first by q_{k-1}, the second by p_{k-1}, and subtract the second from the first to obtain

$$q_k p_{k-1} - p_k q_{k-1} = -(q_{k-1} p_{k-2} - p_{k-1} q_{k-2}).$$

Since $q_1 p_0 - p_1 q_0 = -1$, the result follows.

8. Verify in the case of ϕ that the assertion is true for the first few terms of the sequence and then prove the result by using the law of formation of the convergents. In the case of $1/\phi^2$, use the fact that $1/\phi^2 = 1/(1 + \phi)$.

9. Using the answer to Exercise 6, with $a = 4$, we rapidly find $11/5$, $20/9$, $29/13$, $47/21$, $85/38$, $123/55, \ldots$ Since $1/(e-1) = [0; 1, 1, 2, 1, 1, 4, \ldots]$ we find $2/3$ and $11/19$ as intermediate convergents.

11. For the second part: $(3, 2)$ and $(19, 11)$. Compare Exercises 9 and 12.

12. The parametric equation of the segment for the real number c is

$$x = \frac{c}{a_n} q_n + \left(1 - \frac{c}{a_n}\right) q_{n-2} = c q_{n-1} + q_{n-2}$$

$$y = \frac{c}{a_n} p_n + \left(1 - \frac{c}{a_n}\right) p_{n-2} = c p_{n-1} + p_{n-2}$$

Between the two vertices, $0 < c < a_n$. The lattice points between the two vertices occur at the integer values of c between 0 and a_n. It follows that in the last case $(x, y) = (q_{n,c}, p_{n,c})$.

13. With orthostichy 0, 34, 68, 102, ... we have $c = 3$, $s = 2$, $cm + sn = 34$, $c\mu + s\nu = 13$ and $d \simeq 13/34$.

16. Refer to Figure 5. Since point $q = 16$ can be reached from point $a = 0$ or from point $p = 1$ we have $m\nu = n\mu + 1$. Since point $Q = 25$ can be reached from point $p = 1$ or from point $A = 0$ we have $m\nu = n\mu - 1$.

17. Suppose that $\overline{qp}$ meets $\overline{aA}$ at R, $\overline{Qp}$ meets $\overline{aA}$ at S and that T is the foot of the perpendicular from p to $\overline{aA}$. Then by properties of the similar triangles aqR and aBA we have:

$$\overline{aq}/nl = \overline{qR}/ml^* = \overline{aR}$$

where l and l^* are defined in the text. That is, we have:

$$\nu/n = (\mu l^* + \overline{pR})/ml^* = d + \overline{TR} \cdot (1)$$

It follows that $d \leq \nu/n$. Consider now the similar triangles pSR and aBA. We have:

$$\overline{pR}/ml^* = \overline{SR} = \overline{ST} + \overline{TR},$$

so that $\overline{TR} \leq \overline{pR}/ml^*$. From (1) we obtain $d \geq \mu/m$ (where $m\nu - n\mu = 1$). Working with triangles SQA and aBA, we obtain $\nu/n \leq d \leq \mu/m$ (where $m\nu - n\mu = -1$).

18. By Exercise 17 we have

$$\mu/S_{t,k} \leq d \leq \nu/S_{t,k-1} \quad \text{or} \quad \nu/S_{t,k-1} \leq d \leq \mu/S_{t,k},$$

where $m\nu - n\mu = \pm 1$, that is $S_{t,k}\nu - S_{t,k-1}\mu = \pm 1$. These are diophantine equations whose only solution is $(\nu, \mu) = (F(k-1), F(k))$, since

$$F(k-1)^2 - F(k)F(k-2) = \pm 1,$$

the sign depending on whether k is odd or even (can you prove that?). By a principle known in calculus as the principle of closed nested intervals, we have that the infinite set of nested intervals under consideration contains only one point, since the lengths of these intervals tend towards zero as k tends towards infinity. The point common to every interval is

$$\lim_{k\to\infty} F(k)/S_{t,k} = (t + \phi^{-1})^{-1} = d.$$

20. The abscissa of $F(k)$ in the cylindrical lattice is

$$\phi F(k) - F(k+1) - [\phi F(k) - F(k+1)].$$

In the expression $\phi F(k) - F(k+1)$, replace $F(k)$ and $F(k+1)$ by their values given by *Binet's formula*:

$$F(k) = (\phi^k - (-\phi)^{-k})/\sqrt{5}$$

(can you prove it? induction. . .). This results in

$$\phi F(k) - F(k+1) = (-1)^{k+1}(\phi^2 + 1)/\sqrt{5}\phi^{k+1}.$$

Then show that $\phi^2 + 1 = \sqrt{5}\phi$. It follows that $[\phi F(k) - F(k+1)]$ is 0 or -1 depending on whether $\phi F(k) - F(k+1)$ is positive or negative. So the coordinates of the neighbor $F(k)$ of the Y-axis in the cylindrical lattice are as expected. Now consider in the XY-plane the square of the Euclidean distance from the origin to $F(k)$ and to $F(k+1)$, two neighbors of the Y-axis; that is, $1/\phi^{2k} + F(k)^2r^2$ and $1/\phi^{2k+2} + F(k+1)^2r^2$. The second expression can be made smaller than the first if we choose

$$r^2 < 1/\phi^{2k+1}(F(k+1)^2 - F(k)^2),$$

that is,

$$r < \phi^{-k-(1/2)}(F(k+2)F(k-1))^{-(1/2)}.$$

Finally, the absolute value of the abscissa of $F(k)$ is greater than the absolute value of the abscissa of $F(k+1)$.

21. We must have $d(0, 3) < d(0, 2)$ and $d(0, 5) < d(0, 8)$, where $d(0, x)$ is the Euclidean distance $(x_1^2 + x_2^2)^{1/2}$ from the origin to point $x = (x_1, x_2)$. The coordinates of points 2, 3, 5, 8, as given in the theorem of Section 4.1, correspond to $k = 3, 4, 5, 6$. It follows that

$$1/\sqrt{39}\phi^{11/2} < r < 1/\sqrt{5}\phi^{7/2}.$$

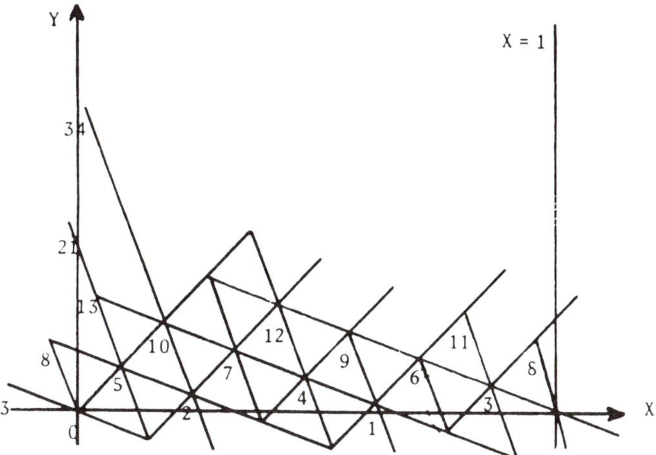

Figure 12. Point 8 has become a neighbor of the origin and the phyllotaxis is rising from 5/3 to 8/5. (From Jean, *Phytomathématique*, 1978.)

The phyllotaxis changes when $d(0, 8) = d(0, 3)$; that is, when $r = 5^{1/4}/\phi^5\sqrt{55}$. Figure 12 is drawn with this value of r. Phyllotaxis passes from $F(k)/F(k-1)$ to $F(k+1)/F(k)$ for

$$r = 5^{1/4}/\phi^k(F(k+1)^2 - F(k-1)^2)^{1/2} = 5^{1/4}/\phi^k(F(2k))^{1/2}.$$

22. Suppose that $d = k_1/k_2$, a rational number. Then leaf k_2 is also on the Y-axis since

$$k_2 = (k_2 d - [k_2 d], k_2 r) = (0, k_2 r).$$

23. For $n \geq 2$ we have

$$q_{n,a_n-1} = (a_n - 1)q_{n-1} + q_{n-2} = q_n - q_{n-1}$$

and

$$q_{n+1,1} = q_n + q_{n-1}.$$

(See the definition of intermediate convergents and the law of formation of the convergents: Section 2.3 and Exercise 12.) It follows that

$$q_{n-1} < q_{n,1} \quad \text{and} \quad q_{n,a_n-1} < q_n.$$

Obviously $q_{n,i} < q_{n,i+1}$, so that we have the result.

24. The theorem in Section 4.1 gives the coordinates of points $F(k)$ and $F(k+1)$. It is known from analytic geometry that two points (x_1, x_2) and (y_1, y_2) make a right angle with $(0, 0)$ if $x_1 y_1 + x_2 y_2 = 0$. It follows that $-\phi^{-2k-1} + F(k)F(k+1)r^2 = 0$ (this formula is demonstrated in Coxeter's *Introduction to Geometry* by a longer way).

25. Draw the visible opposed parastichy triangle belonging to the pair 7/4 and use Bravais's approximation formula. We have

$$cm + sn = 7c + 4s = S(k),$$

so that $(c, s) = (F(k-3), F(k-4))$. Since $\mu = 2$ and $\nu = 1$ ($7\nu - 4\mu = \pm 1$): See Exercise 16) we have $c\mu + s\nu = F(k-1)$. It follows that

$$d = \lim_{k\to\infty} F(k-1)/S(k)$$

and since $S(k) = F(k+1) + F(k-1)$ we have the result. By following the genetic spiral (1, 2, 3, 4, 5, . . .) we have to come back five times to the left to meet 18 points: the phyllotactic fraction is $5/18 = F(5)/S(6)$. More generally, with point $S(k)$, the phyllotactic fraction is $F(k-1)/S(k)$.

26. By Binet's formula (Exercise 20) we have

$$S_{t,k}\phi/(\phi t + 1) = \phi^k/\sqrt{5} + (-1)^k(\phi - t)/\phi^{k-1}(\phi t + 1)\sqrt{5}$$

and $\phi^k = \sqrt{5}F(k) + (-1)^k/\phi^k$. It follows that the expression above has the value

$$F(n) + (-1)^k(\phi + 2)/\phi^k(\phi t + 1)\sqrt{5}.$$

Since $\phi + 2 = \sqrt{5}\phi$, we have the result.

27. The distance of $(S_{t,k}, F(k))$ to $y = (t + \phi^{-1})^{-1}x$ is obtained by putting the line in its normal form. This distance is a constant times $|\phi F(k-1) - F(k)|/(\phi t + 1)$, and Binet's formula gives that the absolute value is ϕ^{-k+1}. Compare with Exercise 26 giving the other distance.

UMAP

Modules in Undergraduate Mathematics and Its Applications

Published in cooperation with the Society for Industrial and Applied Mathematics, the Mathematical Association of America, the National Council of Teachers of Mathematics, the American Mathematical Association of Two-Year Colleges, and The Institute of Management Sciences.

Module 574

Expected Loss in Keno

William Barnier

According to the brochure of one Reno gambling casino, the modern game of keno is based on a lottery game played in China about 1100 B.C. It was played with characters from an ancient poem of luck. Twenty characters were drawn from a possible eighty. Winners were those who placed wagers on the correct characters before drawing.

INTERMODULAR DESCRIPTION SHEET:	UMAP Unit 574
TITLE:	EXPECTED LOSS IN KENO
AUTHOR:	William Barnier Department of Mathematics Sonoma State University Rohnert Park, CA 94928
CLASSIFICATION:	ELEMENTARY PROBABILITY
TARGET AUDIENCE:	Students in courses that introduce probability.
ABSTRACT:	This unit uses a simplified version of keno to explain the method for calculating probabilities and expected value in keno. A casino pay chart and a computer generated table of probabilities are used to find various expected values in keno. The exercises contain applications of probability to card hands, selecting job applicants, and casino tourist incentive coupons, as well as to keno.
PREREQUISITES:	Ability to use and manipulate binomial coefficients. An elementary knowledge of the multiplicative counting principle of probability and expected value.

Expected Loss in Keno

William Barnier
Department of Mathematics
Sonoma State University
Rohnert Park, CA 94928

Table of Contents

Modules and Monographs in Undergraduate Mathematics and Its Applications Project (UMAP)

The goal of UMAP was to develop, through a community of users and developers, a system of instructional modules in undergraduate mathematics and its applications to be used to supplement existing courses and from which complete courses may eventually be built.

The Project was guided by a National Advisory Board of mathematicians, scientists, and educators. UMAP was funded by a grant from the National Science Foundation and is now supported by the Consortium for Mathematics and Its Applications, Inc. (COMAP), a nonprofit corporation engaged in research and development in mathematics education.

The Project would like to thank H. Alan Lasater of the University of Tennessee, Peter A. Lindstrom of North Lake College, Donald F. Shriner of Frostburg State College, and one anonymous reviewer, for their reviews, and all others who assisted in the production of this unit.

This unit was field-tested and/or student reviewed by Robert Brandon of Eastern Oregon State College, Eleanor Kendrick of San Jose City College, and Clement Falbo of Sonoma State University, and has been revised on the basis of data received from these sites.

This material was prepared with the partial support of National Science Foundation Grant No. SED80-07731 and SPE-8304192. Recommendations expressed are those of the author and do not necessarily reflect the views of the NSF or the copyright holder.

1. Introduction

1.1 How Keno is Played

According to the brochure of one Reno gambling casino, the modern game of keno is based on a lottery game played in China about 1100 B.C. It was played with characters from an ancient poem of luck. Twenty characters were drawn from a possible eighty. Winners were those who placed wagers on the correct characters before drawing.

The modern version is similar. A player selects from one to 15 numbers by marking the corresponding box on a ticket which has 80 boxes number 1 through 80. Both the ticket and a wager (commonly $1.00) are turned in before 20 balls are drawn at random from 80 numbered balls in a clear, round plastic container. Possible payoffs are given on a pay chart. Almost all the pay charts I have seen have payoffs identical to those in the pay chart of Table 1. However, most no longer have the .70 column.

Suppose, as a player, you turned in a card with five boxes marked along with a $1.00 wager. You would look in the $1.00 column of the "Mark 5 Spots" section to find the possible payoffs. If three of the 20 numbers drawn were the same as any three of your "spots" (marked boxes), you would get a payoff of $1.00 because you would "catch 3." If you catch 4, you get a payoff of $9.00.

1.2 Two Basic Questions

One reason for the popularity of keno is that a person has a chance to win a very large payoff for a small wager. A $1.00 wager will yield a payoff of $8,100.00 if the player has marked 7 spots and then all seven numbers are among the 20 selected. Similarly a $1.00 wager with a mark 8 spot card will return a payoff of $1,650.00 if the player catches 7.

But what is the probability a player can win the two bets above? Even more important, what is the long run expectation in the game of keno?

In what follows we will analyze and answer two main questions.

1. What is the probability of catching k given the player marked m spots $(m > k)$? This question is discussed in Sections 2 and 3.
2. What is the expected loss on a $1.00 bet in keno? This question is discussed in Sections 4 and 5.

Table 1

Catch	.70	1.00	5.00
1	2.10	3.00	15.00
MARK 2 SPOTS			
2	8.40	12.00	60.00
MARK 3 SPOTS			
2	.70	1.00	5.00
3	29.40	42.00	210.00
MARK 4 SPOTS			
2	.70	1.00	5.00
3	2.80	4.00	20.00
4	79.10	113.00	565.00
MARK 5 SPOTS			
3	.70	1.00	5.00
4	6.30	9.00	45.00
5	574.00	820.00	4,100.00
MARK 6 SPOTS			
3	.70	1.00	5.00
4	2.10	3.00	15.00
5	63.00	90.00	450.00
6	1,260.00	1,800.00	9,000.00
MARK 7 SPOTS			
4	.70	1.00	5.00
5	14.00	20.00	100.00
6	287.00	410.00	2,050.00
7	5,670.00	8,100.00	25,000.00
MARK 8 SPOTS			
5	6.30	9.00	45.00
6	63.00	90.00	450.00
7	1,155.00	1,650.00	8,250.00
8	12,600.00	18,000.00	25,000.00
MARK 9 SPOTS			
5	2.10	3.00	15.00
6	31.50	45.00	225.00
7	234.50	335.00	1,675.00
8	3,290.00	4,700.00	23,500.00
9	12,950.00	18,500.00	25,000.00
MARK 10 SPOTS			
5	1.40	2.00	10.00
6	14.00	20.00	100.00
7	99.40	142.00	710.00
8	700.00	1,000.00	5,000.00
9	3,150.00	4,500.00	22,500.00
10	13,300.00	19,000.00	25,000.00

Catch	.70	1.00	5.00
6	7.00	10.00	50.00
7	52.50	75.00	375.00
8	266.00	380.00	1,900.00
9	1,400.00	2,000.00	10,000.00
10	8,750.00	12,500.00	25,000.00
11	13,650.00	19,500.00	25,000.00
MARK 12 SPOTS			
6	4.20	6.00	30.00
7	19.60	28.00	140.00
8	140.00	200.00	1,000.00
9	595.00	850.00	4,250.00
10	1,680.00	2,400.00	12,000.00
11	9,100.00	13,000.00	25,000.00
12	25,000.00	25,000.00	25,000.00
MARK 13 SPOTS			
6	1.40	2.00	10.00
7	11.20	16.00	80.00
8	54.60	78.00	390.00
9	490.00	700.00	3,500.00
10	2,520.00	3,600.00	18,000.00
11	6,300.00	9,000.00	25,000.00
12	21,000.00	25,000.00	25,000.00
13	25,000.00	25,[illegible]0.00	25,000.00
MARK 14 SPOTS			
6	2.10	3.00	15.00
7	5.60	8.00	40.00
8	22.40	32.00	160.00
9	210.00	300.00	1,500.00
10	560.00	800.00	4,000.00
11	1,750.00	2,500.00	12,500.00
12	8,400.00	12,000.00	25,000.00
13	25,000.00	25,000.00	25,000.00
14	25,000.00	25,000.00	25,000.00
MARK 15 SPOTS			
6	1.40	2.00	10.00
7	5.60	8.00	40.00
8	14.70	21.00	105.00
9	52.50	75.00	375.00
10	168.00	240.00	1,200.00
11	1,680.00	2,400.00	12,000.00
12	5,600.00	8,000.00	25,000.00
13	25,000.00	25,000.00	25,000.00
14	25,000.00	25,000.00	25,000.00
15	25,000.00	25,000.00	25,000.00

2. A Simplified Version of Keno

2.1 Defining $P(m, k)$

To help compute the probabilities needed to answer Question 1, let us consider a simplified version of keno. Suppose five balls are drawn each game from seven balls numbered consecutively 1 through 7.

We will write the probability of catching k given the player marked m spots as $P(m, k)$.

$$P(m, k) = \text{Probability (mark } m, \text{ catch } k).$$

So,

$$P(m, k) = \frac{\text{Number of ways of catching } k \text{ of the given } m \text{ spots}}{\text{Total number of ways the balls can be selected}}.$$

The first number which we need is the total number of ways the balls can be selected. In our simplified version this is just the number of ways five balls can be selected from seven. In other words, the number of combinations of 7 balls taken 5 at a time. This is written

$$\binom{7}{5}.$$

We get

$$\binom{7}{5} = \frac{7!}{5!\,2!} = \frac{7 \cdot 6}{2 \cdot 1} = 21.$$

2.2 An Example Using the Simplified Version

Example 1. Suppose the player marks 3 spots.
(a) What is the probability of catching 3?
We want to compute $P(3, 3)$ and we know

$$P(3, 3) = \frac{\text{Number of ways of catching 3 of the given 3 spots}}{21}.$$

To compute the number of ways of catching 3 of the given spots imagine the player has marked the boxes with even numbers (2, 4, 6). It does not matter which three numbers are marked—the following analysis will yield the same result. For the player to catch all three of these numbers they must be among the five selected. The three marked numbers can occur in

$$\binom{3}{3} = 1 \text{ way.}$$

Also two of the five selected must be from the four odd numbers (1, 3, 5, 7). This can occur in

$$\binom{4}{2} = 6 \text{ ways.}$$

Hence the number of ways of catching 3 of the given 3 spots is equal to

$$\binom{3}{3} \cdot \binom{4}{2} = 6.$$

Therefore $P(3, 3) = 6/21 = 2/7$.

(b) What is the probability of catching 2?

We need to know the number of ways two of these three numbers (say the even numbers again) can be among the five selected. First, note there are

$$\binom{3}{2} = 3 \text{ ways}$$

of getting two of the three marked numbers. Three of the five selected must be from the remaining four odd numbers. This can happen in

$$\binom{4}{3} = 4 \text{ ways.}$$

To compute the number of ways of catching 2 of the given 3 spots we use the multiplicative counting principle and obtain

$$\binom{3}{2} \cdot \binom{4}{3} = 3 \cdot 4 = 12. \quad \text{Hence } P(3, 2) = \frac{12}{21} = \frac{4}{7}.$$

2.3 A Systematic Look at the Example

Let us look more systematically at what happened in Example 1.(b). We can think of the seven numbers as partitioned into two disjoint sets: the marked numbers (m) and the remaining numbers ($7 - m$). Similarly the five selected numbers are partitioned into those the player catches (k) and the other ($5 - k$). In Example 1.(b) we had

$$7 = m + (7 - m) = 3 + 4$$

$$5 = k + (5 - k) = 2 + 3.$$

Since the player catches only marked spots we can further symbolize our analysis in Example 1.(b) by:

$$\begin{array}{l} 7 = 3 + 4 \\ \quad\ \ \downarrow \ \ \downarrow \\ 5 = 2 + 3 \end{array}$$

Note that

$$P(3, 2) = \frac{\binom{3}{2}\binom{4}{3}}{\binom{7}{5}}.$$

Exercises

1. Refer to Example 1.
   (a) Note a player will always catch at least one spot. Why? Use this fact and our computed values for $P(3, 3)$ and $P(3, 2)$ to get $P(3, 1)$.
   (b) Compute $P(3, 1)$ using the same method we used to compute $P(3, 2)$.

2. Suppose a player marks 4 spots in our simplified version of keno (5 balls drawn from 7).
   (a) Compute $P(4, 4)$.
   (b) Compute $P(4, 3)$.
   (c) Note a player must catch at least 2 spots in this game and compute $P(4, 2)$ in two different ways.

3. Keno: The Real Thing

A keno player marks $m(1 \leq m \leq 15)$ of the 80 numbers. We can think of the 80 numbers as partitioned into the marked (m) and the other numbers ($80 - m$). The 20 numbers selected are partitioned into the numbers the player catches (k) and the remaining numbers ($20 - k$).

Symbolically:

$$\begin{array}{c} 80 = m + (80 - m) \\ \quad\ \downarrow \qquad \downarrow \\ 20 = k + (20 - k). \end{array}$$

3.1 An Example Where a Player Marks Five

Example 2. Suppose a player marks 5 spots.
(a) What is the probability of catching all 5?

We have

$$\begin{array}{c} 80 = 5 + 75 \\ \quad\ \downarrow \quad \downarrow \\ 20 = 5 + 15 \end{array}$$

So,

$$P(5, 5) = \frac{\binom{5}{5}\binom{75}{15}}{\binom{80}{20}} = .000645.$$

The computation of $P(5, 5)$ can be done with some judicious cancellation and a hand calculator.

(b) What is the probability of catching 4 of the 5?

We have $\begin{array}{c} 80 = 5 + 75 \\ \quad\ \downarrow \quad \downarrow \\ 20 = 4 + 16 \end{array}$

So,

$$P(5, 4) = \frac{\binom{5}{4}\binom{75}{16}}{\binom{80}{20}} = .01209.$$

(c) What is the probability of catching 3 of 5? (See Exercise 3).

Exercises Using a Hand Calculator

3. Compute $P(5, 3)$.

4. Compute $P(6, 6)$, $P(6, 5)$, $P(6, 4)$ and $P(6, 3)$ using a hand calculator.

3.2 Use of Table 2

To find $P(6, 5)$ in Table 2, look in the row with 6 on the left ($m = 6$) and $k = 5$ to find .309564E − 2. The "E − 2" means "exponent −2" which is short for "multiply by 10^{-2}." So, move the decimal point left by two places to get $P(6, 5) = .00309564$.

Table 2 was generated by a computer at Sonoma State University. (More extensive tables can be found in *Tables of the Hypergeometric Probability Distribution* by G. J. Lieberman and D. B. Owen, Stanford University Press, 1961, pp. 370–371.) It is not surprising the table is not available at a casino where keno is played.

4. Expected Loss for Keno: Simplified Version

Suppose, as before, five balls are selected at random from seven each game. In addition assume the following pay chart is used for this game.

MARK 3 SPOTS

Catch	1.00
3	3.00

Table 2

m	k	$P(m, k)$	m	k	$P(m, k)$
1	1	.25	11	6	.202037E − 1
			11	7	.360781E − 2
2	2	.601266E − 1	11	8	.411417E − 3
			11	9	.283736E − 4
3	2	.138754	11	10	.1058E − 5
3	3	.138754E − 1	11	11	.160303E − 7
4	2	.212636	12	6	.322089E − 1
4	3	.432479E − 1	12	7	.702739E − 2
4	4	.306339E − 2	12	8	.10196E − 2
			12	9	.95401E − 4
5	3	.839351E − 1	12	10	.542799E − 5
5	4	.120923E − 1	12	11	.167272E − 6
5	5	.644925E − 3	12	12	.209091R − 8
6	3	.12982	13	6	.475013E − 1
6	4	.285379E − 1	13	7	.123152E − 1
6	5	.309564E − 2	13	8	.218314E − 2
6	6	.128985E − 3	13	9	.259898E − 3
			13	10	.200623E − 4
7	4	.052191	13	11	.943367E − 6
7	5	.863851E − 2	13	12	.239839E − 7
7	6	.732077E − 3	13	13	.245989E − 9
7	7	.244026E − 4			
			14	6	.657574E − 1
8	5	.183026E − 1	14	7	.198513E − 1
8	6	.236671E − 2	14	8	.418164E − 2
8	7	.160455E − 3	14	9	.608238E − 3
8	8	.434566E − 5	14	10	.597377E − 4
			14	11	.381102E − 5
9	5	.326015E − 1	14	12	.147841E − 6
9	6	.571956E − 2	14	13	.308404E − 8
9	7	.591679E − 3	14	14	.257003E − 10
9	8	.325925E − 4			
9	9	.724277E − 6	15	6	.863481E − 1
			15	7	.298897E − 1
10	5	.514277E − 1	15	8	.733144E − 2
10	6	.114794E − 1	15	9	.126716E − 2
10	7	.161114E − 2	15	10	.15206E − 3
10	8	.135419E − 3	15	11	.123425E − 4
10	9	.612065E − 5	15	12	.649605E − 6
10	10	.112212E − 6	15	13	.206771E − 7
			15	14	.350459E − 9
			15	15	.233639E − 11

Remember $P(3, 3) = 2/7$. So the probability of no payoff (a $1.00 loss) is 5/7. If the game is played seven times a player should expect to win $2.00 (3.00 − 1.00) twice and lose $1.00 five times. The expected loss over seven games is $2.00(2) − 1.00(5) = −1.00. A player should expect to lose $1.00 every seven games. The expected loss on a $1.00 wager is $2.00 (2/7) − 1.00(5/7) = −1.00/7.

In general if a game has n possible outcomes and outcomes occur with probabilities $p_1, \ldots, p_n$, and have payoffs $s_1, \ldots, s_n$, respectively, then the expected payoff of a game,

$$E = \sum_{i=1}^{n} s_i p_i = s_1 p_1 + s_2 p_2 + \ldots + s_n p_n.$$

When the expected value is negative (as in most games of chance) we call E the expected loss.

Exercise

5. Suppose a player marks 4 spots with the following pay chart given.

MARK 4 SPOTS

Catch	1.00
4	5.00

Find the expected loss over seven games and the expected loss on a $1.00 wager.

5. Expected Loss for Keno: The Real Thing

Consider a player who marks 5 and wagers $1.00. From Table 1:

MARK 5 SPOTS

Catch	1.00
3	1.00
4	9.00
5	820.00

The wager must be subtracted from each payoff to get the amount won. So catching 3 gives a net winning of 0, catching 4 a net of $8.00, and catching 5 a net of $819.00. Catching anything other than 3, 4, or 5 results in a loss of $1.00. The probability of losing $1.00 is therefore $1 - P(5, 5) - P(5, 4) - P(5, 3)$. This is

$$1 - .000645 - .012092 - .08393 = .9033.$$

Expected loss on a \$1.00 wager is:

$$819.00 \cdot P(5, 5) + 8.00 \cdot P(5, 4) + 0 \cdot P(5, 3) - 1.00(.9033)$$

$$= -.2784$$

So, a player who plays 100 games should expect to lose almost \$28.00. The expected loss on a \$1.00 wager in roulette is −.0526. Hence keno has an expected loss more than five times that of roulette.

Exercises

6. Find the expected loss on a \$1.00 wager when a player marks 6 spots.

7. Compute the expected losses on a \$1.00 wager for two other games of keno (say mark 4 and mark 7) by using Tables 1 and 2. Compare your answers to those obtained for mark 5 and mark 6 games.

Supplementary Exercises

8. Another simplified version of keno: suppose five balls are drawn each game from nine balls.

Assume a player marks 3 and the following pay chart is given:

MARK 3 SPOTS

Catch	1.00
3	4.00
2	1.00

(a) Compute $P(3, 3)$ and $P(3, 2)$.
(b) Compute the probability of losing the \$1.00 wager.
(c) Compute the expected loss of a \$1.00 wager.

9. Still another simplified version of keno: suppose six balls are drawn from 13. Assume a player marks 4 spots.
(a) Compute $P(4, 4)$, $P(4, 3)$, and $P(4, 2)$.
(b) Find the expected loss on a \$1.00 wager with this given pay chart:

MARK 4 SPOTS

Catch	1.00
4	5.00
3	2.00
2	1.00

In Exercises 10, 11, and 12 the skills you learned in solving the keno problem are applied in other areas.

10. Consider a "deck" of the 13 spades from a standard bridge deck of cards. Suppose six cards are picked at random from this deck of 13.

(a) What is the probability the six will include the four honor cards (Ace, King, Queen, Jack)? 3 of the 4?, 2 of the 4?
(b) What is the probability the six will include none of the four honor cards?

11. Suppose there are 80 job applicants for 20 positions and 15 of the applicants are women. Assume the 20 successful applicants are selected at random.
(a) What is the probability six of the 20 are women?
(b) What is the probability at least six of the 20 are women?
(c) What is the probability none of the 20 is a woman?

12. Suppose you and two other members of your family take part in a study of vitamin C. There are 25 people in the study including the three from your family. Large doses of vitamin C are given to ten of 25 while the other 15 get a placebo. Assume the ten are chosen randomly.
(a) What is the probability your whole family gets the vitamin C?
(b) What is the probability your whole family gets the placebo?
(c) What is the probability at least one of your family gets the vitamin C?
(d) What is the probability one of your family gets the vitamin C?
(e) What is the probability you get the vitamin C?

13. As an incentive for tourists, coupon books for a specific casino are sometimes made available at motels. In one such book was a coupon for keno which when turned in with $.50 would allow the player to make a $1.00 wager. Suppose you use one of these coupons to make a $1.00 wager for a $.50 cost to you. What is your expected "loss" if you mark 5?

6. Answers to All Questions

1. (a) $P(3, 1) = 1 - P(3, 3) - P(3, 2) = 1 - \frac{2}{7} - \frac{4}{7} = \frac{1}{7}$

(b) $P(3, 1) = \dfrac{\binom{3}{1}\binom{4}{4}}{21} = \dfrac{3 \cdot 1}{21} = \dfrac{1}{7}.$

2. (a) $P(4, 4) = \dfrac{\binom{4}{4}\binom{3}{1}}{21} = \dfrac{1 \cdot 3}{21} = \dfrac{1}{7}.$

(b) $P(4, 3) = \dfrac{\binom{4}{3}\binom{3}{2}}{21} = \dfrac{4 \cdot 3}{21} = \dfrac{4}{7}.$

(c) $P(4, 2) = 1 - \dfrac{1}{7} - \dfrac{4}{7} = \dfrac{2}{7},\ P(4, 2) = \dfrac{\binom{4}{2}\binom{3}{3}}{21} = \dfrac{6 \cdot 1}{21} = \dfrac{2}{7}$

3. $P(5, 3) = \dfrac{\binom{5}{3}\binom{75}{17}}{\binom{80}{20}} = \dfrac{5!}{3!\,2!} \cdot \dfrac{75!}{17!\,58!} \cdot \dfrac{20!\,60!}{80!}$

$$= \frac{5 \cdot 4}{2 \cdot 1} \cdot \frac{75!}{58!} \cdot \frac{20!}{17!} \cdot \frac{60!}{80!}$$

$$= \frac{(5 \cdot 4)(75 \cdot 74 \cdots 59)(20 \cdot 19 \cdot 18)}{2(80 \cdot 79 \cdots 61)}$$

$$= \frac{5 \cdot 60 \cdot 59 \cdot 19 \cdot 18}{2 \cdot 79 \cdot 78 \cdot 77 \cdot 76}$$

$$= \frac{5 \cdot 15 \cdot 59 \cdot 3}{2 \cdot 79 \cdot 13 \cdot 77} = .0839.$$

4. $P(6, 6) = \dfrac{\binom{6}{6}\binom{74}{14}}{\binom{80}{20}} = .000129,\ P(6, 5) = \dfrac{\binom{6}{5}\binom{74}{15}}{\binom{80}{20}} = .003096$

$P(6, 4) = \dfrac{\binom{6}{4}\binom{74}{16}}{\binom{80}{20}} = .02854,\ P(6, 3) = \dfrac{\binom{6}{3}\binom{74}{17}}{\binom{80}{20}} = .12982$

5. Expected loss:

(over 7 games) $= 4.00(1) - 1.00(6) = -2.00$

(on a 1.00 wager) $= 4.00\left(\dfrac{1}{7}\right) - 1.00\left(\dfrac{6}{7}\right) = -\dfrac{2.00}{7}$

6. $1799.00(.000129) + 89.00(.003096) + 2.00(.02854) - 1.00(.8384)$
$= -.2737$

7. Mark 4 Expected Loss $= -.2645$

Mark 7 Expected Loss $= -.2773.$

11

8. (a) $P(3, 3) = \dfrac{15}{126}$, $P(3, 2) = \dfrac{60}{126}$

(b) $1 - \dfrac{15}{126} - \dfrac{60}{126} = \dfrac{51}{126}$

(c) $3.00\left(\dfrac{15}{126}\right) - 1.00\left(\dfrac{51}{126}\right) = -\dfrac{6}{126}$

9. (a) $P(4, 4) = \dfrac{3}{143}$, $P(4, 3) = \dfrac{28}{143}$, $P(4, 2) = \dfrac{63}{143}$

(b) $13.00\left(\dfrac{3}{143}\right) - 1.00\left(\dfrac{49}{143}\right) = -\dfrac{10}{143}$

(c) $4.00\left(\dfrac{3}{143}\right) + 1.00\left(\dfrac{28}{143}\right) - 1.00\left(\dfrac{49}{143}\right) = -\dfrac{9}{143}$

10. (a) $\dfrac{\binom{4}{4}\binom{9}{2}}{\binom{13}{6}}, \dfrac{\binom{4}{3}\binom{9}{3}}{\binom{13}{6}}, \dfrac{\binom{4}{2}\binom{9}{4}}{\binom{13}{6}}$

(b) $\dfrac{\binom{4}{0}\binom{9}{6}}{\binom{13}{6}}$

11. (a) Use Table 2 to get $P(15, 6)$.
(b) $P(15, 6) + P(15, 7) + \ldots + P(15, 15)$ and use Table 2.
(c) Compute $P(15,0)$ using a calculator.

12. (a) $\dfrac{\binom{3}{3}\binom{22}{7}}{\binom{25}{10}}$ (b) $\dfrac{\binom{3}{3}\binom{22}{12}}{\binom{25}{15}}$ (c) $1 - \dfrac{\binom{3}{0}\binom{22}{15}}{\binom{25}{15}}$

(d) $\dfrac{\binom{3}{1}\binom{22}{9}}{\binom{25}{10}}$ (e) $\dfrac{\binom{1}{1}\binom{24}{9}}{\binom{25}{10}}$

13. $819.50(.000645) + 8.50(.012092) + .50(.08393) - .50(.9033) = +.2217$. Note: $+.2217 = -.2784 + .50$ (with round off error), so the casino is adding \$.50 to your expected value by giving you the coupon. This is a specific example of a general principle for expected value.

12

UMAP

Modules in Undergraduate Mathematics and Its Applications

Module 607

Determining the Size for a Mussel Farm

Ernest D. True

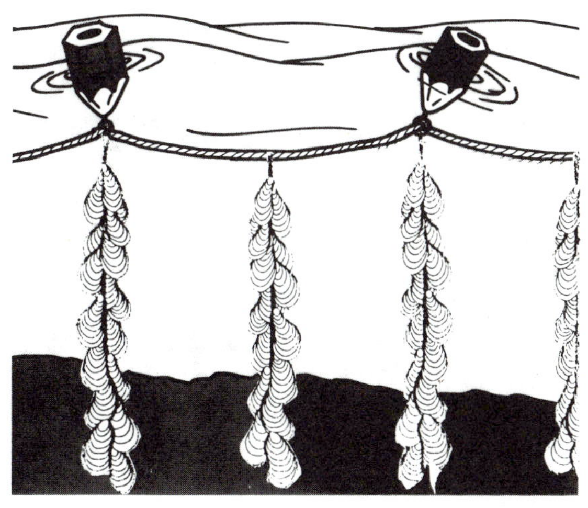

Published in cooperation with the Society for Industrial and Applied Mathematics, the Mathematical Association of America, the National Council of Teachers of Mathematics, the American Mathematical Association of Two-Year Colleges, and The Institute of Management Sciences.

Intermodular Description Sheet:	UMAP Unit 607
Title:	DETERMINING THE SIZE FOR A MUSSEL FARM
Author:	Ernest D. True Department of Mathematics Norwich University Northfield, VT 05663
Math Field:	Precalculus
Application Field:	Marine biology — aquaculture
Target Audience:	Students in a precalculus course.
Abstract:	In recent years, experimental mussel culture farms have been constructed along the coasts of the United States to examine the feasibility of growing mussels in large scale commercial farms. A mathematical model is provided to estimate the size of such a farm which will maximize the harvest for a given location without overly depleting nutrients in a tidal estuary. Students learn: 1) To better understand how simple mathematical models can be used to predict results; 2) To recognize the importance of preliminary research data employed in a mathematical model; 3) To recognize the need for making idealized assumptions and examining ways in which certain assumptions can be altered; and 4) To gain practice in developing skills in computing and using proper units of measurement.
Prerequisite Skills:	1. To be able to use a pocket calculator to compute expressions involving exponentials and logarithms. 2. Recognize and construct terms in a geometric sequence.

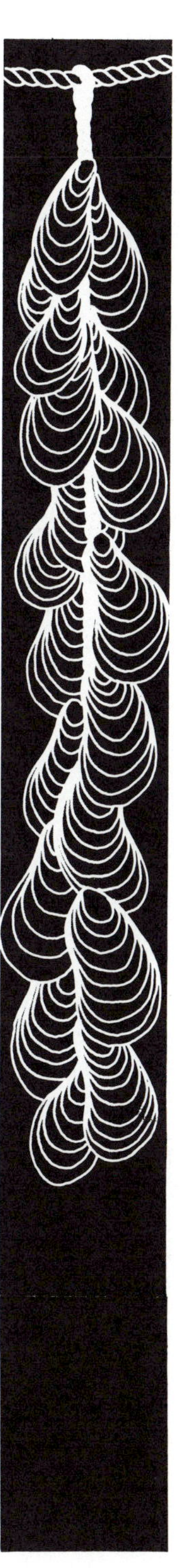

Determining the Size for a Mussel Farm

Ernest D. True
Department of Mathematics
Norwich University
Northfield, VT 05663

Table of Contents

Modules and Monographs in Undergraduate Mathematics and its Applications Project (UMAP)

The goal of UMAP was to develop, through a community of users and developers, a system of instructional modules in undergraduate mathematics and its applications to be used to supplement existing courses and from which complete courses may eventually be built.

The Project was guided by a National Advisory Board of mathematicians, scientists, and educators. UMAP was funded by a grant from the National Science Foundation and is now supported by the Consortium for Mathematics and Its Applications, Inc. (COMAP), a nonprofit corporation engaged in research and development in mathematics education.

This material was prepared with the partial support of National Science Foundation Grant No. SED8007731. Recommendations expressed are those of the author and do not necessarily reflect the views of the NSF or the copyright holder.

1. Blue Mussel Farms: Historical Background

"One crop which has been grown successfully in Europe for generations is that of Mytilus edulis, the edible blue mussel."

We have all heard that the world's oceans may be more useful as a food resource, especially if we can control the crop by growing it in a near-shore area where it can be more easily monitored and harvested. One crop which has been grown successfully in Europe for generations is that of Mytilus edulis, the edible blue mussel. This mussel is about the same size and shape of a steamer clam and is preferred to the clam by many who have eaten both. It can be preserved by canning, freezing, drying, smoking, and pickling. The United States Department of Agriculture *Handbook of the Nutritional Contents of Food* (Watt and Merril, [1975]) compares the nutritional value of 3.5 ounces of raw mussel meat with the same amount of choice T-Bone steak in the following table:

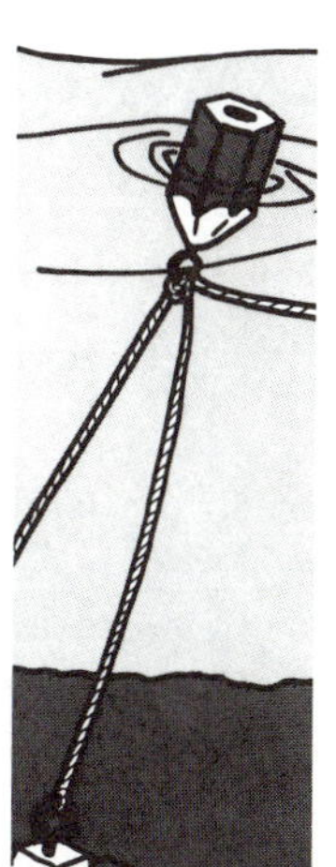

	Blue Mussel		**T-Bone Steak**	
Calories	95		395	
Protein	14.4	grams	14.7	grams
Fat	2.2	grams	37.1	grams
Carbohydrates	3.3	grams	0	grams
Calcium	88	milligrams	8	milligrams
Phosphorus	236	milligrams	135	milligrams
Iron	3.4	milligrams	2.2	milligrams
Thiamin	.16	milligrams	.06	milligrams
Riboflavin	.21	milligrams	.13	milligrams

"...tidal waters bring in nutrients for the mussels..."

The largest commercial mussel farms are in Spain, France, Italy, and the Netherlands. In the Netherlands, where mussel farming is three hundred years old, the mussels are grown in culture plots on the sea bottom in about 15 feet of water, where they are dredged up for market. The plots are then reseeded with young mussels from natural growth areas. In France, the mussel seed is attached to poles which have been driven into the ocean floor. The moving tidal waters bring in nutrients for the mussels which are eventually harvested by picking the mature mussels from these poles. The process in Spain has been the most productive and is being adapted with some modifications in this country. The farming area consists of parallel ropes, called long lines. These are about 50 meters long and are attached to floats on either end. From the long lines at two-meter intervals are suspended shorter ropes upon which the mussels grow. (See Figure 1.)

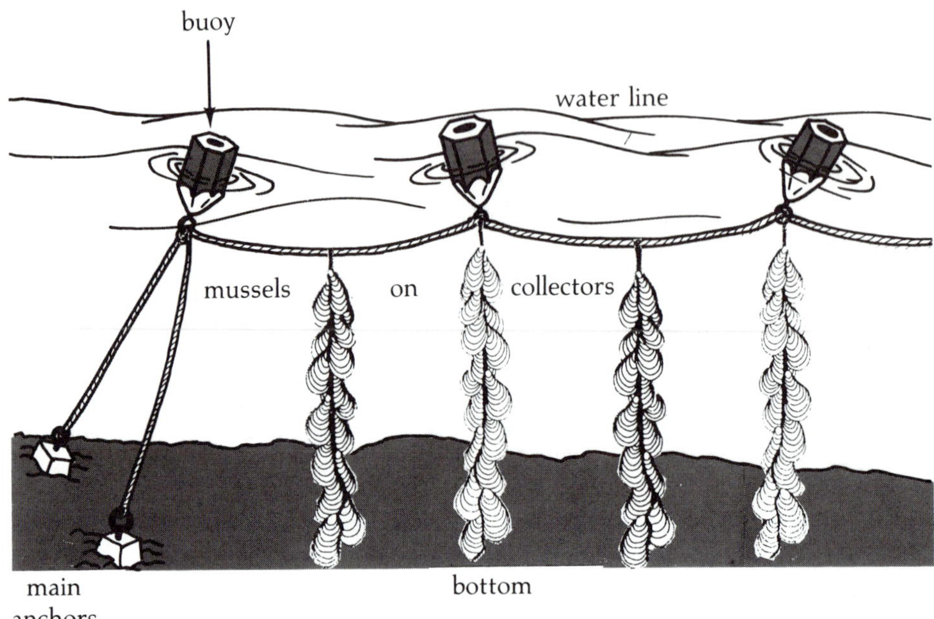

Figure 1. Detail of Long Line, taken from [4].

"... one-quarter of a million pounds of pure meat per year in only one acre..."

The long lines are lifted out of the water as needed so that the mussels can be tended and harvested by boat. In this suspended culture system the mussels reach maturity (50 mm or more in shell length) in about 12 to 18 months, depending on the supply of nutrients which they receive from the incoming tidal waters. In Spain this system of farming has produced as much as one-quarter of a million pounds of pure meat per year in only one acre of ocean water. This is impressive indeed when we compare it with western beef production, which yields less than 100 pounds per acre each year.

The blue mussel grows in abundance along the northern coasts of the United States and Canada. Perhaps commercial farming of this food source has never materialized in this country because there has never really been a need for it. Until recently, other shellfish and finfish have been plentiful and inexpensive, but the increasing demand for protein has led us to search for new sources. In the early 1970s experimental farms were constructed along the Atlantic coast of North America from Newfoundland to Rhode Island to determine the potential for commercial production of mussels using suspended culture systems similar to those which have been so successful in Spain.

2. The Problem

In other countries overproduction sometimes has led to a depletion in available nutrients causing losses to both the farmer and to the surrounding environment. In order to avoid similar problems in this country, scientists have examined the variables which affect the growth rates of the blue mussel, and related them to the physical and biological surroundings of the sea.

"The model we construct will be only as good as the data available to us."

We will examine the problem of determining the largest size a suspended culture farm can be without overtaxing the nutrients present in a given coastal area. A mathematical representation (called a mathematical model) will be constructed to help us. The model we construct will be only as good as the data available to us.

3. Gathering the Data

Information about the nutritional budget of a blue mussel is needed, as is information about the nutritional provisions and requirements of the sea water in a given area.

"Most of the data now available comes from laboratory research."

The diet of a blue mussel, the manner in which it feeds, the average rate of consumption, and minimum nutritional requirements for healthy growth need to be known. Most of the data now available comes from laboratory research. Even though these results may not coincide precisely with those in an estuary or ocean bay, they do provide us with the essential nutrient budget of a blue mussel.

A suitable location for a mussel farm also depends upon the quality of the tidal water. Measurements are needed to determine the velocity of the current, and the seasonal amount and balance of nutrients in the sea water.

4. Formulating the Model

Let's suppose that we want to determine the number of mussels that can be grown safely in a given bay in which all the essential data has been gathered. We will apply the model to a farm that uses the suspended culture system (Fig. 2). As mentioned earlier, this system is made up of rows or tiers of long lines across the surface of the water. The mussels are attached to ropes which are suspended vertically below each long line forming a vertical rectangular plane of mussels. The tiers are usually

"... mussels in the first tier receive the highest concentration of food particles available..."

oriented so that the tidal waters flow in a direction perpendicular to them. As the water flows in, the fortunate mussels in the first tier receive the highest concentration of food particles available in the water. As the water flows literally through the mussels, they filter out a portion of the food particles,which reduces the amount of food in the water as it passes into the next tier of mussels. You can see that the mussels in the last tier must survive on the remaining nutrients flowing into their area, and herein lies our problem. How many tiers can be constructed without reducing the nutrients to less than acceptable limits?

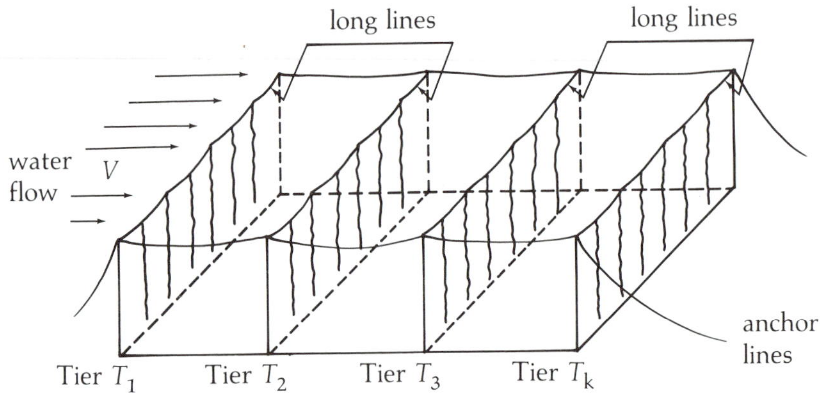

Figure 2. A typical box diagram showing the vertical tiers of mussels (T_1, T_2, ..., T_k) perpendicular to the flow of current (V). The vertical lines in each tier represent the suspended ropes on which the mussels are attached. The long lines are attached to floating rafts (not shown) along the outer edges of the box.

4.1 Assumptions

"... certain idealizations of the parameters involved must be made."

As with most models, certain idealizations of the parameters involved must be made. We will make use of the data provided by marine biologists and physical oceanographers who have measured filter rates and current speeds of tidal waters along our northern coasts.

(a) The concentration of food particles per liter is homogeneous as it enters each tier.

(b) The flow of water is perpendicular to the face of each tier.

(c) The average minimum hourly nutrition intake rate per blue mussel (measured in particles) is b_{min} = 200 mg/hr.

(d) Each mussel, on the average, can filter about 2.4 liters per hour of water.

(e) Each tier contains (approximately) the same number of mussels.

4.2 Terms

(a) A: (in square meters, m^2) the cross-sectional area of a tier perpendicular to the flow.

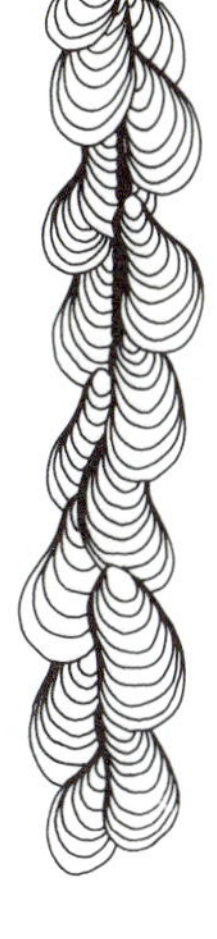

(b) V: (in meters per hour, m/hr) the flow rate of water mass entering perpendicular to a tier.

(c) N: (in liters per hour, ℓ/hr) the volume of water entering a tier per unit time. (Since 10^3 liters = 1 m^3, it follows that $N = V \cdot A \cdot 10^3$ ℓ/hr.)

(d) b_{min}: (in milligrams per hour, mg/hr) the minimum nutrient intake rate required per mussel.

(e) n_k: (in milligrams per liter, mg/ℓ) the concentration of particles per liter flowing into tier T_k, $k = 1, 2, 3, \ldots$.

(f) b_k: (in milligrams per hour, mg/hr) the available particle rate into the kth tier.

(g) M: the number of mussels suspended in each of the tiers. From the assumption that each mussel can filter 2.4 liters per hour, it follows that b_k = (filter rate) · (concentration) = $2.4\, n_k$ (mg/hr).

4.3 Analysis

In each tier, M mussels will filter $2.4\,M$ ℓ/hr as the water passes through. Since there are N ℓ/hr passing through each tier, then $(2.4M)/N$ is the fraction of particles filtered out of the water as it passes through each tier of mussels. Starting with the first tier, T_1, there are $n_1 \cdot N$ mg of particles flowing in per hour, so that

$$\frac{2.4M}{N} \cdot n_1 N = 2.4Mn_1 \text{ mg will be filtered out per hour.}$$

This leaves $n_1 N - 2.4Mn_1 = n_1(N - 2.4M)$ mg/hr which will then flow into the next tier, T_2.

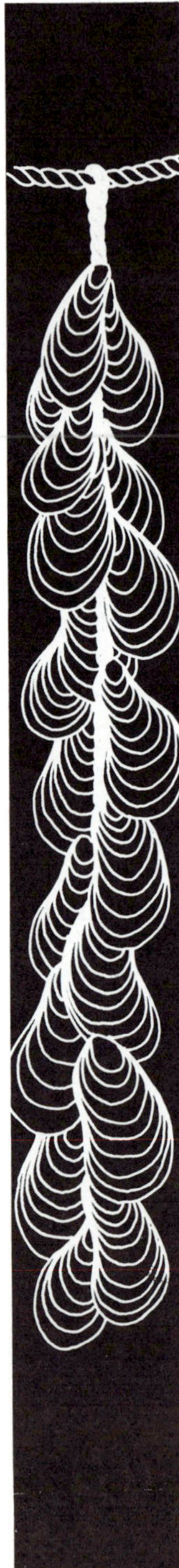

Thus,

$$n_2 = n_1 \left[\frac{N-2.4M}{N}\right] . \tag{4.1}$$

Likewise, following the same argument for the number of particles flowing into tier T_3, we get

$$n_3 = n_2 \left[\frac{N-2.4M}{N}\right] . \tag{4.2}$$

Substituting (4.1) into (4.2) for n_2 yields

$$n_3 = n_1 \left[\frac{N-2.4M}{N}\right]^2 . \tag{4.3}$$

Exercise

1. Use the results from equations (4.2) and (4.3) to determine a formula similar to (4.3) for n_4.

If we continue to use (4.2) and (4.3) for subsequent tiers, we see that the concentration of particles flowing into tier T_k will be

$$n_k = n_1 \left[\frac{N-2.4M}{N}\right]^{k-1}, k = 2, 3, 4, \ldots . \tag{4.4}$$

The quantities $n_1, n_2, n_3, \ldots, n_k$ form a geometric sequence of real numbers in which the first term is n_1 and the geometric ratio is

$$r = \left[\frac{N-2.4M}{N}\right] .$$

The terms in the sequence are a measure of the depletion of nutrients as the tidal waters flow through the individual tiers. The kth term in the sequence tells us how many mg/ℓ of food particles remain in the water that is flowing into the kth tier.

Exercise

2. The dimensions of the cross-sectional area of a culture system are 30m wide and 8m deep. The velocity of the tidal waters flowing into the system is 300 meters per hour. The concentration of particles flowing into tier T_1 is n_1 = 350 mg/ℓ. Each tier contains 200,000 mussels. Find (a) the geometric ratio r for this system, and (b) the number n_4 (mg/ℓ) of particles flowing into the fourth tier.

The terms in the geometric sequence of our model can now be used to determine the number of tiers that can be constructed to meet environmental and nutritional requirements. First, we must require that all mussels receive their minimum hourly requirement; i.e., that $b_k > b_{min}$ for all k. Second, the environment surrounding an aquaculture farm is dependent on nutrients brought in by tidal currents. To be sure the farm does not overly deplete the environment, let's require that concentrations of nutrients passing through a culture system are reduced by no more than one-half. The problem then is to determine the number of tiers k to use so that $b_k \geq b_{min}$ and also so that $n_{k+1} \geq (1/2)n_1$. (Note that n_{k+1} is the concentration of nutrients flowing *out* of tier T_k.) To accomplish this, we set $n_{k+1} = (1/2)n_1$ in equation (4.4) and solve for k.

"...our model can now be used to determine the number of tiers that can be constructed..."

$$n_1 r^k = \frac{1}{2}\, n_1, \text{ where } r = \left[\frac{N-2.4M}{N}\right] .$$

Cancel n_1 and take the logarithm of both sides to get

$$k \log r = -\log 2$$
$$k = -\log 2/\log r . \qquad (4.5)$$

"...current velocity required to support such a system can be determined from our model..."

To obtain the *integer* k which insures that $n_{k+1} \geq (1/2)n_1$, we must round the value of k down to the nearest integer so that $k \leq -\log 2/\log r$.

Exercise

3. Using the same data from Exercise 2 and your answer from part (a), determine the number of tiers, k to be used in this culture system. Be sure to check that $b_k \geq b_{min}$. (Recall: $b_k = 2.4n_k = 2.4n_1r^{k-1}$.)

4.4 Searching for an Appropriate Site

A suspended aquaculture system must be of a size large enough to be economically feasible. Consequently, preliminary measurements must be made along the coast in search for a site which will accommodate a culture operation of given size. If the size of the culture system and the average nutrient concentrations for coastal waters are known, then the current velocity required to support such a system can be determined from our model and an appropriate site can be sought. To do this, we use equation (4.4)

$$n_k = n_1 r^{k-1}, \text{ where again, } r = (N-2.4M)/N$$

and the constraint $n_{k+1} = (1/2)n_1$ to obtain

$$r = \left(\frac{1}{2}\right)^{1/k} = 2^{-1/k}. \tag{4.6a}$$

Next solve $r = (N-2.4M)/N$ for N, since M and (now) r are known, to obtain:

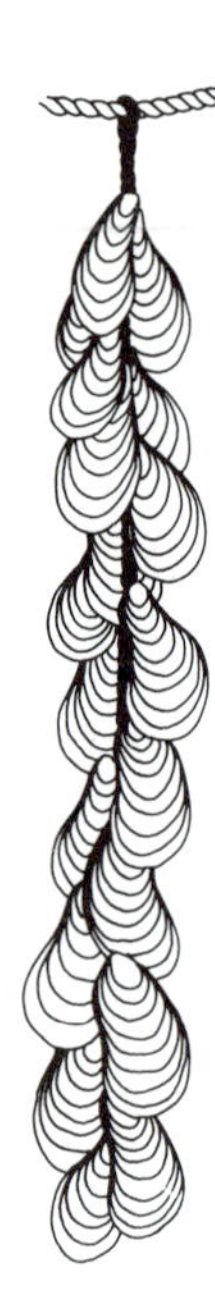

$$N = \frac{2.4M}{1-r} .$$

Finally, solve $N = V \cdot A \cdot 10^3$ (of Section 4.2c) for V, since A and now N are known, to obtain

$$V = \frac{N}{A \cdot 10^3} = \frac{2.4M}{A \cdot 10^3 (1-r)} = \frac{2.4M}{A \cdot 10^3 (1-2^{-1/k})} . \tag{4.6b}$$

Also, since r is now known, equation (4.4) can be used to determine b_k. That is,

$$n_k = n_1 r^{k-1} = n_1 (2^{-1/k})^{k-1} = n_1 \cdot 2^{(1-k)/k}$$

and

$$b_k = (2.4)n_k = (2.4)n_1 2^{(1-k)/k} . \tag{4.6c}$$

Once the size of a mussel farm has been decided upon, M, A, and k become known quantities. Then equations 4.6(a), (b), and (c) are used to compute r, v, and b_k respectively. The site selected would require a current speed V and the condition $b_k \geq b_{min}$ for all k must also be satisfied.

Exercise

4. The dimensions of the cross-sectional area of a culture system are 30m wide and 8m deep. A location is being sought for a farm which will contain 200,000 mussels in each tier, using 20 tiers. If the concentration of particles in the waters being considered is 350 mg/ℓ, what current speed would be appropriate for this size farm? Is $b_{20} \geq b_{min}$ satisfied?

5. Summary

"As we learn more... the model will no doubt become more refined..."

In order to determine the appropriate size for a suspended mussel culture system along our coasts, a mathematical model has been prepared. In order to use the model effectively, certain preliminary local data must be obtained first. The use of the model involves algebraic computations such as the basic laws of exponents and logarithms. The heart of the model is a geometric sequence which is used to provide the answers about the overall capacity of a particular culture system. In certain estuaries along the coast of Maine, it was felt that the experimental suspended culture systems could be enlarged without affecting the growth rates of the mussels. When the data from these regions were incorporated in the model, the model confirmed this conjecture. As we learn more about aquaculture and the needs of the blue mussel, the model will no doubt become refined and probably more complex. The following exercises include some possible modifications.

Exercises

5. In the derivation of equation (4.5), it was assumed that the concentration of nutrients passing through the culture system should not be reduced by more than one-half n_1. Generalize equation (4.5) by assuming that this reduction of nutrients should not be reduced to more than the fraction q of n_1.

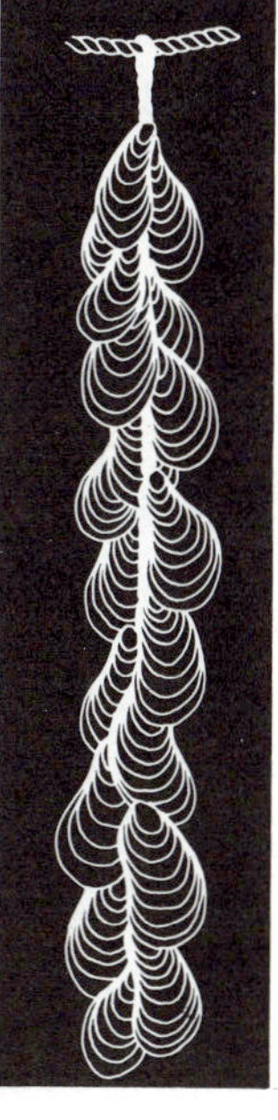

6. In the model, a filter rate of 2.4 ℓ/hr was used. To use another filter rate F ℓ/hr, replace 2.4 everywhere in the equations with F.

   In most systems, the first tiers are frequently filled with young seed mussels with a lower filter rate followed by tiers of larger mussels with larger filter rates. Describe how the equations could be used to determine the number of tiers in such a graded system. (Hint: Suppose the first p tiers are used for seed mussels with filter rate F_1 ℓ/hr. From equation (4.4) the concentration of particles moving into tier p+1 will be

$$n_{p+1} = n_1 \left[\frac{N-F_1M}{N}\right]^p.$$

   If the filter rate in the remaining tiers is F_2 ℓ/hr, regard these remaining tiers as a new system with initial concentration n_{p+1} replacing n_1.)

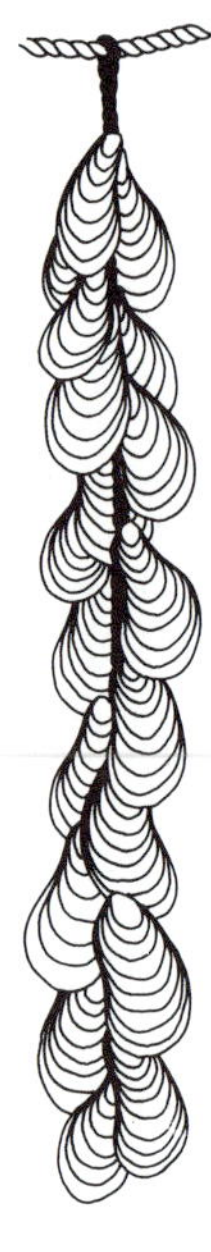

7. (Optional: requires elementary trigonometry and physics.) It may not be convenient to construct the tiers perpendicular to the tidal flow moving into an estuary. Suppose the current makes an angle θ with the tiers. How can the current speed V be adjusted to handle this situation?

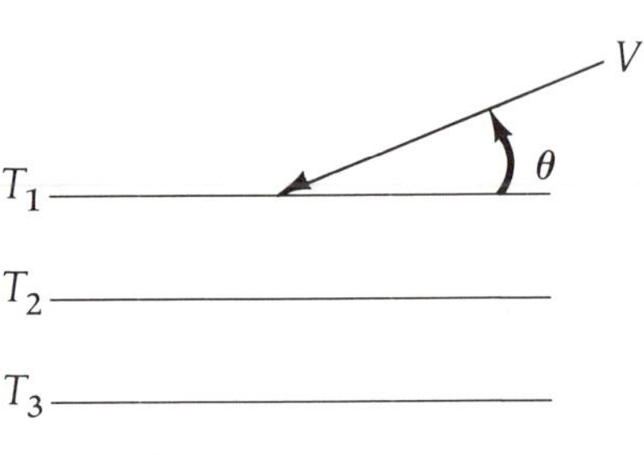

8. In the model for culture systems, the terms $n_1, n_2, \ldots n_k$ in the geometric sequence provide a measure of the depletion of original nutrients as water flows through the tiers. Compare this process with a problem in the depreciation of an automobile which cost $6000 new and depreciates each year by eight percent of its value from the preceding year. What will be the value of the automobile at the end of seven years?

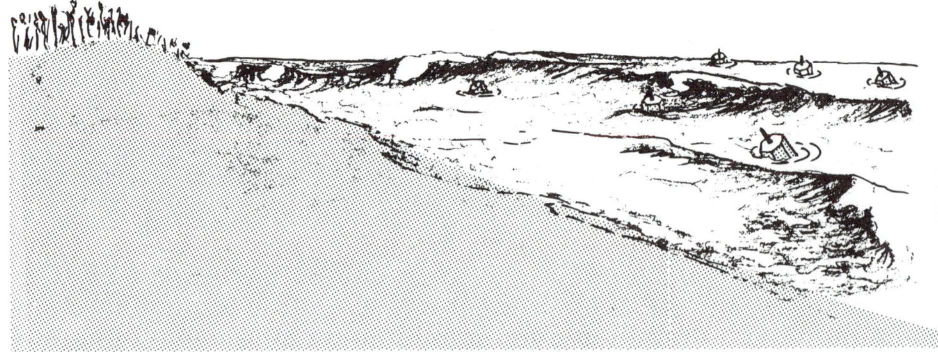

6. Answers to Exercises

1. Replace n_3 and n_2 with n_4 and n_3 respectively in equations (4.2) to get

$$n_4 = n_3 \left[\frac{N-2.4M}{N}\right] .$$

Next, substitute (4.3) for n_3 to obtain

$$n_4 = n_1 \left[\frac{N-2.4M}{N}\right]^3 .$$

2. (a) To compute N, the relationship in Section 4.2(c) yields

$$N = V \cdot A \cdot 10^3 = 300 \cdot (30 \cdot 8) \cdot 10^3 = 72 \times 10^6 \ \ell/\text{hr}.$$

Thus,

$$r = \frac{N-2.4M}{N} = \frac{72 \times 10^6 - 2.4(2 \times 10^5)}{72 \times 10^6} = \frac{149}{150} \simeq .993 .$$

(b) From equation (4.4),

$$n_4 = 350 \left[\frac{149}{150}\right]^3 = 343 \text{ mg}/\ell .$$

3. Using equation (4.5),

$$k = \frac{-\log 2}{\log \left[\frac{149}{150}\right]} = \frac{-.301030}{-.002905} = 103.6^+$$

which is rounded down to 103 tiers. Also,

$$b_{103} = 2.4n_{103} = (2.4)(350) \left[\frac{149}{150}\right]^{102} = 424.6 \text{ mg/hr}.$$

Thus, $b_{103} > b_{min} = 200$ mg/hr from 4.1(c).

4. Using (4.6*a*),

$$r = \left[\frac{1}{2}\right]^{1/20} = 2^{-1/20} .$$

From (4.6b),

$$V = \frac{2.4(2 \times 10^5)}{240(10^3)(1-2^{-1/20})} \simeq 58.7 \text{ m/hr}.$$

5. Set $n_{k+1} = qn_1$ in equation (4.4) and solve for k to get

$$k = \frac{\log(q)}{\log\left[\frac{N-2.4M}{N}\right]}$$

7. The component of the current direction which is perpendicular to the tiers could be used. From trigonometry, the current speed would be $V \sin \theta$.

8. Since the value depreciates by 8%, at the end of the first year the automobile will be worth 92% of $6000, or 6000 (.92). At the end of the second year, it will be worth $6000\,(.92)^2$ and at the end of the kth year it will be worth $6000\,(.92)^k$. When $k = 7$, the value of the automobile will be $6000\,(.92)^7 \simeq \$3{,}347$.

7. References

1. Incze, L. S.; Lutz, R. A.; True, E. D. 1981 *Modeling Carrying Capacities for Bivalve Mollusks in Open, Suspended-Culture Systems:* Proceedings: World Mariculture Society.

2. Muise, B.C. and Macleod, L. L. *Longline Culture of Blue Mussels on the Eastern Shore of Nova Scotia:* Tech. Report No. 8002. Halifax: Nova Scotia Department of Fisheries.

3. *Mussel Culture and Harvest: A North American Perspective;* edited by R. A. Lutz. 1980. New York: Elsevier Scientific Publishing Co.

4. Watt, B. K., and Merril, A. L. 1975. *Handbook of Nutritional Contents of Food,* prepared for U.S.D.A., Dover Publications.

UMAP

Modules in
Undergraduate
Mathematics
and Its
Applications

Published in
cooperation with
the Society
for Industrial
and Applied
Mathematics, the
Mathematical
Association of
America, the
National Council
of Teachers of
Mathematics,
the American
Mathematical
Association of Two-
Year Colleges, and
The Institute
of Management
Sciences.

COMAP

Module 614

Classifying Probability Distribution Functions

John D. Emerson

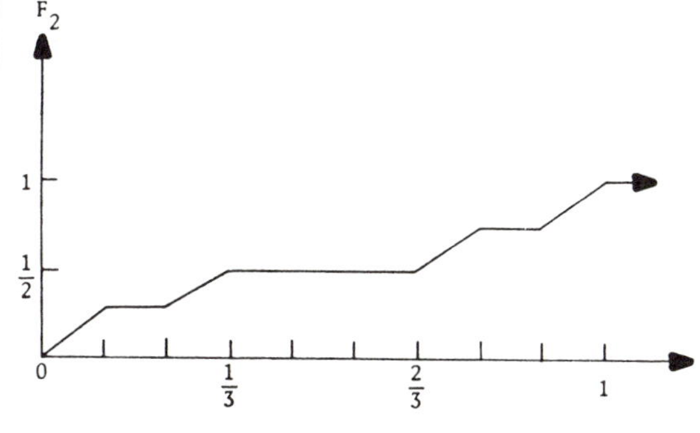

INTERMODULAR DESCRIPTION SHEET: UMAP Unit 614

TITLE: CLASSIFYING PROBABILITY DISTRIBUTION FUNCTIONS

AUTHOR: John D. Emerson
Department of Mathematics
Middlebury College
Middlebury, VT 05753

MATH FIELD: Probability and advanced calculus

TARGET AUDIENCE: Students who are taking a course in advanced calculus, and who have been introduced to some elementary probability theory.

ABSTRACT: At the introductory level, examples that students see of probability distribution functions are generally either discrete or absolutely continuous. In this module, the Cantor set is used to construct a distribution that is not discrete or absolutely continuous. An urn model illustrates a random variable which has the Cantor distribution. This distribution leads naturally to the concept of a singular continuous function. An arbitrary distribution function can always be decomposed uniquely into a convex linear combination of three distributions: discrete, absolutely continuous, and singular continuous. Necessary and sufficient conditions are provided for a distribution function to be absolutely continuous, rather than singular continuous. Some of these results can be generalized to functions other than probability distributions.

PREREQUISITES: Advanced calculus, including some topology of the real line, differentiability, Riemann integration, and sequences of functions. Elementary probability theory, including discrete and absolutely continuous distributions. No measure theory is assumed, although exposure to the concept "measure zero" is helpful.

Classifying Probability Distribution Functions

John D. Emerson
Department of Mathematics
Middlebury College
Middlebury, VT 05753

Table of Contents

Modules and Monographs in Undergraduate Mathematics and Its Applications Project (UMAP)

The goal of UMAP was to develop, through a community of users and developers, a system of instructional modules in undergraduate mathematics and its applications to be used to supplement existing courses and from which complete courses may eventually be built.

The Project was guided by a National Advisory Board of mathematicians, scientists, and educators. UMAP was funded by a grant from the National Science Foundation and is now supported by the Consortium for Mathematics and Its Applications, Inc. (COMAP), a nonprofit corporation engaged in research and development in mathematics education.

This module was developed under the auspices of the UMAP Statistics Panel, Thomas R. Knapp, Chair, University of Rochester. The Project would like to thank the members of the Statistics Panel and Alan H. Schoenfeld of Hamilton College for their reviews, and all others who assisted in the production of this unit.

This material was prepared with the partial support of National Science Foundation Grant No. SED80-07731. Recommendations expressed are those of the author and do not necessarily reflect the views of the NSF or the copyright holder.

Prologue

Some probability theory texts at the undergraduate level (e.g., DeGroot, 1975, p. 78) define a cumulative distribution function, and then specialize the definition to the discrete and absolutely continuous cases. It is natural to wonder what other types of distributions may exist. Is there a classification scheme for distribution functions?

These questions are typically answered in texts (e.g., Chung, 1974 and Billingsley, 1979) that presuppose a measure-theoretic background. But many users of probability and statistics, including some who do graduate study in these or related fields, do not study probability theory at this advanced level.

This module provides insights into the three basic types of probability distributions and the resulting classification of an arbitrary distribution function. It assembles in one place some concepts and results that are scattered in the literature. While undergraduate-level advanced calculus is used to identify various properties and characterizations of the distribution functions, measure theory and other graduate-level concepts are avoided.

After providing a brief review of cumulative distribution functions for the discrete and absolutely continuous cases, this module develops an example that does not belong to either case. The example, the Cantor distribution, offers motivation for a third general type of distribution function—the singular continuous distribution. The addition of this type of distribution provides the capability to classify an arbitrary distribution function in a unique way. The mathematical properties of absolutely continuous distributions are described, and further characterizations are provided. Some of the discussion of distribution functions is generalized to functions of bounded variation. A series of questions that arise naturally concludes the discussion and may stimulate further study of the issues raised.

The aim of this module is not mathematical rigor; references are provided for the proofs of most of the results presented. Rather, the emphasis is on the exposition and illustration of the various types of distribution functions. Theorems and other results needing measure-theoretic proofs are stated in a way which should make them accessible and meaningful to readers without a background in measure theory. Although Lebesgue measure and the Lebesgue integral necessarily underlie much of the material being described, this presentation neither provides nor assumes the related definitions and results.

This module can provide an enrichment unit for undergraduate students in an advanced calculus course who have also seen some probability theory. The material it addresses illustrates why several central concepts and theorems from advanced calculus are needed if one is to classify all cumulative distribution functions for real-valued random variables. Many students seem to find this kind of application of abstract concepts from analysis quite appealing.

1. Introduction

Probability distribution functions, as described and illustrated in undergraduate courses in probability, are usually either discrete or absolutely continuous. It is not hard to imagine situations in which certain random variables combine the two types. For example, the time from turning on a light bulb until the light burns out is continuous but would have a discrete component at time zero if a bulb could fail to light up in the first place. Are there other types of distributions that differ from discrete and continuous distributions in fundamental ways? If so, what are they? Is there an experiment, even a hypothetical experiment, in which they would arise? How can probability distributions be classified as discrete, absolutely continuous, some other type, or "mixtures" of the various types?

Although these questions may not have occurred to you, they are examples of the kinds of questions asked by mathematicians who study probability theory. Their answers, when provided in theoretical detail, involve sophisticated mathematical concepts that you have not yet studied. However, the answers can be described intuitively and even fairly precisely, using some important concepts from calculus courses usually taken by undergraduate mathematics majors. These answers make use of interesting applications of some of the more theoretical material studied in advanced calculus.

2. Distribution Functions

The cumulative distribution function provides a basic way of assigning probabilities to random variables and their related random events. Its mathematical characterization is readily abstracted from the familiar settings you have encountered in elementary probability theory.

Definition 1. A function $F: R \to [0, 1]$ is a *distribution function* if it satisfies:

(a) $\lim_{x\to-\infty} F(x) = 0$ and $\lim_{x\to\infty} F(x) = 1$;
(b) for all x_1 and x_2 in R, if $x_1 < x_2$ then $F(x_1) \le F(x_2)$;
(c) F is "right-continuous": $\lim_{x\to a+} F(x) = F(a)$.

Definition 2. A distribution function F is said to be

(a) *discrete* if F is a step function,

(b) *absolutely continuous* if there is an integrable function f for which the equality

$$F(x) = \int_{-\infty}^{x} f(t)\,dt$$

holds for all x.

By identifying $F(x)$ with $\Pr[X \leq x]$, we can always associate a distribution function F with a random variable X. Conversely, if F is a distribution function, there is a probability space S and associated random variable X such that F is the distribution function of X. While the demonstration of this result is easy in the discrete case, it is more subtle in general (Chung, 1974, pp. 24–29). We assume these results, and so the definitions above are given probabilistic interpretations. In Definition 2(a), if F has a jump at c, then $\Pr[X = c] = F(c) - F(c-)$ so that this probability is the size of the jump at c. In Definition 2(b),

$$\Pr[a < X \leq b] = \int_{a}^{b} f(t)\,dt$$

and f is typically continuous over the region where it is strictly positive.

After an introduction to these preliminaries, probability courses often study separately, though perhaps in parallel, the "discrete case" and the "continuous case." We can now ask a number of specific questions:

Are all distribution functions somehow related to those presented in Definition 2?

If not, what other types of distributions are there and how can an arbitrary distribution function be classified?

What are necessary and sufficient conditions for F to be absolutely continuous? Does it suffice that F have a derivative everywhere?

If F is continuous everywhere and differentiable except on a set whose probability is zero, and if the derivative F' is integrable, must F be absolutely continuous?

We provide answers to all of these questions below. Examples help to make some of these answers more tangible. The discussion and examples should add considerably to your understanding of the nature and true meaning of the phrase *absolutely continuous distributions*.

Exercise 1

A light bulb is defective and, with probability 1/4, fails to light when turned on. If the bulb does light, then the time until burnout is exponentially distributed with a mean time of two months.

(a) Give the cumulative distribution function for the random variable, T, the time that the bulb is lit. Sketch this function.
(b) Explain why this distribution is neither discrete nor absolutely continuous.

Exercise 2
Consider again the distribution function F you described above.
(a) Give F' where it exists.
(b) Explain why F' cannot be a density function.
(c) Can you think of a way to specify a density function for T that has a discrete component and a continuous component?
(d) What is the expected value of T? (*Hint:* You will need to think of a reasonable definition of expected value for a "mixed" distribution.)

Exercise 3
Let F be a discrete distribution function. Show how to define a probability space S and a random variable X so that F is the continuous cumulative distribution function of X.

3. The Cantor Function

Several of the questions we have posed may be answered with the aid of an example called the Cantor function. The example may shatter your notions as to what types of functions are distribution functions.

3.1 Constructing the Cantor Set

First, we review the construction of the Cantor set (Goldberg, 1976, pp. 22–23 and Rudin, 1976, pp. 41–42, 309). Let K_0 denote the interval $[0, 1]$. Remove the open middle third of K_0 to obtain $K_1 = [0, 1/3] \cup [2/3, 1]$. Remove the open middle thirds of these intervals, and let $K_2 = [0, 1/9] \cup [2/9, 3/9] \cup [6/9, 7/9] \cup [8/9, 1]$. By continuing to remove middle thirds of remaining intervals, we obtain K_n as a union of 2^n intervals, each of length $(1/3)^n$. Thus the "cumulative length" of K_n is $(2/3)^n$, and this length approaches 0 as n approaches infinity. The set

$$K = \bigcap_{n=1}^{\infty} K_n$$

is called the *Cantor set*.

Evidently K is contained in each member of a sequence of sets whose cumulative lengths approach zero. Any set with this property is said to have (Lebesgue) *measure zero. So the Cantor set K has cumulative length, or measure, zero.*

The Cantor set is nonempty; it contains all points, like 0, 1/9, and 1, which are endpoints of intervals making up K_n. Since K is the intersection of closed sets, it is closed. It also is bounded so K is compact. We can show that every point of K is a limit point of K, and thus that K contains no isolated points. For, let k be an arbitrary number in K, and let U be an open interval containing k. Let I_n be the closed interval of K_n which contains k. For n sufficiently large, I_n is a subset of U. Choose k_n to be an endpoint of I_n, with $k_n \neq k$. By the construction of K, k_n is in K and so every neighborhood of k contains a distinct point of K. Thus any point k is a limit point of K. Since K is also closed, it is (by definition) a perfect set. By a theorem of analysis (Rudin, 1976, p. 41), non-empty perfect sets are uncountable. *The Cantor set thus provides an example of an uncountable set of measure zero.*

Further insight into the Cantor set is obtained from the base-3 expansions of the real numbers in [0, 1]:

$$x = \sum_{j=1}^{\infty} \frac{a_j}{3^j} = 0 \cdot a_1 a_2 a_3 \ldots \text{ where } a_j = 0, 1, \text{ or } 2.$$

(To make the expansion unique, we can disallow representatives ending in an infinite string of 2s while allowing representatives ending in an infinite string of zeros.) The set K_1 consists of all x in [0, 1] having a base-3 expansion with $a_1 = 0$ or 2. Similarly, K_2 consists of all x in [0, 1] with $a_1 = 0$ or 2 and $a_2 = 0$ or 2. Generally, K_n consists of numbers in [0, 1] with each of the first n elements a zero or a two. Because the Cantor set is the intersection of the sets K_n, it is characterized as the set of all real numbers in [0, 1] having a base-3 expansion that uses only zeros and twos.

3.2 Defining the Cantor Function

We can now construct a distribution function that assigns all probability to the Cantor set (Rudin, 1974, p. 197 and Tucker, 1967, pp. 20–21). This distribution has no discrete component, i.e., it has no "lumps" of probability at any points. You may recall that if E is a set, then the indicator function of E, denoted $I(E)$, is one on E and zero elsewhere. We then define:

$$f_0 = I([0, 1])$$

$$f_1 = I([0, 1/3] \cup [2/3, 1])/(2/3)$$

$$\vdots \qquad \vdots$$

$$f_n = I(K_n)/(2/3)^n$$

$$\vdots \qquad \vdots$$

Clearly,

$$\int_0^1 f_n(t)\,dt = 1$$

for all n. Figure 1 illustrates the definition for $n = 2$.

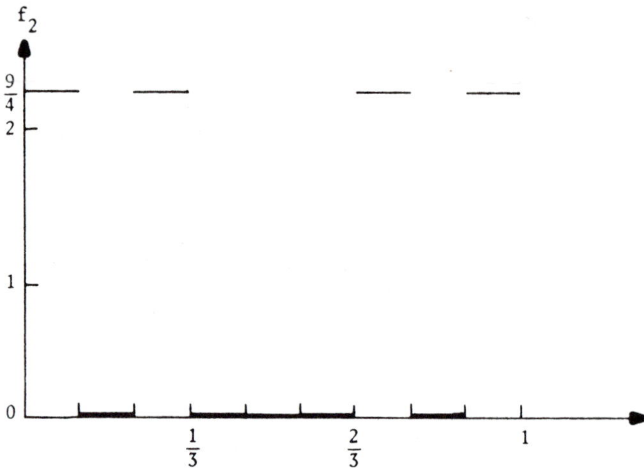

Figure 1. The density function f_2.

Let

$$F_n(x) = \int_{-\infty}^{x} f_n(t)\,dt.$$

Then F_n is an absolutely continuous distribution function. Furthermore, $F_n(0) = 0$, $F_n(1) = 1$, and F_n is constant on each segment of K_n^c the complement of K_n. We illustrate the function F_2 in Figure 2.

We next examine the sequence $\{F_n\}$ of absolutely continuous distribution functions. If I_n is one of the 2^n intervals whose union is K_n, then

$$\int_{I_n} f_n(t)\,dt = \int_{I_n} f_{n+1}(t)\,dt = (3/2)^n(1/3)^n = (1/2)^n.$$

Thus $F_{n+1}(x) = F_n(x)$ on K_n^c.

If $x \in K_n$, let $I_n = [c, d]$ be the subinterval of K_n that contains x. Thus

$$|F_n(b) - F_n(a)| \leq (1/2)^n,$$

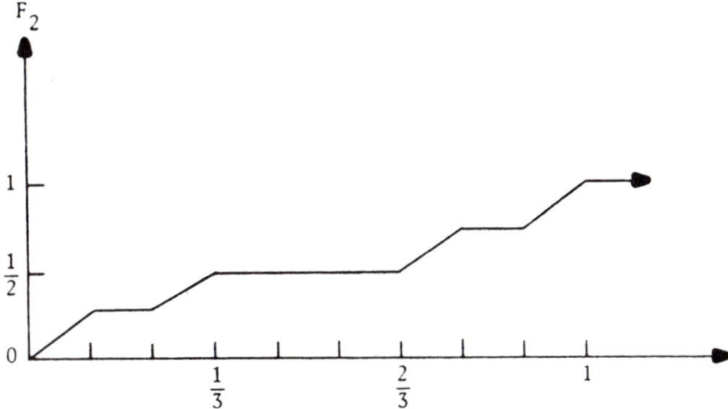

Figure 2. The density function F_2.

and so

$$|F_n(x) - F_{n+1}(x)| \le |F_n(b) - F_{n+1}(a)|$$
$$= |F_n(b) - F_n(a)|$$
$$= (1/2)^n.$$

This inequality guarantees that $\{F_n\}$ is a Cauchy sequence at each x and so converges uniformly to a function F_K which we call the *Cantor distribution.*

Note that F_K is nondecreasing, $F_K(0) = 0$, and $F_K(1) = 1$, because similar properties hold for each F_n. The continuity of each F_n and their uniform convergence to F_K make F_K a continuous function (Rudin, 1976, Theorem 7.12). Furthermore, for all x in K^c, the derivative function $F'_K(x)$ exists and is zero.

3.3 Properties

The Cantor distribution has several intriguing properties. To describe them, we introduce the phrase "almost everywhere." A property is said to hold *almost everywhere* if the set where it fails to hold has accumulated length zero, or (more generally) measure zero. For an absolutely continuous distribution, a property which holds almost everywhere fails only on a set whose probability is zero. This failure is insignificant from a practical probabilistic viewpoint. For example, it makes no practical difference whether a uniform distribution has its density defined to be one on the open interval (0, 1) or on the closed interval [0, 1].

Using this terminology, we have seen that the Cantor function is a continuous function that is differentiable almost everywhere. Its derivative is equal almost everywhere to a Riemann-integrable function: the zero function. Yet the Cantor distribution is not absolutely continuous because it is not the integral of its derivative. The fact that the equation

$$F(x) = \int_{-\infty}^{x} F'(t)\, dt$$

cannot hold for the Cantor distribution makes this distribution fundamentally different from the continuous distributions that you have previously encountered. Thus F_K provides surprising answers to some of the questions we posed in the previous section.

3.4 A Probability Interpretation

As remarked in Section 2, all distributions, including the Cantor distribution, have an associated sample space and random variable. Still, you may wonder whether the random variable associated with F_K has a physical interpretation. One such interpretation can be based on the preceding discussion of the base-3 expansion of numbers in $[0, 1]$ (de Finetti, 1974, p. 21).

Suppose that an urn contains the digits 0, 1, and 2. We can construct a number in $[0, 1]$ by successive random selection, with replacement, of the digits for the base-3 expansion. If the digit 1 is missing from the urn, only the numbers with digits 0 and 2 in the base-3 expansion can be constructed. For $x \in [0, 1]$, let $X(x) = 0 \cdot a_1 a_2 a_3 \ldots$ and observe that the probability for X is uniformly distributed over the Cantor set when the digit 1 is missing from the urn. Finally, F_K is the distribution function of the random variable X.

Exercise 4

A subset A of the real line is called *nowhere dense* if its closure has an empty interior. Show that the Cantor set is nowhere dense.

Exercise 5

Sketch the graphs of f_3 and F_3. List all points at which F_3 does not have a derivative.

Exercise 6

Suppose we had constructed a modified Cantor set by removing, successively, the "open left thirds" from $[0, 1]$.

(a) In what sense would this construction be less convenient than the one used? (*Hint:* Consider base-3 expansions of the remaining numbers.)

(b) In what sense is the "modified Cantor set" very similar to the set K we constructed?

4. Singular Continuous Distributions

The Cantor distribution illustrates a type of probability function that is neither discrete nor absolutely continuous.

Definition

Definition 3. A distribution function F is said to be *singular continuous* if it is a continuous function with derivative F' equal to zero almost everywhere. When F is singular continuous, we denote it F_{sc}.

We have seen that the Cantor distribution is singular continuous. It locates all probability on a set whose measure is 0, namely, the Cantor set.

4.2 A Remarkable Example

We now outline an example, described by Billingsley (1979, pp. 361–363), that is also singular continuous. It is similar to the Cantor distribution in several respects. It is perhaps more remarkable in that the cumulative distribution function is monotone *strictly* increasing on [0, 1], even though the derivative function exists almost everywhere and is 0 where it exists. Because the details of this example are quite complex, we only sketch it; we ask you to "believe it" or to work through the details with the help of the reference provided.

Example 1. Let $X_1, X_2, \ldots$ be independent identically distributed Bernoulli random variables with success probability p for $0 < p < 1/2$. Let

$$X = \sum_{n=1}^{\infty} \frac{X_n}{2^n},$$

and let F be defined by $F(x) = P[X \leq x]$ for all real x. Then F is uniformly continuous, monotone strictly increasing on [0, 1], differentiable except on a set of measure 0, and has an integrable derivative. Yet F is singular continuous and thus has no density function.

Exercise 7
Using a singular continuous distribution already described, construct an example of a cumulative distribution function that has a discrete component at $x = 0$ and a singular continuous component on [0, 1].

5. Absolutely Continuous Distributions

Armed with the knowledge that continuous distribution functions may be differentiable almost everywhere without being absolutely continuous, we return to examine the nature of absolutely continuous distributions.

5.1 A Preliminary Theorem

First, we state a result that applies to all monotonic functions. We will need this result when we prove the classification theorem for distribution functions.

Theorem 1. A monotonic function G is differentiable almost everywhere, its derivative G' is an integrable function and

$$\int_a^b G'(t)\,dt \leq G(b) - G(a)$$

for all real numbers a and b (Billingsley, 1979, p. 358).

In Theorem 1, both the differentiation and the integration are performed using a measure induced by ordinary length, the measure called Lebesgue measure. Therefore this differentiation and integration generalize those studied in calculus courses. Note that the theorem does apply to the Cantor distribution—a function that fails to be differentiable at uncountably many points.

5.2 Relating to the Fundamental Theorem of Calculus

Since F' is an integrable function, we might naturally suspect that its integral closely resembles the function F. For the Cantor distribution, however, the definite integral of F' is identically zero. But a generalization of the Fundamental Theorem of Calculus does hold for an absolutely continuous distribution; indeed, it characterizes such distributions.

Theorem 2. A distribution function F is absolutely continuous if and only if

$$F(x) = \int_{-\infty}^{x} F'(t)\,dt$$

(Rudin, 1974, Theorem 8.18).

Thus the function f of Definition 2(b) may as well be the derivative of F. As you might suspect, two functions that are equal almost everywhere will have the same integral provided they are integrable functions (Rudin, 1976, p. 317).

Corollary. If F is absolutely continuous with

$$F(x) = \int_{-\infty}^{x} f(t)\,dt$$

then $F'(x) = f(x)$ almost everywhere (Chung, 1974, p. 11).

The Cantor distribution is pathological in that it lacks a derivative at uncountably many points. The next result reveals a vastly improved situation when F is everywhere differentiable.

Theorem 3. If a distribution function F is everywhere differentiable, then

$$F(x) = \int_{-\infty}^{x} F'(t)\,dt,$$

and thus F is absolutely continuous (Rudin, 1974, Theorem 8.21).

This result readily generalizes to the case where F is continuous and F' exists except on a finite set: one simply performs the integration piecewise over intervals where the derivative exists. In light of this result and the example provided by the Cantor function, you might ask about a continuous function which lacks differentiability only on a *countable* set. A result which is apparently not well-known says that if F is continuous with an integrable derivative F' at all but a countable set of points, then F is absolutely continuous (Kestelman, 1960, p. 183). Thus the uncountability of the set where the Cantor function lacks a derivative is essential for the lack of absolute continuity exhibited by the function.

The next theorem, the Fundamental Theorem of Calculus, provides a setting in which the ordinary Riemann integral gives the probability.

Theorem 4. Let f be the continuous function for which

$$F(x) = \int_{-\infty}^{x} f(t)\,dt.$$

Then $F'(x) = f(x)$ everywhere (Rudin, 1976, Theorem 6.20).

5.3 An $\varepsilon - \delta$ Characterization

If your course in advanced calculus was typical, you have studied continuous functions and uniformly continuous functions. Both concepts have definitions which may be given in terms of ε's and δ's.

Absolute continuity is an even stronger condition than uniform continuity. To compare these definitions, we reformulate the concept of absolute continuity in terms of ε's and δ's.

Theorem 5. A distribution function F is absolutely continuous if and only if the following condition is satisfied:

For every $\varepsilon > 0$ and for every finite disjoint collection of intervals

$$\{(x_i, x_i') \text{ for } i = 1, \ldots, N\}$$

there is a $\delta > 0$ such that if

$$\sum_{i=1}^{N} (x_i' - x_i) < \delta$$

then

$$\sum_{i=1}^{N} |F(x_i') - F(x_i)| < \varepsilon$$

(Rudin, 1974, pp. 175–177).

The value of N is not fixed in the preceding statement. Setting $N = 1$ shows that absolute continuity implies uniform continuity, but the Cantor distribution provides an example of a uniformly continuous function that is not absolutely continuous. The statement of Theorem 5 may be taken as a definition of absolute continuity for functions from R to R that are not necessarily distribution functions.

Exercise 8

Let f be defined

$$f(x) = \begin{cases} 1/2 \text{ for } x \text{ in } [0, 2] \text{ and } x \neq i/10. \\ 0 \text{ for } x \text{ in } [0, 2] \text{ and } x = i/10. \end{cases}$$

(a) Show that f is a density function for the absolutely continuous case.

(b) If

$$F(x) = \int_{-\infty}^{x} f(t)\, dt,$$

use the definition to show that F is an absolutely continuous distribution function.

(c) Show that $f(x)$ does not equal $F'(x)$. Explain why this fact does not contradict Theorem 4 or the Corollary to Theorem 2.

Exercise 9

We have constructed a distribution function on [0, 1] that is uniformly continuous but not absolutely continuous. Is there a distribution function on [0, 1] that is continuous but not uniformly continuous?

Exercise 10
Is the sum of two absolutely continuous distribution functions also an absolutely continuous distribution?

Exercise 11
If F_1 and F_2 are absolutely continuous distributions and $0 \leq b \leq 1$, show that the function $F = bF_1 + (1-b)F_2$ is also an absolutely continuous distribution.

6. Some Real Analysis: Bounded Variation

The theorems of the preceding section are not results of probability; they are theorems of analysis. As such, they hold for a function G satisfying weaker conditions than those which define a distribution function. A necessary requirement, and one trivially satisfied by a distribution function, is that G not vary too much.

Definition 4. Let G be defined on R. Then G is of *bounded variation on R* if there is a positive number M not depending on N for which

$$\sum_{k=1}^{N} |G(x_k) - G(x_{k-1})| \leq M$$

whenever $-\infty < x_0 < x_1 < \ldots < x_N < \infty$. If G is a function defined on $[a, b]$ with a similar property holding whenever $a \leq x_0 < \ldots < x_N \leq b$, then G has *bounded variation on* $[a, b]$.

Although the concept of bounded variation is somewhat subtle, the following theorem provides an elementary characterization of this property.

Theorem 6. A function defined on $[a, b]$ is of bounded variation on $[a, b]$ if and only if it is the difference of two nondecreasing functions (Billingsley, 1979, p. 368).

If G has bounded variation on R, Theorem 1 holds. The other results of Section 5 assume implicitly that

$$\lim_{x \to -\infty} G(x) = 0.$$

If

$$\lim_{x \to -\infty} G(x) = G(-\infty)$$

exists, then these results hold with $G(x) - G(-\infty)$ replacing $G(x)$ in their statements, for any G which satisfies their conditions. Such a G

is automatically of bounded variation on any bounded interval. The connection between absolute continuity and bounded variation is made precise in the next theorem; it provides yet another characterization of absolutely continuous functions.

Theorem 7. A function G is absolutely continuous if and only if G is continuous, has bounded variation on all bounded intervals of R, and maps sets of measure zero to similar sets (Natanson, 1961, p. 250).

The Cantor distribution function satisfies two of the three conditions for absolute continuity—it is a continuous function and it has bounded variation on R (and so on bounded intervals of R). However, it lacks the third property because it maps a set of measure zero (the Cantor set) onto a set of measure one (the unit interval $[0, 1]$). Similar remarks hold for the singular continuous distribution described in Section 4.

Exercise 12
Use Definition 4 to show that if F is a cumulative distribution function, then F is of bounded variation on R. (*Hint:* the total variation of F on R is 1.)

Exercise 13
Show that a function of bounded variation is a bounded function.

7. The Classification Theorem

We now outline the proof of a theorem which says that discrete, absolutely continuous, and singular continuous distributions classify all distribution functions.

Theorem 8. A distribution function F may be decomposed uniquely as

$$F = c_1F_d + c_2F_{ac} + c_3F_{sc}$$

where

$$0 \leq c_i \leq 1, \sum_{i=1}^{3} c_i = 1,$$

and where F_d is discrete, F_{ac} is absolutely continuous, and F_{sc} is singular continuous (Chung, 1974, pp. 10–12).

Proof. We first obtain F_d. Let D be the set of discontinuities of F. Since F is monotone, D is a countable set. For each t in D, consider

$g(t) = F(t) - F(t-)$. Then define

$$G_d(x) = \sum_{\{t: t \le x, t \in D\}} g(t).$$

The function G_d is monotone increasing and is bounded above by one. The limit

$$\lim_{x \to \infty} G_d(x) = r,$$

r in $[0, 1]$, exists, and is zero only if D is empty, a trivial case. We define $F_d = r^{-1} G_d$ and let $c_1 = r$. Note that F_d is a monotone increasing step function and is right continuous with

$$\lim_{x \to -\infty} F_d(x) = 0$$

and

$$\lim_{x \to \infty} F_d(x) = 1.$$

Thus F_d is a discrete cumulative distribution function.

To obtain F_{ac}, consider $G = F - c_1 F_d$. Then G is right continuous because F and F_d are, and it is also left continuous. Therefore G is continuous. Because F and F_d are distribution functions, G is differentiable almost everywhere. Let

$$G_{ac}(x) = \int_{-\infty}^{x} (F - c_1 F_d)'(t)\, dt.$$

Then G_{ac} is continuous. If $x_1 < x_2$, then consider

$$G_{ac}(x_2) - G_{ac}(x_1) = \int_{-\infty}^{x_2} (F - c_1 F_d)'(t)\, dt - \int_{-\infty}^{x_1} (F - c_1 F_d)'(t)\, dt.$$

But

$$c_1 F_d(x_2) - c_1 F_d(x_1) = \sum_{\{x_j : x_1 < x_j \le x_2\}} F(x_j) - F(x_j -) \le F(x_2) - F(x_1).$$

Thus $G = F - c_1 F_d$ is monotone nondecreasing, so that $(F - c_1 F_d)'(t) \ge 0$ wherever the derivative exists. It follows that G_{ac} is monotone nondecreasing.

Let

$$s = \lim_{x \to \infty} G_{ac}(x) = \lim_{x \to \infty} \int_{-\infty}^{x} (F - c_1 F_d)'(t)\, dt.$$

Then

$$\int_{x_1}^{x_2} (F - c_1 F_d)'(t)\, dt \leq (F - c_1 F_d)(x_2) - (F - c_1 F_d)(x_1)$$

by Theorem 1. But

$$\lim_{x_1 \to -\infty} (F - c_1 F_d)(x_1) = 0$$

and

$$\lim_{x_2 \to \infty} (F - c_1 F_d)(x_2) = 1 - c_1$$

and thus $s \leq 1$. If $s = 0$, there is no absolutely continuous part of F; otherwise let $F_{ac} = (1/s)G_{ac}$. Finally, we let $c_2 = s$ and note that F_{ac} satisfies Definition 2(b) and is an absolutely continuous distribution.

To obtain F_{sc}, we let $G_{sc} = F - c_1 F_d - c_2 F_{ac}$. Because $F - c_1 F_d$ and $c_2 F_{ac}$ are continuous, G_{sc} is continuous. Since

$$c_2 F_{ac}(x) = \int_{-\infty}^{x} (F - c_1 F_d)'(t)\, dt,$$

we have that $(c_2 F_{ac})' = (F - c_1 F_d)'$ almost everywhere, by the corollary in Section 5. Then if $x_1 \leq x_2$,

$$\begin{aligned} G_{sc}(x_2) - G_{sc}(x_1) &= [(F - c_1 F_d)(x_2) \\ &\quad - \int_{-\infty}^{x_2} (F - c_1 F_d)'(t)\, dt] \\ &\quad - [(F - c_1 F_d)(x_1) \\ &\quad - \int_{-\infty}^{x_1} (F - c_1 F_d)'(t)\, dt] \\ &= (F - c_1 F_d)(x_2) - (F - c_1 F_d)(x_1) \\ &\quad - \int_{x_1}^{x_2} (F - c_1 F_d)'(t)\, dt \geq 0, \end{aligned}$$

by Theorem 1. Thus G_{sc} is monotone increasing.

Let

$$F_{sc} = \frac{1}{1 - c_1 - c_2} G_{sc}$$

provided $1 - c_1 - c_2 > 0$. Let $c_3 = 1 - c_1 - c_2$. Then

$$\begin{aligned} \lim_{x \to \infty} F_{sc}(x) &= \frac{1}{c_3} \lim_{x \to \infty} G_{sc} \\ &= \frac{1}{c_3} \lim_{x \to \infty} [F(x) - c_1 F_d(x) - c_2 F_{ac}(x)] \\ &= \frac{1}{c_3} [1 - c_1 - c_2] = 1. \end{aligned}$$

Also,

$$\lim_{x \to -\infty} F_{sc}(x) = 0$$

is clear, and F'_{sc} exists and is 0 almost everywhere because G'_{sc} has these properties. Therefore, F_{sc} is a singular continuous distribution function.

Altogether, the equality $F = c_1 F_d + c_2 F_{ac} + c_3 F_{sc}$ holds and the uniqueness of this decomposition can be seen from the steps of the proof.

Exercise 14

Consider again the distribution function you discussed in Exercises 1 and 2.

(a) Use Theorem 8 to decompose the distribution function.

(b) Discuss again Exercise 2(c) in light of your classification. (*Hint:* The components, F_d and F_{ac}, of your decomposition each have an associated density function.)

Exercise 15

Explain why Theorem 8 does not have an analog for density functions.

8. Discussion

In considering a few questions about probability distributions, we have raised far more questions than we have answered. How is length or measure generalized to sets of real numbers which are not unions of disjoint intervals? Which sets are measurable? Which sets have measure zero? How are the integrals of the discontinuous functions appearing in the various theorems defined? To what extent do the results stated generalize to the multivariate case? You can surely find many more questions that are implicitly posed in this manuscript. Answers to these questions are found in several of the references cited. We hope that some of you will be motivated to pursue the issues raised in this module.

9. References

1. Billingsley, P., *Probability and Measure*, John Wiley and Sons, Inc., New York, 1979.
2. Chung, K. L., *A Course in Probability Theory*, Harcourt, Brace, and World, Inc., New York, 1974.

3. DeGroot, M., *Probability and Statistics*. Addison-Wesley, Reading, Massachusetts, 1975.
4. de Finetti, B., *Theory of Probability*, Volume 1, John Wiley and Sons, New York, 1974.
5. Goldberg, R., *Methods of Real Analysis*, Second Edition, John Wiley and Sons, Inc., New York, 1976.
6. Kestelman, H., *Modern Theories of Integration*, Second Edition, Dover, New York, 1960.
7. Natanson, I. P., *Theory of Functions of a Real Variable* (Translated from Russian), Revised Edition, Ungar, New York, 1961.
8. Rudin, W., *Principles of Mathematical Analysis*, Third Edition, McGraw-Hill, Inc., New York, 1976.
9. Rudin, W., *Real and Complex Analysis*, Second Edition, McGraw-Hill, Inc., New York, 1974.
10. Tucker, H. G., *A Graduate Course in Probability*, Academic Press, Inc., New York, 1967.

10. Answers to the Exercises

1. (a)

$$F(t) = \begin{cases} 0 & t < 0 \\ \frac{1}{4} + \frac{3}{4}(1 - e^{-t/2}) & t \geq 0 \end{cases}$$

(b) F has a discrete component at $t = 0$ and a continuous component on $(0, \infty)$.

2. (a) $F'(t) = \begin{cases} 0 & t < 0 \\ \frac{3}{8}e^{-t/2} & t > 0 \end{cases}$

The derivative does not exist at $t = 0$.

(b) $F'(t)$ is not a density function because its integral over R is $3/4$, not 1.

(c) A "density" for T—loosely speaking—might have a discrete spike of probability $1/4$ at $t = 0$ and a continuous exponential component on $(0, \infty)$ whose total probability is $3/4$. Note, however, that ordinary integration of such a function does not always produce probabilities.

(d)
$$\begin{aligned} ET &= \tfrac{1}{4} \cdot 0 + \tfrac{3}{4} \cdot E(T|T > 0) \\ &= \tfrac{1}{4} \cdot 0 + \tfrac{3}{4} \cdot 2 = \tfrac{3}{2}. \end{aligned}$$

3. Given F, a discrete density function, f, is obtained by letting $f(x) = F(x) - F(x-)$. Thus $f(x)$ is the size of the jump in F at a discontinuity, x, of F. Let $S = \{x_1, x_2, x_3, \ldots\}$ be the set of all values where $f(x_1)$ is nonzero; because F is discrete, the set S is countable. Then if w is in S, define $X(w) = x_i$ if $w = x_i$. Then X is a random variable and $P(X = x_i) = f(x_i)$. Thus f is the discrete density function of X, and F is the associated cumulative distribution function of X.

4. The Cantor set is an intersection of closed sets and so is closed. From the construction it should be clear that K does not contain any interval. Thus, K has an empty interior.

5. The sketches are similar to those shown in Figures 1 and 2. The nonzero part of F_3 has value $(3/2)^3 = 27/8$. The values of x at which F_3 is not differentiable are: 0, 1/27, 2/27, 1/9, 2/9, 7/27, 8/27, 1/3, 2/3, 19/27, 20/27, 7/9, 8/9, 25/27, 26/27, 1.

6. (a) The limiting set would not correspond to numbers in $[0, 1]$ whose base-3 expansions contain only the digits 1 and 2. For example, while 0 would remain in the set, its base-3 expansion cannot be given without using the digit 0. Similarly, 1/3 is in the set but it has no base-3 expansion without using the digit 0.

(b) Call the modified set K'. Then there exists a one-to-one, onto function $f: K \to K'$. Thus K and K' have the same cardinality. In fact, K' is uncountable and has measure zero for the same reasons that K has these properties.

7. Let F_K denote the Cantor distribution and let F_0 be the discrete distribution function that places all probability at $x = 0$. Then the function $F = cF_0 + (1 - c)F_K$, for $0 < c < 1$, is an example of a distribution with discrete and singular continuous components.

8. (a) The total integral of f is

$$\int_{-\infty}^{\infty} f(x)\,dx = \sum_{k=1}^{20} \int_{(k-1)/10}^{k/10} 1\,dx$$

$$= 1/10 + 1/10 + \ldots + 1/10 = 1.$$

Since f is a non-negative real-valued function, it is a density for the absolutely continuous case. Note that $F(x) = x/2$ for $0 \le x \le 2$ and thus that $F'(x) = 1/2$, for $0 < x < 2$, is a density function that is probabilistically equivalent to f. In fact, F' and f are equal almost everywhere: they differ at exactly 19 points and these points have probability 0.

(b) $$F(x) = \int_{-\infty}^{x} f(t)\,dt = x/2 \quad \text{for } 0 \le x \le 2.$$

Furthermore, $F(x) = 0$ for $x < 0$ and $F(x) = 1$ for $x > 2$. It is now obvious that F satisfies Definitions 1 and 2b.

(c) We have seen in (a) above that f and F' differ at 19 points. Theorem 4 is not contradicted because f is not continuous. The corollary holds because f and F' are equal almost everywhere.

9. There is no distribution function on $[0, 1]$ that is continuous but not uniformly continuous. These two types of continuity are equivalent on compact sets, and $[0, 1]$ is compact.

10. Let F and G be absolutely continuous distribution functions. Then Theorem 2 holds for both F and G so

$$(F + G)(x) = \int_{-\infty}^{x} (F' + G')(t)\,dt.$$

Although this condition makes $F + G$ absolutely continuous, it clearly cannot be a distribution function because it approaches 2 as $x \to \infty$.

11. An argument similar to that given for Exercise 10 shows that for

$$F = bF_1 + (1 - b)F_2, \quad F(x) = \int_{-\infty}^{x} F'(t)\,dt.$$

It is easy to see that F satisfies the conditions of Definition 1 whenever F_1 and F_2 do.

12. Let $x_0, x_1, \ldots, x_N$ be given as in Definition 4. Since F is monotone nondecreasing,

$$\begin{aligned}\sum_{k=1}^{N} |F(x_k) - F(x_{k-1})| &= \sum_{k=1}^{N} [F(x_k) - F(x_{k-1})] \\ &= F(x_N) - F(x_0) \le 1.\end{aligned}$$

Thus take $M = 1$. Note that as $x_N \to +\infty$ and $x_0 \to -\infty$, $F(x_N) - F(x_0) \to 1$ so that $M = 1$ is the largest possible variation of F on R.

13. We show the result for f of bounded variation on $[a, b]$. If $a < x < b$, then

$$\begin{aligned}|f(x)| &= |f(x) - f(a) + f(a)| \\ &\le |(f(x) - f(a)| + |f(a)| \\ &\le M + |f(a)|.\end{aligned}$$

Thus f is bounded on $[a, b]$.

14. (a) Let $F_d(t) = \begin{cases} 1 & t \geq 0 \\ 0 & t < 0 \end{cases}$

and let

$$F_{ac}(t) = \begin{cases} 1 - e^{-t/2} & t > 0 \\ 0 & t \leq 0. \end{cases}$$

Then

$$F = \tfrac{1}{4}F_d + \tfrac{3}{4}F_{ac}.$$

Thus, in Theorem 8, we take $c_1 = 1/4$, $c_2 = 3/4$, and $c_3 = 0$.

(b) Both F_d and F_{ac} have associated density functions:

$$f_d(t) = \begin{cases} 1 & t = 0 \\ 0 & t \neq 0 \end{cases}$$

and

$$f_{ac}(t) = \begin{cases} (1/2)\, e^{-t/2} & t > 0 \\ 0 & t \leq 0. \end{cases}$$

It is probably unwise to form the function $(1/4)f_d + (3/4)f_{ac}$ because fundamentally different operations are needed to go from f_d to F_d and from f_{ac} to F_{ac}.

15. Theorem 8 has no analog for density functions because singular continuous distributions can have no densities.

UMAP

Modules in Undergraduate Mathematics and Its Applications

Module 626

Regression Methods and Problem Banks

David E. Booth

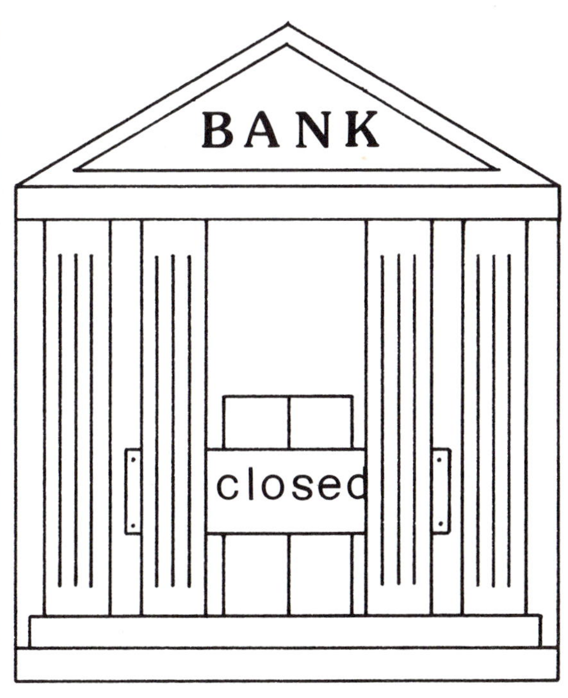

Published in cooperation with the Society for Industrial and Applied Mathematics, the Mathematical Association of America, the National Council of Teachers of Mathematics, the American Mathematical Association of Two-Year Colleges, and The Institute of Management Sciences.

COMAP

INTERMODULAR DESCRIPTION SHEET:	UNIT 626
TITLE:	REGRESSION METHODS AND PROBLEM BANKS
AUTHOR:	David E. Booth
MATH FIELD:	Statistics
APPLICATION FIELD:	Management Science
TARGET AUDIENCE:	Students of Statistics
ABSTRACT:	This module is designed to help the student understand regression analysis. A model (using real data) is developed to identify potential problem banks. In applying the model, the student is introduced to many techniques that are commonly required in practice. The application itself is also of importance.
PREREQUISITES:	Multiple regression, elementary calculus, derivatives (only required if the theory is considered in depth).

Regression Methods and Problem Banks

David E. Booth

Department of Administrative Sciences
Graduate School of Management
Kent State University
Kent, Ohio

Table of Contents

MODULES AND MONOGRAPHS IN UNDERGRADUATE MATHEMATICS AND ITS APPLICATIONS PROJECT (UMAP)

The goal of UMAP was to develop, through a community of users and developers, a system of instructional modules in undergraduate mathematics and its applications to be used to supplement existing courses and from which complete courses may eventually be built.

The Project was guided by a National Advisory Board of mathematicians, scientists, and educators. UMAP was funded by a grant from the National Science Foundation and is now supported by the Consortium for Mathematics and Its Applications, Inc. (COMAP), a nonprofit corporation engaged in research and development in mathematics education.

We would like to thank Professor Thomas R. Knapp for reviewing the manuscript and making many valuable suggestions. Thanks also are due Mitch Pollack, Anne Hower, and Joan Gutta, students at Bucknell University, who edited the manuscript and made excellent suggestions which have been incorporated.

This material was prepared with the partial support of National Science Foundation Grant No. SPE8304192. Recommendations expressed are those of the author and do not necessarily reflect the views of the NSF or the copyright holder.

The author would like to thank Dr. K. Berk, Dr. J. Dossey, Dr. J. Ingles, and the UMAP reviewers for reading the manuscript and making many valuable suggestions. The author would also like to thank Dr. R. Lenth for providing the original computer program. This work was supported in part by a grant from the Illinois State University Instructional Development Program.

1. Introduction

The eight largest bank failures in U.S. history have occurred since 1973. The largest, Franklin National Bank of New York, was at the time of its failure in 1974 the twentieth largest U.S. bank, with total deposits of $1,445 million dollars. The purpose of this unit is to discover how regression models can be used as a tool in identifying potential bank failures and further, to see if the use of these models has any advantage over the current periodic examination procedure.

A problem bank can be defined as a bank that has a large volume of high risk assets in comparison to its total capital and reserves. It can be thought of as a bank that is performing poorly when compared to other banks of a similar size and, in the extreme case, as a potential failure. Currently, these banks are being identified by use of the periodic examination process. Depending on the bank's charter, Federal Reserve Membership, etc., a bank is subject to one of three regulatory agencies, the U.S. Comptroller of the Currency, the Federal Reserve Board or the Federal Deposit Insurance Corporation. Each bank must submit to the appropriate regulatory agency, at four designated times each year, a full financial report consisting of Report of Income, Report of Condition, and other information that may be required for the particular bank. In addition, the regulatory agency periodically conducts a full examination of each bank. For details see Sinkey (1978) and Spong and Hoenig (1979). If the results of that examination indicate the bank is not doing well, it is then placed on the agency's problem list. At that point, further work is undertaken to prevent greater deterioration of the bank's position.

"... a bank that has a large volume of high risk assets in comparison to its total capital and reserves... can be thought of as a bank that is performing poorly when compared to other banks of a similiar size..."

It is clear that this procedure would be improved if a method were available to flag potential problem banks prior to the periodic examination, thus allowing two things to happen.

1. examiners could be allocated more efficiently, and

2. more time would be available to prevent a potential failure.

Our goal is to present a hypothesis that, if true, would lead to these results and to then examine a statistical procedure that is a consequence of it. It will be seen that the method is successful and in the process you will learn to apply several statistical methods that you have studied previously.

The hypothesis in the problem bank case can be stated in the following manner: If a bank is a problem, it must be doing poorly in comparison to similar banks. The necessary facts for identifying it as a problem should be visible in the bank's financial data. Hence, if we compare a problem bank with a group of non-problem banks, we expect to find that the problem bank exhibits characteristics different from non-problem ones. In statistics, one would say that the problem bank is an outlier. We will now digress to study the statistics of dealing with outliers. This is an important topic for a great number of other applications, in addition to identifying problem banks, as we will see. Once we have the procedures in hand we will return to the problem bank case and attempt to develop a model to deal with that situation.

"... we expect to find that the problem bank exhibits characteristics different from non-problem ones... one would say that the problem bank is an outlier."

2. Outlying Data Points

We wish to give a qualitative definition of the term "outlier" in order to begin to build an intuitive feeling for when a point is or is not an outlier. Following that, we will introduce examples of outliers.

DEFINITION 1: We say that a data point is an *outlier* if it is not likely to be representative of the rest of the data or if it causes problems in a standard statistical procedure.

It is important to realize that definition 1 is very qualitative. A point that is an outlier in one analysis may not be in another, that uses a different statistical procedure. We will illustrate this concept with some examples later.

"A point that is an outlier in one analysis may not be in another..."

We will now examine the related concept of robustness. As Huber (1981) says "for our purposes, robustness signifies insensitivity to small deviations from the assumptions". Since we are primarily concerned with outlying points in our applications, the assumption we will be concerned with is that of normality. We may write a linear statistical model in the form: $Y = X\beta + \epsilon$, where X is a fixed $n \times p$ matrix, Y is an $n \times 1$ vector of observed values, β is a $p \times 1$ vector of undetermined coefficients and ϵ is an $n \times 1$ vector of random variables, with mean $\underset{\sim}{0}$ and covariance matrix $\sigma^2 I_n$, where σ^2 is constant and I_n is the $n \times n$ identity matrix. In addition to the above, we usually add the assumption that the components of ϵ, ϵ_i, are normally distributed.* Under this additional

*References 22-24 give details.

assumption of normality, the usual *OLS* (ordinary least squares) estimator has a number of desirable properties. Unfortunately (from the point of view of statistical inference, but fortunately for our application), the presence of outliers indicates a distribution of ϵ_i that is likely to have "bigger tails" than the normal. We will see examples as we proceed.

DEFINITION 2: Let $\hat{\theta}$ be an unbiased estimator of θ, some population parameter. We say $\hat{\theta}$ is *robust* if a large change in one sample point produces only a small change in $\hat{\theta}$.

We now illustrate definitions 1 and 2 with the following example.

EXAMPLE. Consider the sample consisting of the numbers 1, 2, 3. Let $\bar{X}$ be the sample mean and $\tilde{X}$ be the sample median. Clearly $\bar{X} = \tilde{X} = 2$. Now suppose the sample comes from measurements made by a particular instrument, and that (unknown to us) just before the third measurement was made, the instrument broke, causing the third point to be erroneous. Further, suppose that this results in the sample: 1, 2, 33. Clearly $\bar{X} = 12$, but $\tilde{X} = 2$. Since this is a general property of $\tilde{X}$, we say that $\tilde{X}$ is robust and that 33 is an outlier. Notice the change in the histograms in Fig. 1.

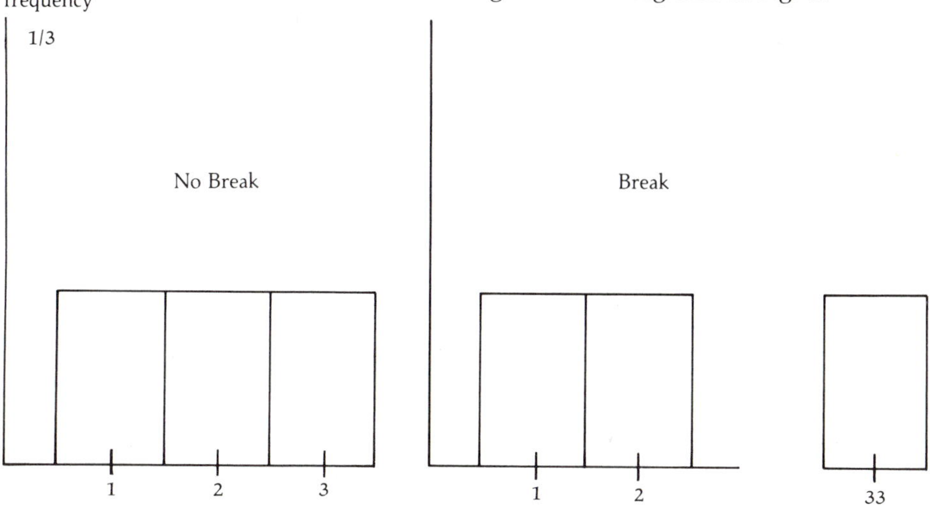

Figure 1. Measurement Histograms

Also, notice that the difficulty arises if we do not know that the instrument was defective at the time of the last measurement. If we did know we would, of course, simply ignore the 33. We usually believe that $\bar{X}$ is a better estimator of μ, the population mean, than is $\tilde{X}$, though it is clear that this is not the case here.

What we desire is a procedure that would: 1) indicate that such a happening may have occurred by indicating the 33 is "different" from the other points in the data, and 2) allow us to make a good estimate of μ, the population mean, even if the "different" point or outlier is included in the data. We will now develop such a procedure, called the *Method of M-estimators.*

PROBLEM. Consider the samples consisting of:

a) 1, 5, 7, 9, 58 and
b) 90, 91, 97, 16, 98

1. Find the mean and median for both samples.

2. For each sample, which values would you consider to be outliers? Why?

3. Compare and contrast the sample means and medians as estimators of the respective population means.

3. M-estimators, the univariate case.

The *M*-estimator procedure is based on a generalization of least squares estimation. Essentially, we wish to treat the sample points that are not outliers, as we usually do in calculating $\bar{X}$. The outliers, we wish to treat as we do in calculating $\tilde{X}$, based on the previous example. Suppose we wish to estimate μ, the mean of a population, using ordinary least squares, (*OLS*). The appropriate linear model is:

$$y = \beta o + \epsilon = \mu + \epsilon$$

where y is the vector of observed values. The corresponding prediction equation is $\hat{y} = \hat{\mu}$. Proceeding as usual, we wish to minimize *SSE*, where

$$SSE = \Sigma(y_i - \hat{y}_i)^2 = \Sigma(y_i - \hat{\mu})^2 \tag{1}$$

By the usual calculus procedure:

$$\frac{\partial SSE}{\partial \hat{\mu}} = \Sigma[-2(y_i - \hat{\mu})] = 0, \tag{2}$$

which implies

$$\Sigma(y_i - \hat{\mu}) = 0 \text{ or } \Sigma y_i = n\hat{\mu}$$
$$\text{or} \quad \hat{\mu} = \frac{\Sigma y_i}{n} = \bar{y} \tag{3}$$

Now we must perform our modification. Since we want to revise the calculational algorithm to treat outliers in the same manner as the median, and the rest of the data as ordinary least squares does, we must modify *SSE*. We adopt the following notation (and illustrate it with the *OLS* case, first):

$$SS\rho = \Sigma(y_i - \hat{\mu})^2 = \Sigma 2\rho\,(y_i - \hat{\mu}), \tag{4}$$

where

$\rho(X) = \frac{X^2}{2}$, (the 2 in the denominator is added for convenience)

The graph of $\rho(X)$ is shown in Fig. 2.

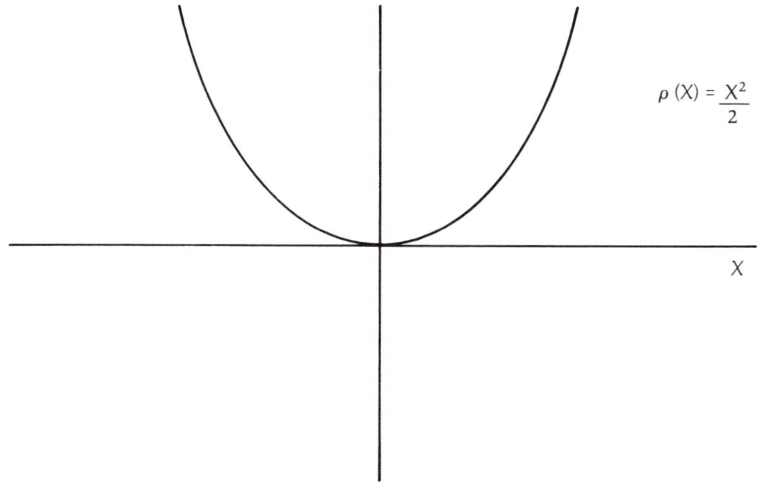

Figure 2. ρ for ordinary least squares

Now let $\psi(X) = \frac{d\rho(X)}{dX}$. Hence in (4), $\psi(X) = X$, and its graph is given in Fig. 3.

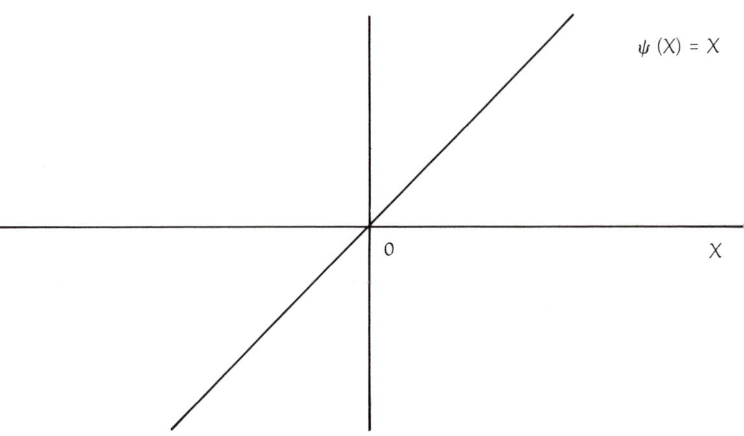

Figure 3. $\psi(X)$ for ordinary least squares

Now consider the median. The median, $\tilde{Y}$, is not a least squares estimator of μ, but is a least absolute deviation estimate. (Randles and Wolfe, 1979, p. 234). Consider the following: Suppose we wish to minimize $E = \sum_i |y_i - \hat{\mu}| = \sum_i \rho\,(y_i - \hat{\mu})$.

The graph of $|kX|$ is given in Fig. 4.

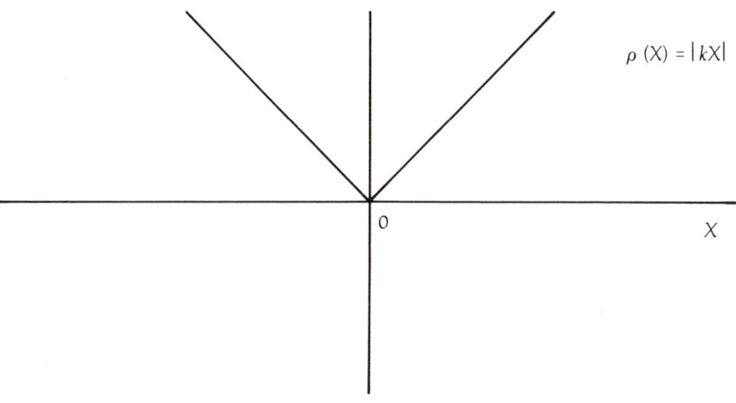

Figure 4. The graph of $|kX|$

Hence for $X > 0$, $\frac{d\rho}{dX} = |k| > 0$, for $X < 0$, $\frac{d\rho}{dX} = -|k| < 0$. For $X = 0$, $\frac{d\rho}{dX}$ does not exist. Notice that E is of this form. Now return to the minimization of E. We wish to compute $\frac{\partial E}{\partial \hat{\mu}}$.

$$\frac{\partial E}{\partial \hat{\mu}} = \frac{\partial}{\partial \hat{\mu}} \left(\Sigma_i | y_i - \hat{\mu} | \right)$$

$$\text{for } y_i - \hat{\mu} < 0 \quad \frac{\partial E}{\partial \hat{\mu}} = -1$$

$$(\text{or } y_i < \hat{\mu}), \quad \frac{\partial E}{\partial \hat{\mu}} = -1$$

$$\text{for } y_i > \hat{\mu}, \quad \frac{\partial E}{\partial \hat{\mu}} = +1 \tag{5}$$

and hence we have for the case of $\tilde{Y}$, $\psi(X)$ as shown in Fig. 5.

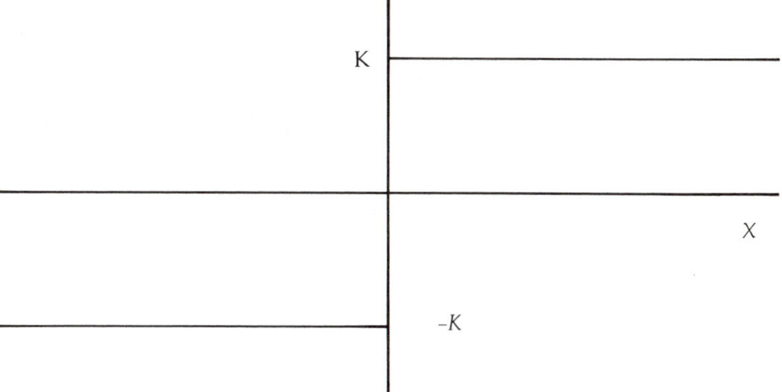

Figure 5. $\psi(X)$ Corresponding to the Sample Median

Notice that this is exactly what one would expect since by definition, $\tilde{Y}$, divides the sample into an upper group and a lower group.

If we combine the two functions, we obtain the function of Fig. 6, called Huber's ψ function. The most important thing to notice about this function is that it treats outliers differently, from other points in the sample. We indicate where to stop one treatment and start the other by choosing a value for *k*. We will consider this in detail later.

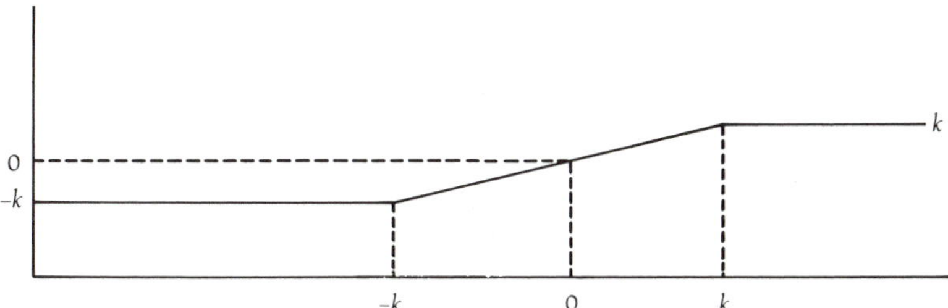

Figure 6. Huber ψ function

The equation of the Huber ψ function is given by:

$$\psi(X) = \begin{cases} -k, & X < -k \\ X, & -k \leq X \leq k \\ k, & X > k \end{cases}$$

Use of this function implies that

$$\sum_{i=1}^{n} \psi(y_i - \hat{\mu}) = 0, \text{ (the robust analogue to (2))} \tag{6}$$

must be solved by iterative methods. Before continuing with the solution, we vill need to consider the following example, taken from Hogg (1979a). Suppose that we obtain a solution, $\hat{\mu}$ from (6) for a particular sample. Suppose then, that a new $\hat{\mu}$ was computed, in which some of the elements of the sample were replaced by some in which the deviations were tripled. The new $\hat{\mu}$ would not necessarily be the same as the old. In other words, the estimator may not be scale invariant. To make the solution scale invariant, we divide $y_i - \hat{\mu}$ by a robust "standard deviation," d. Then we have:

$$\sum_{i=1}^{n} \psi\left(\frac{y_i - \hat{\mu}}{d}\right) = 0 \tag{7}$$

Notice that $\frac{y_i - \hat{\mu}}{d}$, is of the same form as the usual, $Z = \frac{X - \mu}{\sigma}$.

Our "standard deviation", d, is given by:

$$d = \frac{\text{median} \mid y_i - \text{median}\ (y_i) \mid}{0.6745} \tag{8}$$

The constant 0.6745 is included so that d is a consistent estimator of σ, if the underlying distribution is normal (i.e. $\lim_{n \to \infty} d = \sigma$). $0.6745 = F^{-1}(1/2)$, where F is the cumulative normal distribution function. See references 17 and 25.

PROBLEM. For the sample consisting of 1, 2, 3, 20 compute d and the sample standard deviation. Compare and contrast the two. Further, notice how the function $\psi(X)$ treats data points. Since $\frac{y_i - \hat{\mu}}{d}$ is a distance measure, if y_i is an outlier, a large distance results. Applying the definition of $\psi(X)$, it is clear that ψ assigns either k or $-k$ to outliers and $\frac{y_i - \hat{\mu}}{d}$ to all other points in the sample. A sample point is treated as an outlier if $\left|\frac{y_i - \hat{\mu}}{d}\right| > k$. This is an important fact to remember because we will use it several times later in the unit. We must now make a choice for k. Clearly we want most elements of the data set to satisfy $\left|\frac{y_i - \hat{\mu}}{d}\right| < k$. (i.e., most data points are not outliers).

Suppose the underlying distribution is normal. After standardization, we wish Prob $(-k \leq Z \leq k) \simeq 1$, i.e., most data points are not outliers. Suppose we choose $k = 1.5$. The Prob $(-1.5 \leq Z \leq 1.5) = 2(.4332) = .8664$. Prior to standardization, this corresponds to Prob $(\mu - 1.5\sigma \leq X \leq \mu + 1.5\sigma) = .8664$. Similarly, Prob $(\mu - 2\sigma \leq X \leq \mu + 2\sigma) = 2(.4772) = .9544$. Both of these say that there are only a few outliers in the data. Now consider the distance from $-k$ to k. In the first case, to choose k we note that $2k \simeq 3$ hence $k \simeq 1.5$. In the second case $2k \simeq 4$, hence $k \simeq 2$. This indicates that the choice of k is somewhat arbitrary. Choices in this range (about 1.5) are common. We will usually take $k = 1.5$ as our criterion for whether or not a point is to be treated as an outlier. We must now find a way to solve (7) under these conditions.

"...to obtain the parameter estimate... use a method known as iterative reweighting."

In order to do the necessary computation to obtain the parameter estimate we will use a method known as iterative reweighting. By this we mean that we will compute an initial set of weights that will lessen the effect of the outlying points, based on an initial solution of (7). We will then continue making repetitions that generate modified solutions and weights, until the solution converges.

Consider:

$$\sum_{i=1}^{n} \psi\left(\frac{y_i - \hat{\mu}}{d}\right) = 0 \tag{9}$$

where $\hat{\mu}$ is an initial estimate of μ, and $d \neq 0$. For $y_i \neq \hat{\mu}$, we may write:

$$\sum_{i=1}^{n} \frac{\psi\left(\frac{y_i - \hat{\mu}}{d}\right)}{\left(\frac{y_i - \hat{\mu}}{d}\right)} \left(\frac{y_i - \hat{\mu}}{d}\right) = 0 \tag{10}$$

Multiplying both sides by d gives:

$$\sum_{i=1}^{n} \frac{\psi\left(\frac{y_i - \hat{\mu}}{d}\right)}{\left(\frac{y_i - \hat{\mu}}{d}\right)} (y_i - \hat{\mu}) = 0 \tag{11}$$

If we define a set of weight functions by:

$$W_i = \frac{\psi\left(\frac{y_i - \hat{\mu}}{d}\right)}{\left(\frac{y_i - \hat{\mu}}{d}\right)}, \; y_i \neq \hat{\mu}, \, d \neq 0 \tag{12}$$

Then we may write (11) as:

$$\sum_{i=1}^{n} W_i (y_i - \hat{\mu}) = 0 \tag{13}$$

(Compare equations (13) and (3))

Now since (13) corresponds to the usual least squares estimate of μ, except that the points are weighted, we know that the solution to (13) is given by the weighted mean:

$$\hat{\mu} = \frac{\Sigma W_i y_i}{\Sigma W_i} \tag{14}$$

We will now consider an example calculation.

EXAMPLE. Suppose we have obtained the following data set: 1, 2, 3, 33, where the 33 arose from instrument failure. We wish to estimate μ, without discarding the outlier. We first note that $\tilde{y} = 2.5$, $\bar{y} = 9.75$ and $\bar{y} = 2$ with the 33 deleted, where $\tilde{y}$ is the sample median and $\bar{y}$ is the sample mean. We will apply the weighted algorithm, using $\tilde{y}$ as an initial estimate of $\hat{\mu}$. Therefore, $\hat{\mu}_o = 2.5$. We next compute d.

y_i	$y_i - \tilde{y}$	$\lvert y_i - \tilde{y} \rvert$
1	-1.5	1.5
2	-0.5	0.5
3	0.5	0.5
33	30.5	30.5

10

$d = \dfrac{1.0}{.6745} = 1.48$, which we will hold fixed *only as a convenience.*

Now by definition:

$$W = \frac{\psi(Z)}{Z} = \begin{cases} 1 & |Z| \leq 1.5 \\ \dfrac{1.5}{|Z|} & 1.5 < |Z| \end{cases}$$

Therefore:

iteration 1

y	$Z = \dfrac{y_i - \hat{\mu}_o}{d}$	W
1	−1.014	1
2	− .338	1
3	.338	1
33	20.61	.0728

$$\hat{\mu}_1 = \frac{\Sigma W_i\, y_i}{\Sigma W_i} = \frac{1 + 2 + 3 + (.0728)\,(33)}{3.0728} = 2.734$$

iteration 2

y	$Z = \dfrac{y_i - \hat{\mu}_1}{d}$	W
1	1.172	1
2	.496	1
3	.180	1
33	20.45	.0733

$$\hat{\mu}_2 = \frac{\Sigma W_i\, y_i}{\Sigma W_i} = \frac{1 + 2 + 3 + (.0733)\,(33)}{3.0733} = 2.739$$

We can continue the process as long as we like. Notice two things about this example. First, the solution has converged to two decimal places in only two iterations (convergence is usually somewhat slower). Second, notice the weight assigned to the outlier. Our goal is to weight the outlier less in our estimate of μ since it is less likely to be representative. Therefore our weight function gives it less effect. This is clear if we recall the previous discussion of $\psi(Z)$, for $|Z| = \left|\frac{y_i - \hat{\mu}}{d}\right| > k$. Also notice that if we did not already know that 33 was an outlier we would now know by examining the weights. Recall that $W = \frac{1.5}{|Z|}$ for an outlier. By its definition an outlier must have a large $|Z|$ ($>k$) and hence W is small for an outlier. In other words, the further away from the rest of the data a point is, the lower the weight assigned to it. Thus, we have a method that we can use to identify outliers. To become familiar with this procedure, you should solve the following:

PROBLEMS. Given the samples **a)** 2, 4, 6, 68 and **b)** –50, –5, –4, 1, 2, estimate μ using the weighted M-estimator procedure. Continue the process for two iterations.

ANSWERS.

a) $d = 2.965$, $\hat{\mu}_2 = 5.48$

b) $d = 7.413$, $\hat{\mu}_2 = -4.29$

4. *M*-estimators, the general linear regression model

We must now extend these results to the regression case. We consider the constructed bivariate example,

X	Y
1	5
2	7
3	8
4	9
5	22
6	11

under the usual *OLS* assumptions, using the model $Y = \beta_0 + \beta_1 X + \epsilon$

PROBLEM. Graph Y versus X, compute the *OLS* regression coefficients and plot the residuals against $\hat{Y}$, using an *OLS* program.

The results clearly indicate that the fit is not good (R^2 = .45, large prob values). Notice that the point (5,22) lies away from the others on both plots.

PROBLEM. Delete (5,22) and repeat the last problem. Notice the change in the plots and in the statistics (R^2 = .979 prob values small). Removing the clearly outlying point improved the fit a great deal.

Now draw both prediction equations (with and without the outlier) on the graph of Y versus X for all six points. Do you notice the effect of the outlier? It pulls the line toward it and makes the fit erroneous, giving rise to misleading results, as in the univariate case, assuming, of course, that the outlier really shouldn't be there.

Clearly, we must do something about points such as these. One idea that has been advanced is to simply discard them. There are two problems with the suggestion:

"Both the plot of the data and the residuals indicated the point was an outlier, but these plots are not always clear..."

(1) An extreme point may be giving us useful information of one sort or another and hence should not be discarded.

(2) How can we be sure a particular point is an outlier and not just one of the approximately five per cent that we expect to find more than two standard deviations from the mean under the normal assumption?

Both the plot of the data and the residuals indicated the point was an outlier, but these plots are not always clear, especially when a number of predictor variables are in the model. We will now proceed in a similar manner to our previous univariate M-estimator method and attempt to develop a procedure that will deal with these problems.

In the regression case, we wish to minimize $SS\rho$, where $SS\rho$ =

$$\sum_{i=1}^{n} \rho\,(Y_i - \sum_{j=1}^{P} (\hat{\beta}_j X_{ij})) \qquad (15)$$

If $\rho(X)\ \alpha X^2$, then we have OLS regression, and $SS\rho = SSE$. If we wish an M-estimate, then we proceed in the same manner as in section III. We again want our estimate to be scale invariant and hence we modify (15) as we did (6), giving

$$SS\rho = \sum_{i=1}^{n} \rho \left(\frac{(Y_i - \sum_{j=1}^{P} (\hat{\beta}_j X_{ij}))}{d} \right), \text{ where}$$

d will be our robust "standard deviation." We now proceed as in the derivation of the *OLS* normal equations, as we did in the univariate case. Doing the minimization by differentiating with respect to $\hat{\beta}_j$

$$- \frac{\partial SS\rho}{\partial \hat{\beta}_j} = \sum_i \psi \left(\frac{Y_i - \Sigma(\hat{\beta}_j X_{ij})}{d} \right) \frac{X_{ij}}{d} = 0 \qquad (16)$$

where:

$$\psi(t) = \frac{d\rho}{dt}$$

or:

$$\sum_i \psi \left(\frac{\Delta_i}{d} \right) X_{ij} = 0 \qquad j = 1, 2, \ldots, P \qquad (17)$$

where Δ_i is the numerator in (16).

If we choose to use iterative weighting as in the univariate case, we may rewrite this as:

$$\sum_i \frac{\psi(\Delta_i/d)}{\Delta_i/d} \frac{\Delta_i}{d} X_{ij} = 0 \qquad (18)$$

or:

$$\sum_i \frac{\psi(\Delta_i/d)}{\Delta_i/d} \Delta_i X_{ij} = 0 \qquad (19)$$

letting

$$W_i = \frac{\psi(\Delta_i/d)}{(\Delta_i/d)} \text{ yields}$$

$$\sum_i W_i \Delta_i X_{ij} = 0 \qquad j = 1, \ldots, P \qquad (20)$$

which we solve iteratively as before. As Hogg (1979b) suggests, we may take

$$d = \underset{\substack{\text{(nonzero} \\ \text{(deviations)}}}{\text{median}} \left[\frac{|\Delta_i|}{.6745} \right],$$

where Δ_i is the ith residual, computed using the latest approximation of $\hat{\beta}$ in the iterative scheme. d is computed using non-zero values to avoid the possibility of d itself being zero. Now, we must start the iterative scheme. A relatively good solution is given by *OLS*. The ψ function may be Huber's function, as before or one of several others. Note that:

$$\sum_i W_i \Delta_i X_{ij} = 0 \qquad j = 1, 2, \ldots, P$$

is simply a weighted set of normal equations and hence:

$$\hat{\beta} = (X'WX)^{-1} X'WY \tag{21}$$

where W is the diagonal matrix of weights.*

There are other possible ψ functions besides Huber's. We will consider only one more, the one due to Andrews. The function is defined by:

$$\psi(X) = \begin{cases} \sin(X/a), & |X| \leq a\pi \\ 0, & |X| > a\pi \end{cases}$$

Here the constant a serves the same purpose as k in Huber's ψ. A function of the form of Andrews ψ is called a descending M-estimator, since it goes to zero at $\pm a\pi$. Notice that this means that points that are greater than $a\pi$ or less than $-a\pi$ are assigned a weight of zero. It is important to note that the use of the Andrews ψ requires a robust starting value in the iterative scheme. If this is not provided it is possible for the algorithm, using-Andrews ψ, to converge to an incorrect result. In our case, we will generally use *OLS* to start the Huber process and then use the Huber process to start the Andrews process.

*See reference 23 for details.

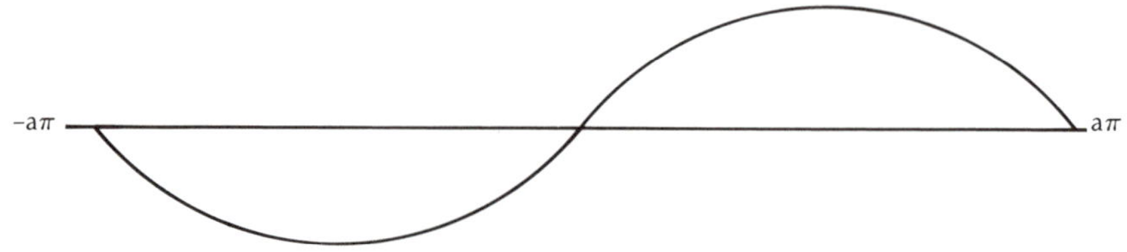

Figure 7. Andrews ψ function

PROBLEM. In the univariate case, we saw that the weights gave outlying points less influence in our estimate of μ. The similar result is true in the regression case. That is, the weights will decrease the influence of outlying points on our estimate of β. Write a paragraph explaining how this fact can be used to detect outliers.

We now wish to consider the use of robust regression with real data. The data set we choose is known as the "Brownlee Data" (Brownlee, 1965). The data are from 21 days of operation of a plant oxidizing ammonia to nitric acid. The variables are:

X_1 — Airflow, i.e., the rate of operation of the process.

X_2 — Cooling Water Inlet Temperature.

X_3 — Acid concentration, i.e., the concentration of nitric acid in the absorbing liquid (coded by subtracting 50 and multiplying by 10 each observation).

Y = Stack loss, i.e., the percent of the ingoing ammonia that is lost by escaping in the unabsorbed nitric oxides (these go up a stack, hence the name). This is an inverse measure of the nitric acid yield for the plant. We wish to predict Y for the X variables, i.e., we would wish to determine the conditions under which we get a maximum yield from the process, as the company data analyst. Here, of course, our goal is to examine the situation with respect to outliers.

PROBLEM. Do an *OLS* analysis of this data using an available computer program.

Include a residual plot. Notice that in the *OLS* analysis nothing is clearly wrong, except the residual plot does not look quite "right."

We will now run the data in a robust regression program. Our program uses an *OLS* start, Hubers ψ and Andrews ψ. The data and the program are in Appendix 2.

5. Problem Bank Identification

Problem: We will now try to pull all of this together with a case study. You should use the computer program in Appendix 2 and the case 1 data to follow the steps in the next section. Then repeat these steps with data from one or the other cases in Appendix 1. Compare your results with those given in section 6.

Now, how does all of this relate to identifying problem banks? Remember that the hypothesis was that problem banks should be outliers. Suppose we ran a data set containing variables that are important to a bank's success and isolated the points with low weights. These points would be outliers, but will they be problem banks? The only way to know is to conduct an examination. The suggestion that the banks that receive low weights, should be examined first, since they have a greater chance of being problems than the others. There is one further consideration. A bank may receive a low weight not because it is doing poorly, but because it is doing better than the average in its group. How can we tell the difference? The answer is by considering the sign of the residual point produced by the bank, as well as by the weight it receives. Points with different residual signs lie on opposite sides of the prediction equation.

We will now try to pull all of this together with a case study.

6. Problem Bank Model Study

This section of the unit is a summary of a study that was carried out to determine if robust regression would provide a useful method of identifying problem banks. In particular, we will study Franklin National Bank of New York. References used in this study are listed at the end of the unit.

6.1 Methodology of the Study

We will first review what we have learned and then see exactly how it applies in the case of problem bank identification. Recall that robust regression has two purposes. The first is to pinpoint outliers in the data by assigning lower weights to outlying points than to representative sample points. Thus, outliers may be detected by simply inspecting the weight each sample point receives. The iterative procedure that we discussed previously and will apply again in this study will result in maximum possible weights at convergence of 1. Outliers will therefore have weights of less than 1 at convergence. The second purpose of robust regression is to provide a solution to the regression problem while the outlying points are still in the data set. The lower weights for the outliers make this solution possible.

"...robust regression is to provide a solution to the regression problem while the outlying points are still in the data set."

The robust regression algorithm that we use is called the H-algorithm, in the form described by Lenth (1976), i.e., the program CUTHREG. This algorithm uses the Huber ψ function and the Andrews' ψ function. Both of these functions contain an adjustable parameter C, (corresponding to our k and a in Figures 6 and 7). In this work, the chosen value of C was 1.4. Small changes in the chosen value of C will change the magnitude of the reported weights, but not their relative order.

The data set used in this work is a modification of the one used by Sinkey (1977). A list of the 46 largest United States banks (based on total assets, as of December 31, 1973) was obtained from *The American Banker* (Boostein 1978). The reports of income and condition of these banks for the years ending December 31, 1972 and December 31, 1973 were obtained from the Federal Reserve Board or the Comptroller of the Currency, depending on the individual bank. The values of the variables to be studied (listed in Table 1) were taken directly from these reports. The variables and years considered are summarized in Table 1. The data sets are in the Appendix. The linear model to be used is obtained in the following manner. The original model to be considered is of the form:

$$Y = \beta o + \beta_1 X + \epsilon \tag{1}$$

where Y and X are variables from Table 1 and ϵ is a random error component. One of the most important assumptions of this model is that of constant error variance. If this assumption is not met, the conclusion that a particular point is or is not an outlier will depend on the X coordinate of the point thus introducing the possibility of an erroneous result.

The assumption of constant error variance can be checked in two different ways in each case. The first is to simply plot Y versus X for each case in Table 1 and observe the spread of the data. It should be noted that the cases listed in Table 1 give approximately linear plots. The second method is to do an ordinary linear least squares fit (using the model given by equation (1)) and then observe the resulting residual pattern, as plotted against

X, for signs of non-constancy of error variance. In all six cases from Table 1, both procedures indicate that the error variance is not constant. The standard corrective method to be used in such cases is a weighted least squares procedure. Neter and Wasserman (1974, p. 131), however, point out that there are data transformations that are equivalent to the use of weighted least squares. The transformation method is the one adopted for use in this study. The appropriate transformation can be determined in the following manner. Plots of the *absolute values* of the residuals, obtained from the ordinary least squares fit of equation (1), versus the X variables from Table 1 are obtained for all cases studied. These plots are graphs of the functions to be used in the transformation. These plots indicate that in all cases a suitable transformation is to multiply through equation (1) by $X^{-1/2}$. This yields the model actually used in the study:

$$YX^{-1/2} = \beta'_0 X^{-1/2} + \beta'_1 X^{1/2} + \epsilon' \qquad (2)$$

where X and Y are as described in Table 1. This model will meet the requirement of constant error variance, as must be demonstrated after each robust regression analysis by plotting the resulting residuals against $X^{-1/2}$ and $X^{1/2}$. Note that the residual plots used here are equivalent to plotting the residuals against $\hat{Y}$.

For purposes of convenience, the values of the X and Y variables have been multiplied by a constant (the X multiplier and the Y multiplier of Table 1). These values are the ones in the Appendix prior to the actual regression analysis.

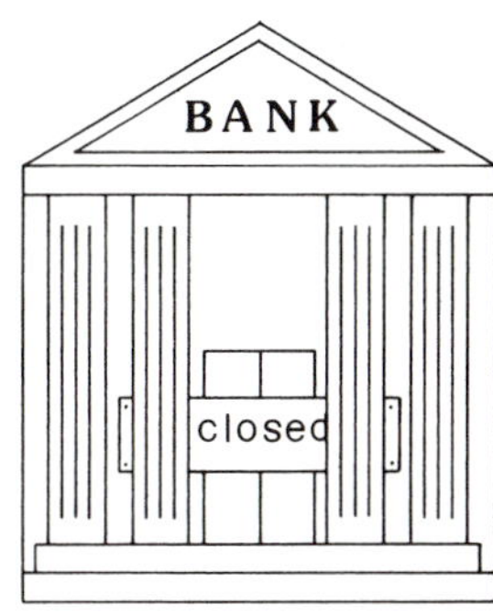

Variables Used in the Model*

Case	Y (abbreviation)	X (abbreviation)	Year	Multipliers Y	Multipliers X	Missing Data Bank Number
1	Net Income (*NI*73)	Total Assets (*TA*73)	1973	10^{-6}	10^{-9}	38
2	Net Income (*NI*72)	Total Assets (*TA*72)	1972	10^{-6}	10^{-9}	—
3	Net Operating Income (*NOI*73)	Total Assets (*TA*73)	1973	10^{-6}	10^{-9}	38
4	Net Operating Income (*NOI*72)	Total Assets (*TA*72)	1972	10^{-6}	10^{-9}	—
5	Net Loan Losses (*NLL*73)	Total Loans (*TL*73)	1973	10^{-6}	10^{-9}	38
6	Net Loan Losses (*NLL*72)	Total Loans (*TL*72)	1972	10^{-6}	10^{-9}	42,

*The importance of these particular variables has been described by Sinkey (1977).

Table 1

Outliers with Residuals Having the
Same Sign as Franklin National Bank of N.Y.

Case	Bank Code	H Algorithm Weight (C=1.4)	Residual Sign
1.	*B*	0.54	—
	A	0.74	—
	C	0.76	—
	Franklin	0.78	—
2.	*B*	0.65	—
	C	0.77	—
	Franklin	0.80	—
	D	0.81	—
	E	0.85	—
3.	*A*	0.58	—
	B	0.62	—
	Franklin	0.64	—
	D	0.76	—
4.	Franklin	0.56	—
	B	0.59	—
	E	0.65	—
5.	*F*	0.00	+
	G	0.19	+
	Franklin	0.46	+
	H	0.64	+
	I	0.65	+
6.	*J*	0.00	+
	K	0.33	+
	G	0.47	+
	Franklin	0.58	+

Table 2

Outliers with Residuals Having the Opposite Sign as Franklin National Bank of N.Y.

Case	Bank Code	H Algorithm Weight (C=1.4)	Residual Sign
1.	AA	0.00	+
	BB	0.38	+
	CC	0.59	+
	DD	0.61	+
	EE	0.73	+
	FF	0.75	+
2.	AA	0.00	+
	BB	0.73	+
	DD	0.76	+
	EE	0.78	+
	GG	0.80	+
3.	AA	0.00	+
	CC	0.47	+
	HH	0.74	+
	BB	0.75	+
4.	AA	0.00	+
	HH	0.54	+
	BB	0.64	+
	JJ	0.67	+
5.	II	0.32	—
	AA	0.51	—
	EE	0.73	—
6.	EE	0.8	—

Table 3

6.2 Results

The following is a description of one person's conclusions. The primary results of this study are given in Tables 2 and 3. All banks with the exception of Franklin are listed only by a code letter. Table 2 summarizes those outliers having the same sign residual as Franklin National Bank of New York, (an outlier in each case studied), while Table 3 lists those outliers having opposite sign residuals. It should be noted that Sinkey (1977) found Franklin to be an outlier in all of these cases. Note also that all outliers for each case are determined with only one computer run.

If a bank has the same sign residual as Franklin, it must lie on the same side of the regression curve as Franklin. Consider Case 4 of Table 2. Franklin has a weight of 0.56 (and is thus an outlier) and a negative residual sign. This implies, by the definition of residual (i.e., $Y_i - \hat{Y}_i$), that Franklin's net operating income for 1972 is less than is predicted from the other banks, given Franklin's 1972 total asset size.

By similar reasoning, Cases 1 and 2 of Table 2 indicate that in 1973 and 1972 Franklin's net income was less than would have been expected, for its total asset size. Again, in Cases 5 and 6, it can be seen that Franklin's net loan losses were higher than would have been predicted on the basis of the data from the average of the other banks in the study, given the size of Franklin's loan portfolio. Clearly Franklin had a problem with respect to these variables in those years.

"... the method for identifying a problem bank using robust regression procedure is to determine if the bank is an outlier..."

The results of Table 2 indicate that there may be other potential problem banks in this data set, e.g., *A*. Clearly, as the weights observed become lower and as the number of cases in which this finding occurs increases (given the residual sign situation of Table 2), it becomes more and more important for the bank under consideration to be examined by the appropriate regulatory agency, since the bank's financial difficulty is clearly increasing. In summary then, the method for identifying a problem bank using the robust regression procedure is to determine if the bank is an outlier by observing the weight assigned by the algorithm and then using the sign of its residual for the particular variable set under consideration, to determine if it is doing better or worse than would be predicted for it. If it is doing worse, it is a potential problem bank. A serious problem bank will show this condition for a series of different variables.

A question that occurs from these results is "Why didn't banks with lower weights than Franklin (and similar residual signs) also fail?" There are many possible answers. Some examples of them are: the bank suffered only a temporary setback and recovered, a bailout of some sort occurred, etc. (see Booth, 1982). It is clear, however, that poor-performing banks are more likely to fail than better performers. The goal of our model is to obtain a method that will allow an earlier examination of institutions that are approaching difficulty than is now available. The robust regression approach does this. Once these banks have been flagged by the procedure, they need to be examined by the appropriate regulatory agency so that failure prevention activities can take place.

"The use of a particular residual's sign and the definition of residual gives an immediate indication of whether a particular bank is doing better or worse than average."

Table 3 shows a positive side to the picture, however. By similar reasoning to the above, using the residual sign, these banks are doing better financially than the average bank in the data set, with respect to the studied variables. The use of a particular residual's sign and the definition of residual gives an immediate indication of whether a particular bank is doing better or worse than average. By being able to pinpoint which banks are performing better or worse than average, it becomes possible to study their management techniques and hopefully eventually increase our understanding of bank management methods.

6.3 Conclusion

The essential conclusion is that the robust regression procedure indicates that Franklin National Bank is an outlier in the cases considered. Since Franklin also failed, it was clearly a problem bank.

Appendix 1 Data Sets

The data sets used in this unit provide some interesting problems prior to the actual data analysis. These data were obtained from the original reports of income and condition, as described in the main text. However, the two agencies don't provide exactly the same type of material. In one case, the reports were computer printouts of data tapes, which contained at least one obvious decimal point error. In the other case, the reports were photocopies of the originals. Some of these were handwritten and some contained corrections. Most reports contain 30-day averages for several of the Table 1 variables, but not all do. In addition, some reports were amended later, thus changing values of important variables. The question one is left with is, "What value do we assign for a particular variable from a particular bank, if there is more than one possibility?" In general, the following guidelines were adopted:

1. Use 30-day averages whenever possible.

2. Use corrected values when given.

In the first analysis (Booth, 1981b), a minimal number of significant digits was included, to minimize the effect of later amendments. In the data given here, more digits were kept and some values that were missing from the earlier study have since been obtained , giving Franklin National Bank Mahalanobis distance weights of 0.542 and 0.554 for 1972 and 1973, respectively.

The modified data sets as described in Table 1 are given below. The banks are ordered by 1973 total asset size, and number 20 is Franklin National Bank of New York. The table values were truncated, not rounded.

1972

	Total Assets	Total Loans	Net Operating Income	Net Income	Net Loan Loss
1.	40.845	19.253	267.864	189.191	48.776
2.	33.747	20.627	290.123	206.532	45.041
3.	30.891	16.892	197.967	157.724	47.833
4.	11.208	4.866	187.930	121.801	5.102
5.	12.169	6.408	119.951	76.097	10.996
6.	12.345	7.180	73.300	60.884	22.446
7.	9.326	5.164	74.929	59.261	19.268
8.	12.287	6.604	100.326	80.659	8.325
9.	11.061	6.762	93.963	66.447	14.469
10.	11.688	6.156	84.449	55.968	17.278
11.	8.933	5.198	51.658	36.753	12.281
12.	7.180	3.985	45.336	34.027	8.726
13.	5.511	2.628	49.235	43.674	2.639
14.	6.450	3.876	45.069	32.727	13.205
15.	4.908	2.197	34.688	22.495	1.097
16.	3.185	1.450	11.446	13.810	7.090
17.	5.900	2.572	70.590	41.339	11.332
18.	6.148	2.575	40.801	35.097	2.444
19.	3.804	2.470	41.986	32.464	6.904
20.	3.589	1.820	10.952	14.244	11.301
21.	4.042	2.175	30.245	20.208	8.311
22.	3.649	1.673	26.452	20.017	7.140
23.	3.179	1.558	29.135	23.212	6.304
24.	3.216	1.856	28.233	22.315	6.123
25.	3.147	1.376	31.615	22.342	3.609
26.	2.495	1.338	25.050	18.587	1.610
27.	2.622	1.234	24.674	17.073	2.868
28.	3.090	1.668	34.126	29.042	4.351
29.	2.129	1.108	23.507	17.918	.237
30.	2.352	1.392	19.653	17.201	5.316
31.	2.575	1.403	20.332	16.628	1.751
32.	2.099	1.336	31.478	21.711	10.005
33.	2.655	1.491	7.818	8.087	7.304
34.	2.642	1.652	17.417	16.099	4.661
35.	2.266	.987	21.430	14.558	2.140
36.	2.585	1.349	22.419	18.703	.874
37.	2.676	1.697	24.239	18.465	16.126
38.	2.414	1.427	17.439	14.158	2.133
39.	2.514	1.266	16.358	14.372	3.420
40.	2.306	1.320	20.955	15.491	2.511
41.	2.155	.978	20.836	18.200	2.770
42.	1.870	1.117	17.437	15.477	—
43.	2.094	1.003	11.100	8.329	1.295
44.	1.869	.891	21.971	15.048	1.016
45.	2.225	.854	26.749	22.649	1.715
46.	1.950	1.145	20.645	15.049	10.078

1973	Total Assets	Total Loans	Net Operating Income	Net Income	Net Loan Loss
1.	49.034	24.614	334.138	218.795	77.344
2.	42.284	25.759	352.152	265.645	76.533
3.	36.317	21.641	256.799	170.862	84.963
4.	13.150	6.544	222.333	144.177	3.017
5.	13.497	7.767	149.387	96.867	15.463
6.	14.206	8.667	88.106	63.592	21.316
7.	11.769	6.901	77.805	53.554	32.949
8.	16.440	9.589	106.508	85.892	4.114
9.	14.854	8.965	127.640	88.098	18.556
10.	13.435	7.797	89.504	60.897	25.303
11.	11.600	6.853	56.074	42.857	15.146
12.	9.531	4.888	35.030	32.378	9.856
13.	9.363	3.950	66.245	68.335	2.566
14.	7.188	4.647	44.755	32.206	15.439
15.	6.004	3.230	46.363	28.936	6.794
16.	3.362	1.686	29.932	22.216	7.215
17.	7.532	3.592	82.996	48.616	30.058
18.	6.692	3.213	57.159	42.654	2.731
19.	4.641	2.876	54.668	40.663	9.179
20.	3.804	2.171	11.565	13.761	15.493
21.	4.359	2.633	30.671	21.597	11.311
22.	4.214	1.861	26.919	21.408	6.540
23.	3.969	2.074	32.181	25.561	6.258
24.	3.896	2.166	30.997	23.978	5.860
25.	3.884	1.549	36.571	26.317	1.349
26.	3.087	1.543	35.888	23.066	2.417
27.	3.653	1.604	29.474	20.971	4.278
28.	3.397	1.882	43.957	35.993	4.694
29.	2.576	1.454	29.990	18.498	1.517
30.	2.655	1.531	21.901	18.370	6.773
31.	3.196	1.626	26.251	19.669	2.187
32.	2.793	1.765	24.996	22.361	16.146
33.	3.080	1.698	8.220	6.478	9.926
34.	2.938	1.824	13.284	14.891	3.699
35.	2.993	1.143	23.301	16.630	1.643
36.	2.844	1.624	32.828	23.024	2.639
37.	2.887	1.721	31.786	21.557	9.927
38.	—	—	—	—	—
39.	2.647	1.390	24.542	18.086	3.002
40.	2.632	1.516	28.758	19.749	4.134
41.	2.618	1.088	28.522	23.849	5.150
42.	1.969	1.240	23.483	19.089	3.477
43.	2.481	1.248	12.224	9.213	1.798
44.	1.827	1.071	29.337	18.502	2.248
45.	2.336	.961	30.374	22.780	1.742
46.	2.098	1.329	19.178	14.347	6.217

APPENDIX 2 Computer Program

This appendix contains a robust regression program for use in solving the problems in this unit. The program listing contains the Brownlee Data. The order of the variables is Stack loss, Air Flow, Inlet Temp., Acid Conc. This program is converted and slightly modified from a FORTRAN program originally published by R. Lenth (1976). This BASIC version has been tested on both a DEC VAX 11/780 and a TI 99/4A. Output and full program details are available from the author at Kent State University or at:

205 Mecherle Drive
Bloomington, IL 61701

```
105 REM CUTHREG
110 DIM X(60, 7), W(60), D(20)
115 DIM Y(60), XY(20), UDU (20)
120 EPS=1.E-6
125 REM
140 REM
145 REM ADJUST C IN 150, 1363, N=#OF
    OBS, K=#OF PREDTS W/ CONST
150 CC=1
160 CA=1.1*ÇC
180 N=21
181 REM
182 K=4
185 FOR I=1 TO N
186 READ X(I, 5), X(I, 2), X(I, 3), X(I, 4)
187 PRINT X(I, 5); X(I, 2); X(I, 3); X(I, 4)
188 NEXT I
190 FOR I=1 TO N
192 REM FOR BANKS (1972, 73) ADD
    FOLLOWING REMS
193 REM DROP CONST TERM BY
    DROPPING 200
195 REM
196 REM
197 REM X(I, 1)=1./SQR ((X(I, 2))
198 REM X(I, 2)=SQR(X(I, 2))
199 REM X(I, 3)=X(I, 3)*X(I, 1)
200 X(I, 1)=1
202 W(I)=1
220 NEXT I
235 K1=K+1
240 NPK=N+K
245 KM1=K-1
250 N1=N+1
265 REM X(I, K1)=Y(I),
    PUT IN DATA STATEMENT
```

```
275 FOR I=1 TO K
280 FOR J=1 TO K1
285 X(I+N, J)=0
288 NEXT J
290 X(I+N, I)=-1
292 NEXT I
295 REM SWEEP X
300 FOR I=1 TO KM1
305 D(I)=0
310 XY(I)=0
315 IP1=I+1
320 FOR L=1 TO N
325 D(I)=D(I) + X(L, I)*X(L, I)
330 NEXT L
350 D(I)=1./D(I)
355 FOR J=IP1 TO K
360 B=0
365 FOR L=1 TO N
370 B=B+X(L, I)*X(L, J)
375 NEXT L
380 B=B*D(I)
385 FOR L=1 TO NPK
390 X(L, J)=X(L, J)-B*X(L, I)
395 NEXT L
425 NEXT J
430 NEXT I
440 D(K)=0
445 XY(K)=0
450 FOR L=1 TO N
455 D(K)=D(K)+X(L, K)*X(L, K)
460 NEXT L
465 D(K)=1./D(K)
470 FOR I=1 TO K
475 UDU(I)=0
480 FOR J=1 TO K
485 UDU(I)=UDU(I)+D(J)*X(N+I, J)*X(N+I, J)
490 NEXT J
495 NEXT I
530 REM ITERATE FOR SOLN
540 ITER=-1
550 MO=1
560 ITER=ITER+1
565 IF ITER >50 THEN 840
570 BMAX=0
572 WTCHG=0
574 SSE=0
576 PSN=0
590 FOR J=1 TO K
595 B=0
600 FOR I=1 TO N
620 B=B+X(I, J)*X(I, K1)*W(I)
625 NEXT I
630 IF (D(J)*B*B) >BMAX THEN 635
    ELSE 640
635 BMAX=D(J)*B*B
640 XY(J)=XY(J)+B
645 B=B*D(J)
650 FOR I=1 TO NPK
655 X(I, K1)=X(I, K1)-B*X(I, J)
660 NEXT I
665 NEXT J
680 FOR I=1 TO N
685 PSN=PSN+W(I)*W(I)
690 SSE=SSE+X(I, K1)*X(I, K1)*W(I)*W(I)
695 NEXT I
700 IF ITER < >0 THEN 760
705 PRINT "****"
710 PRINT "OLS SOLN"
715 PRINT
720 FOR I=N1 TO NPK
721 PRINT "ORDER IS SAME AS
    VARIABLES IN X MATRIX, CONST
    1ST, ETC"
725 PRINT "B(";I;")=";X(I, K1)
730 NEXT I
735 PRINT "SSE= ";SSE
745 PRINT "*****************"
750 PRINT "RUNNING"
760 RS=SQR ((PSN-K) /SSE)
765 FOR I=1 TO N
770 Z=ABS(RS*X(I, K1))
773 XX=Z
775 GOSUB 1319
777 WW=WGT
780 IF ABS(WW-W(I)) >WTCHG THEN
    782 ELSE 810
782 WTCHG=ABS (WW-W(I))
810 W(I)=WW
815 NEXT I
820 IF MO=1 THEN 821 ELSE 830
821 MO=2
830 IF BMAX > (SSE*EPS) THEN 560
    ELSE 831
831 IF (WTCHG*WTCHG) >EPS THEN
    560 ELSE 840
832 REM IF ITER < 20 THEN 560
833 PRINT "SEE #832, 830, 831"
840 PRINT
842 PRINT "BMAX= ";BMAX; "WTCHG=
    ";WTCHG
850 PRINT "SOLUTION AFTER ";ITER;
    "ITERATIONS"
860 PRINT
870 PRINT "*** ANALYSIS OF REGRESSION
    COEFFICIENT"
875 PRINT
910 XMSE=SSE/(PSN-K)
915 SSR=0
```

```
920 FOR I=1 TO K
930 SSS=XY(I)*XY(I)*D(I)
935 SSR=SSR+SSS
960 PSS=X(I+N, K1)*X(I+N, K1)/UDU(I)
965 FS=SSS/XMSE
980 FP=PSS/XMSE
990 PRINT "NO. = ";I; "SEQSS = "; SSS;
    "SEQF = ";FS
995 PRINT "PARTIAL SS = "; PSS; "PART
    F = ";FP
997 NEXT I
1010 DF=K
1015 XMSR=SSR/DF
1020 F=XMSR/XMSE
1025 PRINT
1027 PRINT "SUMMARY ANOVA"
1035 PRINT
1040 PRINT "SOURCES ARE REGN, ERROR,
     TOTAL"
1045 PRINT "REGN, DF = ";DF; "SSR = ";SSR;
1050 PRINT " MS = ";XMSR; "F = ";F
1055 DF=PSN-K
1060 PRINT
1065 PRINT "ERROR, DF = ";DF; "SSE = ";SSE
1070 PRINT "MS = "; XMSE
1075 REM TO HAVE NO CONST DROP
     LINE 200
1080 SST=SSR+SSE
1085 PRINT
1090 PRINT "TOTAL, DF = ";PSN;
     "SST = "; SST;
1095 PRINT
1105 PRINT
1115 PRINT "** REGN COEFFICIENT **"
1120 PRINT
1125 PRINT "NO. "; TAB(15); "COEF", TAB
     (30); "VAR"
1140 FOR I=1 TO K
1150 V=XMSE*UDU(I)
1160 COF=X (I+N, K1)
1165 PRINT I; TAB(9); COF; TAB (21); V
1175 NEXT I
1185 INPUT "CONT"; GGGGG ‡
1190 PRINT "ROBUST RESULTS"
1195 PRINT
1200 PRINT "OBS";TAB(15); "RESID"; TAB
     (30); "WEIGHT";
1205 PRINT
1210 FOR I=1 TO N
1230 PRINT I; TAB (9); X(I, K1);
     TAB (21); W(I)
1240 NEXT I
1245 IF MO=3 THEN 5000
1250 ITER=0
1255 MO=3
1258 PRINT "***"
1260 PRINT "DESCEND M-EST"
1265 PRINT "C= ";CA
1267 PRINT "NOW RUNNING"
1270 GOTO 560
1280 REM MOST MICROS REQUIRE AN
     END HERE
1319 REM FUNCTION WT
1320 REM XX=ABS(RESDIDS/X)
1322 REM MO (MODE)=1 DROPS OUTLIERS
1323 REM =2 HUBER
1324 REM =3 ANDREWS
1325 REM D.BOOTH-AFTER LENTH, U OF
     IA TECH REPORT 53,1/76
1360 REM SET C(ASCC)
1363 CC=1.0
1365 CA=1. 1*CC
1367 CP=3.141593*CA
1370 WGT=1
1380 IF MO=1 THEN 1385  ELSE 1400
1385 IF XX > (CC-.3) THEN 1386 ELSE 1387
1386 WGT=0
1387 RETURN
1400 IF MO=2 THEN 1410 ELSE 1420
1410 IF XX > CC THEN 1412 ELSE 1415
1412 WGT=CC/XX
1415 RETURN
1420 IF MO=3 THEN 1425  ELSE 1455
1425 IF XX<.001 THEN 1426 ELSE 1430
1426 RETURN
1430 WGT=0
1435 IF XX >CP THEN 1440 ELSE 1445
1440 RETURN
1445 WGT=CA*SIN(XX/CA)/XX
1450 RETURN
1455 PRINT "MO OUT OF RANGE"
1457 RETURN
2997 REM INPUT DATA AS INDICATED
     BY 186
2999 REM BROWNLEE DATA
3000 DATA 42., 80, 27, 89
3001 DATA 37, 80, 27, 88
3002 DATA 37, 75, 25, 90
3003 DATA 28, 62, 24, 87
3005 DATA 18, 62, 22, 87
3007 DATA 18, 62, 23, 87
3009 DATA 19, 62, 24, 93
3011 DATA 20, 62, 24, 93
3013 DATA 15, 58, 23, 87
3015 DATA 14, 58, 18, 80
3017 DATA 14, 58, 18, 89
3019 DATA 13, 58, 17, 88
3021 DATA 11, 58, 18, 82
```

```
3023 DATA 12, 58, 19, 93
3025 DATA 8, 50, 18, 89
3027 DATA 7, 50, 18, 86
3029 DATA 8, 50, 19, 72
3031 DATA 8, 50, 19, 79
3033 DATA 9, 50, 20, 80
3035 DATA 15, 56, 20, 82
3037 DATA 15, 70, 20, 91
5000 END
```

In order to run the bank data sets, the following changes should be made:

1. Change N to the appropriate number of observations in line 180, and delete line number 200.

2. Then: Remove REM from lines 197-199 and replace these lines

```
150 CC = 1.4/REM CC is the adjustable parameter
182 K = 2
184 FOR I = 1 TO. N/READ X(I, 2)/NEXT I
185 FOR I = 1 TO N
186 READ X(I, 3)
187 PRINT X(I, 2); X(I, 3)
1363 CC = 1.4
2999 REM Data order is X, Y by variables
```

   REPLACE the current data by the bank data in the order indicated by 2999.

Bibliography

1. Boostein, P. (1978), *American Banker*, 525 W. 42nd St., New York, NY 10036, personal communication.

2. Booth, D.E. (1981a) "A Note on the Introduction of Robust Regression in the Elementary Statistics course," *Journal of the CUNY Mathematics Discussion Group* 8, pp. 25-35.

3. Booth, D.E. (1981b), "The Analysis of Outlying Data Points Using Robust Regression: I. A Model for the Identification of Problem Banks," *Industrial Mathematics* 31(2), pp. 85-98.

4. Booth, D.E. (1981b), "A Multivariate Problem Bank Identification Model," *Proceedings of the Business and Economic Statistics Section*. Washington, DC: American Statistical Association.

5. Booth, D.E. (1981c), "The Identification of Problem Banks — An Application of Robust Regression," *Proceedings of the 13th Annual Meeting*, Vol. 2, Atlanta, GA: American Institute for Decision Sciences.

6. Booth, D.E. (1982), "The Analysis of Outlying Data Points Using Robust Regression: A Multivariate Problem Bank Identification Model," *Decision Sciences* 13, pp. 71-81.

7. Brownlee, K. (1965). *Statistical Theory and Methodology in Science and Engineering* (2nd Ed.), New York: John Wiley and Sons.

8. Daniel, C. and Wood, F. (1971). *Fitting Equations to Data*, New York: Wiley-Interscience. (1977)

9. Dutter (1977) "Numerical Solution of Robust Regression Problems: Computational Aspects, a Comparison," *Journal of Statistical Computation and Simulation*, 5, pp. 207-238.

10. Hill, W. and Holland, P.W. (1977), "Two Robust Alternatives to Least Squares Regression," *Journal of the American Statistical Association*, 72, pp. 828-833.

11. Hill, R. and Holland, P.W. (1978), "Corrigendum," *Journal of the American Statistical Association*, pp. 73, 455.

12. Hogg (1977a) "An Introduction to Robust Procedures," *Communications in Statistics*, A6(9), pp. 789-794.

13. Hogg, R.V. (1977b) "Robust Statistical Procedures," Notes from *A Short Course in Statistics*, given at the January 1977 American Mathematical Society meeting, St. Louis, MO (1977).

14. Hogg, R.V. (1978). "Statistical Robustness: On Its Use in Applications Today," Technical Report Number 60, Department of Statistics, The University of Iowa, Iowa City, IA 52242

15. Hogg, R.V. (1979a), "Statistical Robustness: One View of its Use in Applications Today," *American Statistician* 33, pp. 108-116.

16. Hogg, R.V. (1979b), "An Introduction to Robust Estimation," in Launer, R.L. and Wilkinson, G.N. (Eds), *Robustness in Statistics*, New York: Academic Press.

17. Hampel, F. (1974), "The Influence Curve and Its Role in Robust Estimation," *Journal of the American Statistical Association* 69, pp. 383-393.

18. Huber, P.J. (1977), *Robust Statistical Procedures*, Philadelphia, PA: Society for Industrial and Applied Mathematics.

19. Huber, P.J. (1981). *Robust Statistics*. New York: Wiley-Interscience.

20. Kennedy, Jr., W.J. and Gentle, J.E. (1980). *Statistical Computing*, New York: Marcel Dekker.

21. Lenth, R.V. (1976), "A Computational Procedure for Robust Multiple Regression," Technical Report Number 53, Department of Statistics, The University of Iowa, Iowa City, IA 52242

22. Morris, C.N. and Rolph, J.E. (1981), *An Introduction to Data Analysis and Statistical Inference*. Englewood Cliffs, NJ: Prentice-Hall.

23. Neter, J. and Wasserman, W. (1974). *Applied Linear Statistical Models*. Homewood, IL, Richard D. Irwin.

24. Ott, L. (1977). *An Introduction to Statistical Methods and Data Analysis*. Belmont, California: Duxbury.

25. Randles, R. and Wolfe, D.A. (1979). *Introduction to the Theory of Nonparametric Statistics*. New York: Wiley-Interscience.

26. Seber, G.A.F. (1977). *Linear Regression Analysis*. New York: Wiley-Interscience.

27. Sinkey, Jr., F. (1977) "Identifying Large Problem/Failed Banks: The Case of Franklin National Bank of New York," *Journal of Financial and Quantitative Analysis*, 12, pp. 179-800.

28. Sinkey Jr., J.F. (1978), "Identifying Problem Banks," *Journal of Money, Credit and Banking* 10, pp. 184-193.

29. Sinkey Jr., J.G. (1979). *Problem and Failed Institutions in the Commercial Banking Industry*. Greenwich, CT: JAI Press.

30. Spong, K. and Hoenig, T. (1979). "Bank Examination Classifications and Loan Risk." *Federal Reserve Bank of Kansas City Economic Review*, June 1979, pp. 15-25.

UMAP

Modules in Undergraduate Mathematics and its Applications

Module 649

Continuous Time, Discrete State Space Markov Chains

Frederick Solomon

Published in cooperation with the Society for Industrial and Applied Mathematics, the Mathematical Association of America, the National Council of Teachers of Mathematics, the American Mathematical Association of Two-Year Colleges, and The Institute of Management Sciences.

COMAP

INTERMODULAR DESCRIPTION SHEET: UMAP Unit 649

TITLE: CONTINUOUS TIME, DISCRETE STATE SPACE MARKOV CHAINS

AUTHOR: Frederick Solomon
Division of Natural Science
College at Purchase
State University of New York
Purchase, NY 10577

MATH FIELD: Probability

APPLICATION FIELD: Management Science

TARGET AUDIENCE: Students in a probability or a linear algebra course.

ABSTRACT: This unit develops a model for the number of components operating in a multicomponent device. Using the number of bulbs lit in a movie theatre sign as an example, the unit works toward a general model beginning with the exponential distribution.

PREREQUISITES: Knowledge of Linear Algebra through finding eigenvalues and eigenvectors of matrices, Calculus through straightforward Differential Equations, and a knowledge of Probability including the Poisson Distribution, the Central Limit Theorem, and the Law of Large Numbers.

Continuous Time, Discrete State Space Markov Chains

Frederick Solomon
Division of Natural Sciences
College at Purchase
State University of New York
Purchase, New York 10577

Table of Contents

Modules and Monographs in Undergraduate Mathematics and its Applications Project (UMAP)

The goal of UMAP was to develop, through a community of users and developers, a system of instructional modules in undergraduate mathematics and its applications to be used to supplement existing courses and from which complete courses may eventually be built.

The Project was guided by a National Advisory Board of mathematicians, scientists, and educators. UMAP was funded by a grant from the National Science Foundation and is now supported by the Consortium for Mathematics and Its Applications, Inc. (COMAP), a nonprofit corporation engaged in research and development in mathematics education.

The author would like to thank Dr. K. Berk, Dr. J. Dossey, Dr. J. Ingles, and the UMAP reviewers for reading the manuscript and making many valuable suggestions. He would also like to thank Dr. R. Lenth for providing the original computer program. This work was supported in part by a grant from the Illinois State University Instructional Development Program. Thanks are also due Mitch Pollack, Anne Hower, and Joan Gutta, students at Bucknell University, who edited the manuscript and made excellent suggestions which have been incorporated.

This material was prepared with the partial support of National Science Foundation Grant No. SPE8304192. Recommendations expressed are those of the authors and do not necessarily reflect the views of the NSF or the copyright holder.

1. Introduction

This unit develops a model that is interesting and applicable in its own right and also serves as an introduction to the general theory of Continuous Time, Discrete State Space Markov Chains. The general theory is covered in standard probability textbooks (several of which are listed in the bibliography); and, although we will develop our model with no background in the general theory assumed, our development is consistent with a more general approach. In fact, all of our results can be generalized, so our model can provide intuition into the general theory.

Consider a movie marquee that consists of a large number N of light bulbs. Each of the bulbs burns independently of the others, but will of course burn out at some finite time. The replacement policy is to replace all the burned out bulbs when *fewer than n* bulbs are operating. Among the questions we might want a mathematical analysis to answer are: How much time elapses between replacements? What is the fraction of the time during which 80 percent, say, of the bulbs are operating? As n decreases, how does the time between replacements increase?

2. The Exponential Distribution

Consider the case of one light bulb that burns for a random length of time. We'll assume the *Lack of Memory* property which will imply that the lifetime of the light bulb is exponentially distributed. The Lack of Memory property states that no matter how long the bulb has been operational, the probability that it will last an additional time s is independent of the time that it has already been burning. In terms of conditional probabilities

$$P(T > t + s \mid T > t) = P(T > s) \tag{1}$$

for t, s non-negative times and where T is the random variable that is the lifetime of the light bulb. The Lack of Memory property is equivalent to the assumption that the bulb undergoes no aging: given that it has lasted till time t, it behaves just as though it were brand new. Do actual light bulbs actually obey this property? At first glance it seems obvious that any real device should not since there is always aging with time and greater likelihood of failure. On the other hand, suppose that a device fails only due to some external circumstance—a power surge, for example. Then no matter

"...no matter how old the device is, its age has no bearing on its subsequent functioning."

how old the device is, its age has no bearing on its subsequent functioning. For example, a set of dishes will break only when dropped; each dish eventually 'fails,' but its breakage is completely independent of its present condition. (Not totally accurate because very new and very old dishes will be treated with more care.) Thus we have the phenomenon of one or two dishes in the set continuing to last long after the rest have broken; each time a dish is used it is brand new so far as its breakage is concerned. The Lack of Memory property actually does apply to any 'device' whose failure is due to some circumstance which cannot be known by knowing only its internal state. At any rate, we will assume that the lifetimes of the light bulbs in the marquee obey the Lack of Memory property; even if there is some aging present, our model may still serve as an approximation to the correct model and thereby provide insight.

Let us use (1) to obtain the density for the random variable T. Let $G(t) = P(T > t)$ for $t > 0$. We develop a differential equation for $G(t)$:

$$
\begin{aligned}
G(t+s) &= P(T > t + s) \\
&= P(T > t + s \text{ and } T > t) \\
&= P(T > t + s \mid T > t) \cdot P(T > t) \qquad (2) \\
&= P(T > s) \cdot P(t > t) \\
&= G(s) \cdot G(t).
\end{aligned}
$$

The second equality follows since the events $\{T > t + s\}$ and $\{T > t + s \text{ and } T > t\}$ are the same; the third equality invokes the definition of conditional probability; the next to last equality uses the Lack of Memory property. Subtracting $G(s)$ from the extreme sides of (2), dividing by s, and letting s approach 0 yields $G'(t)$ on the left side. On the right we obtain

$$G'(t) = \lim_{s \to 0} G(t) \cdot \frac{G(s) - 1}{s}$$

after factoring out $G(t)$. Noting that $G(0) = P(T > 0) = 1$ (assuming that the bulb is not originally defective) and that we obtain $-\lambda = G'(0)$

$$G'(t) = -\lambda \cdot G(t)$$

The solution to this differential equation with the initial condition that $G(0) = 1$ is

$$G(t) = e^{-\lambda t}. \quad (3)$$

Problem

1. The above derivation assumes that G is differentiable and that $G(0) = 1$. This problem outlines a rigorous derivation based on less restrictive assumptions. Assume $G(0) = 1$, $G(t + s) = G(t)\,G(s)$ for non-negative t, s, and G is continuous near 0.

   (a) For positive integer m and $x > 0$ show that

   $$G(mx) = G(x + x + \ldots + x) = G(x)^m.$$

   (b) For positive integer n take $x = 1/n$ in **(a)** to show that

   $$G(1/n) = G(1)^{1/n}.$$

   (c) For rational $r = m/n$ where $m, n > 0$ show that **(a)** and **(b)** imply

   $$G(r) = G(m/n) = G(1)^{m/n}.$$

   (d) Since G is continuous near 0 and $G(0) = 1$, there is an integer n so that $G(1/n) > 0$. Use **(c)** with $r = 1/n$ to conclude that

   $$G(1)^{1/n} = G(1/n) > 0.$$

   Hence $G(1) > 0$.

   (e) Since G is continuous near 0 show that **(c)** implies

   $$G(x) = G(1)^x$$

   for all $x > 0$.

   (f) Since $1 > G(1) > 0$, there is a $\lambda > 0$ so that $G(1) = e^{-\lambda}$.

   (g) Hence **(e)** and **(f)** imply for all $x > 0$

   $$G(x) = (e^{-\lambda})^x = e^{-\lambda x}.$$

Let F be the *exponential distribution function with parameter* λ; that is $F(t) = P(T \leq t) = 1 - G(t)$. We have shown

$$F(t) = \begin{cases} 0, \text{ for } t < 0 \\ 1 - e^{-\lambda t}, \text{ for } 0 \leq t. \end{cases} \qquad (4)$$

Problem

2. Let $f(t) = F'(t)$ be the exponential density. Show that the expectation and variance of the lifetime T are

$$\mu = \int \quad tf(t)\ dt = 1/\lambda$$

$$\sigma^2 = 1/\lambda^2.$$

3. The Classical Poisson Distribution

"When this device wears out, it is immediately replaced by another device with identical lifetime distribution; and the process continues on this way."

Now we return to the movie marquee model; after the excursion into the exponential distribution—which will be assumed to be the distribution of the lifetime of each light bulb—we can readily answer the relevant questions when $N = 1$. Consider, therefore, a 'system' consisting of one device whose lifetime has distribution (4). When this device wears out, it is immediately replaced by another device with identical lifetime distribution; and the process continues in this way. We will show that this model leads to the classical Poisson Distribution with parameter λ. Let $T_1, T_2, \ldots$ denote the lifetimes of devices 1, 2, ... We assume that these random variables are independent and that each has the exponential distribution with parameter λ. We want to find the distribution of N_t = number of failures in the time interval $(0, t]$. The derivation is standard in probability texts so we give an outline only in the language of our specific model. Now, as soon as a device fails, it is instantly replaced. Thus the Lack of Memory property implies that a device fails in any time interval of length s with probability equal to the distribution in (4), $F(s) = 1 - e^{-\lambda s}$. For small s we use the Taylor Series for the exponential function to approximate this probability. Since

$$e^x = 1 + x + x^2/2! + x^3/3! + \ldots$$

$$= 1 + x + O(x^2)$$

where $O(x^2)$ denotes terms—a function—that are of order x^2 or higher. (The technical definition of $O(x^2)$ is that it is any function which when divided by x^2 remains bounded as x tends to 0.) So the probability that a device fails in a time interval of length s is $F(s) = 1 - e^{-\lambda s} = \lambda s + O(s^2)$; the probability of no failure in time s is $1 - F(s) = e^{-\lambda s} = 1 - \lambda s + O(s^2)$. Consequently the probability of more than one failure in time s is $O(s^2)$. If n devices have failed in the time interval $(0, t]$, then in the next small interval of length s, 1 or 0 devices may fail with probabilities λs and $1 - \lambda s$ to first order terms in s. Let $P_n(t) = P(N_t = n) = P(n$ devices fail in $(0, t])$. Then by the law of total probability

$$
\begin{aligned}
P_n(t + s) &= P_n(t) \cdot P(\text{no failures in } (t, t + s]) \\
&\qquad + P_{n-1}(t) \cdot P(\text{one failure in } (t, t + s]) \\
&\qquad + O(s^2) \\
&= P_n(t) \cdot (1 - \lambda s) + P_{n-1}(t) \cdot (\lambda s) + O(s^2)
\end{aligned}
$$

for $n > 0$. And for $n = 0$

$$
\begin{aligned}
P_0(t + s) &= P_0(t) \cdot P(\text{no failures in } (t, t + s]) \\
&= P_0(t) \cdot (1 - \lambda s) + O(s^2).
\end{aligned}
$$

Subtracting $P_n(t)$ from both sides (in both cases $n > 0$ and $(n = 0)$, dividing by s, and letting s tend to 0 imply

$$
\begin{aligned}
\frac{d}{dt} P_n(t) &= -\lambda P_n(t) + \lambda P_{n-1}(t), \qquad \text{for } n > 0 \\
\frac{d}{dt} P_0(t) &= -\lambda P_0(t).
\end{aligned}
\tag{5}
$$

Problems

3. Note that the initial conditions to this *system* of differential equations are $P_0(0) = 1$ and $P_n(0)$ for $n > 0$ since the process begins with no devices failed. Check that the solution to (5) is

$$
P_n(t) = e^{-\lambda t} \frac{(\lambda t)^n}{n!}, \qquad \text{for } n \geq 0 \tag{6}
$$

by substituting (6) into (5). Show that the expectation and the variance of the random variable N_t with distribution (6) are both λt. (Hint: To find the variance, first find $E(N_t(N_t - 1)) = E(N_t^2) - E(N_t)$).

4. For $t = 1$ sketch several terms of the *Poisson Distribution with parameter* λ for $\lambda = .5, 2,$ and 10. Notice that the maximum occurs when the integer n is approximately λ. Show that for fixed t, $Pn(t)$ is increasing with n if and only if $t > n$.

The Law of Large Numbers and the Central Limit Theorem both apply to the Poisson Distribution. The Law of Large Numbers states that the average of n independent, identically distributed random variables approaches the common expectation as $n \to \infty$. Symbolically, if $X_1, X_2, \ldots$ are independent, identically distributed with $\mu = E(X_i)$, then

$$\frac{X_1 + \ldots + X_n}{n} \to \mu \qquad \text{as } n \to \infty.$$

In our case we can consider the time interval $(0, t]$ to be subdivided into many small time intervals of length h; the number of subintervals is $n = t/h$. By the Lack of Memory property the *numbers of device failures in non-overlapping time intervals are independent.* The average number of device failures in time intervals of length h is λh by Problem 3. Since there are $n = t/h$ such subintervals and since the total number of device failures is the sum of the numbers in each subinterval, the Law of Large Numbers implies

$$\lim_{t \to \infty} \frac{N_t}{t} = \lambda. \tag{7}$$

That is, the average number of device failures per unit time is λ. This is intuitively clear since $1/\lambda$ is the mean time till failure of each device (each device is exponentially distributed with parameter λ and mean $1/\lambda$) so, intuitively speaking, the number of devices per unit time is λ.

The Central Limit Theorem does not have such an obvious interpretation. Recall that this result applies to sums of independent, identically distributed random variables each with mean μ and variance σ^2. If S_n is such a sum, then $(S_n - n\mu)/\sqrt{n}\sigma$ is approximately Normally distributed, mean 0, variance 1 for n large. In our case the total number of device failures in $(0, t]$ is, as in the Law of Large Numbers, the sum of n contributions—each being the number of device failures in a subinterval of time of length h. Since the number of device failures in time h has mean λh and variance

λh by Problem 3, and since non-overlapping time intervals are independent, the Central Limit Theorem implies that $(N_t - n\lambda h)/\sqrt{n\lambda h}$ is approximately Normally distributed for large n. Now $t = nh$ (the number of subintervals multiplied by the length of each subinterval is the total time.), so

$$P\left(\frac{N_t - \lambda t}{\sqrt{\lambda t}} \leq x\right) \simeq \Phi(x) \tag{8}$$

for t large where $\Phi(x)$ denotes the Normal Distribution, mean 0, variance 1.

Problem

5. Let $\lambda = 1$. With $t \doteq 20$ find

$$P(N_{20} \leq 16) = P(\text{no more than 16 failures in } (0, t]).$$

For $\lambda = 1$ we expect t device failures in the interval $(0, t]$; for $t = 100, 1000, 10000$ use the Central Limit Theorem to find x so that

$$P(|N_t - t| \leq x) = .95.$$

4. The General Markov Chain with Two States

"... the system can be in either of two states — an 'on' or operational and an 'off' or down state."

Now consider this generalization of the model of the previous section: As before when one light bulb (device) fails, it is replaced; and the system consists of just one bulb. Only now we assume that it takes a certain amount of time to change the bulb rather than immediate replacement. More specifically, suppose the system can be in either of two states—an 'on' or operational and an 'off' or down state. The 'on' state lasts an exponential time with parameter α, mean $1/\alpha$; that is, each 'on' time is a random variable with Exponential Distribution. The 'off' state lasts an exponential time with parameter β, mean $1/\beta$. So the system consists of one bulb which burns for a random time and the 'fix-it' time is also random. We also assume independence of the 'on' and 'off' times. It is convenient to define the random variable X_t = state of the system at time t;

$X_t = 0$ or 1 if the system is on or off respectively at time t. Let P^t be the 2x2 matrix whose ij^{th} entry is

$$P^t_{ij} = P(X_t = j \mid X_0 = i)$$

for $i, j \in 0, 1$.

Problem

6. Use the Lack of Memory property to derive the *Chapman-Kolmogorov Equations*

$$P^{t+s}_{ij} = \sum_{k=0}^{1} P^t_{ik} \cdot P^s_{kj} \quad . \tag{9a}$$

That is, in terms of *matrix multiplication*

$$P^{t+s} = P^t \cdot P^s . \tag{9b}$$

(The Lack of Memory property for this system states that no matter what the state of the system at any time before time t, the future state at any time after t only depends on the present state at time t). To solve this problem it may be useful to prove the following equality for conditional probabilities: Let A, B, and C be events; then

$$P(A \text{ and } B \mid C) = P(A \mid B \text{ and } C) \cdot P(B \mid C).$$

To derive (9a) justify the following

$$\begin{aligned}
P^{t+s}_{ij} &= P(X_{t+s} = j \mid X_0 = i) \\
&= P(X_{t+s} = j \text{ and } X_t = 0 \mid X_0 = i) \\
&\qquad + P(X_{t+s} = j \text{ and } X_t = 1 \mid X_0 = i) \\
&= P(X_{t+s} = j \mid X_t = 0 \text{ and } X_0 = i) \cdot P(X_t = 0 \mid X_0 = i) \\
&\qquad + P(X_{t+s} = j \mid X_t = 1 \text{ and } X_0 = i) \cdot P(X_t = 1 \mid X_0 = i) \\
&= P(X_{t+s} = j \mid X_t = 0) \cdot P(X_t = 0 \mid X_0 = i) \\
&\qquad + P(X_{t+s} = j \mid X_t = 1) \cdot P(X_t = 1 \mid X_0 = i)
\end{aligned}$$

$$= P^s_{0j} \, P^t_{i0} + P^s_{1j} \, P^t_{i1}$$

$$= \sum_{k=0}^{1} P^t_{ik} \cdot P^s_{kj} \; .$$

We derive and solve differential equations for P^t in much the same that the Poisson Distribution was derived in the last section. Let s be so small that the probability that more than one transition between states in time s is negligible (of order $O(s^2)$). Since the system is in state 0 (off) an exponential length of time with parameter β, and the system is in state 1 (on) an exponential length of time with parameter α,

$$\begin{aligned} P^s_{00} &= 1 - \beta s + O(s^2) \\ P^s_{01} &= \beta s + O(s^2) \\ P^s_{11} &= 1 - \alpha s + O(s^2) \\ P^s_{10} &= \alpha s + O(s^2). \end{aligned} \tag{10}$$

Let Q be the 2x2 matrix

$$Q = \begin{bmatrix} -\beta & \beta \\ \alpha & -\alpha \end{bmatrix}.$$

Equations (10) can be written in the matrix form

$$P^s = I + sQ + O(s^2) \tag{11}$$

where $O(s^2)$ denotes a 2x2 matrix each of whose entries are $O(s^2)$ and I is the identity 2x2 matrix

$$I = \begin{bmatrix} 1 & 0 \\ 0 & 1 \end{bmatrix}.$$

To derive a system of differential equations substitute (11) into (9b), subtract P^t from both sides, and divide by s to obtain

$$\frac{P^{t+s} - P^t}{s} = P^t \cdot Q + \frac{P^t \cdot O(s^2)}{s}$$

where now each of the terms is a 2x2 matrix. Letting s tend to 0 implies

$$\frac{d}{dt} P^t = P^t \bullet Q \qquad (12)$$

where the *derivative of a matrix is the matrix obtained by taking the derivative of each entry in the matrix.* The initial condition for this matrix differential equation is $P^0 = I$ since $P(X_0 = j \mid X_0 = i)$ is obviously 1 or 0 depending on whether $i = j$ or $i \neq j$. The solution to this equation is $P^t = e^{tQ}$, but in order to prove or apply this we must interpret the exponential of a matrix. For an $n \times n$ matrix Q, by definition

"... the derivative of a matrix is the matrix obtained by taking the derivative of each entry in the matrix."

$$e^{tQ} = I + tQ + t^2Q^2/2! + t^3Q^3/3! + \ldots$$

That is, we extend the definition of the exponential of a matrix by using the Taylor Series for e^x.

Problem

7. Use this definition of e^{tQ} and formal term by term differentiation to show that

$$(e^{tQ})' = e^{tQ} \bullet Q$$

$$(e^{tQ})' = Q \bullet e^{tQ}.$$

Problem

8. Let Q be a diagonal n x n matrix;

$$Q = \begin{bmatrix} a_1 & & \\ & \ddots & \\ & & a_n \end{bmatrix} .$$

Show by computing Q^n for each integer n and using the definition that

$$e^{tQ} = \begin{bmatrix} e^{ta_1} & & \\ & \ddots & \\ & & e^{ta_n} \end{bmatrix} .$$

Problem 8 shows that it is straightforward to compute e^{tQ} for a diagonal matrix Q: e^{tQ} is obtained as the diagonal matrix whose ii^{th} entry is the exponential of the ii^{th} entry of Q. In general to obtain e^{tQ} requires that we invoke some theorems from Linear

Algebra. The idea is this: Suppose we want to find e^{tQ} for an $n \times n$ matrix Q; and suppose we can find a matrix M so that $M^{-1}QM = D$ is diagonal. Then

$$D^n = M^{-1}QM \cdot M^{-1}QM \cdots M^{-1}QM$$

$$= M^{-1}Q^nM$$

since the interior M's cancel with the M^{-1}'s. Multiplying this last equation by M^{-1} on the right, M on the left, and by the scalar t^n yields

$$(tQ)^n = M(tD)^nM^{-1}. \tag{13}$$

The conclusion is that if we could find a 'diagonalizing' matrix M then (13) together with the definition can be used to compute e^{tQ}. Now to find a matrix M we state a theorem from Linear Algebra:

> Let Q be an $n \times n$ matrix which has n independent eigenvectors. Let M be an $n \times n$ matrix whose *columns* are these eigenvectors. Then $M^{-1}QM = D$ is a diagonal matrix with the eigenvalues of Q as its entries along the main diagonal.

Problem

9. Let $Q = \begin{bmatrix} -\beta & \beta \\ -\alpha & -\alpha \end{bmatrix}$ where α, β are fixed non-negative numbers with at least one positive. The problem is to find the matrix $P^t = e^{tQ}$.

   (a) Find the eigenvectors and eigenvalues of Q: Show that the solutions to the *characteristic equation* $\det(xI - Q) = 0$ are $x = 0, -(\alpha + \beta)$. Show that an eigenvector associated with $x = 0$ is $\begin{bmatrix} 1 \\ 1 \end{bmatrix}$ and that $\begin{bmatrix} -\beta \\ \alpha \end{bmatrix}$ is an eigenvector associated with $x = -(\alpha + \beta)$.

   (b) Let $M = \begin{bmatrix} 1 & \beta \\ 1 & -\alpha \end{bmatrix}$. Find M^{-1}. Show that

   $$M^{-1}QM = D = \begin{bmatrix} 0 & 0 \\ 0 & -(\alpha + \beta) \end{bmatrix}$$

   where the diagonal entries of D are the eigenvalues of Q.

(c) Now D is diagonal; use the remarks above or the definition to find e^{tD}.

(d) Show that

$$e^{tQ} = \sum_{n=0} \frac{(tQ)^n}{n!} \tag{14}$$

$$= \sum_{n=0} \frac{M(tD)^n M^{-1}}{n!}$$

$$= M \left(\sum_{n=0} \frac{(tD)^n}{n!} \right) M^{-1}$$

$$= M\, e^{tD}\, M^{-1}$$

$$= \frac{1}{\alpha + \beta} \begin{bmatrix} \alpha + \beta e^{-t(\alpha + \beta)} & \beta - \beta e^{-t(\alpha + \beta)} \\ \alpha - \alpha e^{-t(\alpha + \beta)} & \beta + \alpha e^{-t(\alpha + \beta)} \end{bmatrix}$$

$$= \frac{1}{\alpha + \beta} \begin{bmatrix} \alpha & \beta \\ \alpha & \beta \end{bmatrix} + \frac{e^{-t(\alpha + \beta)}}{\alpha + \beta} \begin{bmatrix} \beta & -\beta \\ -\alpha & \alpha \end{bmatrix}. \tag{14a}$$

Note that in part (**d**), once having found D and the matrix of eigenvectors M, e^{tQ} is found using the formula

$$e^{tQ} = M\, e^{tD}\, M^{-1}. \tag{15}$$

The final result of Problem 9 is a formula for the *matrix of transition probabilities* $P^t = e^{tQ}$ where $P^t_{ij} = P$(state is j at time t | state is i at time 0). There are several interesting consequences of this result. First, note that as $t \to \infty$ the matrix P^t tends to the constant matrix by (14a)

$$P^t \to \frac{1}{\alpha + \beta} \begin{bmatrix} \alpha & \beta \\ \alpha & \beta \end{bmatrix}$$

with constant rows. To give an interpretation of this let $q^0 = [q^0_0, q^0_1]$ be an *initial probability vector;* that is $q^0_0 + q^0_1 = 1$ and $q^0_0, q^0_1 \geq 0$. Now, given the initial probabilities q^0 of being in state 0 or 1 at time 0, the probabilities of being in these states t time units later can be computed using P^t; namely

$$P(X_t = i) = P(X_t = i \mid X_0 = 0) \cdot P(X_0 = 0)$$

$$+ P(X_t = i \mid X_0 = 1)\, P(X_0 = 1)$$

$$= q_0^0\, P_{0i}^t + q_1^0\, P_{1i}^t \; .$$

Hence in terms of matrix multiplication

$$q^t = q^0 P^t \tag{16}$$

where q^t denotes the probability vector at time t whose components are the probabilities of the system being in states 0, 1 at time t.

Problem

10. Show that $q^t = [q_0^t, q_1^t]$ where

$$q_0^t = [\alpha + (\beta q_0^0 - \alpha q_1^0)\, e^{-t(\alpha + \beta)}]/(\alpha + \beta)$$

$$q_1^t = [\beta - (\beta q_0^0 - \alpha q_1^0)\, e^{-t(\alpha + \beta)}]/(\alpha + \beta)$$

using equations (14) and (16); and hence show that

$$q = \lim_{t \to \infty} q^t = [\alpha, \beta]/(\alpha + \beta)$$

regardless of the initial probability vector q^0.

Problem 10 shows that $P(X_t = i) = q_i^t$ tends to $\alpha/(\alpha + \beta)$ and $\beta/(\alpha + \beta)$ independently of how the system started. This is intuitively clear since the system 'on' time is exponential with mean $1/\alpha$ and the 'off' time is exponential with mean $1/\beta$. Hence one expects the system to be 'on' an average of

$$(1/\alpha)/((1/\alpha) + (1/\beta)) = \beta/(\alpha + \beta)$$

and similarly one expects the system to be down an average of $\alpha/(\alpha + \beta)$.

Problems

11. As a multiple of $\alpha + \beta$, how large must t be so that

$$| q_0^t - \alpha/(\alpha + \beta) | < .001$$

$$| q_1^t - \beta/(\alpha + \beta) | < .001$$

for any choice of initial probability vector q^0?

12. Let S_t be the total time in $(0, t]$ during which the light bulb is on. Now $X_t = 0, 1$ if the bulb is off, on at time t. Hence

$$S_t = \int_0^t X_s \, ds.$$

So

$$E(S_t) = E(\int_0^t X_s \, ds) = \int_0^t E(X_s) \, ds.$$

(Actually you know that the expectation of a finite sum is the sum of the expectations. It is also true under very general conditions that the expectation of an integral is the integral of the expectations.) Now for each s

$$E(X_s) = 1 \bullet P(X_s = 1) + 0 \bullet P(X_s = 0) = q_1^s.$$

Now find $E(S_t)$.

Just as in the Poisson Distribution section, we want to derive a Law of Large Numbers and a Central Limit Theorem for the system with one bulb and exponential on and off times. To do so, we first introduce some notation. Suppose the system starts at time 0 in the 'on' state ($X_0 = 1$). Let the successive 'on' and 'off' times be labeled $U_1, V_1, U_2, V_2, \ldots$ Hence each U_i is exponential with parameter α and each V_i is exponential with parameter β. As with the Poisson Distribution we look for the distribution of N_t = number of burnouts in $(0, t]$. Let $W_i = U_i + V_i$ be the time of a complete 'cycle'—that is, time $i + 1$st bulb installed − time ith bulb installed where we say that the first bulb is installed at time 0. Note that $W_1, W_2, \ldots$ are independent, identically distributed with

$$\begin{aligned} E(W_i) &= E(U_i) + E(V_i) \\ &= (1/\alpha) + (1/\beta) \\ &= \frac{\alpha + \beta}{\alpha\beta}. \end{aligned}$$

Thus the Law of Large Numbers implies

$$\lim_{n \to \infty} \frac{W_1 + \ldots + W_n}{n} = \frac{\alpha + \beta}{\alpha\beta}. \tag{17}$$

To translate this to a result concerning N_t = the number of burnouts in $(0, t]$, note that the event $\{N_t = n\}$ is the event that in time t, n bulbs have failed ($U_1 + V_1 + \ldots + U_n \leq t$), but $n + 1$ have *not* ($U_1 + V_1 + \ldots + U_{n+1} > t$). That is, if the event $\{N_t = n\}$ occurs, then

$$W_1 + \ldots + W_{N_t - 1} < t < W_1 + \ldots + W_{N_t + 1}. \tag{18}$$

In other words, the time for $N_t - 1$ complete cycles ('on' to 'off' and back to 'on') must be less than t which, in turn, must be less than the time for $N_t + 1$ cycles. Dividing both sides of equation (18) by N_t and letting N_t tend to ∞ implies that the right and left sides of (18) each tend to $(\alpha + \beta)/\alpha\beta$. This is so because of equation (17) and the fact that $N_t \to \infty$ as $n \to \infty$; that is, we use (17) with N_t playing the role of n to conclude from (18) that t/N_t is squeezed between two numbers both of which tend to $(\alpha + \beta)/\alpha\beta$. The conclusion is

$$\lim_{n \to \infty} \frac{N_t}{t} = \frac{\alpha\beta}{\alpha + \beta}. \tag{19}$$

This is the Law of Large Numbers for N_t. Compared with its proof which is fairly sophisticated, it has a straightforward interpretation: The average time to complete one cycle is

$$(1/\alpha) + (1/\beta) = (\alpha + \beta)/\alpha\beta;$$

so N_t/t—the average number of cycles per time—tends to the reciprocal.

To obtain a Central Limit Theorem for N_t we reason as follows: Let $W_i = U_i + V_i$ = time for the ith cycle as before. Let $\Sigma_n = W_1 + \ldots + W_n$; now $W_1, W_2, \ldots$ are independent, identically distributed each with expectation and variance

$$\mu = E(W_i) = E(U_i) + E(V_i) = \alpha^{-1} + \beta^{-1} = \frac{\alpha + \beta}{\alpha\beta}$$

$$\sigma^2 = \text{Var}(U_i) + \text{Var}(V_i) = \alpha^{-2} + \beta^{-2}$$

by Problem 2. The Central Limit Theorem claims that

$$P\left(\frac{\Sigma_n - n\mu}{\sqrt{n}\,\sigma} \le x\right) \simeq \Phi(x) \tag{20}$$

for large n where $\Phi(x)$ is the Normal Distribution function with mean 0, variance 1. The task now is to translate (20) into an approximation involving N_t rather than Σ_n.

Since the event $\{N_t \ge n\}$ means that in $(0, t]$ there have been at least n failures, $\{N_t \ge n\}$ is equivalent to $\Sigma_{n-1} + U_n \le t$. Hence

$$\begin{aligned} P(N_t \ge n) &= P(\Sigma_{n-1} + U_n \le t) \\ &= P(\Sigma_n - V_n \le t) \\ &\sim P\left(\frac{\Sigma_n - n\mu}{\sqrt{n}\,\sigma} \le \frac{t - n\mu}{\sqrt{n}\,\sigma}\right) \\ &\sim \Phi\left(\frac{t - n\mu}{\sqrt{n}\,\sigma}\right) \end{aligned} \tag{21}$$

for large n. (The first approximation is by subtracting $n\mu$ from both sides of the inequality in the event on the second line, dividing by $\sqrt{n}$, and noting that $V_n/\sqrt{n}$ will be negligible if n is large since V_n is the *finite* nth 'fix-it' time.) We want to derive a more memorable result. Given $x \ge 0$, choose the largest integer n so that $n\mu + \sqrt{n}\,\sigma \le x$ and let $t = n\mu + \sqrt{n}\,\sigma x$. So, in particular, t is now a function of x and n. From (21)

$$\begin{aligned} P\left(\frac{N_t - t/\mu}{\sqrt{t}} \ge \frac{n - t/\mu}{\sqrt{t}}\right) &= P(N_t \ge n) \\ &\simeq \Phi\left(\frac{t - n\mu}{\sqrt{n}\,\sigma}\right) \\ &\simeq \Phi(x) \end{aligned} \tag{22}$$

for large n. But as $n \to \infty$

$$\frac{n - t/\mu}{\sqrt{t}} \to -\sigma x/\mu^{3/2}. \tag{23}$$

Problem

13. Use the definition of t in terms of n and x to show this.

Therefore

$$P\left(\frac{N_t - t/\mu}{\sqrt{t}} \geq -\frac{x\sigma}{\mu^{3/2}}\right) \simeq \Phi(x)$$

for large n. And therefore

$$P\left(\frac{N_t - t/\mu}{\sqrt{t\sigma^2/\mu^3}} < x\right) = 1 - P\left(\frac{N_t - t/\mu}{\sqrt{t\sigma^2/\mu^3}} \geq x\right) \tag{24}$$

$$\simeq 1 - \Phi(-x)$$

$$= \Phi(x).$$

For the very last equality the symmetry of the Normal Density is being used. To summarize (finally) we have that

$$\frac{N_t - t/\mu}{\sqrt{t\sigma^2/\mu^3}} \tag{25}$$

is approximately Normally distributed, mean 0, variance 1 for large t.

Problem

14. (a) Let $\alpha = 1$ and $\beta = 1$; then $\mu = 2 = \sigma^2$. Find x so that $P(\mid N_t - t/2 \mid < x) = .90$ for $t = 100, 1000, 10000$.

(b) If $\alpha = \beta$, then the 'off' time has the same distribution as the 'on' time; they are both exponential with parameter $\alpha = \beta$. This model can be considered to be the Poisson Distribution with 'on' corresponding to 'odd number bulb now operating' and 'off' corresponding to 'even number bulb now operating.' Show that with this equivalence the two Central Limit Theorems (8) and (25) for the two processes are the same.

5. The General Marquee Model

We can now generalize to the model mentioned in the introduction. A movie theatre sign consists of N light bulbs; each burns for a length of time independently of the others with an exponential distribution with parameter α (mean $1/\alpha$). The replacement policy is to replace all burned out bulbs at the moment when the nth bulb has just failed, that is, at the first instant that fewer than n bulbs are operational. Thus at each replacement $N - n + 1$ bulbs are replaced. Let c be the cost of each new bulb and let d be the additional replacement cost; each time there is a replacement the cost is $(N - n + 1)c + d$. (d might represent wages to the bulb changer.)

The state of the system X_t can be taken to be the number of lighted bulbs at time t. Then X_t can take on any of the values $n, n + 1, \ldots, N$. Only transitions from states i to $i - 1$ can occur for $i = n + 1, \ldots, N$; a transition from n to N is the only possible transition out of state n since the length of time required to replace the failed bulbs is considered negligible compared with the lifetime of the individual bulbs.

"...a transition from n to N is the only possible transition out of state n since the length of time required to replace the failed bulbs is considered negligible..."

Problems

15. Let $Z_1, Z_2, \ldots, Z_j$ be independent, each exponentially distributed with parameter α. Let $M = \min\{Z_1, \ldots, Z_j\}$ be the minimum of the j random variables. Show that

$$
\begin{aligned}
P(M > t) &= P(Z_1 > t, \ldots, Z_j > t) \\
&= P(Z_1 > t) \cdots P(Z_j > t) \\
&= e^{-j\alpha t}
\end{aligned}
$$

for positive t. Conclude that M is exponentially distributed with parameter $j\alpha$ (mean $1/j\alpha$).

Problem 15 gives a very concrete way to think about this process: If the marquee starts with N lighted bulbs, then the system cycles through the states

$$N \to N - 1 \to N - 2 \to \ldots \to n + 1 \to n \to N$$

where the 'sojourn' time in state i — the length of time that exactly i bulbs remain operational — is exponential with parameter $i\alpha$.

As in the previous section let P^t be the matrix of transition probabilities; P^t is the $(N - n + 1) \times (N - n + 1)$ matrix (there are exactly $N - n + 1$ states) whose ij^{th} entry is

$$P^t_{ij} = P(X_t = j \mid X_0 = i).$$

Note that the indices i and j here correspond with the states from n to N rather than ranging from 1 to N. And, as in the previous sections, differential equations govern the evolution of the matrix P^t as a function of t. Let s be so small that more than one transition in a time interval of length s is negligible (that is, or order $O(s^2)$). Then

$$\begin{aligned} P^{t+s}_{ij} &= P(X_{t+s} = j \mid X_0 = i) \qquad (26) \\ &= P(X_{t+s} = j \mid X_t = j+1) \cdot P(X_t = j+1 \mid X_0 = i) \\ &\quad + P(X_{t+s} = j \mid X_t = j) \cdot P(X_t = j \mid X_0 = i) \\ &\quad + O(s^2) \\ &= (j+1)\alpha s P^t_{i,\,j+1} + (1 - j\alpha s) P^t_{ij} + O(s^2) \end{aligned}$$

where $j + 1$ should be interpreted as n if $j = N$.

Problem

16. Justify these steps. Note that if s is small, to first order terms in s a transition from $j + 1$ to j occurs with probability $(j + 1)\alpha s$; this is so since the time spent in state $j + 1$ is exponential with parameter $(j + 1)\alpha s$. Hence the probability of *no* transition in time s is $e^{-(j+1)\alpha s} \sim 1 - (j + 1)\alpha s$.

As before subtract P^t_{ij} from both sides of (26), divide by s, and let s tend to 0 to obtain

$$\frac{d}{dt} P^t_{ij} = (j+1)\alpha P^t_{i,\,j+1} - j\alpha P^t_{ij} \quad . \qquad (27)$$

To write this as a *matrix* equation introduce Q as the matrix whose off-diagonal entries give the probabilities of transitions. For example, since in time s a transition from $i + 1$ to i occurs with probability $(i + 1)\alpha s + O(s^2)$, the corresponding entry of Q is set to $(i + 1)\alpha$. In fact, the *transition scheme* to first order terms in s is

$i \to i-1$	with probability	$i\alpha s$	
$i \to j$	with probability	0,	for $j \neq i-1, i$
$i \to i$	with probability	$1 - i\alpha s$	

for $i > n$. And for $i = n$

$n \to N$	with probability	$n\alpha s$	
$n \to j$	with probability	0	for $j \neq n, N$
$n \to n$	with probability	$1 - n\alpha s.$	

The matrix Q codes this information. By definition

$$Q = \begin{bmatrix} -n\alpha & 0 & 0 & 0 & n\alpha \\ (n+1)\alpha & -(n+1)\alpha & 0 & 0 & 0 \\ 0 & (n+2)\alpha & -(n+2)\alpha & 0 & 0 \\ \cdot & \cdot & \cdot & \cdot & \cdot \\ \cdot & \cdot & \cdot & \cdot & \cdot \\ 0 & 0 & 0 & N\alpha & -N\alpha \end{bmatrix} .$$

Then the system of differential equations (27) becomes

$$\frac{d}{dt} P^t = P^t \bullet Q \tag{28}$$

Problem

17. Verify this. Show that

$$\frac{d}{dt} P^t_{ij} = \sum_{k=0}^{\infty} P^t_{ik} Q_{kj}$$

agrees with the system (27).

The initial conditions for (28) are

$$P^0_{ij} = P(X_0 = j \mid X_0 = i) = 0, 1$$

for $i \neq j$, $i = j$. That is, $P^0 = I =$ identity matrix. As in Section 4 the solution is $P^t = e^{tQ}$. However, it is much more difficult to find e^{tQ} explicitly.

Let $q^0 = [q_n^0, \ldots, q_N^0]$ be an initial probability vector; $0 \le q_i^0 = P(X_0 = i) \le 1$ for each i. As in Section 4, and for the same reasons, the probability vector at time t is

$$q^t = q^0 P^t = q^0 e^{tQ} \tag{29}$$

where the components of q^t are $q_i^t = P(X_t = i)$.

Problem

18. If $n = N - 1$, we can solve the equations by interpreting this model in terms of the last section. The system is 'on' if N bulbs are operating; the system is 'off' if $N - 1$ bulbs are operating. 'On' time is exponential with parameter $N\alpha$; 'off' time is exponential with parameter $(N - 1)\alpha$. What are q^t and q of Problem 10 in this case?

Although it is difficult to solve for P^t, q^t, and $q = \lim_{t \to \infty} q^t$ directly, another method will show that q is straightforward to calculate. *Assume* that for any initial probability vector q^0,

$$q = \lim_{t \to \infty} q^0 P^t = \lim_{t \to \infty} q^t$$

exists and is independent of q^0. In such as case q is called the *stable probability vector*. Assuming this q exists, then

$$qP^s = \lim_{t \to \infty} q^0 P^t P^s = \lim_{t \to \infty} q^0 P^{t+s} = \lim_{t \to \infty} q^0 P^t = q.$$

That is, q is a (left) eigenvector of each of the transition probability matrices P^s with eigenvalue 1. Differentiating implies

$$0 = q' = \frac{d}{ds} qP^s = q \cdot \frac{d}{ds} P^s = qP^sQ = qQ$$

using (28) for the next to last equality. The result is that the stable probability vector is a probability vector q which is also a (left) eigenvector of Q with eigenvalue 0:

$$qQ = 0. \tag{30}$$

Now we apply this to the movie marquee model: the vector equation (30) together with the description of Q on page 20 implies

$$
\begin{aligned}
-nq_n \;+\; (n+1)q_{n+1} \qquad\qquad\qquad\qquad &= 0\\
-(n+1)q_{n+1} \;+\; (n+2)q_{n+2} &= 0\\
\cdots\cdots\cdots\cdots\cdots\cdots &\\
nq_n \;+\; \qquad\qquad\qquad -Nq_N &= 0
\end{aligned}
\tag{31}
$$

Problem

19. Show that the unique solution to (31) with $q_n + \ldots + q_N = 1$ and $q_i > 0$, for all i is

$$q_i = C/i, \quad \text{for } i = n, \ldots, N$$

where

$$C = \left(\frac{1}{n} + \frac{1}{n+1} + \ldots + \frac{1}{N}\right)^{-1}.$$

The logic has shown that *if* a stable probability vector exists, then q is given as above; however, there is no guarantee that such a q exists. On the other hand, it is intuitively clear that this is the case. For no matter what probability distribution the process begins with at time 0, no matter whether there are N or n bulbs operational at time 0, after enough time has elapsed all trace of the initial distribution is gone. For large times t $P(X_t = i) \sim q_i$ regardless of the initial number of defective bulbs. And a passerby can *expect* to see this number of bulbs operational

$$
\begin{aligned}
E = E(X_t) &\sim \sum_{i=n}^{N} iq_i\\
&= (N - n + 1)C
\end{aligned}
\tag{32}
$$

To gain intuition consider two special cases—the case where N is much larger than n and the case where n is small. For $N >> n$

$$
\begin{aligned}
\frac{1}{n} + \frac{1}{n+1} + \ldots + \frac{1}{N} &\simeq \int_n^{N+1} 1/x\,dx\\
&= \ln(N+1) - \ln(n)\\
&\simeq \ln(N/n)
\end{aligned}
\tag{33}
$$

where the first inequality follows since the sum on the left is an approximation to the area under the $1/x$ curve. Using $1n(N/n)$ as an approximation to C, equation (32) yields

$$E(X_t) \simeq (N - n + 1)/1n(N/n) \simeq N/1n(N/n)$$

for n much smaller than N. If n is 1 or close to 1, then a good approximation to $1n(N/n) = 1n(N) - 1n(n)$ is simply $1n(N)$. Hence for n close to 1, the approximate number of bulbs lit is $E(X_t) = N/1n(N)$.

N	$\sim N/1n(N)$
100	22
1000	145
10000	1086
100000	8686

On the other hand, suppose that $n \sim N$ so that replacement occurs when very few bulbs have burned out. We can expect to see this number of bulbs operational:

$$\begin{aligned} E(X_t) &= (N - n + 1)C \\ &= (N - n + 1)/(\frac{1}{n} + \frac{1}{n+1} + \ldots + \frac{1}{N}) \\ &\sim (N - n + 1)/((N - n + 1) \bullet (1/N)) \\ &= N \end{aligned}$$

for n close to N—which proves the obvious fact that if bulbs are replaced often, then there will always be close to N bulbs operating.

Problems

20. Let $q_i = P(X_t = i)$ be the stable probability found in Problem 19. Now q_i can be interpreted as the fraction of time that i bulbs are operational. Assume that N is large and n is close to 1 so that $C \sim 1n(N)^{-1}$. For $N = 1000$ find j so that 50 percent of the time at least j bulbs are operational; do the same for 25 percent and 75 percent. For fraction α find j_α so that at least $100 \bullet \alpha$ percent of the time j_α of the bulbs are lit. Graph j_α against α. Do the same for $N = 10000$ and $n = 100000$. It might be useful to use the approximation

$$\frac{1}{j} + \ldots + \frac{1}{N} \simeq 1n(\frac{N+1}{j})$$

for large N as was done in equation (33).

A Law of Large Numbers and a Central Limit Theorem can be obtained by methods almost identical with those used in the last section. Let $S_1, S_2, \ldots$ be the successive 'cycle' times: S_1 = time till first replacement, S_2 = time from S_1 till second replacement; S_n = time between $n - 1^{st}$ and n^{th} replacements. By the Lack of Memory property which holds for each bulb, $S_1, S_2, \ldots$ are independent. If we also assume (though this isn't necessary for the final results derived) that the process starts with N bulbs operational, then $S_1, S_2, \ldots$ are identically distributed. Actually, in any case $S_2, S_3, \ldots$ are identically distributed. Now each S_i is the sum of $N - n + 1$ independent random variables

$$S_i = T_N + T_{N-1} + \ldots + T_n$$

where T_j is the time for one among j remaining bulbs to burn out. We have already seen by Problem 15 that T_j is exponentially distributed with parameter $i\alpha$. Hence

$$\mu = E(S_i) = \frac{1}{N\alpha} + \frac{1}{(N-1)\alpha} + \ldots + \frac{1}{n\alpha}$$

$$= \frac{1}{\alpha} \bullet (\frac{1}{n} + \ldots + \frac{1}{N}) \qquad (34)$$

$$\sigma^2 = \mathrm{Var}(S_i) = \frac{1}{\alpha^2} \bullet (\frac{1}{n^2} + \ldots + \frac{1}{N^2}).$$

Then the Law of Large Numbers implies

$$\lim_{n \to \infty} (S_1 + \ldots + S_n)/n = \mu \qquad (35)$$

and the Central Limit Theorem implies

$$P(\frac{S_1 + \ldots + S_n - n}{\sqrt{n}\sigma} < x) \simeq \Phi(x) \qquad (36)$$

By the methods of the previous section if N_t denotes the number of replacements in the time interval $(0, t]$, then

$$\frac{N_t}{t} \sim \frac{1}{\mu} \tag{37}$$

$$P\left(\frac{N_t - t/\mu}{\sqrt{t\sigma^2/\mu^3}} \leq x\right) \sim \Phi(x) \tag{38}$$

to large t.

Problems

21. μ in equation (34) is the expected time between replacements. Graph μ as a function of n with N *fixed*.

22. The total cost is the time interval $(0, t]$ is

$$TC = [(N - n + 1)c + d] \cdot N_t.$$

Show that

$$\lim_{t \to \infty} \frac{TC}{t} = \frac{(N - n + 1)c + d}{\mu}.$$

Call this the *average cost per time*. For $N = 1000$ graph the average cost per time as a function of n for the two special cases: *i)* c = 0 (light bulbs are free) and *ii)* $d = 0$ (wages to the bulb changer are 0).

6. Final Note

The intention of this unit is to provide a preview to some of the methods used in Continuous Time, Discrete State Space Markov Chains. Although we have not developed the properties of these Markov Chains in general, many of the techniques used are the same as we used for our marquee model. There are many sources of information on the general theory; we list a few here which seem particularly lucid:

Bibliography

1. Breiman, Leo, *Probability with a View Toward Applications*, Houghton Mifflin, Boston, MA, 1969, Chapter 7.

2. Feller, William, *An Introduction to Probability Theory and Its Applications*, Vol. 1, John Wiley & Sons, Inc., New York, NY, 1968, Chapter XVII.

3. Hoel, Port, and Stone, *Introduction to Stochastic Processes*, Houghton Mifflin, Boston, MA, 1972, Chapter 3.

4. Parzen, Emanuel, *Stochastic Processes*, Holden-Day, Inc., San Francisco, CA, 1962, Chapter 7.

UMAP

Modules in Undergraduate Mathematics and Its Applications

Module 660

Applications of High School Mathematics in Geometrical Probability

Richard Dahlke

Robert Fakler

Published in cooperation with the Society for Industrial and Applied Mathematics, the Mathematical Association of America, the National Council of Teachers of Mathematics, and the American Mathematical Association of Two-Year Colleges.

COMAP, INC.

INTERMODULAR DESCRIPTION SHEET:	UMAP Unit 660
TITLE:	Applications of High School Mathematics in Geometrical Probability
AUTHORS:	Richard Dahlke Robert Fakler
CLASSIFICATION:	Geometry
TARGET AUDIENCE:	High School students in an algebra class or a plane geometry class
PREREQUISITES:	Algebra I, plane geometry, and the graphing of absolute value and quadratic inequalities as well as solving equations in quadratic form.

Applications of High School Mathematics in Geometrical Probability

Table of Contents

Modules and Monographs in Undergraduate Mathematics and its Applications Project (UMAP)

The goal of UMAP was to develop, through a community of users and developers, a system of instructional modules in undergraduate mathematics and its applications to be used to supplement existing courses and from which complete courses may eventually be built.

The Project was guided by a National Advisory Board of mathematicians, scientists, and educators. UMAP was funded by a grant from the National Science Foundation and is now supported by the Consortium for Mathematics and Its Applications, Inc. (COMAP), a nonprofit corporation engaged in research and development in mathematics education.

1. Introduction

1.1 What is Geometrical Probability?

Geometrical probability deals with probability on infinite sample spaces where each outcome of the experiment in question is equally likely to occur. It allows us to calculate the probability of an event occurring at random in a single trial of an experiment by identifying the sample space with a geometric region R and the event with a subregion r of R. We can then proceed to use geometry to find the desired probability.

1.2 Why is it Interesting and Profitable to Study?

Geometrical probability is replete with interesting problems that apply to all levels of high school mathematics, from elementary algebra through trigonometry (and even calculus, although we shall not consider such problems here). Solving problems in geometrical probability can require such concepts as finding the area of a trapezoid, graphing inequalities, or using the Pythagorean Theorem. A particular nice feature of geometrical probability is that its definition is very intuitive and can be presented in a short time, thus allowing you to begin working on significant problems almost immediately.

Geometrical probability can serve to develop your skills in problem solving which should be the primary focus of your mathematics study. Each applied problem requires translating the situation into a mathematical model. Making such translations lies at the very foundation of problem solving, and any additional exposure you can get to this kind of thinking will indeed be valuable.

Finally, geometrical probability is a type of probability dealing with continuous, as opposed to discrete, sample spaces and events. It is this type of probability which is the basis for the ever-so-important calculus-based probability and statistics which you may study at the college level. Your exposure now to this subject should help you better understand what may come later.

2. Geometrical Probability Model

2.1 Defining Some Basic Terms

We need to define some basic terms of probability that we shall be using. The set of all possible outcomes of an experiment is called the *sample space* of the experiment. An *event* is a subset of the sample space. With a given event in mind, we say an outcome is a *success* if it belongs to the event and a *failure* if it does not.

2.2 Modeling A Specific Type of Real World Experiment

Beginning with a real-world experiment whose outcomes occur at random, and an event, we want to find the probability of a success on a single trial of the experiment. Our first step toward this goal is to associate each outcome of the experiment with a point in geometric region. For us, a geometric region will be either a curve segment (a one-dimensional region) or a planar region (a two-dimensional region). Once we have done this, it can be seen that an outcome of the real-world experiment occurring at random corresponds to a point being chosen at random in the geometric region representing the sample space of the experiment. This mathematical experiment of choosing a random point in a geometric region is the *mathematical model* of the real-world experiment that we shall use to determine our probabilities. We shall use R to denote the geometric region that represents the sample space of our experiment. An event will then be represented by a subregion r of R. These notions are summarized in Figure 1.

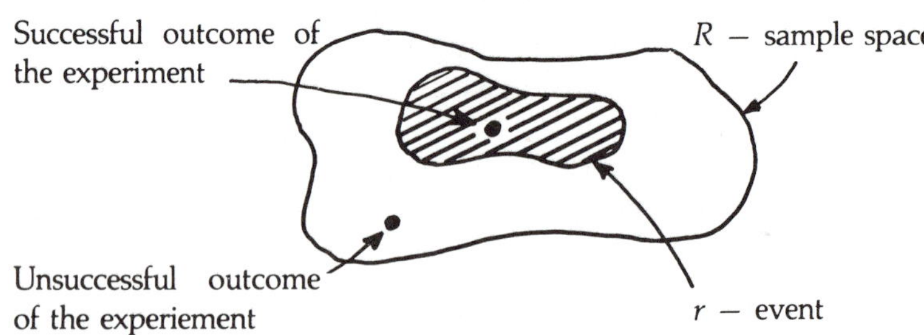

Figure 1. **Experiment:** Randomly choosing a point in R.

Successful outcome: The point belongs to r.

Unsuccessful outcome: The point does not belong to r.

EXAMPLE 1. An experiment is conducted by randomly cutting a 5-meter piece of string into two parts. Consider the event that both parts of the string will be at least 1 meter long. Identify the sample space with a line segment of length 5. The corresponding experiment is choosing a point at random from R. The region R and the subregion r representing the successful outcomes of the experiment are shown in Figure 2. (Notice that for a successful outcome the string must be cut at a point more than 1 meter from either end of the string. In other words, the randomly chosen point must belong to r,

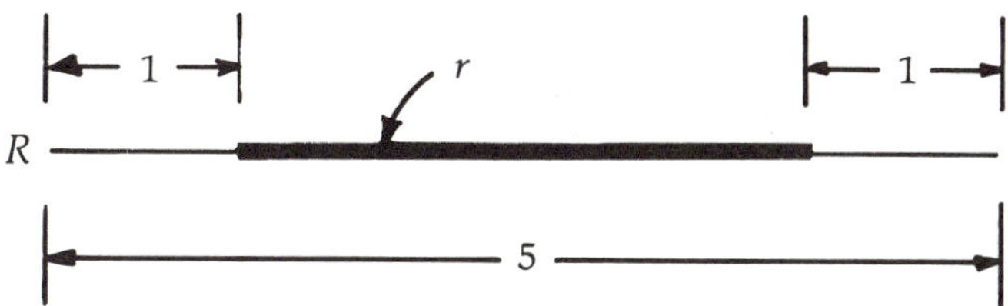

Figure 2. One-dimensional sample space R and event r.

EXAMPLE 2. A dartboard consists of a square of side 1 meter that is divided into four squares of side 1/2 meter. Consider the experiment of tossing a dart so that the dart hits inside the shaded square shown in Figure 3. This experiment corresponds to the mathematical experiment of choosing at random a point in a square region R of side 1 unit, and the event corresponds to the chosen point belonging to the shaded square. The region R and the subregion r representing a success are shown in Figure 3.

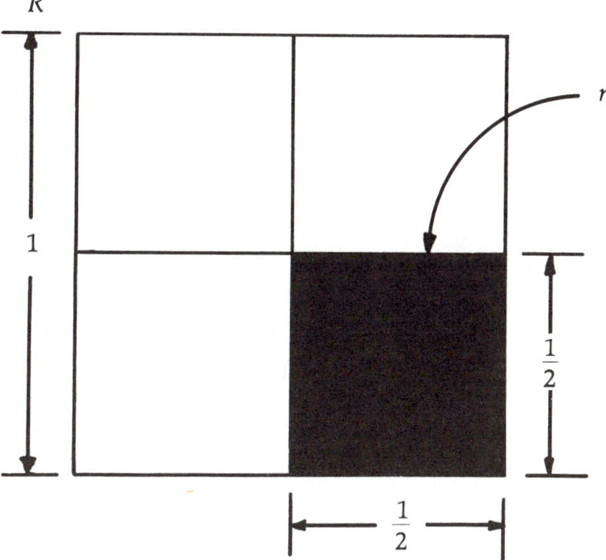

Figure 3. Two-dimensional sample space R and event r.

2.3 Defining the Geometrical Probability Model

Once a real-world experiment has been transformed into a corresponding mathematical experiment with sample space R, the probability of a given event occurring in the real-world experiment will be the probability of the corresponding event r occurring in the mathematical experiment, that is, of a randomly chosen point in R belonging to r. Looking back at Examples 1 and 2, what is the probability of the given event occurring in each? In Example 1 it seems reasonable that if a random point is chosen in R, the probability p of the point belonging to r is

$$p = \frac{\text{length of } r}{\text{length of } R} = \frac{3}{5} = 0.60 = 60\%.$$

(Since r is of length 3 and R of length 5, we would expect, in the long run, to average 3 successes out of every 5 trials or 60 successes out of every 100 trials. As this example illustrates, a probability can be expressed as a fraction, decimal or percent.)

In Example 2, following the above line of reasoning, the probability p of a point randomly chosen inside the larger square being also inside the smaller square is

$$p = \frac{\text{area of } r}{\text{area of } R} = \frac{\frac{1}{2} \cdot \frac{1}{2}}{1 \cdot 1} = \frac{\frac{1}{4}}{1} = \frac{1}{4}.$$

Thus, we will deduce that for a general mathematical experiment, that is, randomly choosing a point in a region R, the probability that the point chosen will belong to a given subregion r of R is

$$p = \frac{\text{measure of } r}{\text{measure of } R},$$

where measure means length if R is one-dimensional and area if R is two-dimensional. (What would measure mean if R were three-dimensional?)

2.4 Determining Probability Bounds

Since event r is a subregion of sample space R, we have

$$0 \leq \text{measure of } r \leq \text{measure of } R.$$

Thus, dividing the members of these inequalities by the measure of R (which is assumed to be positive) gives

$$\frac{0}{\text{measure of } R} \leq \frac{\text{measure of } r}{\text{measure of } R} \leq \frac{\text{measure of } R}{\text{measure of } R},$$

that is, $0 \leq p \leq 1$. This inequality shows that geometrical probabilities are bounded below by 0 and above by 1. Notice that for $p = 0$ the measure of r must be 0 (a point has length 0 and a curve has area 0), and for $p = 1$ the measure of r must equal the measure of R.

We now introduce another symbol for the probability of r occurring, namely, $p(r)$. This symbol is read "p of r" and indicates that the probability we have defined is a function. (What is the domain and range of the probability function $p(r)$?)

EXAMPLE 3. A sample space R and an event r are represented in Figure 4. Find the probability that a randomly chosen point in R belongs to r.

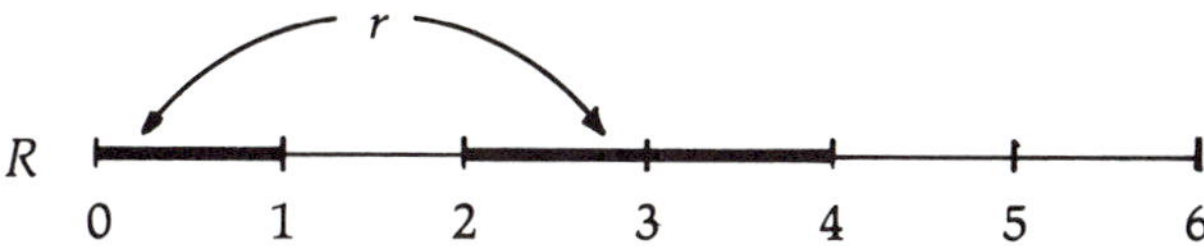

Figure 4

Solution. $$p(r) = \frac{\text{length of } r}{\text{length of } R} = \frac{1 + 2}{6} = \frac{1}{2}.$$

Example 4. A sample space R and an event r are represented in Figure 5. Find the probability that a randomly chosen point in R belongs to r.

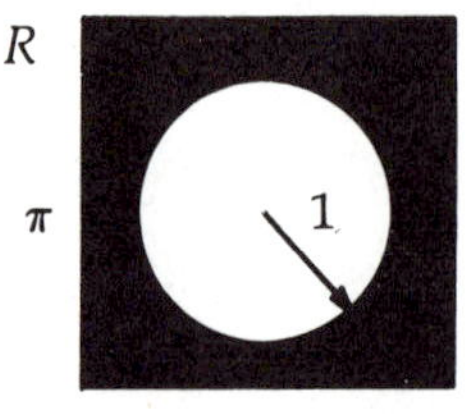

Figure 5

r = shaded region

Solution. $p(r) = \dfrac{\text{area of } r}{\text{area of } R} = \dfrac{3\pi - \pi(1)^2}{3\pi}$

$= \dfrac{2\pi}{3\pi} = \dfrac{2}{3}.$

2.5 Exercise Set I

For each exercise, a region R and one of its subregions (darkened portion) are represented. Calculate the probability that a randomly chosen point in R also belongs to r.

1. R: Square region

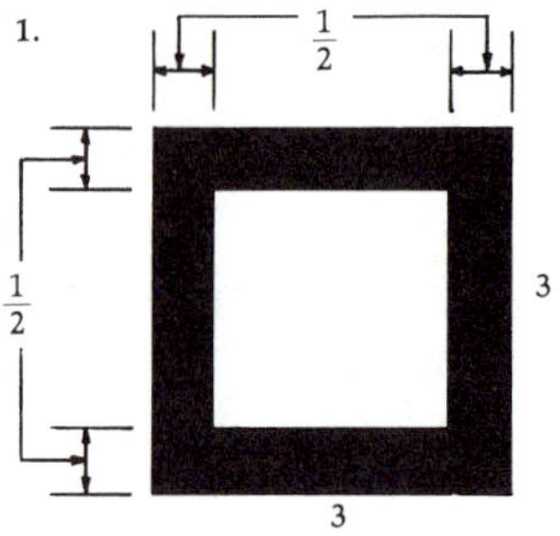

2. R: Rectangular region

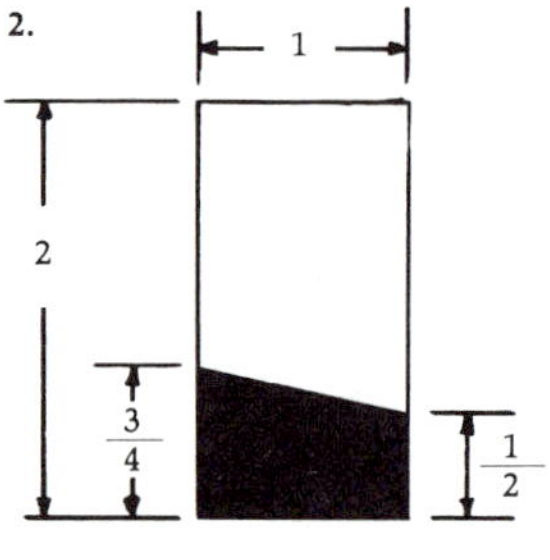

3. R: Triangular region

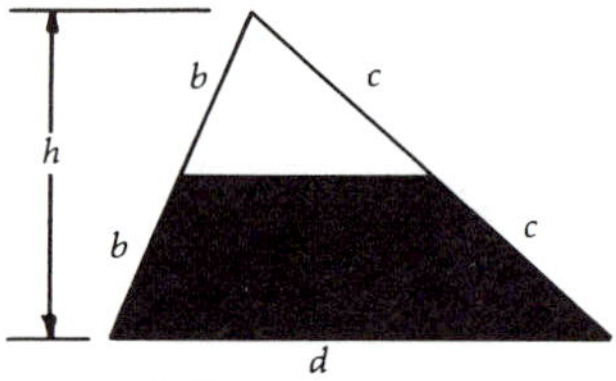

4. R: Circle

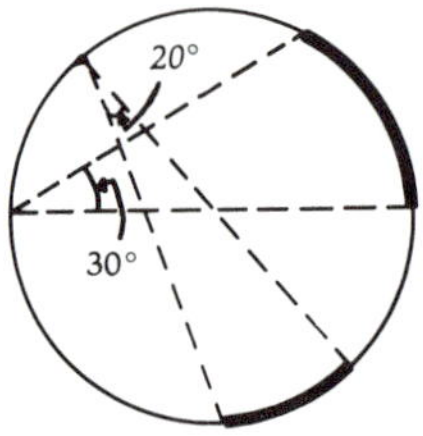

5. R: Circle

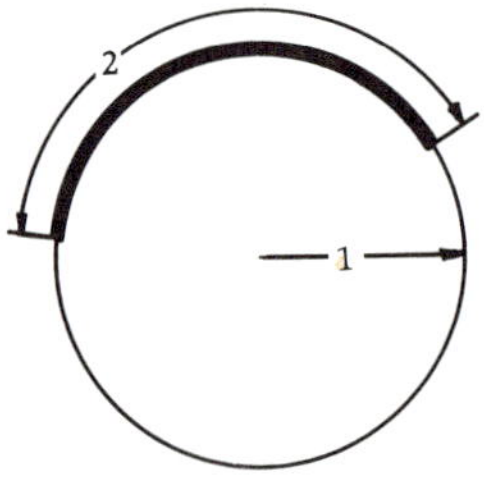

6. R: Intersecting Chords

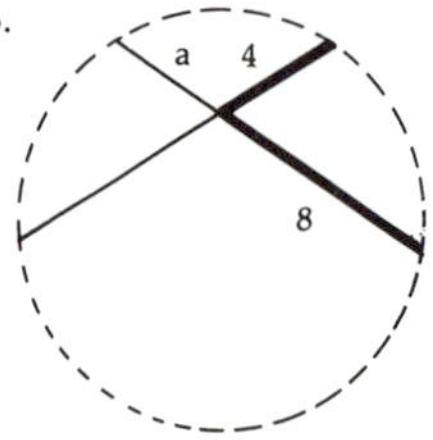

7. R: Circular region

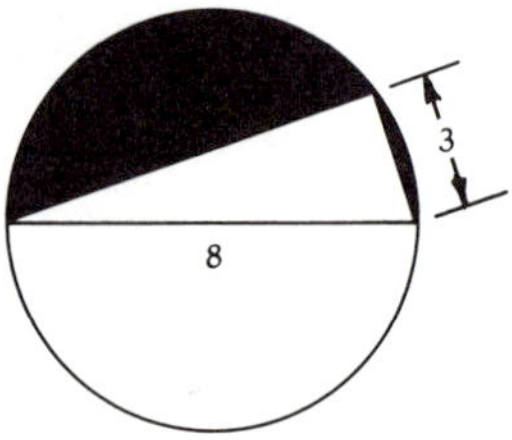

8. R: Triangle

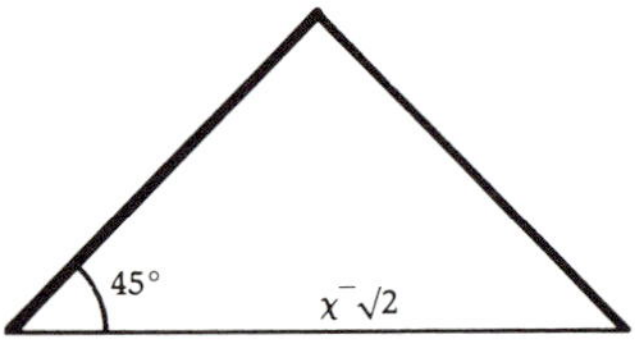

3. Applications

3.1 Beginning Applications

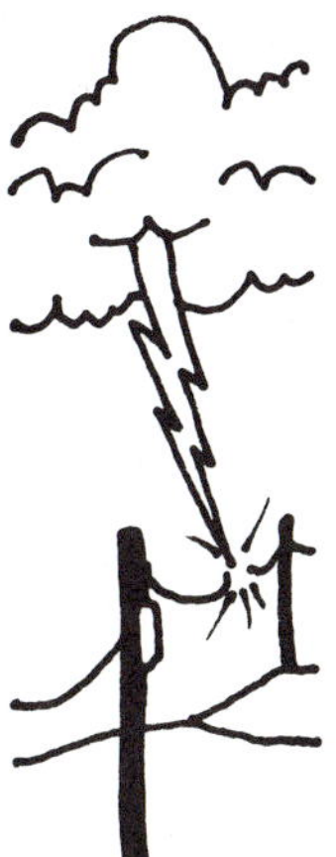

EXAMPLE 5 (TELEPHONE LINE PROBLEM). A telephone line 50 meters long is suspended between two poles, one containing a transformer. Due to a storm, a break occurs at a random point on the telephone line. Find the probability that the break is at a distance not less than 20 meters from the transformer.

Solution. Represents the telephone by a line segment R of length 50. The line segment R representing the sample space of the experiment and the success region r (those points on the line segment at a distance of not less than 20 from the end representing the pole containing the transformer) are shown in Figure 6.

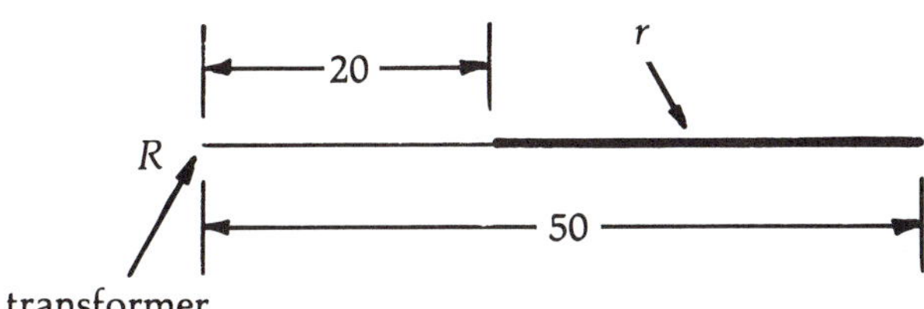

Figure 6

Thus,

$$p(r) = \frac{\text{length of } r}{\text{length of } R} = \frac{30}{50} = 0.60 = 60\%.$$

EXAMPLE 6 (PIZZA PROBLEM). Sam's Pizza Parlor has a square dart board of side 18 cm hanging on a wall near the front door. For a quarter, a customer has the opportunity to win one of three types of pizzas by making one throw of a dart at the board. The dart board contains three concentric circles with their centers being the center of the board. The prize for sticking the dart in the circular region (the bull's eye) of radius 1 cm is a large pizza; the circular region of radius 2 cm (excluding the bull's eye), a medium pizza; and the circular region of radius 3 cm (excluding the other two circular regions), a small pizza. A customer loses out entirely if the dart sticks in any other portion of the board. We shall assume that a randomly thrown dart will hit the board, that the circular arcs have no width, and that the dart does not stick in one of the arcs. What is the probability that a customer will

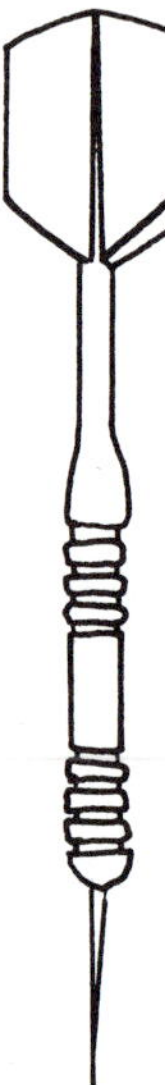

(a) win a large pizza?
(b) win a medium pizza?
(c) win a small pizza?
(d) lose out entirely?

Solution. The sample space of our experiment can be represented by a square of side 18. Figure 7 shows R and the subregions r_1, r_2, r_3, and r_4, which represent the events of winning a large, medium, or small pizza, or losing out entirely, respectively.

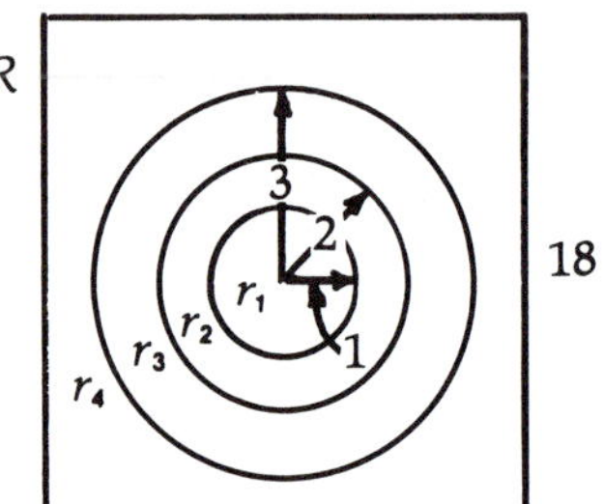

Figure 7

$$\text{(a)}\quad p(r_1) = \frac{\text{area of } r_1}{\text{area of } R} = \frac{\pi(1^2)}{18^2} = \frac{\pi}{324} = 0.01.$$

$$\text{(b)}\quad p(r_2) = \frac{\text{area of } r_2}{\text{area of } R} = \frac{\pi(2^2) - \pi(1^2)}{324} = \frac{3\pi}{324} = 0.03.$$

$$\text{(c)}\quad p(r_3) = \frac{\text{area of } r_3}{\text{area of } R} = \frac{\pi(3^2) - \pi(2^2)}{324} = \frac{5\pi}{324} = 0.05.$$

$$\text{(d)}\quad p(r_4) = \frac{\text{area of } r_4}{\text{area of } R} = \frac{324 - \pi(3^2)}{324} = 0.91.$$

EXAMPLE 7 (TAPE RECORDER PROBLEM). Joe and Moe had a half-hour conversation on their activities of the previous night. Unknown to them at the time, the conversation was being audiotaped. The FBI gained access to the tape and discovered that a 10-second interval on the tape contained information incriminating to Joe and Moe. It was later discovered that a portion of this interval was erased by an FBI agent, who said she accidentally pushed the wrong button and erased all of the tape from that moment on. What is the probability

that a portion of the incriminating conversation was accidentally erased if the 10-second interval began at a half-minute into the tape?

Solution. We represent the 30-minute tape by a line segment R of length 30. The line segment R and the segment representing the 10-second (= 1/6 minute) interval containing the incriminating evidence are shown in Figure 8. We have a success if the point at which the erasure starts is in, or to the left of, the interval containing the incriminating evidence. Thus the success region r is the segment of length $1/2 + 1/6 = 2/3$ starting at the left end of the line segment R. Thus,

$$p(r) = \frac{\text{length of } r}{\text{length of } R} = \frac{2/3}{30} = \frac{2}{90} = 0.02.$$

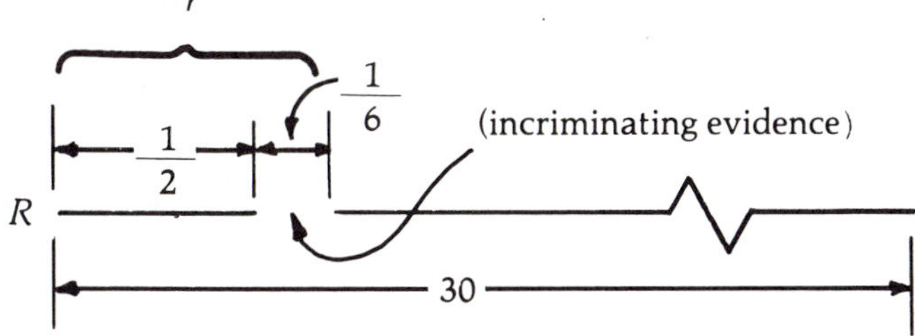

Figure 8

Example 8 (Bomber Problem). In an attempt to wipe out a munitions area, a bomber is to drop bombs inside a 1-kilometer-square field. At each corner of the field is an abandoned building. If a bomb falls within 1/3 kilometer of any building, it will be destroyed. Assuming that one bomb is randomly dropped on the field, what is the probability that (a) none of the buildings are destroyed? (b) one building is destroyed? (c) more than one building is destroyed? (d) the bomb falls exactly 1/4 kilometer from a particular building?

Solution. The contact of the bomb tip with the field will be identified with a point, and the field will be represented by a square of side 1.

(a) There is a success (none of the buildings is destroyed) if the distance from the point where the bomb lands to any vertex of the square is at least 1/3 kilometer. The square region representing the sample space of the experiment and the success region r are both shown in Figure 9. The area of the sample space is 1, whereas the area of the success

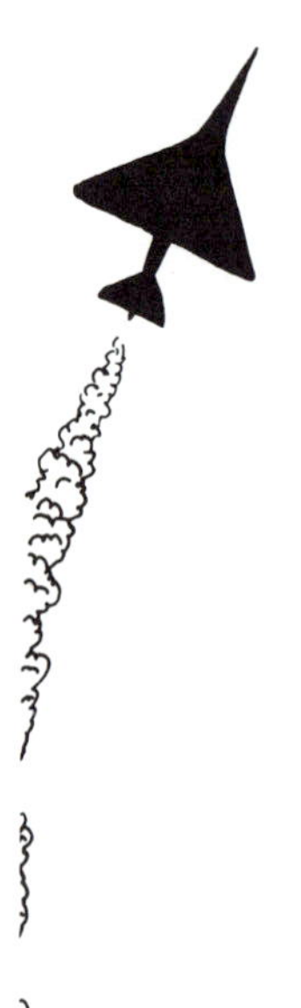

region can be obtained by subtracting the area of the failure region from 1. (The failure region is the complement of the success region. Denote the complement of r by r'.) Now, the area of $r' = \pi(1/3)^2 = \pi/9$. Thus, the area of the success region is $1 - (\pi/9)$ and

$$p(r) = p(\text{not destroying a building})$$

$$= \frac{\text{area of } r}{\text{area of } R} = \frac{1 - (\pi/9)}{1} = 1 - (\pi/9) = 0.65.$$

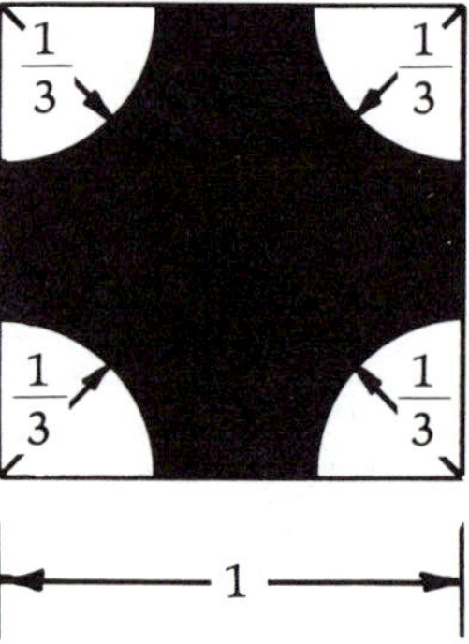

Figure 9

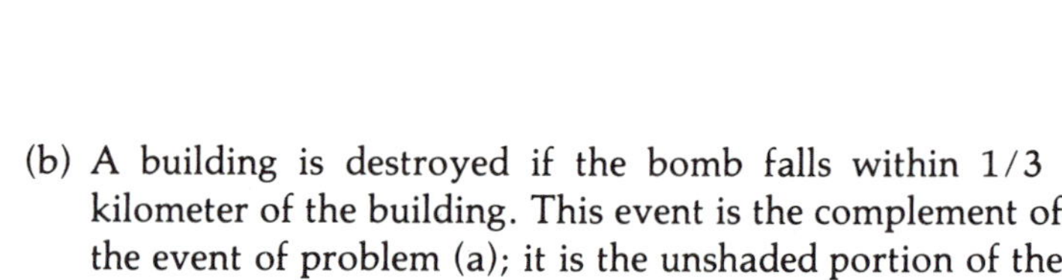

(b) A building is destroyed if the bomb falls within 1/3 kilometer of the building. This event is the complement of the event of problem (a); it is the unshaded portion of the diagram in Figure 9. Thus,

$$p(r') = \frac{\text{area of } r'}{\text{area of } R} = \frac{\pi/9}{1} = \pi/9 = 0.35.$$

(c) There is no point of the sample space that is within 1/3 kilometer of at least two buildings. Hence, the event that more than one building is destroyed is an impossible event. The region identified with the event is ϕ, the empty region, and its area is defined to be 0. Thus,

$$p(\phi) = \frac{\text{area of } \phi}{\text{area of } R} = \frac{0}{1} = 0.$$

(d) The success event is a quarter arc of a circle (see Figure 10). The area of the arc is 0; thus, the probability is 0. Symbolically,

$$p(r) = p(\text{bomb falls exactly } 1/4 \text{ mile from building})$$

$$= \frac{\text{area of } r}{\text{area of } R}$$

$$= \frac{0}{1} = 0.$$

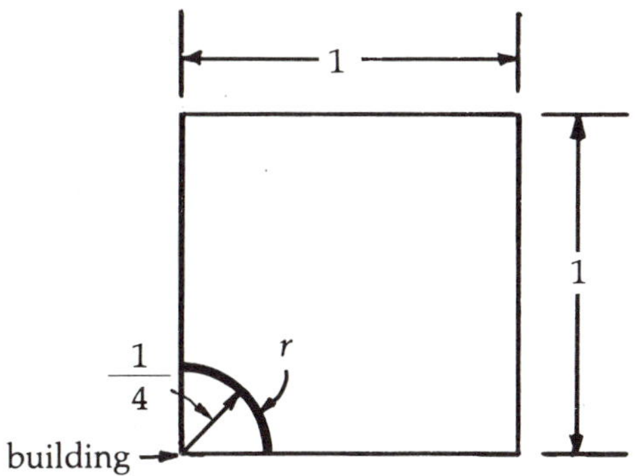

Figure 10

3.2 Exercise Set II

9. Consider Example 5 *(Telephone Line Problem).*

   (a) What is the probability if 20 is replaced by 40? by 49? by 50?

   (b) Find the probability if X is substituted for 50 and x for 20.

   (c) By viewing the sample space and successful outcomes, determine what is happening to the probability as x approaches X in value.

   (d) By viewing the formula obtained in (**b**), determine what is happening to the probability as x approaches X in value. Does this agree with your answer in (**c**)?

   (e) Graph the probability formula obtained in (**b**), where p (the probability) is the dependent variable, x is the independent variable, and X is 15. From the graph, analyze the vehavior of p as x varies over its domain.

10. For Example 6 *(Pizza Problem)*, what would the radius of the largest of the three circles have to be so that the probability of losing out entirely is 0.215?

11. For Example 7 *(Tape Recorder Problem)*, where would you relocate the 10-second interval on the tape so that (**a**) the probability is 0.75; (**b**) you get the largest possible probability (What is this probability?); (**c**) you get the smallest possible probability (What is this probability?).

12. For Example 8 *(Bomber Problem)*, suppose that a building is destroyed if the bomb falls within $1/\sqrt{3}$ km of a building. Find the probability that a randomly dropped bomb will destroy:

(**a**) none of the buildings. (The challenge in this problem is to find the area of the success region. The failure region consists of four regions of equal area. Each of these regions can be divided into a pair of triangular regions and a sector of a circle (see Figure 11). You have enough information to find the area of these regions.)

(**b**) exactly two buildings.

(**c**) exactly one building.

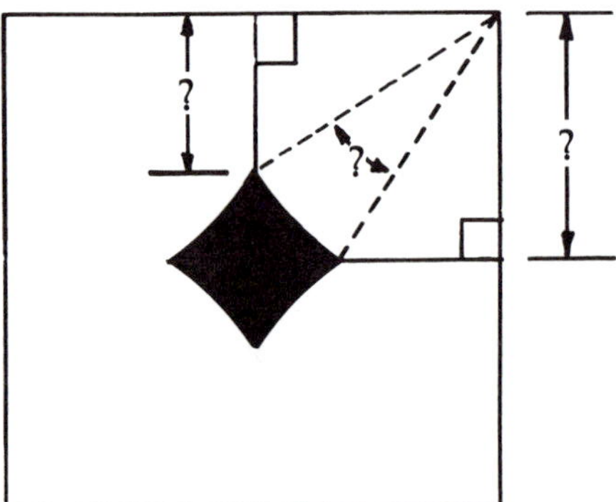

Figure 11

13. For Example 8 *(Bomber Problem)*, suppose that a building is destroyed if the bomb falls within x km of a building. What should x be to be certain that (**a**) at least one building is destroyed? (**b**) at least two buildings are destroyed? (**c**) at least three buildings are destroyed? (**d**) all four buildings are destroyed?

14. For Example 8 *(Bomber Problem)*, suppose that the field has the shape of an equilateral triangle of side s and that there are three buildings, one at each corner. What is the probability that a bomb randomly dropped on the field will destroy one building if the bomb's destroying radius is $s/3$?

15. It is known that an airplane crashed during a storm at some time between 12:00 noon and 12:30 P.M. Find the probability that, within the half-hour interval, the time before the crash *and* the time after the crash were both less than (**a**) 20 minutes, (**b**) 15 minutes, (**c**) 10 minutes, (**d**) 25 minutes, (**e**) 30 minutes. (Hint: Draw the sample space and the set of successful outcomes — the success event — for each part. Notice that each success event is the intersection of two events.)

16. Television station WGPR interrupts its programming to announce a tornado warning the instant it hears about a tornado being sighted. Assume that a tornado warning is announced during the broadcast of a football game. What is the probability that, at the time of the announcement, the portion of the game already played or the portion to be played is at least two times as great as the other portion of the game if there is (**a**) no half-time intermission, (**b**) a half-time intermission equal in time to one of the quarters?

3.3 Further Applications

It is now time to look at some real-world problems that require a bit more ingenuity in relating the real-world outcome of an experiment to its mathematical counterpart — that of randomly choosing a point in a region. One such problem is a game of chance that you may have played at a carnival and may have wondered about your chances of winning.

Example 9 (County Fair Problem). At a county fair a game is played by tossing a coin onto a large table ruled into congruent squares. If the coin lands entirely within some square, the player wins a prize. What is the probability that a random toss of the coin will result in a win if (a) the coin's diameter is 2 centimeters and the squares have sides of 5 centimeters? (b) the coin's diameter is a and the squares are of side b, where $a < b$? (It will be assumed that the markings on the table have no thickness.)

Solution. If possible, translate this problem into one of randomly picking a point from a region. That is, to use geometrical probability the experiment must be equivalent to randomly choosing a point in a region. This is accomplished by focusing our attention on where the coin's *center* lies on the table. Thus, *each outcome of the experiment will be the position of the coin's center on or within whatever square it falls.* Such a square is shown in Figure 12. Since this square and its interior is the sample space, it is isolated in Figure 13.

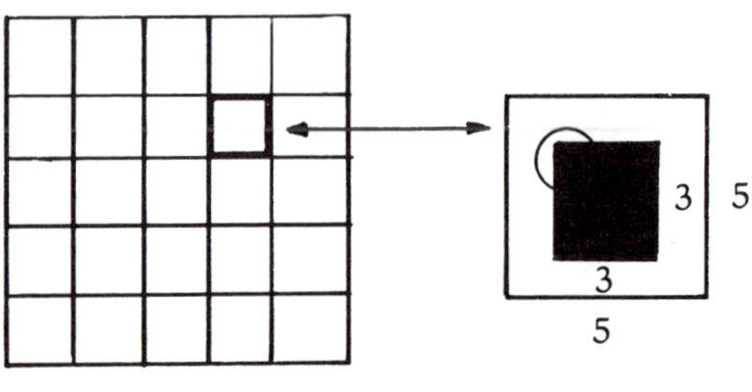

Figure 12 Figure 13

(a) A subregion containing the successful outcomes must be found. To have a success (that is, the coin is interior to the square), the center of the coin must lie at least the radius length (that is, 1 centimeter) from the boundary of the square region. The success region is the square region in Figure 13 of side $5 - (1 + 1) = 3$. Therefore,

$$p = \frac{3^2}{5^2} = \frac{9}{25} .$$

(b) For a success, the center of the coin must lie at least $a/2$ units (the radius length) from the boundary of the square. The success region is the square region in Figure 14 of side $b - (a/2 + a/2) = b - a$. Therefore,

$$p = \frac{(b - a)^2}{b^2} .$$

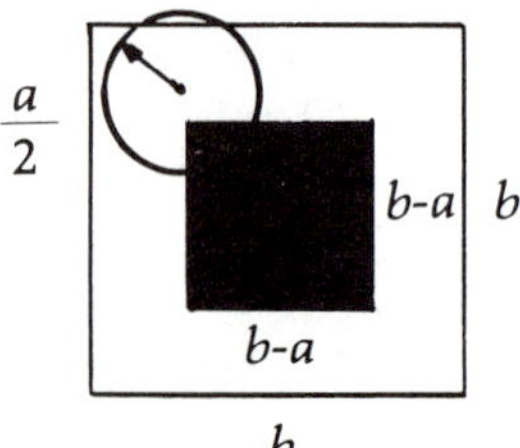

Figure 14

Example 10 (Storm Sewer Problem). A child walking over a storm sewer grating in a street accidentally drops a ball she is carrying onto the grating. Suppose the ball has radius a inches and is randomly dropped into the grating composed of steel bars of width c inches crossing one another at right angles so as to leave square openings of side b inches ($a < b$). Find the probability that the ball will go through the grating (without hitting the grating). (Hint: View the grating as being composed of openings with borders of width c on the bottom and right-hand sides.)

Solution. We shall view each outcome of the experiment as the position of the center of the ball as it arrives at the grating. We can and will focus our attention on an arbitrary opening, together with the bars on the bottom and right-hand sides. (Note: Any dropping of the ball will result in the ball going through a particular opening or hitting bars on the bottom and right-hand sides of the opening, thus not going through.) For a success to occur, the center of the ball must lie at least the length of its radius, $a/2$ units, from any bar. The sample space R can be represented by the square of side $b + c$ as shown in Figure 15 and the success region r is the square region of side $b - a$, as shown in Figure 15. The area of the success region is $(b - a)^2$, and the area of the large square representing the entire sample space is $(b + c)^2$. Therefore,

$$p(r) = \frac{(b - a)^2}{(b + c)^2}.$$

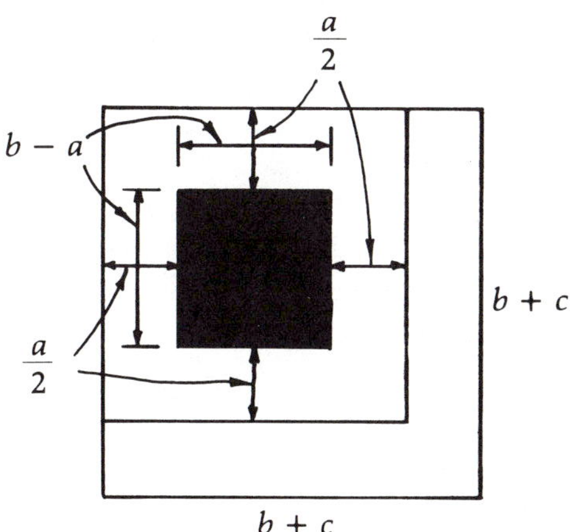

Figure 15

3.4 Exercise Set III

17. These exercises are based on Example 9 *(County Fair Problem).*

    (a) Discuss, by viewing Figure 14, how the probability varies as the coin's diameter approaches in length the side of a square. Also, discuss how the probability varies as the coin's diameter approaches 0. Then, support your answers by analyzing the formula $p = (b - a)^2/b^2$ as a approaches b and as a approaches 0.

    (b) Graph the formula in (a) where b is 4, a is the independent variable, and p is the dependent variable. (Note: $0 < a < 4$.)

    (c) If $b = 1/2$ cm, what size coin should a customer throw so that the probability of winning a prize is 0.36?

    (d) If $a = 1/4$ cm, what should a side of a square be so that the probability of a failure is 0.19?

    (e) What is the probability of winning a prize if the table is ruled into r by s rectangles, and the coin has diameter t, where $t < r$ and $t < s$?

    (f) Use the probability formula obtained in (e) to determine the diameter of a coin that will give a probability of 0.5 if a rectangle has dimensions 1 inch by 2 inches.

    (g) What is the probability of winning a prize if the table is ruled into equilateral triangles of side s and the coin's diameter is a, where $0 < a < s\sqrt{3}/3$?

18. (a) Use Figure 16 as a hint for finding another method for calculating the probability formula $p = (b-a)^2/(b+c)^2$ associated with Example 10 *(Storm Sewer Problem).*

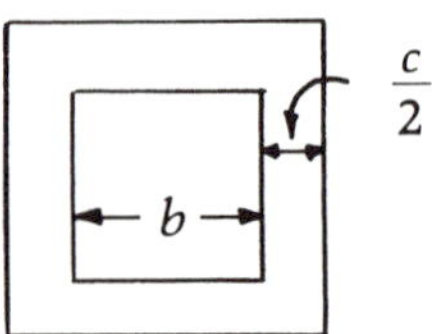

Figure 16

(b) Let $c = 0$ in the formula $p = (b-a)^2/(b+c)^2$.

Compare the formula you just derived with the formula determined in Example 9 *(County Fair Problem)*. Argue that the solution to the *Storm Sewer Problem* would be the same as the solution to the *County Fair Problem* if the latter problem did not ignore the condition that the markings on the table have non-zero width.

(c) For the *Storm Sewer Problem*, determine the relationship that exists between the diameter of the ball and the side of the storm sewer grating, if the width of the bars is the same as the diameter of the ball, and the probability that the ball will go through the grating is 1/2.

(d) Solve the *Storm Sewer Problem* if the holes through which the ball may fall are equilateral triangles of sides s, c is the width of the bars, and a is the diameter of the ball, where $0 < a < s\sqrt{3}/3$.

19. A disk of diameter a is thrown onto a table ruled with parallel lines a distance b apart, where $a < b$. Find the probability that the disk crosses a line.

20. *Turkey-Shoot Problem*. A village has an annual turkey-shoot. A circular target 1 inch in diameter is attached to a wall. Each contestant pays a quarter a shot and wins a turkey if the bullet is completely within the target. A contestant randomly fires at the target and makes a bullet hole 1/4 inch in diameter in the wall. If her shot hits the target, what is the probability that she will win a turkey?

3.5 Applications Using Coordinate Systems

For the following examples a coordinate system (one- or two-dimensional) is used to construct a representation of the sample space and the success event.

EXAMPLE 11 (TRIANGLE PROBLEM).

A line segment $\overline{AB}$, with midpoint M, has length a. A point X is randomly chosen interior to the segment. What is the probability that $\overline{AX}$, $\overline{BX}$, and $\overline{AM}$ can be the sides of a triangle?

Solution. Coordinatize segment $\overline{AB}$, where A is labeled with 0, B with a, and X with x. Thus, M has coordinate $a/2$ (see Figure 17). The sample space consists of all points with coordinate x, where $\overline{AX}$, $\overline{BX}$, and $\overline{AM}$ can be the sides of a triangle. What is a necessary and sufficient condition for these segments to be the sides of a triangle? The answer lies in a plane geometry result, namely, the sum of the lengths of any two sides must be greater than the length of the third side. Since the length of $\overline{AX} = x$, the length of $\overline{BX} = a - x$, and the length of $\overline{AM} = a/2$,

Figure 17. Coordinate model with labels

$$x + (a - x) > \frac{a}{2}$$

$$x + \frac{a}{2} > a - x$$

$$(a - x) + \frac{a}{2} > x \quad .$$

(See Figure 18.) This system of linear inequalities is equivalent to the system

$$a > \frac{a}{2} \qquad \text{(which is always true)}$$

$$x > \frac{a}{4}$$

$$x > \frac{3a}{4}$$

Writing this another way, a success occurs if the point selected has coordinate x, where $a/4 < X < 3a/4$. The sample space R and success region r are shown in Figure 19. We get

$$p = \frac{\frac{3a}{4} - \frac{a}{4}}{a} = \frac{\frac{a}{2}}{a} = \frac{1}{2} .$$

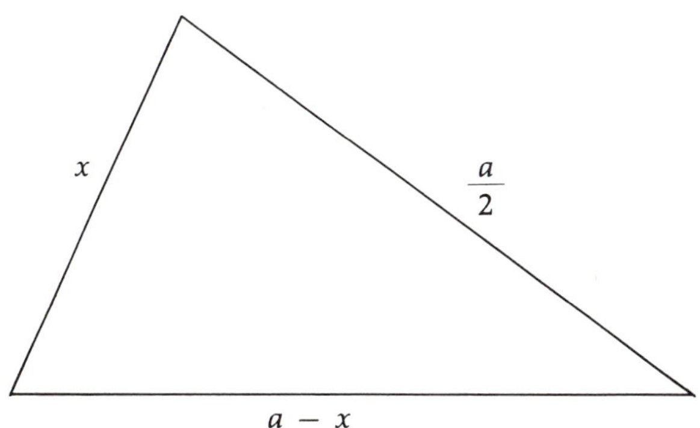

Figure 18. Lengths of the sides of the triangle

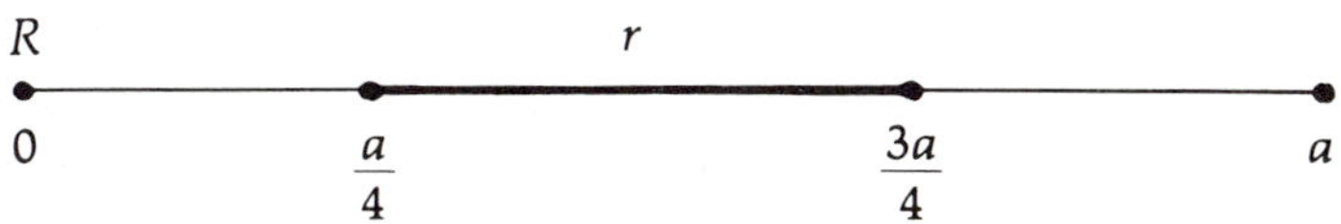

Figure 19

EXAMPLE 12 (CB RADIO PROBLEM). Two CB (Citizen Band) radio operators, Tiger Lily and Huge Huey, work for Carl's Trucking. The range of their CB radios is 25 km. Tiger Lily is traveling toward the base from the east and at 3:00 P.M. is somewhere within 30 km of the base. Huge Huey is traveling toward the base from the north and at 3:00 P.M. is somewhere within 40 km of the base. What is the probability that they can communicate with each other at 3:00 P.M.?

Solution. Let x and y represent the distances that Tiger Lily and Huge Huey are from the truck base, respectively. Hence $0 \leq x \leq 30$ and $0 \leq y \leq 40$. Now, the set of all pairs of distances can be represented by the set of ordered pairs (x,y), with the given restrictions on x and y. The graph of this set of ordered pairs is our sample space. Each point of the graph represents a particular combination of positions for Tiger Lily and Huge Huey. They can communicate over their radios if the distance between them is not more than 25 km (see Figure 20). Thus, the points of the sample space that constitute a success are represented by the ordered pairs satisfying the inequality $\sqrt{x^2 + y^2} < 25$, which is equivalent to $x^2 + y^2 < 625$. The region representing the sample space and the shaded success region are shown by Figure 21. The area of the region representing the sample space is 1200 km², and the area of the success region is $(1/4)\ \pi(25)^2 = 625\ \pi/4$. Thus,

$$p = \frac{\frac{625\pi}{4}}{1200} = \frac{625\pi}{4800} = 0.41.$$

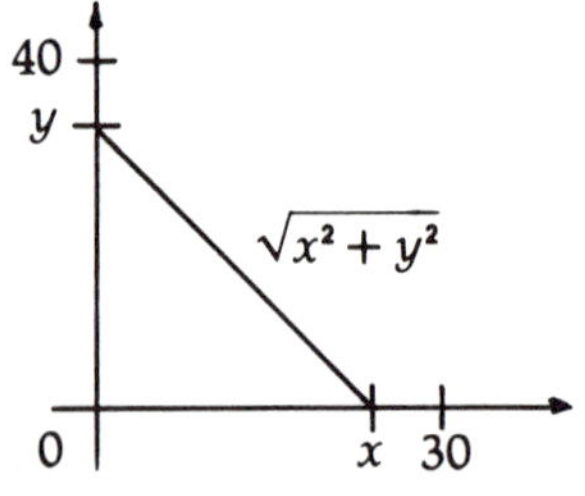

Figure 20

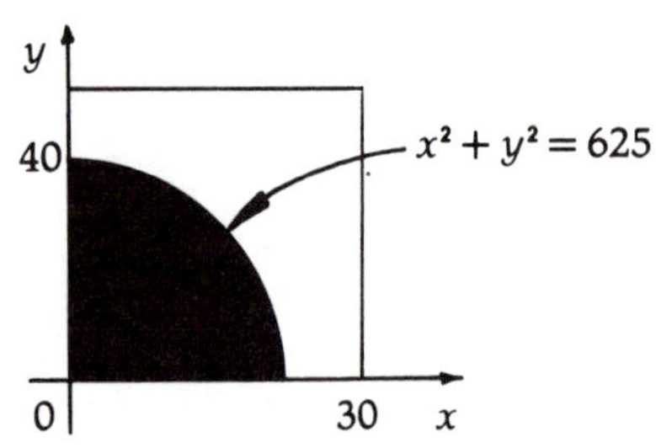

Figure 21

EXAMPLE 13 (HUSBAND-WIFE ENCOUNTER PROBLEM). A husband and wife on a shopping expedition agree to meet at a specified street corner between 4:00 and 5:00 P.M. The one who arrives first agrees to wait 15 minutes for the other, after which that person will leave to continue shopping. What is the probability that the couple will meet, assuming that their arrival times are random within the hour?

Solution. Let x and y be the number of minutes after 4:00 P.M. that the husband and wife arrive, respectively. All the possible pairs of arrival times can be represented by the set of ordered pairs (x,y) where $0 < x < 60$, and $0 < y < 60$. The members of the sample space are the points inside a square of side 60 (see Figure 22). In order for the couple to meet, their arrival times must be within 15 minutes of each other. This observation is symbolized by the absolute value inequality $|x - y| < 15$. (If the wife, for example, should arrive 14 minutes after the husband, they will meet. To see this, we notice that $x - y = -14$, which gives $|x - y| = 14$; thus the inequality is satisfied.) The graph of $|x - y| < 15$, within the confines of the sample space, constitutes the success region. The shaded success region r and sample space R are shown in Figure 22. Therefore,

$$p(r) = \frac{60^2 - \frac{45^2}{2} - \frac{45^2}{2}}{60^2}$$

$$= \frac{3600 - 2025}{3600}$$

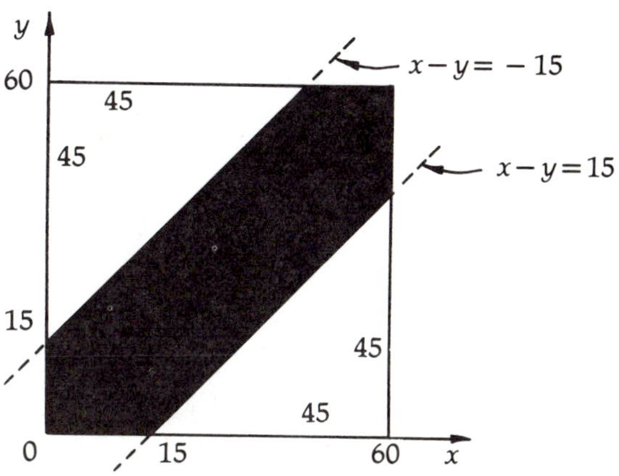

Figure 22

Example 14 (Swimmer Problem). A swimmer starts from the beach in a fog and swims 500 yards in a straight line in a random direction. She then stops swimming and turns around several times but is unable to see land, after which she sets off in a random direction. Assuming the coastline is straight and there is no tidal movement, what is the probability that she will reach the beach before going another 500 yards?

Solution. The final position of the swimmer is determined by choosing angles ϕ and θ such that $0 < \phi < \pi$ and $0 < \theta < 2\pi$, as shown in Figure 23.

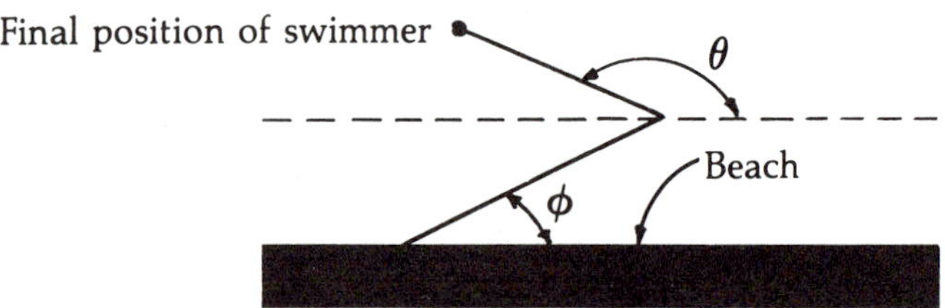

Figure 23. Direction angles of swimmer

We see from Figure 24 that the swimmer will reach the beach if

$$0 < \phi < \pi/2 \text{ and } \pi + \phi < \theta < 2\pi - \phi\,,$$

or, from Figure 25, if

$$\pi/2 < \phi < \pi \text{ and } 2\pi - \phi < \theta < \pi + \phi.$$

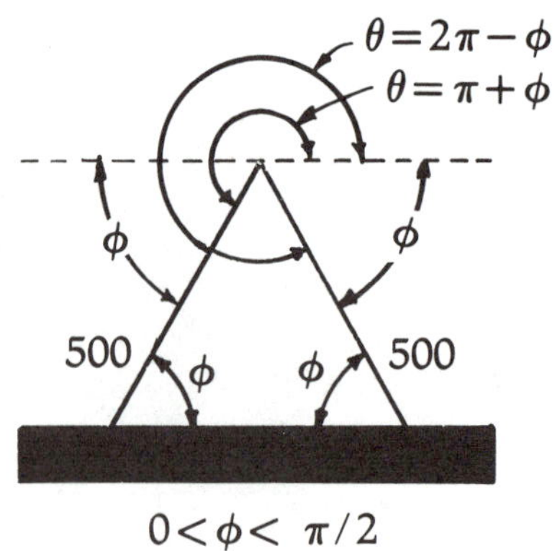

Figure 24. Swimmer's path if initial direction angle is acute

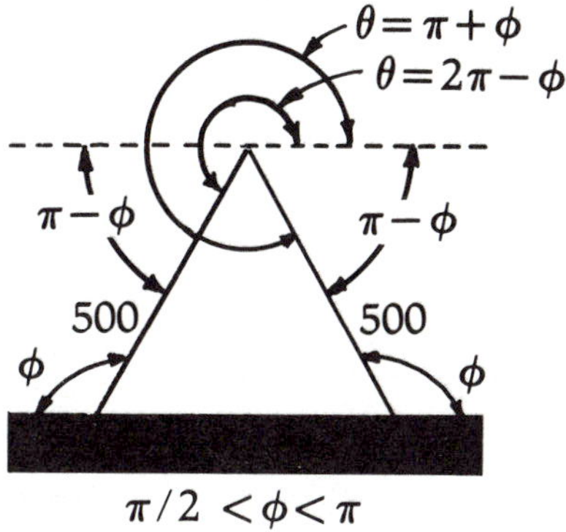

Figure 25. Swimmer's path if initial direction angle is obtuse

The sample space R of the experiment can be represented by the rectangular region

$$\{(\phi,\theta) \mid 0 < \phi < \pi,\ 0 < \theta < 2\pi\}.$$

This region and the shaded success region r are shown in Figure 26. The area of the rectangular region representing the entire sample space is $(2\pi)(\pi) = 2\pi^2$, and the area of the success region is $\pi^2/2$. We get

$$p(r) = \frac{\pi^2/2}{2\pi^2}$$

$$= \frac{1}{4} = 0.25$$

$$= 25\%.$$

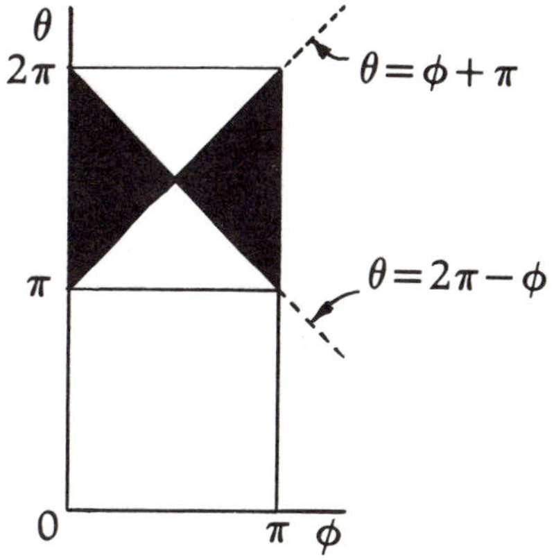

Figure 26

3.6 Exercise Set IV

21. A line segment $\overline{AB}$ of length has a fixed point C belonging to its interior.

(**a**) If a point X is randomly chosen interior to $\overline{AB}$, what is the probability that $\overline{AX}$, $\overline{XB}$, and $\overline{AC}$ can form a triangle? An equilateral triangle? (Hint: Let b (a constant) and x be the coordinates of C and X, respectively.)

(**b**) Use the probability you obtained as the answer to (**a**) to verify the answer obtained in Example 11 *(Triangle Problem)* where C is the midpoint of $\overline{AB}$.

22. A point X is chosen at random from the interior of a line segment of length 1 cm.

(**a**) What is the probability that the product of the lengths of the two segments formed is less that 3/16? Less than 1/4? Less that 1/8? Greater than 1/16?

(**b**) In (**a**), replace 3/16 by k. What value of k will give a probability of 1/10? (Hint: Use the quadratic formula to find the roots of the related quadratic equality in terms of k, and realize that the roots are boundary points of the success event.)

23. A line segment of length 8 is divided into three parts by randomly choosing two points of the segment. Find the probability that the three line segments formed are the sides of some triangle. Does the probability change if the line segment is of a different length?

24. Two points are randomly selected on a line segment of length 10 so as to be on opposite sides of the midpoint of the segment. Find the probability that the three segments (from one endpoint to the first selected point, from the first selected point to the second selected point, and from the second selected point to the other endpoint) form the sides of a triangle.

25. For Example 13 *(Husband-Wife Encounter Problem)*, find the probability that the husband's arrival time is closer to his wife's arrival time than it is to 4:00 P.M. Is this probability changed if 4:00 P.M. is replaced by 5:00 P.M.?

26. A bus line A arrives at a station every four minutes and a bus of line B every six minutes. A potential passenger of line A just arrived at the station and is hoping that the next bus back to the station is from line A. What is the probability that the next bus arriving is from line A? That a bus of any line arrives within two minutes? (Hint: Let x and y be the number of minutes the passenger has to wait for a bus of line A and a bus of line B, respectively.)

27. José and Juanita Juarez have a joint checking account in the amount of $200. One day, unknown to each other, they each write checks on this account for random amounts not to exceed $200. Find the probability that

    (**a**) more than $50 remains in the account.

    (**b**) their account is overdrawn.

    (**c**) their account is not overdrawn by more than $200.

28. A swimmer starts from the beach at an angle of 75° and swims for 40 meters. She then swims off in a random direction. What is the probability that she will reach shore before swimming 40 more meters?

29. Two rival automobile manufacturers agree to have a public competition in which each of them will try to prove that its own compact car (Car A or Car B) gets the better gas mileage. The winning car is to be the one going farther on 5 gallons of gas. Due to an error in filling the cars, each car has less than 5 gallons in its tank. If each of the cars is short a random amount (up to one gallon), what is the probability that Car A wins if Car A gets 25 miles per gallon and Car B gets 30 miles per gallon?

30. For the equation $ax + b = 0$, the coefficient a is chosen at random between 1 and 2 and the coefficient b at random between -1 and 1. What is the probability that the solution of the equation will be greater than 0.25?

31. A state police officer patrols Highway 8 from the state police post to a town located due east. Another state police officer patrols Highway 8 from the post to a town located due west. The post is located midway between the towns and the distance between the towns is 80 km. Assuming that the two patrol cars can be anywhere on their patrol beat at any given instant, find the probability that they are at least 20 km apart.

32. A businessman is expecting two telephone calls. Brown is equally likely to call anytime between 2:00 P.M. and 4:00 P.M., and Jones is equally likely to call anytime between 2:30 P.M. and 3:15 P.M. What is the probability that

(**a**) Brown calls before Jones?

(**b**) the calls are less than 10 minutes apart?

(**c**) Brown calls first, the calls are less than 10 minutes apart, and both are received before 3:00 P.M.

33. *Intersecting Curves Problem.* Suppose we choose u at random from $[0,2]$ and v at random from $[1,2]$. Find the probability that the circle $x^2 + y^2 = u^2$ intersects the hyperbola $xy = v^2$ (see Figure 27). (Hint: Obtain an inequality in u and v by simultaneously solving the equations for x and then analyzing the discriminant.)

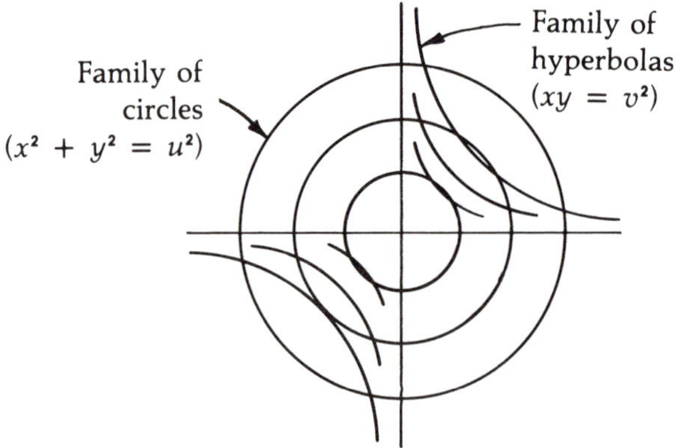

Figure 27

4. Simulating Experiments

It would be beneficial for you to simulate, by means of a real-world or computer model, some of the experiments defined by the examples and exercises. The following sections show two examples of how this might be done.

4.1 Real-World Simulation

A *real-world simulation* of the experiment defined by Example 9 *(County Fair Problem)* is an example of an experiment performed on a real-world model of the experiment. What you can do here is take a large piece of cardboard and rule it into congruent squares. Then toss a coin (whose diameter is less than the side of a square) many times onto this surface and record the number of times you toss and the number of successes obtained. An *experimental probability* is determined by dividing the number of successes by the number of *trials* (i.e., by the number of tosses).

4.2 Computer Simulation

A *computer simulation* of the experiment defined by Example 13 *(Husband-Wife Encounter Problem)* is an example of an experiment performed on a mathematical model of the experiment. What you do here is write a computer program instructing the computer to select randomly two values between 0 and 60, one representing the number of minutes after 3 P.M. that the husband arrives and the other representing the same information for the wife. Then instruct the computer to find the absolute value of the difference of these two values and determine if it is less than 15 (thus constituting a success). Finally, have the computer divide the number of successes by the number of times it performed the experiment. This answer is an experimental probability via a computer simulation.

You are encouraged to compare and combine your simulation results with those determined by other students. Also, compare your simulation results with your mathematical results (i.e., with the geometrical probabilities you calculated when working through this module). A discussion with your classmates or instructor on which type of probability (experimental or mathematical) you place more faith in may be lively.

5. Answers to Exercises

1. 5/9.

2. 5/16.

3. 3/4.

4. 5/18.

5. $1/\pi$.

6. $4/(a + 4)$.

7. $(16\pi - 3\sqrt{55})/32\pi$.

8. $2/(2 + \sqrt{2})$.

9. (a) 1/5, 1/50, 0.

   (b) $\dfrac{X - x}{X}$.

   (c) It is approaching 0.

   (d) It is approaching 0, yes.

   (e) $p = \dfrac{15 - x}{15}$, $x \in [\,0,15\,]$.

We see from the graph that, as x varies from 0 to 15, p varies linearly from 1 to 0.

10. 9 cm.

11. (a) Have it begin 22.33 minutes into the tape.

    (b) the last 10 seconds of the tape, 1.

    (c) the first 10 seconds of the tape, 0.006.

12. (**a**) $1 - (1/\sqrt{3}) - (\pi/9) = 0.07$.

(**b**) $(2\pi/9) - 1/\sqrt{3} = 0.12$.

(**c**) $2/\sqrt{3} - \pi/9 = 0.81$.

13. (**a**) $\geq 1/\sqrt{2} = 0.71$.

(**b**) ≥ 1.00.

(**c**) $\geq \sqrt{5}/2 = 1.12$.

(**d**) $\geq \sqrt{2} = 1.41$.

14. $2\pi/(9\sqrt{3}) = 0.40$.

15. (**a**) 1/3.

(**b**) 0.

(**c**) 0.

(**d**) 2/3.

(**e**) 1.

16. (**a**) 2/3.

(**b**) 8/15.

17. (**a**) As a approaches b (i.e., the coin's diameter approaches in length a side of the square), we see that $(b - a)^2$ approaches 0; as a approaches 0 (i.e., the coin's diameter approaches 0), we see that $(b - a)^2$ approaches b—hence, p approaches 1.

(**b**)

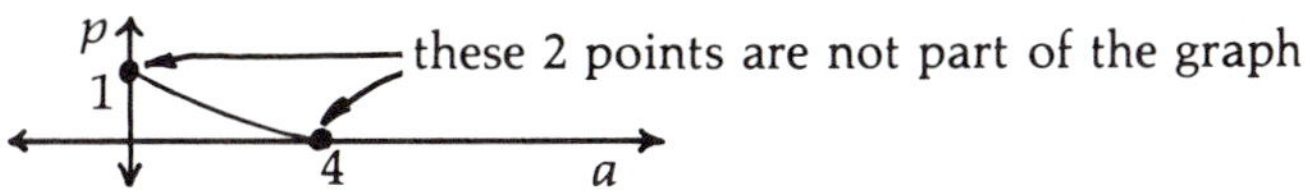

(**c**) 0.20 cm.

(**d**) 2.50 cm.

(**e**) $\dfrac{(s - t)(r - t)}{rs}$.

(f) $\dfrac{3 - \sqrt{5}}{2} = 0.38.$

(g) $\dfrac{(s - \sqrt{3}\,a)^2}{s^2}.$

18. **(a)** The sample space is a square of side:

$$b + \frac{c}{2} + \frac{c}{2} = b + c\ .$$

The success region is a square of side:

$$b - \frac{a}{2} - \frac{a}{2} = b - a\ .$$

Therefore,

$$p = \frac{(b - a)^2}{(b + c)^2}\ .$$

(b) If we let the rulings on the table have width c, then a geometrical model of this different County Fair Problem is identical to that of the Storm Sewer Problem (see Figure 16), ignoring the depth of the bars of the grating.

(c) $b = (3 + 2\sqrt{2})a$

(d) $\dfrac{(s - \sqrt{3}a)^2}{(s + \sqrt{3}c)^2}$

19. a/b.

20. 9/25.

21. (a) b/a, 0.
(b) If c is the midpoint of $\overline{AB}$, then $b = \dfrac{a}{2}\cdot$ Hence,

$$p = b/a = \frac{a/2}{a} = 1/2.$$

22. (a) 1/2, 1, $(2 - \sqrt{2})/2 = 0.29$, $\sqrt{3}/2 = 0.87$.

(b) $19/400 = 0.0475$.

23. 1/4, no.

24. 1/2

25. 3/4, no (by symmetry, the probabilities should be the same).

26. 2/3, 2/3.

27. (**a**) 9/32 = 0.28.

(**b**) 1/2.

(**c**) 1.

28. 1/12 = 0.083

29. 1/60 = 0.02.

30. 5/16 = 0.31.

31. 7/8 = 0.875.

32. (**a**) 7/16 = 0.44.

(**b**) 1/6 = 0.17.

(**c**) 1/18 = 0.056.

33. $(3\sqrt{2} - 4)/4 = 0.06$.

6. Model Exam

1. A baseball player was tagged out while running from first to second base, a distance of 90 feet. Assuming the tag was made at a random place between the two bases, determine the probability that she was tagged out within 5 feet of either base.

2. Suppose the lengths of the two legs of a right triangle are chosen randomly between 0 and 1. Find the probability that the length of the hypotenuse is less than 3/4.

3. Helen is shooting arrows at a circular target with diameter 1 foot and with a bull's eye of diameter 1/2 foot. If, in a particular shot, she hits the target at a random spot, what is the probability that she will not get a bullseye?

4. In the given figure, calculate the probability that a randomly chosen point in R (triangle ABC and its interior) belongs to r (triangle ADE and its interior).

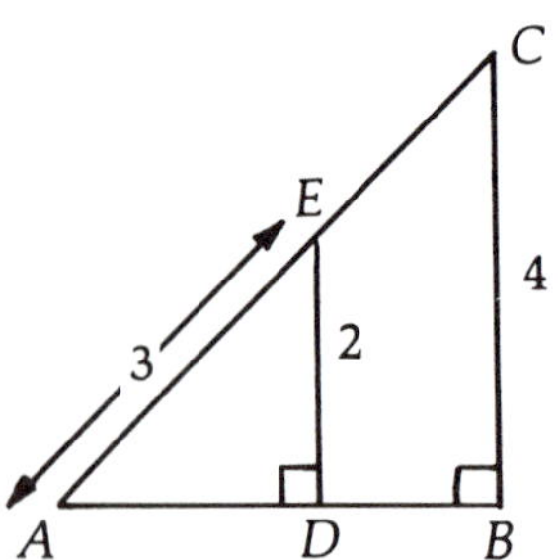

5. A plant has two machines operating independently of each other. Each machine breaks down, on an average, once every 24 hours. If it takes 1 hour to repair machine A and two hours to repair machine B, determine the probability that production will stop (i.e.;both machines will be down at the same time) during a particular 24-hour period, assuming that the breakdown times occur randomly within this time period.

6. The point (a,b) is chosen at random in the rectangle $0 \le a \le 2$, $0 \le b \le 1$. What is the probability that the equation $ax + 2\sqrt{b}x + (3/2) = 0$ has two real roots?

7. An electric company, Great Lakes Power, has a generating station and headquarters for its repair trucks in City A. A transmission line carries electricity from this generating station to City B, which is 8 miles away. Anticipating a storm which is likely to cause a break in the transmission line, Great Lakes Power decides to station one of its repair trucks at a random location between City A and City B. If the line does break at a random point between City A and City B during the storm, what is the probability that this repair truck will be closer to the break than a truck starting from its home base in City A?

7. Answers to Model Exam

1. 1/9.

2. $9\pi/64$.

3. 3/4.

4. 1/4.

5. 0.12.

6. 1/6.

7. 3/4.

UMAP

Modules in Undergraduate Mathematics and Its Applications

Module 668

Adders and Their Design

Jo Ann Fellin, OSB

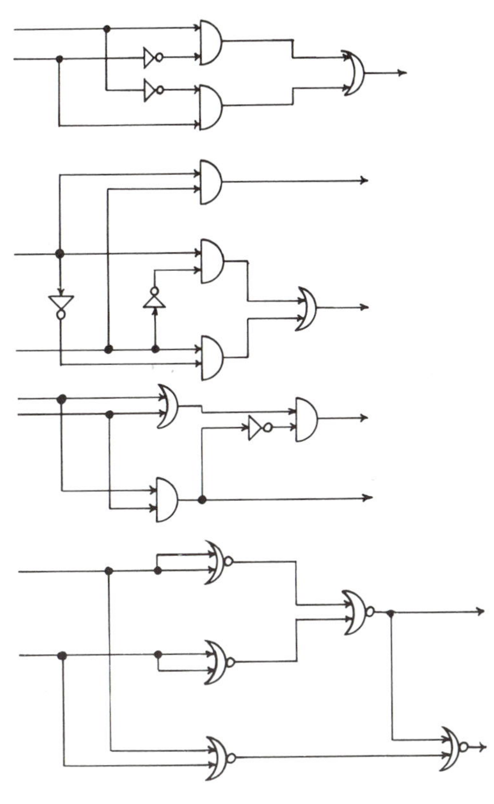

Published in cooperation with the Society for Industrial and Applied Mathematics, the Mathematical Association of America, the National Council of Teachers of Mathematics, the American Mathematical Association of Two-Year Colleges, and The Institute of Management Sciences.

COMAP

INTERMODULAR DESCRIPTION SHEET	UMAP Unit 668
TITLE:	Adders and Their Design
AUTHOR:	Jo Ann Fellin, OSB Department of Mathematics and Computer Science Benedictine College Atchison, Kansas 66002
CLASSIFICATION:	APPL OF LOGIC AND ALGEBRA TO COMPUTER DESIGN
TARGET AUDIENCE:	This module is an appropriate supplement for an abstract algebra computer science course.
ABSTRACT:	In this unit we discuss the logic behind adders. We look at the circuitry used in their realization and the various design methods for creating fast-adders. Inherent in these advances in computer technology has been the mathematics of residue number systems, Boolean algebra, and group theory.
PREREQUISITES:	Elementary group theory, two-element Boolean algebras.
RELATED UNITS:	Primitive Shift Registers (Unit 310)

Adders and Their Design

Jo Ann Fellin, OSB
Department of Mathematics and Computer Science
Benedictine College
Atchison, Kansas 66002

Table of Contents

Modules And Monographs In Undergraduate Mathematics And Its Applications Project (UMAP)

The goal of UMAP is to develop, through a community of users and developers, a system of instructional modules in undergraduate mathematics and its applications that may be used to supplement existing courses and from which complete courses may eventually be built.

The Project is guided by a National Advisory Board of mathematicians, scientists, and educators. UMAP is funded by a grant from the National Science Foundation to the Consortium for Mathematics and Its Applications, Inc. (COMAP), a nonprofit corporation engaged in research and development in mathematics education.

The Project would like to thank Philip S. Straffin and Paul W. Campbell of Beloit College and Zaven A. Karian and Carolyn R. Mahoney of Denison University for their reviews, and all others who assisted in the production of this unit.

1. Introduction

One reason for the increased use of computers has been the increase in the speed of the arithmetic unit, one of the basic units of a digital computer. The most important part of the arithmetic unit is the adder. Thus, logic designers have been challenged by the task of minimizing the addition time needed for an adder to do its task.

In this unit we discuss the logic behind adders. We look at the circuitry used in their realization and the various design methods for creating fast-adders. Inherent in these advances in computer technology has been the mathematics of residue number systems, Boolean algebra, and group theory.

1.1 The Binary System

The components in high-speed computers can assume two possible conditions. This two-fold option can be illustrated in various ways—the on-and-off of an electric switch, the presence or absence of current in a transistor, a magnetic core that is magnetized in a clockwise or counterclockwise direction, a place on a card that can be punched or unpunched. This twofold characteristic is the reason behind the use of the binary system in digital computers.

"... the binary system has only two symbols, 0 and 1 ... called bits."

In contrast to the decimal system, the binary system has only two symbols, 0 and 1. These *b*inary dig*its* are called *bits*. Numbers can be represented in the binary system in a manner similar to the decimal representation, using the idea of place value. In the binary system we work with powers of 2 rather than powers of 10. For example, in the decimal system the symbol 18 indicates 1 group of ten and 8 units.

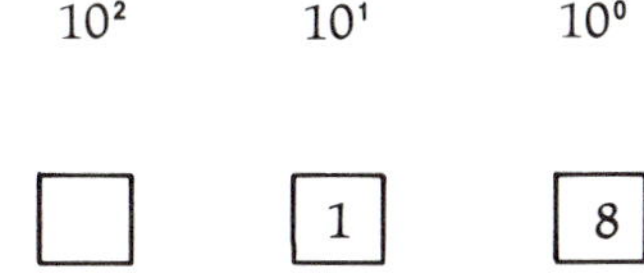

That same number can be represented in the binary system by 10010, 1 group of sixteen and 1 group of two.

2^4	2^3	2^2	2^1	2^0
1	0	0	1	0

We will use the binary representation of numbers throughout the unit.

Exercises

1. Represent the decimal numeral 25 in the binary system.
2. Represent the binary numeral 101101 in the decimal system.
3. Count from one to ten in the binary system. Read 1 as "one," 10 as "one zero," 11 as "one one," and so on.

1.2 Two-element Boolean Algebra

We can consider the symbols 0 and 1 from another point of view as elements of a Boolean algebra. In 1854 George Boole developed a system of symbolic logic now called Boolean algebra. It involves a set of symbols that satisfy certain properties under two binary operations and one unary operation. A typical Boolean algebra is the algebra of subsets of a set with binary operations of union and intersection and the unary operation of complementation. In 1938 C. E. Shannon demonstrated that the properties of bistable electrical switches can be modeled by a two-element Boolean algebra. Designers use Boolean algebra to convert electrical circuit diagrams to algebraic expressions. The application of Boole's work to computer design is known as *switching theory.*

"...the properties of bistable electrical switches can be modeled by a two-element Boolean algebra."

The logic operations on {0,1} are summarized in Table 1. Logic value true is symbolized by "1," while "0" indicates false.

Table 1

Logic Operations on the set {0,1}

	NOT
A	A′
0	1
1	0

		AND	OR
A	B	A•B	A+B
0	0	0	0
0	1	0	1
1	0	0	1
1	1	1	1

We are working with two-value logic, in which the conjunction of two statements is true only if both are true, and the disjunction of two statements is true except when both statements are false. The mathematical multiplication symbol is used for "and" while the addition symbol indicates the disjunction "or."

The symbols used in circuit diagrams for these logic operations are displayed in Fig. 1. These circuit symbols are also called logic gates.

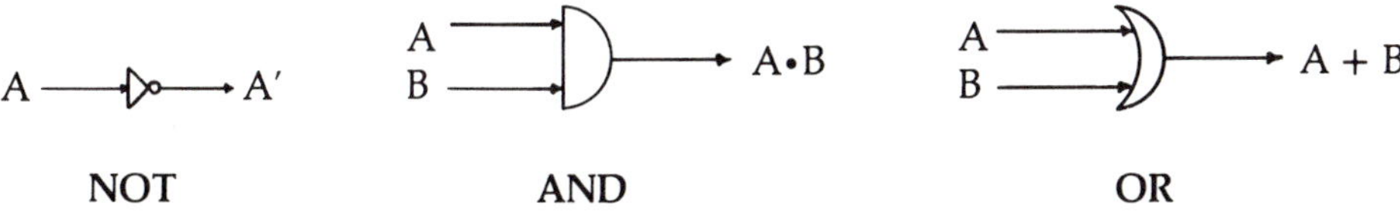

Figure 1. Circuit diagram symbols for the logic operations.

NAND and NOR are shortened forms for "not and" and "not or." NAND and NOR gates, combinations of the basic gates shown in Fig. 1, are displayed in Fig. 2.

Figure 2. The circuit symbols for NAND and NOR.

Exercises

4. Complete the tables showing the truth values for the NAND and NOR expressions.

A	B	NAND $(A \cdot B)'$	NOR $(A + B)'$
0	0		
0	1		
1	0		
1	1		

5. Complete the table below for what are commonly called DeMorgan's laws:

$(A \cdot B)' = A' + B'$ and $(A + B)' = A' \cdot B'$

A	B	A'	B'	$A' + B'$	$A' \cdot B'$
0	0				
0	1				
1	0				
1	1				

6. a) Express output C in terms of inputs A and B for the following circuit:

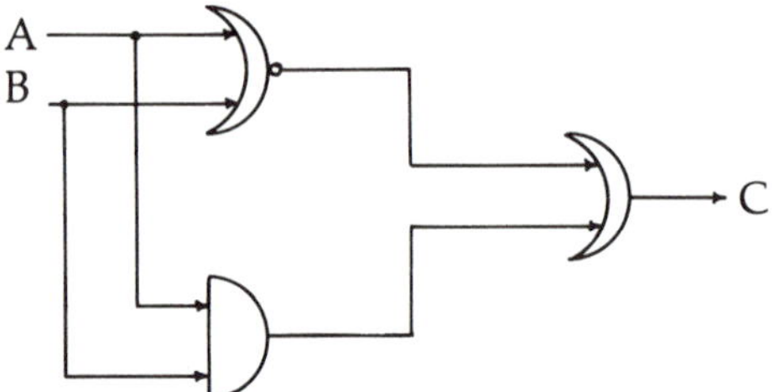

b) Complete the table for the circuit pictured above:

A	B	C
0	0	
0	1	
1	0	
1	1	

7. Draw a circuit diagram for the logic expression:

$$C = (A \bullet B') + (A' \bullet B).$$

1.3 Switching Functions

Consider the following truth table:

A	B	C
0	0	0
0	1	1
1	0	1
1	1	0

The expression C is true in two of the four cases—namely, when A is false and B is true, or when A is true and B is false. We can express this situation in equation form as $C = A'B + AB'$, the equation given in Exercise 7, it being customary to omit the dots between the letters. C is called a Boolean or *switching function*, since it is an expression involving binary variables and the operators AND, OR, and NOT. Since C is a function of variables A and B, it is called a two-variable switching function. When a logic expression is written, like C, as a sum of products of the input variables and their complements, it is said to be in *disjunctive normal form* (also called *standard* or *canonical form*). When a switching function is given in disjuctive normal form, it can be implemented with a *two-level* circuit in which the first level contains the AND gates (the products) and the second level contains OR gates (the sum). Note that the circuit diagram in Exercise 6 is a two-level implementation, even though the function is not in disjunctive normal form.

2. Design for Column Addition

The addition of two numbers in both binary and decimal representation is shown below:

binary addition	decimal addition
1 0 1 1	11
1 1 0 1	13
1 1 0 0 0	24

The usual method for column addition of the bits or digits on the far right involves only two inputs. Each of the other columns involves three inputs: the two bits or digits from the numbers and the carry bit or digit from the previous column.

2.1 Half Adder

We now consider the far right column of the binary addition shown above. We design an adder, called a *half adder*, to add the two one-bit binary numbers, resulting in a sum bit s and a carry bit c as outputs.

There are four possible input combinations to consider. Table 2 gives these possibilities, along with the sum bit and the carry bit for each case.

Table 2

Truth Table for the Half Adder

x	y	s	c
0	0	0	0
0	1	1	0
1	0	1	0
1	1	0	1

Using the values for s and c in the table, we can write the sum and carry as switching functions of x and y as follows:

$s = x'y + xy'$ and $c = xy$

The *half adder* is defined by the values in Table 2 and is represented with inputs and outputs in the block diagram of Fig. 3.

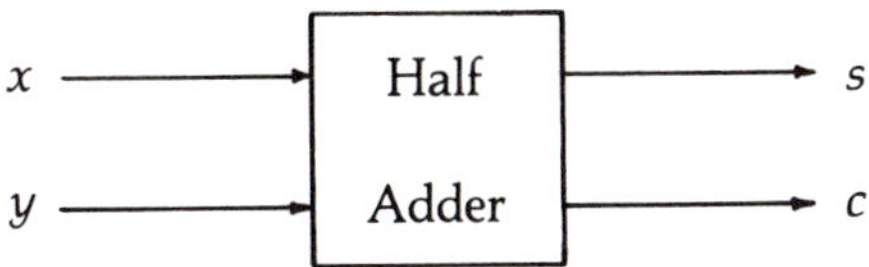

Figure 3. Block diagram for the half adder.

A half adder's inputs usually originate from devices that store bits. One such device is called a *flipflop*, in which both inputs and their complements are available. Fig. 4 below is one possible logic realization of the half adder, showing both complemented and uncomplemented variables as inputs. Note that the s output is the same as the switching function in Exercise 7 and is in disjunctive normal form.

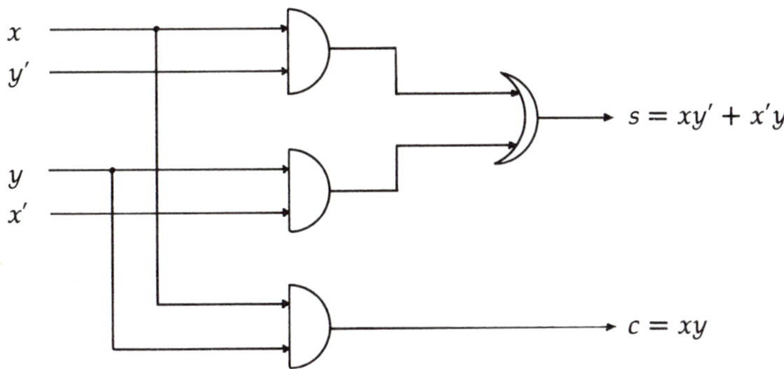

Figure 4. This logic implementation of the half adder has four inputs: the variables x and y and their complements x' and y'.

Exercises

8. **a)** Show an implementation of the half adder that has only uncomplemented inputs but has AND, OR, and NOT gates available.

b) Show an implementation of the half adder that has only uncomplemented inputs and only one NOT gate.

9. Design a half adder using five NAND gates or five NOR gates but not both. Assume only uncomplemented inputs are available. [Hint: $x + x = x$]

2.2 Full Adder

The *full adder* is a circuit that contains three binary inputs in order to add columns that include carry bits. In Exercise 10 you will construct the truth table that defines the full adder. Fig. 5 shows a block diagram for this adder in which c and c° denote the carry-in and carry-out bits, respectively.

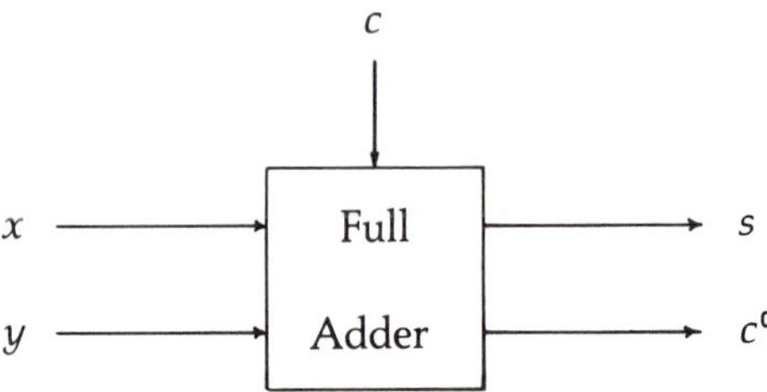

Figure 5. A block diagram for the full adder.

Exercises

10. Construct a truth table that defines the input-output functional relationship for the full adder.

11. Derive the switching functions for the sum and carry-out from the truth table as sums of products of the inputs.

12. The switching function $s = x'y + xy'$ of the half adder is the logic expression called the *exclusive-or*, denoted $x \oplus y$. Verify that the following equations hold for the full adder:

a) $s = x \oplus y \oplus c =$ sum

b) $c^0 = xy + xc + yc =$ carry-out

13. Show a two-level implementation of a full adder using AND and OR gates only. (Assume that both complemented and uncomplemented variables are available.)

14. Verify that the network below, constructed from two half-adders and one OR gate, is equivalent to a full adder.

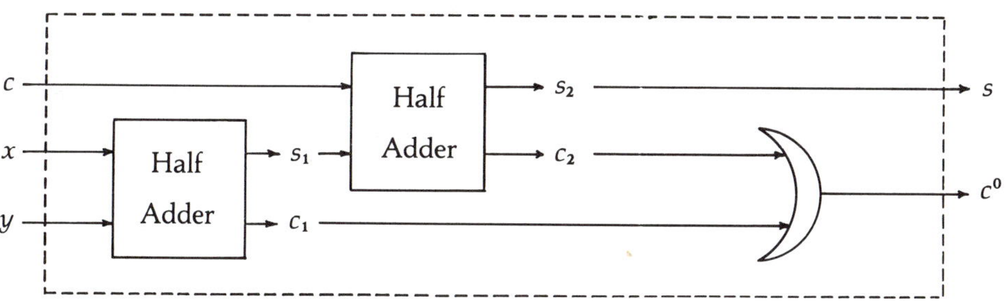

15. Verify that the network shown below is a NAND realization of a full adder.

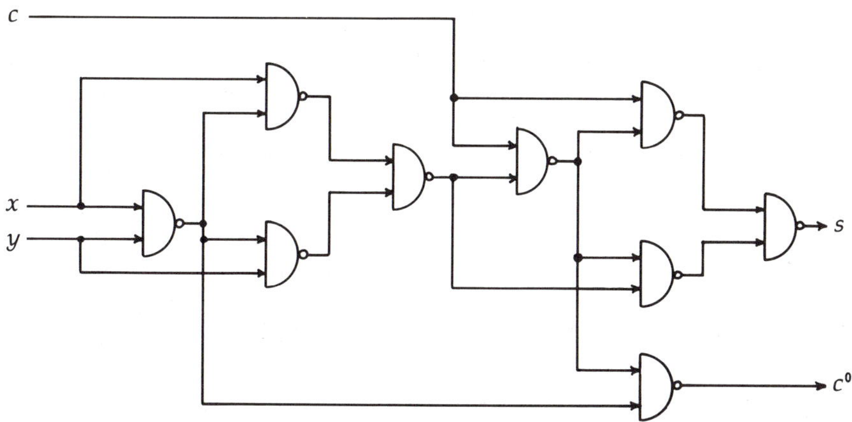

16. Construct a full adder using only NOR gates. (Assume that both complemented and uncomplemented variables are available.)

3. Three-Column Addition

To compare the design of addition devices we use a simplified illustration in this section—the addition of two 3-bit binary numbers, 101 (5 base 10) and 111 (7 base 10). With the usual addition method we calculate the sum and carry bits as shown below:

carry ---------→		1	1			
		1	0	1	=	5
		1	1	1	=	7
Sum --------→	1	1	0	0	=	12

3.1 Parallel Adder

We can realize this method by placing three full adders *in parallel,* meaning that all the bits of the numbers to be added are available for computation at the same time. The specific 3-bit binary number inputs and the output sum for our example are shown in registers at the left of Fig. 6 and on the diagram itself.

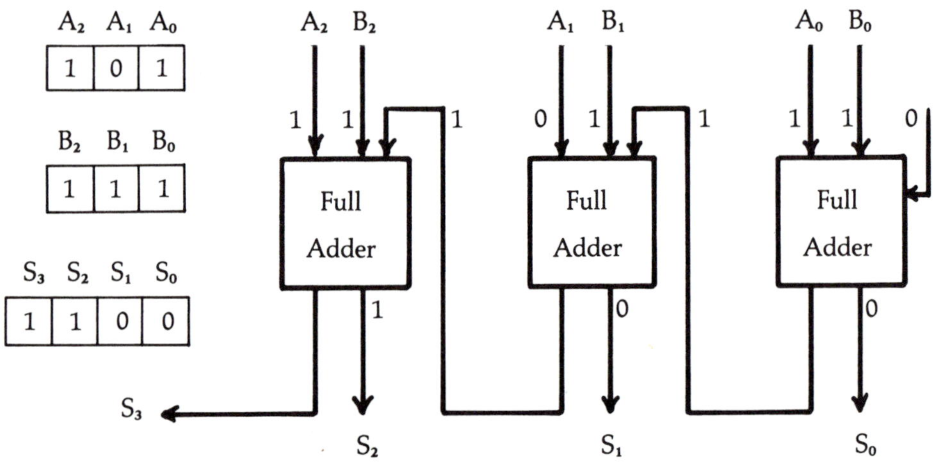

Figure 6. Parallel 3-bit adder.

Although the rightmost adder in Fig. 6 could be a half adder, since the carry-in bit is always zero (sometimes called a *forced carry*), it is a full adder in actual computer systems. We will continue to treat the rightmost adder as a full adder, since doing so makes possible the use of the hardware for the operation of subtraction as well. (Subtraction is generally accomplished by the addition of the inverted subtrahend or by the 2's complement, depending upon the type of machine [6].) Note that the output register must have four bit positions for the addition of two arbitrary 3-bit binary numbers.

Exercises

17. Draw a diagram of a parallel adder to show the addition of 23 and 19.

18. What bit length must the sum register have for the addition of two n-bit binary numbers?

3.2 Serial Adder

The usual addition method can be implemented by a serial adder that adds the two binary numbers serially, i.e., bit by bit. It is constructed from only one full adder and a single delay unit. In the diagram in Fig. 7, the notation used indicates that the adder operates at discrete time intervals, e.g., by a time pulse. The binary number input bits and the sum bit at time t are denoted $x(t)$, $y(t)$, and $s(t)$, respectively. The carry-in and carry-out bits at time t are denoted $c(t)$ and $c^0(t)$, respectively.

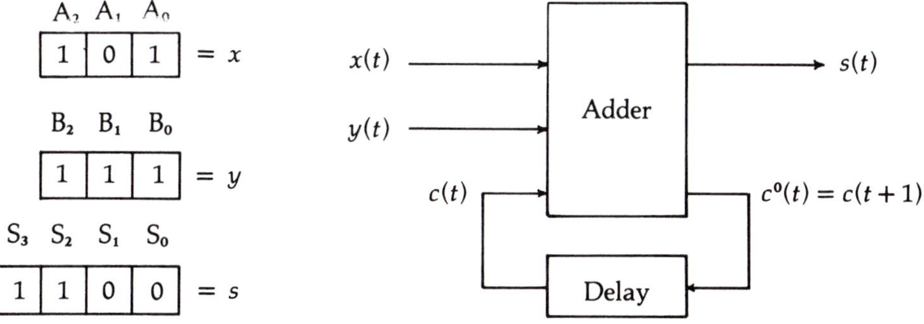

Figure 7. Serial adder.

The least significant bits, A_0 and B_0, are fed in first with the forced carry. The function of the delay is to cause the carry-out bit generated at time t to be an input to the adder at time $t+1$. The registers are shift registers that shift each of the entries one bit to the right at each shift signal [3].

3.3 Circuitry Comparison

"The essential difference between the two adders... lies in the difference between the two basic types of circuitry — combinational and sequential."

In the descriptions above, the parallel adder was constructed with one full adder for each bit addition, while the serial adder contained a single adder and processed the bits sequentially. The essential difference between the two adders, however, lies in the difference between the two basic types of circuitry—combinational and sequential.

The parallel adder has *combinational* circuitry, i.e., the outputs are functions of only the present circuit inputs.

The outputs of a serial adder are functions of both the inputs of the numbers to be added and the internal state of the machine as represented by the carry stored in the delay unit. Such circuitry is termed *sequential* circuitry. The sequential circuit is constructed with a memory capability not available in the combinational circuit.

The diagram of the parallel adder in Fig. 8 illustrates the fact that the outputs are functions of present external inputs. The adders in the diagram are arranged to show the delay time for carry propagation in the addition example considered in the section on parallel adders. We note that the bits of the numbers to be added are fed in simultaneously. Thus the computation time is dependent upon the *carry propagation time*, i.e., the time needed for the carries to be propagated through the system.

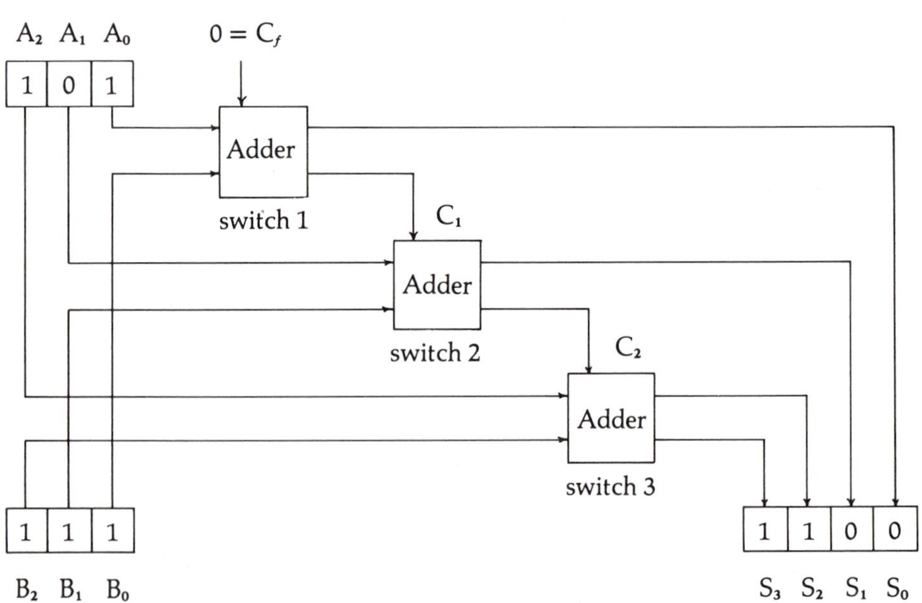

Figure 8. Parallel adder and delay time.

4. Minimizing Addition Time

4.1 Effect of Network Design on Speed

"... the propagation delay is the product of n *and the switching delay."*

For the sum of two n-bit binary numbers, the full adders are activated consecutively, necessitating n delays. If the switching delay is, say, 1 nanosecond (a billionth of a second), then the propagation delay is n nanoseconds. In general, the propagation delay is the product of n and the switching delay. In contrast to the parallel adder, the serial adder by its very construction requires n units of time. Thus, we see that if the switching delay time is smaller than the clock frequency, the speed of the parallel adder exceeds that of the serial adder.

According to Kohavi [6] all high-speed adders are constructed with parallel adders. This is understandable, since the parallel adder has the advantage of speed of operation, whereas the serial adder has the advantage of involving less hardware circuitry. We will concern ourselves with parallel adders and their design.

A number of the choices made by the designer working with the parallel adder will affect computation time. After deciding the size of the output register, the designer chooses the number representation and the addition method to be employed. Thus far we have considered only the conventional addition method used in hand calculation and the conventional binary representation. Other methods and representations will be discussed in Section 5.

4.2 Ripple-carry Addition

Let us consider the sum of two n-bit binary numbers. We can realize this addition with a parallel adder having n full adders. Fig. 9 indicates that the carry-out of one stage is the carry-in of the next stage. The sum and carry-out functions are given by the following equations:

$$S_i = A_i \oplus B_i \oplus C_i$$

and

$$C_{i+1} = A_iB_i + A_iC_i + B_iC_i$$

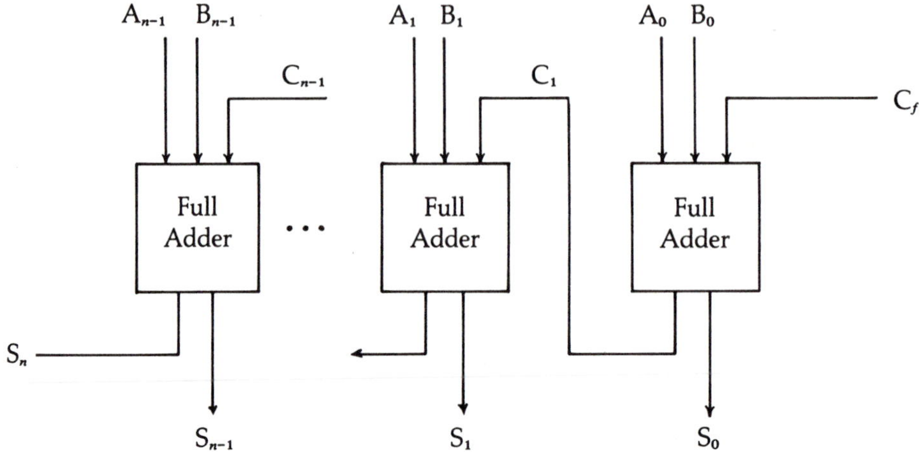

Figure 9. Ripple-carry adder with n stages.

As seen previously in the 3-bit example, this implementation simulates the algorithmic procedure used in hand calculation. Such a parallel adder is called a *ripple-carry* parallel adder, since the carry propagates, or "ripples through," the individual adders. The time needed to perform the addition depends upon the time needed for the propagation (or ripple) of the carries through the entire system.

Exercises

19. Verify that no more than two levels of circuitry are needed to realize a full adder when complemented and uncomplemented variables are both available.

20. If t denotes propagation time for one level of circuitry, then what is the fixed number of time units that must be allotted for the n-stage ripple-carry adder to have the capability of adding any two n-bit binary numbers?

It is desirable to shorten the carry propagation time in order to increase the speed of computation. Consider the example illustrated in Fig. 8. The inputs of the third adder are A_2, B_2, and C_2. The adder cannot begin its operation until C_2 arrives at the adder. This carry was generated in the first full adder and propagated or "rippled" through the second full adder. If C_2 can be given in terms of the A_i and B_i, then it can be available immediately to the third full adder through a carry-anticipation circuit, rather than carried to the third adder through the first two adders. This method would allow the third adder to produce S_2 and S_3 at the same time that the first two adders are producing S_0 and S_1, with a possible gain in time over the full ripple-carry addition.

4.3 Carry-lookahead Addition

Let us again consider the addition of two 3-bit binary numbers and examine the design of an adder in which the carries are anticipated in all stages. Such an adder is called a *carry-lookahead adder*. Each full adder is separated into two sections—the sum network (SN) and the carry network (CN), as shown in Fig. 10.

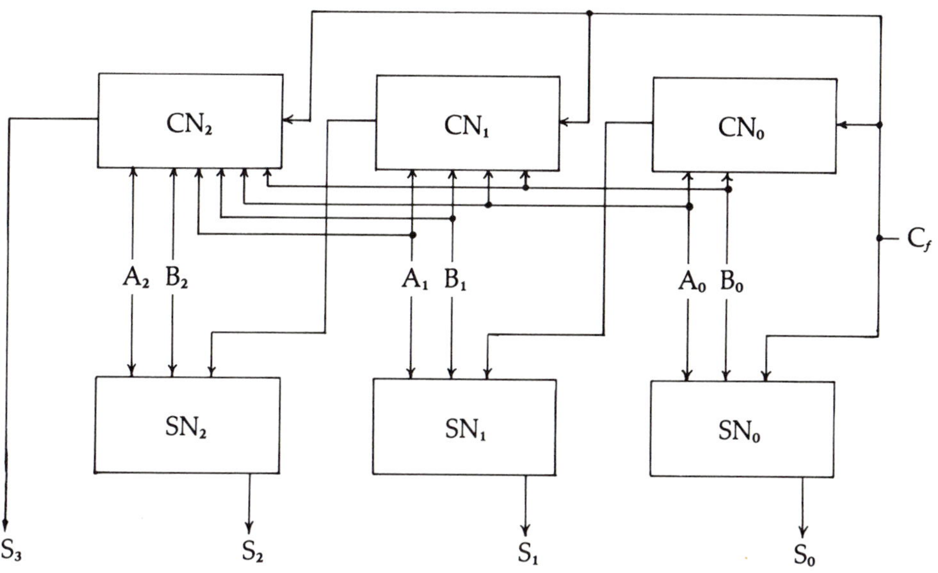

Figure 10. Carry-lookahead adder.

We notice that the carry networks can be executed simultaneously, and afterwards the sum networks can be executed simultaneously. Thus the maximum time for the complete addition will be the maximum time needed by any sequence CN_i and SN_{i+1}. Notice that in the case of the 3-bit carry-lookahead adder, we have no gain in speed over the ripple-carry adder. Each requires six levels of circuitry, as will become clear in the exercises in Section 4.4. If t denotes the propagation time for one level, then each adder requires $6t$ time units. The gain occurs with the n-bit case for $n > 3$. For example, with $n = 8$ the ripple-carry may require as many as $16t$ time units, while the carry-lookahead still requires $6t$ time units. We further note that the carry networks increase in complexity as the number of bits increases. For example, the carry network CN_7, for the addition of 8-bit numbers in a carry-lookahead adder, requires 16 inputs and numerous gates. As the number of inputs and gates increases, the hardware complexity expenditure may override the gain in speed of operation.

A combination scheme using both the ripple-carry and carry-lookahead concepts may be employed to advantage, as explored in the next section. Before we proceed to such a compromise, however, let us look more closely at the carry-out function in general. Originally we defined it recursively as:

$$C_{i+1} = A_iB_i + A_iC_i + B_iC_i .$$

The possible values for C_{i+1} are given in Table 3.

Table 3

Carry Output

A_i	B_i	C_{i+1}
0	0	0
0	1	C_i
1	0	C_i
1	1	1

The carry-out value of 1 can be produced in two distinct ways. The carry-out is said to be *generated* if it is independent of the carry-in, as it is when $A_i = B_i = 1$. If the carry-out is dependent upon the carry-in, the carry-out is said to be *propagated*.

Let $G_i = A_iB_i$ and $P_i = A_i'B_i + A_iB_i' = A_i \oplus B_i$. Then the carry-out function can be given in terms of G_i and P_i by the equation:

$$C_{i+1} = G_i + P_iC_i ,$$

from which it follows that

$$C_{i+1} = G_i + P_i(G_{i-1} + P_{i-1}C_{i-1})$$

$$= G_i + P_iG_{i-1} + P_iP_{i-1}C_{i-1} .$$

Continuing the iteration, we obtain the carry-out in non-recursive form:

$$C_{i+1} = G_i + P_iG_{i-1} + P_iP_{i-1}G_{i-2} + \ldots + P_iP_{i-1}P_{i-2} \ldots P_0C_f.$$

This equation illustrates that the carry-out is 1 if the carry was generated in that stage, i.e., if $G_i = 1$, or if it originated in some preceding stage and was propagated in all subsequent stages. For example, the carry-out $C_6 = P_5P_4P_3G_2 = 1$ says that the carry was generated by $A_2 = B_2 = 1$ and propagated in each succeeding stage. The equation also shows that the carry-out is expressed completely in terms of external inputs, the A_i and B_i of the preceding stages, and the forced carry. In the ripple-carry the carry-out was given in terms of external inputs and the previous carry.

4.4 A Good Compromise

To add two n-bit binary numbers, we may take advantage of the anticipated carry to increase the speed of operation and yet partially retain the ripple-carry, to lessen the complexity of a complete carry-lookahead adder. The n stages of the adder may be divided into groups in such a way that each group is handled with a carry-lookahead scheme, while a ripple-carry is set up between the groups. For example, Fig. 11 shows a 12-bit adder composed of four groups of three stages each. Thus, each group is a carry-lookahead adder (CLA) like the one in Fig. 10.

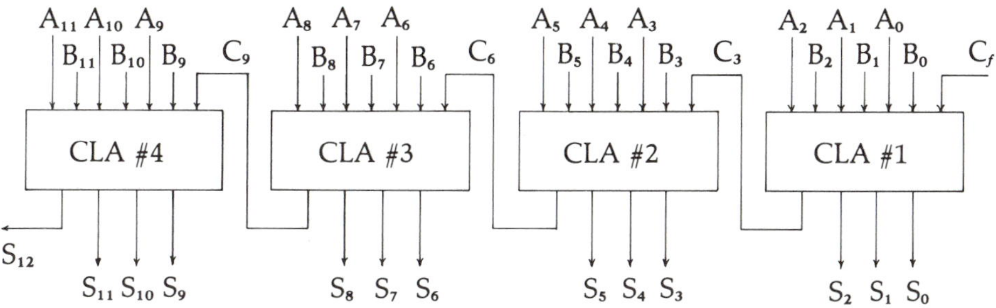

Figure 11. Four carry-lookahead adders with ripple-carry connection.

Exercises

21. Draw a two-level carry network for C_3 using G_i, P_i, and C_f as inputs ($i = 0, 1, 2$).

22. How many time units are needed to execute P_i? (Let t denote the propagation time for one level of circuitry.)

23. At most how many time units are required to obtain C_3? How many for C_6? (Hint: the necessary signals G_i and P_i are already available, since that part of CLA #2 can operate at the same time that CLA #1 operates.)

24. CLA #4 cannot execute sum bits S_i for $i = 9, 10, 11$, and 12 in $2t$ time units. For what reason will an additional $2t$ time units be needed in the final sum stage?

25. What is the longest propagation time for the 12-bit adder, divided into four 3-stage groups, with carry-lookahead within each group and ripple-carry between groups?

26. How does the time arrived at in Exercise 25 compare with the time required for a 12-bit ripple-carry adder?

5. Unconventional Methods and Representation

5.1 Conditional-sum Addition

The conditional-sum addition method exploits the division of the n-bit numbers into groups so that several additions may be computed simultaneously. The results are used in the final result only if they apply. We examine this method through an example — the addition of the two 6-bit binary numbers $x = 101011$ and $y = 110111$. We form three addition problems and use ripple-carry adders to perform each addition: A — the addition of the three least significant bits; B — the addition of the next three higher bits with a carry-in of 1; C — the addition of the same bits as in B but with a carry-in of 0. The use of the B and C results in the final step depends upon the carry-out from A. Since A propagated a carry-out, namely $C_3 = 1$, B is the correct choice. B is combined with A and the final resulting sum is 1100010.

Table 4

Conditional Sums

Addition C	Addition B	Addition A
0	1	
101	101	011
110	110	111
1011	1100	$C_3$010

Exercises

Assume that the switching delay time for a full adder is 10 nanoseconds, i.e., $t = 5$ nanoseconds, and assume that the final combination step takes 10 nanoseconds.

27. How much time is needed to complete problems A, B, and C?

28. How much time is needed to add $x = 101011$ and $y = 110111$ using

a) the conditional-sum method?

b) ripple-carry addition?

c) two 3-stage groups, with carry-lookahead within the groups and ripple-carry between the two groups?

29. a) Describe a conditional-sum method for the addition of two 12-bit binary numbers using 3-bit full adders.

b) Compare the time required for your conditional-sum method with that of the ripple-carry adder.

5.2 Residue Representation

The time required for an arithmetic operation depends on the number representation. We have examined carry propagation time in the case of conventional binary representation. We now look at a number representation that shortens carry time, namely residue representation, and comment on how it might affect computer design.

"The number of numbers in any computer must necessarily be finite... a computer's arithmetic is completed in some modular system for some large n, denoted Z_n."

The number of numbers in any computer must necessarily be finite, which means that a computer's arithmetic is completed in some modular system for some large n, denoted Z_n. For clarity we first illustrate with the clock arithmetic system, Z_{12}. According to Kline [5], Digital Equipment Corporation's PDP-11 and IBM's System/370 have n-size of 16 and 32, respectively.

Since decimal number representation is more familiar and compact than binary number representation, we represent the elements of Z_{12} in decimal form. As a consequence of the Chinese remainder theorem, the cyclic group Z_{12} is isomorphic to a direct product of cyclic groups of prime power order, namely $Z_4 \times Z_3$. The isomorphism can be established by the map θ given by $\theta(k) = < k \bmod 4, k \bmod 3 >$ and called the *residue representation* of k. The residue representations are listed in Table 5.

Table 5

Residue Representation of Integers in Z_{12}

0	<0,0>	4	<0,1>	8	<0,2>
1	<1,1>	5	<1,2>	9	<1,0>
2	<2,2>	6	<2,0>	10	<2,1>
3	<3,0>	7	<3,1>	11	<3,2>

Addition in the decomposition, denoted by $\oplus$, is componentwise—namely, addition mod 4 in the first component and addition mod 3 in the second. (Addition mod n is denoted by $+_n$.) The map θ preserves the operation of addition, i.e.,

$$\theta(x +_{12} y) = \theta(x) \oplus \theta(y).$$

For example, if $x = 7$ and $y = 6$, we have

$$\theta(7 +_{12} 6) = \theta(1) = <1,1> = <3,1> \oplus <2,0> = \theta(7) + \theta(6).$$

The method for converting from conventional representation to residue representation is quite clear from the definition of θ. For use in the computer, however, we need to be able to convert residue representation into conventional representation. This can be accomplished by establishing weights for the unit vectors $<1,0>$ and $<0,1>$ and making use of linear combinations as shown in the following example for converting $<3,2>$ to 11 without the use of the entire table. The unit vectors are assigned the weights $<1,0> \sim w_1 = 9$ and $<0,1> \sim w_2 = 4$, and the number corresponding to $<3,2>$ is $(3w_1 +_{12} 2w_2) = (3 \cdot 9 +_{12} 2 \cdot 4) = 11$. This latter process involves additions mod 12.

Exercises

30. **a)** Express Z_{90} as a product of cyclic groups of prime-power order.

b) Determine the weights for decoding elements of the direct product into elements of Z_{90}.

c) Using the residue representations find the sum 11 + 57 + 23 mod 90, i.e., encode using θ, perform the addition in the direct product, and then decode using θ^{-1} to obtain the sum.

31. Repeat Exercise 30 for the system Z_{290}.

32. **a)** State a method for converting from residue representation to conventional representation for Z_n.

b) Prove that the method is valid.

The following exercises relate this section to previous sections.

33. Prove: $2^n - 1 = \sum_{i=0}^{n-1} 2^i$ for all integers $n \geq 1$.

34. What is the largest decimal number that can be represented by 8 binary bits? [Hint: Use Exercise 33.]

35. How many binary bits are needed to represent the decimal number 43 in conventional binary representation?

36. a) How many bits are needed to represent all mod 11 symbols in conventional binary representation?

b) What is the carry propagation time required for a Z_{11} ripple-carry adder?

37. a) How many bits are needed to represent all mod 4620 symbols in conventional binary representation?

b) What is the carry propagation time required for a Z_{4620} ripple-carry adder?

The decomposition of Z_n just described allows us to perform addition in Z_n by adding within several systems with moduli smaller than n. For example,

$$Z_{4620} \approx Z_4 \times Z_3 \times Z_5 \times Z_7 \times Z_{11} .$$

This residue representation allows us to add in Z_{4620} by using additions in Z_k whose moduli are small in comparison to 4620. The time required for the addition, aside from encoding and decoding, is the maximal time required in the mod systems Z_k, which execute the additions simultaneously as illustrated in Fig. 12.

Let us look at the addition process in Z_{11} using binary representation and the ripple-carry adder. We can represent the eleven elements of Z_{11} as binary 4-tuples using conventional binary representation. Consider the 5 and 9, whose sum in Z_{11} is 3:

decimal	binary
5	101
9	1001

The ripple-carry adder shows the sum to be 1110, which is not an element of Z_{11}. We say that we have an *overflow*. We need to retain the remainder upon division by the modulus. This operation can be accomplished with a device called a shift register [3]. We find that 1110 divided by 111 has remainder 101. With this residue-system addition, the total time involved must include not only the ripple-carry adder time, but also the final division operation time (or the time needed for some method to find the correct residue, such as a table look-up operation). The advantages of the residue representation are somewhat offset by the need for magnitude comparison and overflow detection. These added factors and methods for handling them influence the use of residue representation by computer designers.

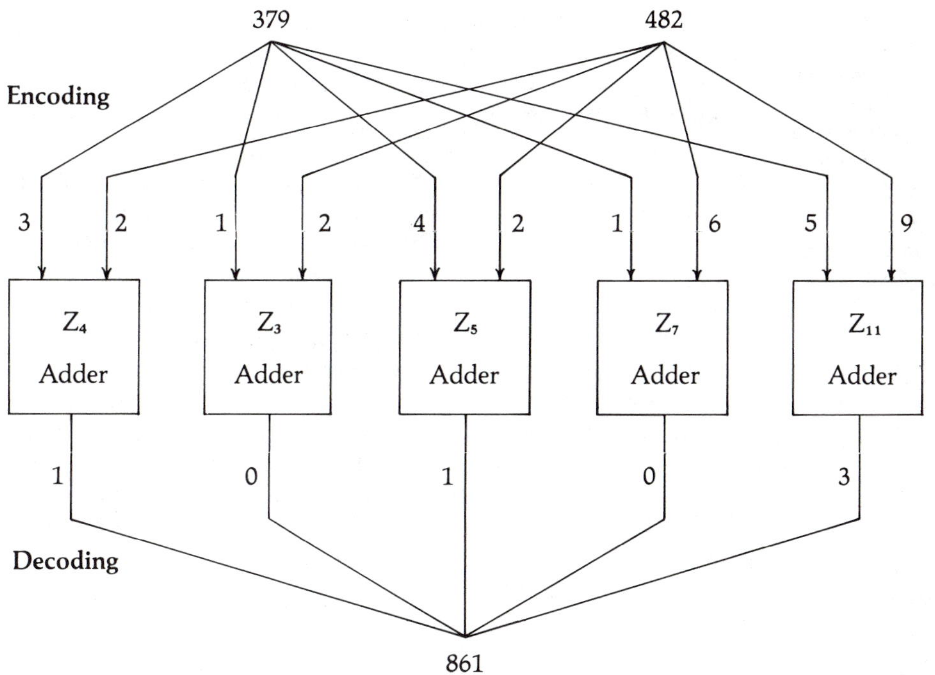

Figure 12. Addition using residue representation.

6. The Theoretically Best Fast Adder

Designers are interested in developing fast adders. Winograd's theory [10] gives the theoretically-best fast adder. He establishes a lower bound for computation time that enables designers of fast adders to have some gauge by which to measure the effectiveness of their results.

We discuss here some factors that influence the design of fast adders, state and illustrate some results relating these factors to computation time, and cite Winograd's lower bound. See Stone [8] or Dornhoff and Hohn [2] for a more extensive treatment.

"The sum of products implementations was a two-level design with two imputs to each gate device and one output from each gate device."

Recall that the sum and carry of the half adder were expressed as 2-variable switching functions. The sums of products implementation was a two-level design with two inputs to each gate device and one output from each gate device. In our discussion of the various adders, the number of levels was seen to be an important factor in computation time. Thus far we have ignored the fact that each gate device has a limit on the number of inputs, called the *fan-in* number and denoted by r. For reasons related to hardware, a common fan-in restriction is that r be less than or equal to 4.

In the discussion that follows, we relate the fan-in number r and the number of switching variables m to the computation time.

The tree network in Fig. 13 illustrates an m-variable switching function f with $m = 11$ and $r = 3$. There are at most $r = 3$ inputs at the bottom level. The next level up can have at most 3 times the number of inputs at the bottom level, or 9. This branching continues to hold as we move up the network from level to level until we have t levels with $11 \leq 3^t$. In this case, $t = 3$ suffices because $11 = 3^3 = 27$.

"If the network with fan-in number r is to compute an m-variable switching function, it must have at least t levels, with m $\leq$ r^t."

If the network with fan-in number r is to compute an m-variable switching function, it must have at least t levels, with $m \leq r^t$.

The notation $\lceil x \rceil$ is called the "ceiling of x" and denotes the smallest integer value that is greater than or equal to x. For example, $\lceil 3.5 \rceil = 4$. Note how the symbol for the "ceiling of x" differs from the usual notation $[x]$ for the greatest integer function, which is sometimes called the "floor of x."

From the inequality $m \leq r^t$ we obtain $\log_r m \leq t$. Thus, for the addition of two m-bit binary numbers using the conventional method of addition, at least $\lceil \log_r 2m \rceil$ time units are necessary, because the left-most sum bit is dependent upon all $2m$ bits of the numbers being added.

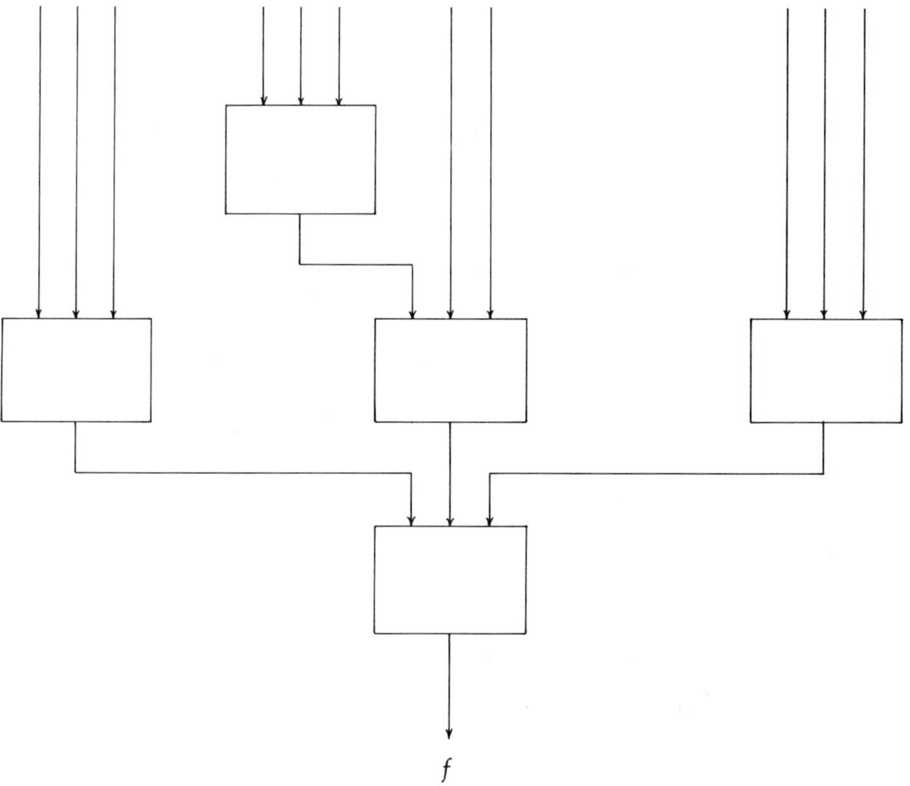

Figure 13. Three-level design for an 11-variable switching function f.

To add modulo n with conventional binary addition, you need to be able to write all the mod n integers as distinct m-bit binary numbers. For this, $n \leq 2^m$ or $m \geq \log_2 n$. Hence $m \geq \lceil \log_2 n \rceil$ and the addition takes at least $\lceil \log_r (2 \lceil \log_2 n \rceil) \rceil$ time units.

This bound of $\lceil \log_r (2 \lceil \log_2 n \rceil) \rceil$ can be further improved. In Section 5.2 we looked at the decomposition of the modulo system Z_n into a direct product of prime-power-order modulo systems to speed up computation time. The advantage of the residue representation results from Winograd's theory on computation time. Winograd's theorem establishes a lower bound for the computation time for addition in Z_n for those n for which the modulo system contains a special element called a *ubiquitous element*. Winograd extends the theorem to obtain a lower bound on computation time for any n.

Group theory plays a vital part in Winograd's development. In any group G, a non-identity element is called *ubiquitous* if it is contained in every non-identity subgroup of the group G. The modulo system Z_n under addition is a cyclic group. It can be shown that a cyclic group of order n has a ubiquitous element if and only if n is a power of a prime.

"In any group G, a non-identity element is called* ubiquitous *if it is contained in every non-identity subgroup of the group G."

The bound for modulo systems Z_n that contain ubiquitous elements is $\lceil \log_r(2\lceil \log_2 n \rceil)\rceil$ and is not dependent upon the representation. The improvement on the bound may be concluded from the further result of Winograd. If Z_n does not have a ubiquitous element but contains a subgroup of order q that does, then the time needed for addition must be at least $\lceil \log_r(2\lceil \log_2 q \rceil)\rceil$ time units.

If $t(n)$ is the order of the largest subgroup of Z_n that has a ubiquitous element, then addition in Z_n must take at least $\lceil \log_r(2\lceil \log_2 t(n) \rceil)\rceil$ time units. Thus, if we can find a representation such that $t(n)$ is considerably less than n, we will see an improvement in computation time. It can be shown that for $n = P_1^{\alpha 1} P_2^{\alpha 2} \ldots P_r^{\alpha r}$, the number $t(n)$ is the largest of the prime power factors. For example, if $n = 12$ and $r = 3$, Winograd's lower bound is $\lceil \log_3(2\lceil \log_2 4 \rceil)\rceil = \lceil \log_3(4)\rceil = 2$ time units.

Exercises

38. Evaluate Winograd's lower bound for devices with fan-in of 3 and for addition in Z_n when

a) $n = 2^{13}$

b) $n = 2^5 - 1$

c) $n = 2^8 - 1$

39. Compare the lower bound found in Exercise 38a with the 13-bit ripple-carry adder examined before.

40. Compare the lower bound found in Exercise 38c with the lower bound for $n = 2^5$.

41. Evaluate Winograd's lower bound for devices with fan-in 3 and for addition in Z_n when

a) $n = 2^{36}$

b) $n = 2^{48}$

Through the exercises you have found that the computation time for $n = 255$ was the same as the computation time for $n = 32$. You might ask, then, why designers have used moduli that are powers of 2. Recall that addition is always done in some modulo system but answers are correct only if there is no overflow. Winograd proved that no number base can increase the speed of overflow indication beyond that achieved by base 2. This result further explains our comments in Section 5.2 on the use of residue representation in computer design of adders. According to Winograd [9], one common adder handles numbers with magnitudes near 2^{36}, roughly one billion, and still another adder uses numbers with magnitudes near 2^{48}, greater than 100 trillion, without creating an overflow.

We have seen that the designer has several choices which influence computation time—first, the size of the output register, and next, the number representation and addition method. Winograd's results give designers a way to compare the computation times of their designs with that of the ideally best fast adder.

7. Solutions to Exercises

1. 11001

2. 45

3. 1, 10, 11, 100, 101, 110, 111, 1000, 1001, 1010.

4.

1	1
1	0
1	0
0	0

5.

1	1	1	1
1	0	1	0
0	1	1	0
0	0	0	0

6. **a)** $C = (A + B)' + A \bullet B$

b) 1
0
0
1

7. A
B
C

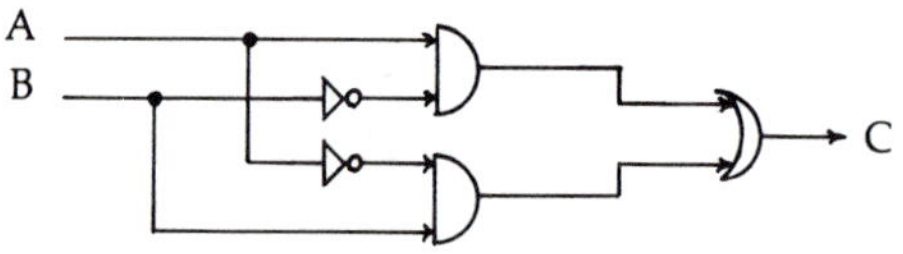

8. **a)**
$c = xy$
x
$s = xy' + x'y$
y

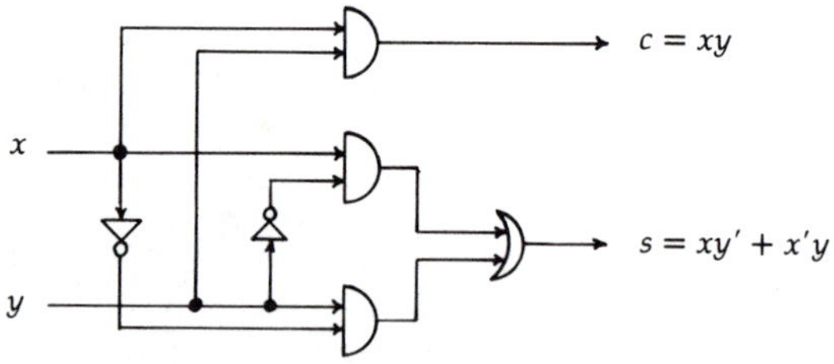

b) x
y
$s = xy' + x'y$
$c = xy$

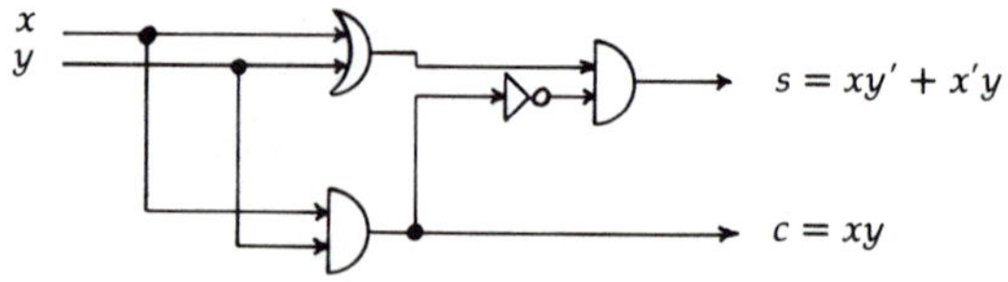

9.

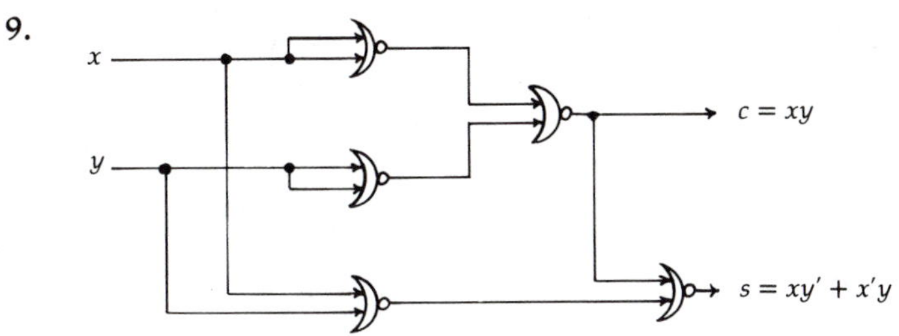

5 NOR gates

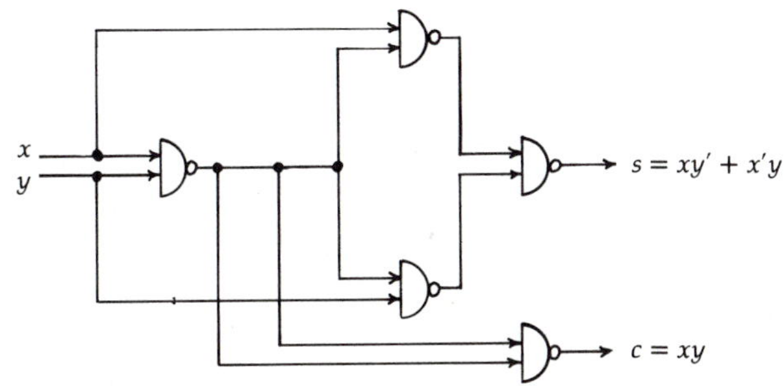

5 NAND gates

10.

x	y	c	s	c^0
0	0	0	0	0
0	0	1	1	0
0	1	0	1	0
0	1	1	0	1
1	0	0	1	0
1	0	1	0	1
1	1	0	0	1
1	1	1	1	1

11.

$$s = x'y'c + x'yc' + xy'c' + xyc$$

$$c^0 = x'yc + xy'c + xyc' + xyc$$

12. **a)** $s = x \oplus y \oplus c = (x \oplus y) \oplus c$

$= (x \oplus y)c' + (x \oplus y)'c$

$= (xy' + x'y)c' + (xy' + x'y)'c$

$= xy'c' + x'yc' + (x' + y)(x + y')c$

$= xy'c' + x'yc' + x'y'c + xyc$

b) $c^0 = x'yc + xy'c + xyc' + xyc$

$= x'yc + xy'c + xy(c' + c)$

$= x'yc + xy'c + xy = (x \oplus y)c + xy$

$= (x + y)(xy)'c + xy$

$= (x + y)c + xy$

$= xc + yc + xy$

alternate methods: truth tables or Karnaugh maps.

13.

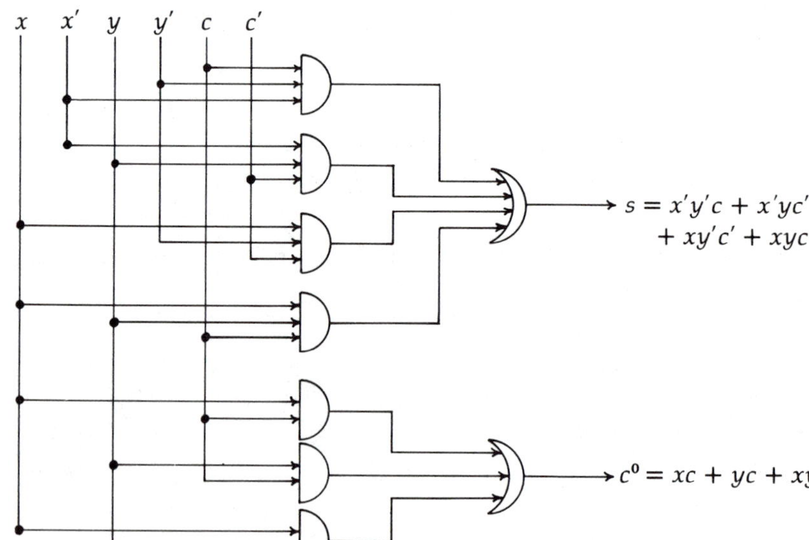

14.

$$s_1 = x \oplus y$$

$$s_2 = s_1 \oplus c = x \oplus y \oplus c = s$$

$$c_1 = xy$$

$$c_2 = (x \oplus y)c$$

$$c^0 = c_1 + c_2 = xy + (x \oplus y)c$$

$$= xy(c + c') + (x'y + xy')c$$

$$= xyc + xyc' + x'yc + xy'c$$

15.

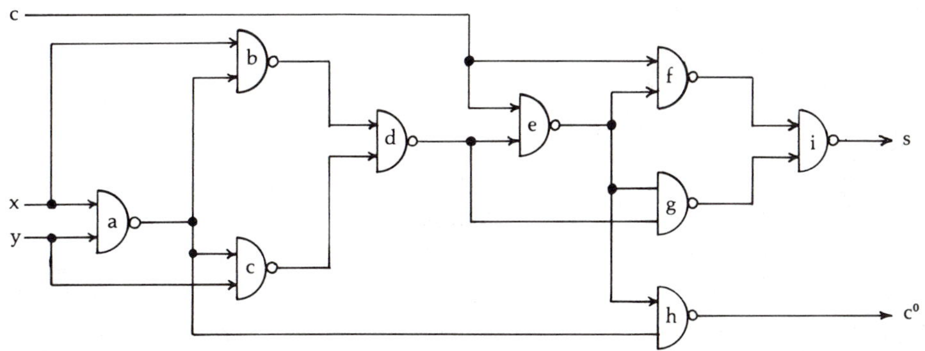

The outputs for the NAND gates are:

a. $(xy)'$

b. $[(x' + y')x]' = xy + x' = x' + y$

c. $[(xy)'y]' = xy + y' = x + y'$

d. $[(x' + y)(x + y')]' = (xy + x'y') = x \oplus y$

e. $[(x \oplus y)c]'$

f. $[([x \oplus y]c)'c]' = c(x \oplus y) + c'$

g. $[(x \oplus y)([x \oplus y]c)']' = (x \oplus y)' + c(x \oplus y)$

h. $[([x \oplus y]c)'(xy)']' = (x \oplus y)c + xy = c^0$

i. $[(c[x \oplus y] + c')([x \oplus y]' + c[x \oplus y])]'$

$= [c'(x \oplus y)' + c(x \oplus y)]'$

$= [(c \oplus [x \oplus y])']' = c \oplus x \oplus y = s$

16.

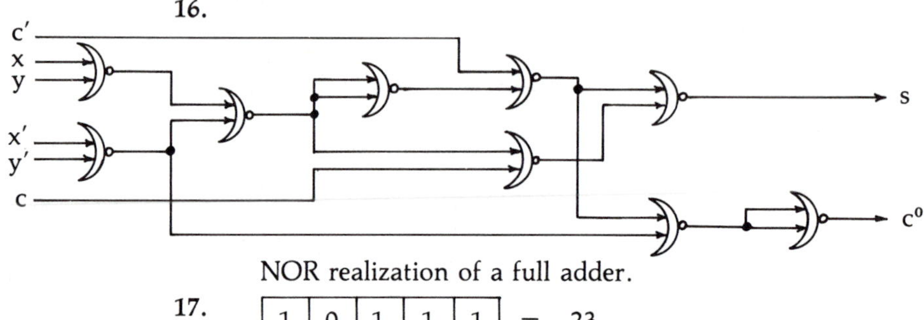

NOR realization of a full adder.

17.

1	0	1	1	1	= 23

1	0	0	1	1	= 19

1	0	1	0	1	0	= 42

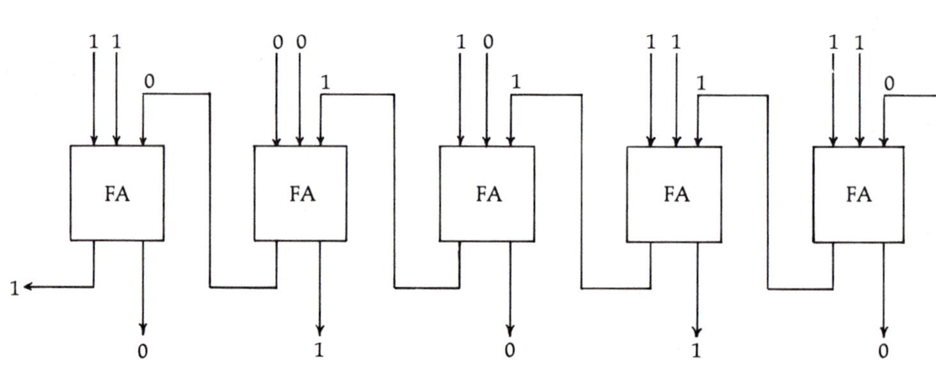

18. $n + 1$

19. Such a realization is shown in the solution to Exercise 13 on full adders.

20. $n(2t)$

21. $C_3 = G_2 + P_2G_1 + P_2P_1G_0 + P_2P_1P_0C_f$

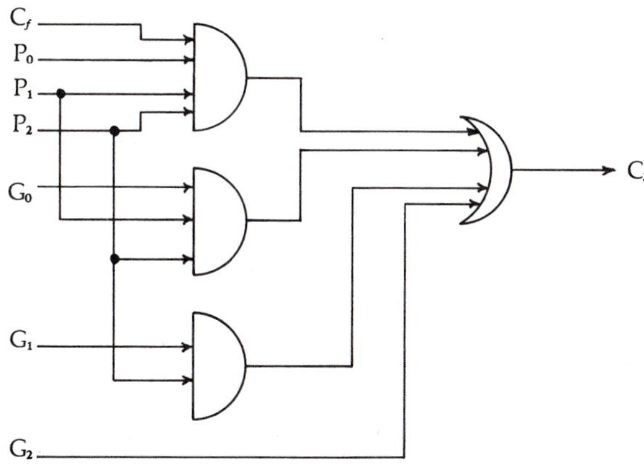

22. $P_i = A_i \oplus B_i = A_iB_i' + A_i'B_i$

$2t$ time units are needed to execute P_i.

23. At most $4t$ are required to obtain C_3.

$$C_6 = G_5 + P_5G_4 + P_5P_4G_3 + P_5P_4P_3G_2 + P_5P_4P_3P_2G_1 + P_5P_4P_3P_2P_1G_0 + P_5P_4P_3P_2P_1P_0C_f$$

At most $2t$ are required to obtain C_6.

24. After C_9 arrives at CLA #4, S_9 requires only $2t$ time units since $S_9 = A_9 \oplus B_9 \oplus C_9$. The determination of S_{10} requires $4t$ time units, since C_{10} is not available at the time C_9 arrives. Similarly, S_{11} requires $4t$ time units but CN_1 can be executing at the same time as CN_0. Thus, S_{11} can be obtained during the same interval as S_{10}, i.e., in $4t$ time units. The computation of $S_{12} = C_{12}$ takes only $2t$ time units. Thus, CLA #4 requires only $4t$ time units to produce all S_i.

25.

CLA	#1	$4t$	
CLA	#2	$2t$	at most $12t$ time units
CLA	#3	$2t$	
CLA	#4	$4t$	

26. For the 12-bit ripple-carry adder, $2(12)t = 24t$ time units. The compromise adder takes half the amount of time.

27. $(2)(3)t = 30$ nanoseconds

28. **a)** 40 ns **b)** 60 ns **c)** 40 ns

29. **a)** Form seven addition problems, denoted A through G, with B, D, and F with carry-in of 1, and C, E, and G with carry-in of 0, e.g.,

	F,G	D,E	B,C	A
x	100	111	000	111
y	111	000	111	000

After the seven additions are completed simultaneously, three choices must be made to obtain the correct sum. These choices must be made in succession.

b) Each of A through G takes 30 ns, but these problems are executed simultaneously. The choices in succession take an additional 30 ns. Total time for conditional-sum method is 60 ns. Time for full ripple-carry is 120 ns, which is twice that needed for the conditional-sum method.

30. **a)** $Z_{90} \approx Z_2 \times Z_5 \times Z_9$

b) $w_1 = 45,\ w_2 = 36,\ w_3 = 10$

c) $\theta(11) = <1,1,2>,\ \theta(57) = <1,2,3>,\ \theta(23) = <1,3,5>,$
$\theta(s) = <1,1,1>$

Sum $= s = \theta^{-1}(<1,1,1>) = 45 + 36 + 10 \pmod{90} = 1$

31. **a)** $Z_{290} \approx Z_2 \times Z_5 \times Z_{29}$

b) $w_1 = 145,\ w_2 = 116,\ w_3 = 30$

c) $\theta(11) = <1,1,11>,\ \theta(57) = <1,2,28>,\ \theta(23) = <1,3,23>,$
$\theta(s) = <1,1,4>$

Sum $= s = \theta^{-1}(<1,1,4>) = 145 + 116 + 120 \pmod{290} = 91$

32. **a)** Let $Z_n \approx Z_{p_1^{\alpha 1}} \times \ldots \times Z_{p_r^{\alpha r}}$ where $n = p_1^{\alpha 1} \ldots p_r^{\alpha r}$. Let θ be the residue representation map.

$\theta(a) = <a_1, a_2, \ldots, a_r>$ where $a \equiv a_i \bmod p_i^{\alpha i}$.

Let w_i be the inverse image of the ith unit vector. Given the residue representation

$$\theta(b) = <b_1, b_2, \ldots, b_r>,$$

then $b = b_1w_1 + \ldots + b_rw_r$ in conventional representation.

b) $\theta^{-1}(<b_1, b_2, \ldots, b_r>) = b_1w_1 + b_2w_2 + \ldots + b_rw_r$

33. Prove $2^n - 1 = \sum_{i=0}^{n-1} 2^i$ for all $n \geqslant 1$.

For $n = 1$, the equality holds. Assume true for $n = k$.

$$\text{Then } 2^{k+1} - 1 = 2^k 2 - 1 = (2^k - 1)2 + 1 = \left(2 \sum_{i=0}^{k-1} 2^i\right) + 1$$

$$= \left(\sum_{i=0}^{k-1} 2^{i+1}\right) + 1 = \left(\sum_{j=1}^{k} 2^j\right) + 1$$

$$= \left(\sum_{j=1}^{k} 2^j\right) + 2^0 = \sum_{j=0}^{k} 2^j$$

34. $\sum_{j=0}^{7} 2^j = 2^8 - 1 = 255$

35. $2^5 - 1 = 31$, $2^6 - 1 = 63$

To represent 43, six bits are needed.

36. a) 4 bits, b) $8t$

37. a) 13 bits, since $2^{12} - 1 = 4095$, $2^{13} - 1 = 8191$, and $4095 < 4619 < 8191$.

b) $26t$

38. a) $n = 2^{13}$, power of a prime, $\lceil \log_3 26 \rceil = 3$ time units.

b) $n = 2^5 - 1 = 31$, a prime, $\lceil \log_3 (2 \lceil \log_2 31 \rceil) \rceil = \lceil \log_3 10 \rceil = 3$ time units.

c) $n = 2^8 - 1 = 3 \cdot 5 \cdot 17$, 17 largest prime, $\lceil \log_3 (2 \lceil \log_2 17 \rceil) \rceil = \lceil \log_3 10 \rceil = 3$ time units.

39. The Winograd lower bound for addition in $Z_{2^{13}} = Z_{8193}$ is 3 time units. The Z_{8193} symbols can be represented with 13 bits. Thus, 26 time units must be allotted for addition in Z_{8193} using the ripple-carry adder.

40. The Winograd lower bound for addition in Z_{255} is the same as the Winograd lower bound for addition in Z_{32}, since for $n = 32$ the number of time units required is at least $\lceil \log_3(2 \log_2 2^5) \rceil = 3$.

41. a) power of a prime

lower bound $= \lceil \log_3(2 \log_2 2^{36}) \rceil = \lceil \log_3 72 \rceil = 4$ time units

b) power of a prime

lower bound $= \lceil \log_3(2 \log_2 2^{48}) \rceil = \lceil \log_3 96 \rceil = 5$ time units.

8. References

1. Chu, Y., *Digital Computer Design Fundamentals*, McGraw-Hill, 1962.

2. Dornhoff, L. L., and F. E. Hohn, *Applied Modern Algebra*, Macmillan, 1978.

3. Fellin, Jo Ann, "Primitive Shift Registers," UMAP Module Unit 310, 1981.

4. Gilbert, W. J., *Modern Algebra with Applications*, John Wiley and Sons, 1976.

5. Kline, R. M., *Digital Computer Design*, Prentice-Hall, 1977.

6. Kohavi, Z., *Switching and Finite Automata Theory*, McGraw-Hill, 1970.

7. Laufer, Henry B., *Discrete Mathematics and Applied Modern Algebra*, Prindle, Weber, and Schmidt, 1984.

8. Stone, H. S., *Discrete Mathematical Structures and Their Applications*, Science Research Associates, Inc., 1973.

9. Winograd, S. "How Fast Can the Computer Add?," *Computers and Computation*, Chapter 14, W. H. Freeman and Company, 1968.

10. Winograd, S., "On Time Required to Perform Addition," *Journal of the Association for Computing Machinery*, *12* (1965), 277-285.

The *UMAP Modules, Tools for Teaching* is published annually by the Consortium for Mathematics and Its Applications, Inc. (COMAP, Inc.), 60 Lowell Street, Arlington, MA 02174, in cooperation with the American Mathematical Association of Two Year Colleges (AMATYC), the Mathematical Association of America (MAA), the National Council of Teachers of Mathematics (NCTM), the Society for Industrial and Applied Mathematics (SIAM), and The Institute of Management Sciences (TIMS). The *UMAP Modules, Tools for Teaching* acquaints readers with a wide variety of professional applications of the mathematical sciences and provides a forum for discussion of new directions in mathematical education.

(ISBN 0-912843-08-X)

United States individual subscription $35.00

Foreign individual subscription $42.00

Institutional membership subscription $120.00

As an institutional member, you will receive:

* Two (2) subscriptions to *The UMAP Journal*, issued quarterly
* Two (2) *UMAP Modules, Tools for Teaching*, issued annually
* Our annual Catalog
* Our quarterly tabloid, *Consortium*; a popular teaching tool
* A 20% discount on additional subscriptions to *The UMAP Journal*
* A 10% discount on selected orders of UMAP Modules and Monographs

All order must be prepaid.

Second class postage rates paid at Boston, MA.

POSTMASTER: Send address changes to

UMAP Modules, Tools for Teaching
COMAP, Inc.
60 Lowell Street
Arlington, MA 02174